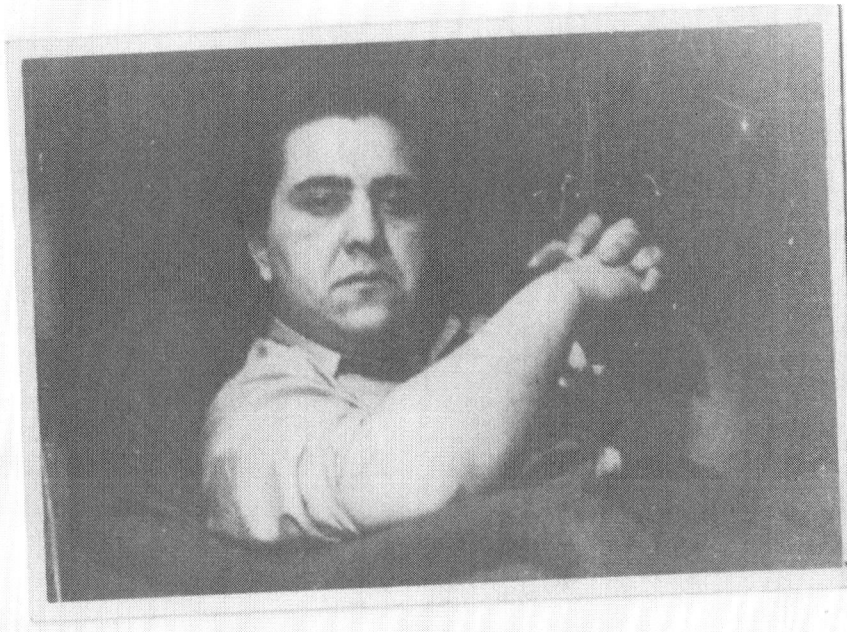

G. LEGMAN 1943

MUSICK TO MY SORROW

BEING BOOK FOUR OF G. LEGMAN'S

AUTOBIOGRAPHY OF INNOCENCE,
PEREGRINE PENIS

FAITHFULLY TRANSCRIBED BY JUDITH
EVANS LEGMAN

PUBLISHED BY CREATESPACE 2018

ISBN-13:
978-1984077745

ISBN-10:
1984077740

DEDICATED TO ALL MY SONS AND
DAUGHTERS

Thanks to Steve Gertz of Booktryst for the attractive
picture of books on the front cover.

The portrait of G. Legman in his middle-twenties on
the back cover is by his friend, Jack Kray.

TOM O' BEDLAM

From the Hagg & Hungry Goblin.

4

When I short haue shorne my sowce face
É swigged my horny barrel,
In an oken Inne I pound my skin
As a suite of guilt apparel,
The Moon's my constant Mistresse
& the lowlie owle my morrowe.
The flaming Drake and ye Nightcrowe make
Mee musicke to my sorrowe.

While I doe sing, any food, any feeding,
Feeding, drink or clothing?'
Come dame or maid, be not afraid:
Poor Tom will injure nothing.

From "Loving Mad Tom," Bedlamite Verses of
the XVI and XVII Centuries, London:
Fanfrolico Press, 1927. Page 24.

TABLE OF CONTENTS

CHAPTER 37

IRINA

WHILE THE WAR went on, more and more men — and women too — were being mustered into the service, song collecting became very much easier. The men needed to sing. In New York City I would seldom hear bawdy songs sung openly any longer in bars. There was too much competition from the juke-boxes, on which the barroom owners got a cut of the take. Big, boomy machines, making loud, bad, non-music. Still, it was easy to talk to the soldiers and sailors there, and to learn their songs. Sometimes they would sing them between juke-box items, or even in competition, though in a less noisy tone. This made it hard to get the tunes, but I would write out the words, and often the singers would repeat them to help me get them right.

The main problem was that most of them assumed that another man not in uniform talking to a soldier was simply a homosexual trying to pick the soldier up. A surprisingly large proportion of the soldiers were also amenable to being picked up in this way. As they explained it to me frankly, they "got their nuts off" with the homosexual, without the trouble and expense of trying to pick up and seduce nice girls, who never came into bars unaccompanied and were very suspicious of servicemen anyhow. Rightly too, as even the songs admitted. On the other hand, a homosexual naturally bought all the drinks and gave the soldier some money as well.

The soldiers hardly thought of what they were doing as prostitution, as long as all the homosexual wanted to do was to suck them off and pay for the privilege. One soldier even claimed that it was no different from being a semen-donor in a hospital. No matter who paid *who*, most of them maintained that it was the homosexual who was the prostitute. He was the queer, the freak and the fag, and anything unworthy about the transaction was therefore his fault and his blame. If, however, the homosexual was of the less common type who wanted to bugger or be buggered, there was more likely to be trouble. Being buggered was obviously a submissive act, and if one were paid for that then one was a male whore and knew it. The proper response to that – and sometimes to being sucked off – was to beat up and roll the homosexual afterward, sometimes actually killing him in the process, and always self-righteously grabbing all his money. That made one a man again.

Often, when I was out fishing up songs and singers, after leaving the library late in the evening, and stopping into various off-Broadway bars and along Sixth Avenue for that purpose, servicemen who would talk to me would be puzzled by my interest only in the songs they knew. And they would say something to me phrased in different ways, but always adding up to: "What do you do, Jack?" At first I would innocently answer, "I'm a medical researcher for the Army." And they would counter impatiently, "No; what do you want to *do*?" Sometimes even adding, "– and how much are you going to give me?" There was even a gag form of this: "Who does what to who, and who pays?" This was so frequent that eventually I had a standard response: "Well, I never pay for songs, and that's all I want." Actually, I often did pay the singers a small sum, especially if they wrote out the words for me. And I naturally paid for their beer and cigarettes too. Pretty low pay, I admit. If it had to be much higher I wouldn't have been able to collect the songs at all.

The Army knew that the soldiers sang, especially on the march, and that it was good for their morale and discipline. But no formal songbooks appeared that I knew of, under Army auspices, as there had in World War I, since almost all the songs the men really sang were of course highly bawdy. Where the songs were not too graphic, for instance "Roll Me Over in the Clover," servicewomen and nurses on leave would join in on the singing in bars, especially in England I was told, where the competition of the juke-boxes didn't exist or was much less. But there weren't many songs that mild.

Coming down one day on the subway, I found a small book of service songs for sale on the newsstands, all lightly expurgated, and credited to the editing of someone named Erich Posselt. He wasn't in the phone book, but a letter to him at the publisher's address, offering more songs for his next edition, got an answer right away as I expected it would. He was in New York, in an apartment down near Broadway and 23rd street, and naturally I thought of the old days with my favorite swindler, Carlo Flumiani, vanity publisher of Fortuny Books, when I passed the Flatiron Building there.

Posselt was evidently a European, probably Viennese originally, and spoke excellent if accented English. He was extremely nervous and jittery, and nothing I could say would put him at ease, so I finally decided it wasn't me that was making him nervous. I showed him a sheaf of the songs I had collected, all typed up, and he looked them over rapidly.

"But these are all too dirty!" he objected.

"Well, that's the way the soldiers sing them," I said.

"Yeah, sure," he admitted, "but I'll have to fix them all up."

"That's up to you," I said. "I write them down the way I hear them."

He was less than affable about it when I then suggested that perhaps he could give me in exchange some of the songs he had collected too. But when I assured him I only wanted the original, non-fixed-up form, he cheered up. Anyhow, he told me, he had already thrown away the to-him useless original texts of the songs he had already *improved* for publication. I enjoyed for a moment the exquisite humor of this obvious foreigner, with his well-grained German accent and name, expurgating for publication the folksongs with which American soldiers & sailors were keeping their courage up in a war of which the basic purpose was to keep bloodlusting Germans from conquering the world. Well, of course, I reminded myself, the man before my eyes was a good German or Austrian. It was the others who were the bad ones. And the proof of his basic goodness was certainly his wonderful sensitivity to the cleanliness or dirtiness of folksongs, and toé" the saleability of the clean ones and the unsaleability of the dirty ones.

Posselt did, however, have a very small sheaf of soldiers' songs which were intrinsically too bawdy for his type of fixing-up, and these he gave me freely, telling me that he could not hope to use them in his forthcoming enlarged edition, which would appear under the pseudonym of 'Edgar Palmer' for another competing publisher. I wondered about the ethics of that, but said nothing, as he already clearly had his course fixed. He nevertheless clarified the matter further by mentioning that his old edition would be sold to a new publisher before the new edition came out, if possible. And in fact it was. Or, at least both editions were on sale competing with each other, under two different publishers' imprints. And all the songs perfectly clean. Who was expected actually to sing these two different but similar, booksful of expurgated bawdy songs I never did figure out. I guess it's like the bad black-market cigarettes sold and traded in Europe during the war which were not for smoking but for trading. These songs were for selling and not for singing. A lot of purported folksong books are like that.

Just for fun, I mixed in with the authentic folksongs I gave to this man a copy of my own satirical creation, or rather adaptation of a famous Australian poem called "Bloody!" or "The Great Australian Adjective," which I entitled simply, "The Cowboy." This was intended to mock the current rash of dull Army profanity, in which every sentence included the Army adjective-of-all-work, *fuckin'*. I wanted to see if there could possibly be any feedback, and if I would ever actually hear anyone sing or recite it after Posselt would publish it. Well, he did publish it, in the 'Palmer' edition, but of course omitting all the fuckin's of which at least one appeared in every single line of this rather long poem; where he replaced them all with chastely non-committal dashes, though I did suggest to him he could at least use "bloody." He also omitted the final or punch-line stanza altogether, as too essentially erotic to be "fixed" in his usual fashion, so similar to the fashion in which dogs and farm animals are likewise "fixed" by veterinarians. This left the piece without much meaning, as the whole point was in the culminating interruptive tmesis or Irish Bull, ending: *"And there, with all his fuckin' force, had sexual fuckin'-intercourse!"* Naturally Posselt's text also omitted my signature at the end, in which I carried the joke to its final step and reprised the nom de guerre I had signed to *Oragenitalism*, signing the poem now: *"R.-M. de La Fuckin' G., Nineteen-fuckin'-Forty-three."*

A dozen years later, to my great surprise, this poem reappeared almost word for word as Posselt had printed it, and again or still without the last stanza, using *"bloody"* instead of dashes throughout, to clean up the *fuckin's*, in a book called *Air Force Airs* edited by one William Wallrich, in his section of "Korean War Beer-Call Ballads." The editor admits it's only a recitation, but says it is his favorite. I never did find out whether he actually collected it "in the field" in Korea, as claimed, and wish I could believe that something I wrote had really become folklore in this way. But I still can't believe it. Twenty years later I had much better luck with "Make Love, Not War!" which made the tour of the world. But that's only a motto or catch-phrase, nor is any country in the world really trying it seriously.

Someone else did succeed in doing this – creating or becoming folklore – in recent years. William Soskin, later a book publisher, was the author of the song, "Violate Me In Violet Time," which he originally wrote for a satirical revue in the 1930s. It was first published in *The Bedroom Companion*, edited for Rinehart & Co. just before World War II by Philip Wylie, who however didn't sign his name to the book. Thousands of soldiers must have sung "Violate Me In Violet Time," which tickled them just where they lived, in its pretended accents of uncontrollable feminine passion. It still lives on now at college beer-busts, where college girls sing it happily with their dates. That doesn't mean, of course, that any girl really wants to get raped. Not if she has any idea of what rape is actually like. But it's fun pretending.

When Hamish Henderson, the Scottish folklorist and poet, was fighting in his Highland Regiment in North Africa, he wrote the extraordinary "Ballad of King Farouk," an unsigned piece which became the favorite bawdy song of the British troops there. As it was set to the tune of the Egyptian national anthem, *"Salaam el-Malik; Hail to the King,"* played at the end of every movie-showing, when the lights went on, the British troops used the hair-raisingly obscene and libellous piece, with plenty of bawdy Arabic words rhymed into it, for the purpose of starting fights with the local population on the way home. So don't ever say that folksong doesn't help world peace.

By the end of the war, especially in the Pacific theatre of the fighting, all the retooled folknik singers who had been in the Communist Party, or the maritime unions, were pressed into service in travelling shows that went around entertaining the soldiers in outlying places and islands. They avoided anything bawdy, of course, as the shows drew an audience not only of soldiers but also of officers and top-brass, and of course servicewomen and nurses who were essentially the superior officers' harem or sex-pool, as everyone knew, but only the soldiers had the nerve to say so and bitch about it. This had been exactly the same in World War I.

The war-time entertainer-singers' choice of properly titillating but only semi-bawdy songs was tough to make. The usual solution was to take charming items from *Pills to Purge Melancholy*, or other properly ancient sources, and expurgate even them where necessary. At least the tunes were authentic. Betty Sanders, who was of course not a Communist but a theatre entertainer, used to sing the beautiful "Wedding & Bedding" song from *Pills* to the troops, and they loved its tender sentimentality. She apparently left out only one verse, with the line "All night within my arms shalt be," and came in for a smash ending, which several correspondents wrote to me about enthusiastically, where the girl alludes to the fact that she has no dowry except "What Nature gave," and offers:

My heart and all's at thy command, though I've never an acre of land;
It's six fat ewes and one milk-cow, I think my love is wealthy now.

A wheel, six platters and a spoon, a jacket edged in blue galoon;
My cloak is thine, my smock and shawl, and something under, best of all!

That certainly must have cheered up the lonely GI soldiers to hear, and you can bet they applauded like mad the gallant girl singer who was willing to remind them, almost frankly this way, of what they were all dreaming about. But it was just as certainly infinitely far from anything that themselves actually sang. Which was more likely to be the British Airforce anthem, "Fuck 'Em All!" politely debited over the radio as "Bless 'Em All!" with its cynically realistic refrain:

Fuck 'em *all!* Fuck 'em *all!* Fuck 'em *ALL!*
The long and the short and the tall;
When you're a civilian, it's one in a million,
But when you're in camp, fuck 'em *all!*

MY LESBIAN FRIEND Irina Naxos had taken a job on Dickinson's research project about then. It was a pleasure to have lunch and talk with her often at the Academy of Medicine, a great silent mausoleum otherwise filled only with people impossible to talk to owing to their being puffed up with the usual medical snobbery, vain self-importance and elitism. Why she took the job I don't know. I doubt that her legart paintings for calendars weren't selling well to the calendar printers. She probably found the project too attractive sexually to refuse, when the part she was being offered was explained to her.

Dr. Dickinson had made thousands of sketch drawings of his women patients' external genital organs, over the decades of his career as the leading American gynecologist and obstetrician. He saw all the rich white ladies discreetly undressed in his private practice in fashionable Brooklyn and later New York City; and all the other races and lesser incomes in the clinics he served. These genital drawings were usually made rapidly on an art-pad held at the woman's pelvic level while Dickinson would be examining her, under a cloud of white sheet. He believed in mercifully giving the woman patient plenty of crisp white sheet to cling to under her chin and over the breasts, even though the rest of her had to be completely denuded for the doctor's examination. I thought that was very gallant. Other gynecologists, such as Dr. Gérard Zwang, and numerous "men's" magazines, intended to appeal sexually to male readers, have used genital color photography in the same way more recently. Some of Dickinson's drawings were actually made then by tracing the form and appearance of the spread vulva, on a heavy glass square with taped edges pressed up against the woman's pubis, while she lay with her knees up and spread in the stirrups on the gynecological table.

Obviously, despite the cold touch of the glass pane, the women patients didn't know that the portraits of their genital parts were being taken in this way for the benefit of science. Dickinson felt, and I believe so do most other physicians in the world, that guinea-pig patients should pay in this way part of the inherent human cost of the medical research which will eventually help, at least theoretically, all the other patients and themselves too. Dickinson was also very keen on trying to create or discover, from these drawings of his, the hypothetical *average* forms of the women's external genital organs. In the same way, statistically-minded propagandists on the style of Professor Alfred Kinsey later tried to set up equally hypothetical average sex-lives or phantom figures, by extrapolating the few hundred or thousand case-histories they were able to gather, onto enormously larger populations of hundreds of millions of people whom of course they would never be able to reach or examine. Like Don Giovanni's "one thousand and three" female conquests – and that only in Spain.

This is the same method necessarily used by all the pollsters for psyching the American presidential elections – usually wrongly, as everyone has observed – and for peddling radio and television programs to the well-bamboozled advertisers. Most people, and especially the media milch-cow advertisers, are not aware and have been kept carefully in ignorance of the fact that all the polls and pollstering are essentially moonshine or feedback propaganda, intended to make the whole population believe some lie or other by pretending that a preponderant majority of them believe it already, and backing up this second lie by means of faked and "weighted" figures and statistical manipulations. Pure hogwash.

One thing that is surely true is that it is extremely difficult to do population sampling, whether of opinions or of facts, honestly and scientifically. I believe the decennial *U. S. Census Reports* are the only honestly sampled and presented statistics of this kind. Most of the other stuff presented to the public as reliable statistics or authentic "poll-taking" is crudely faked or weighted, and is invariably based on ludicrously insufficient or grossly tendentious sampling techniques. This is a lucrative and effective racket, which has been around quite a while now, and is not going to change or disappear either today or tomorrow. When Kinsey, whose statistical method had all this wrong with it, and much more, arrived on the highly publicized popular psychology scene in the late 1940s with considerable advance publicity whoop-te-do of its own, Dr. Dickinson's sanctifying voice was one of the loudest. He just naturally welcomed Kinsey like the long-lost brother and propaganda successor he'd been seeking for decades.

When averaging methods as irresponsible as these were then tried pictorially or schematically with human genital anatomy, as Dickinson tried, even a statistical amateur like me could see instantly that all the fascinating human *differences* were being purposely overlooked, "smoothed," or averaged out of existence, by concentrating instead on the crude and hypothetical outline *similarities*. The purpose being frankly to create or imagine models for teaching purposes, and then, somewhat less honestly, to simplify down to the non-human and almost robotized nubbit, for presentation as pictorial "fact," in the proposed new edition of Dickinson's *Human Sex Anatomy*, a theoretically normal genital anatomy that no living woman or man ever really showed, or that had been authentically drawn, traced, or photographed by Dickinson or anyone else. All the parts, yes. But none of the particularities: like a dressmaker's dummy.

As Dr. Dickinson was always in the process of creating little anatomical clay-and-plaster models and bits of statuary, sometimes in break-apart rubber halves, for teaching and demonstrating to medical classes in gynecology and obstetrics, it was certainly necessary for him to decide in a practical way what conformation to give especially to the female parts on his teaching models. But in the end he came dangerously close to believing in the actual reality of the theoretical and schematised "normal" or average shapes he was creating, originally only for teaching purposes. Meanwhile reserving the right to consider that anything else smacked too much of mere art.

His staff sculptors, first Fortunato and then Belskie, were visibly stunned when Dickinson had them construct an intertwined model of the Dionne quintuplets, then in the popular public news, as they had presumably lain in their mother's womb, but based almost entirely on Dickinson's perhaps shrewd imagining of what their foetal positions might have been. No actual facts were available as A. R. Dafoe, the Canadian country doctor who delivered the quintuplets, had his hands too full when the babies "came popping out," as he told the news-reporters, to take or keep any notes on their presumed positions, or even on what order the five girls were born in. The intertwined model was entirely Dr. Dickinson's after-the-fact imagining, a sort of prettily entangled Vassar daisy chain of five little naked girl-babies, immortalized in fired clay. As this was presented in the form of a uterine cornucopia, I suggested that it should be called "The Horn of Plenty," and this pleasantry was so successful that eventually everyone but the abashed sculptors who had been asked to lie-in-clay seemed ready to overlook the obvious fact that the cornucopia of the Dionne quints was really just a work of the imagination: a lovely piece of anatomical art, surely, but just as surely not of obstetrical science as implied.

A British medical visitor a few years later, a Dr. Norman Haire, himself an outrageous publicity liar in his magazine of pretended sex-letters and questions from the public, observed to me that Dr. Dickinson was considered in England to be a bit of a charlatan, for publicity devices like the Dionne quintuplets cornucopia. Just jealousy, probably: one medical Ananias piqued by another one's success. Of course, he was right too, but in a way it's simply a question of the effective presentation of materials. Shock 'em! and sock 'em – or at least surprise 'em and make 'em laugh – is certainly the oldest didactic and publicity rule in the book, at least since the millennia of the Egyptian magician-priests and the competing miracles of the Old and New Testaments. What about Moses' snake-rod gobbling up the snake-rods of Pharaoh's priests, and the loaves & fishes and walking on the water reported of Jesus Christ? Hit 'em where they live.

Since every artist and writer – especially of gospel-true Testaments – has apparently the god-given right to jazz up and simplify the impact of his materials in this way, why not scientists? The representations of atomic particles and DNA chains in schematic molecular drawings, and of the stars in heaven in popular planetariums, are certainly pretty far from the absolute atomic and sidereal truth – both infinitely large and small. But one assumes nevertheless that they're all based originally on very real information and measurements, or at least on reliable hypotheses, however schematised. That was where the rub came, with Dickinson's phantom "normal" gynecological forms. The original drawings and rare measurements were doubtless as close to exact as he could come. It was what was to be done with them afterwards, to create or discover presumed or pretended averages, that was very dubious.

It was this same criticism that should have been made of Kinsey's indefensible extrapolations as to sex practices of unsampled populations and in fact of the entire "human" (White Anglo-Saxon Protestant) race. Real statisticians, some of them much less squeamish about their scientific sexual vocabularies than Kinsey was, did so criticize his work at the time, in fact, practically removed him from the field of science or statistics to that of publicity where he really belonged. But their voices, and pained outcries in learned statistical journals, were of course quickly lost in the happy welcoming huzzas of the general public and most sexual propagandists like Dr. Dickinson. They basically adored Kinsey's not-very-well-hidden message of wild-cat sexual liberation and the "normality" of the abnormal, and didn't give a damn one way or the other about his statistical hokum. This was in any case, not very different from the equally faked "science" that newspaper and radio advertising media had been habitually feeding them for a century or more.

As to Dickinson's anatomical averages, these were achieved, in fact, in minor part by actual measurement, and mostly by means of his career-long stockpile of genital drawings made during clinical examinations, and further tracings and generations of tracings to be made from these drawings. The artist, in this case Irina Naxos, was supplied with some hundreds of Dickinson's quick sketches of spread-open female genitals, and these had to be taken off on tracing paper, marking the position – real or hypothetical – of the pubic bone or point, once poetically known as the *share-bone*, as in ploughshare. Every five such tracings would then be lined up over one another in a pile over a lighted glass plate, with the pubic points superimposed, and a further tracing would be made then of their dark or median show-through line. Every five such secondary tracings would than be lined up on the pubic points over the glass plate and etc., etc., etc. The idea was that in this way the thousands of Dickinson's vulva drawings could be overlayered time after time, finally to produce a phantom drawing or drawings of standard sexual parts. Well, that's democracy, folks. The Majority is always right, and the Average is King. Or in this case, Queen. If you don't like it, you can just go right back where you came from – right into that Standard Sexual Part.

Irina must have thought at first that it would be great fun, being a lesbian after all, as she was proud to admit and brag of, to sit there for a couple of months doing nothing but handling drawings of female sexual parts of every imaginable size, shape and pigmentation: from pussy pink to tawny chocolate, though the intrinsic colors were generally only rather poorly shown by cross-hatching. The day of the glorious split-beaver color photographs of the genital beauties of Denmark, later also in American and other European men's magazines and erotic movies, had of course not yet dawned. But when she actually sat down to it, Irina found the work very tiresome and uninteresting.

It was certainly not work for an artist. At the very most for a draftsman – or draftswoman. Also the work was basically impossible to do at all, unless a careful division of the thousands of drawings were to have been organized beforehand by main types and general forms. Otherwise the outlines did not coincide closely enough, and the expected median dark show-through line simply did not show through; and no sincere one-for-five tracings could be made. Dickinson had never made any such organization of his materials, though he did recognize that it was necessary. He just threw the job and all the drawings at Irina in a lump. After, all, he was now nearly eighty, and was very seriously looking for other people to carry on his work. That was precisely why he would accept even dubious and wholly non-medical characters like Irina, and like me.

By way of discretion, Irina was given Dickinson's little private office upstairs to work in, which was on a different floor from the public office of the National Committee for Maternal Health, as Dickinson's organization was called, and which was also at the other end of the Academy of Medicine from his enormous museum studio behind the lecture auditorium. Irina could therefore work there in private with the stacks of genital drawings. She had the file of his original drawings and a large supply of tracing paper half sheets

– cut in half by Dickinson himself to save money. Also pencils and a glass-topped light box on which to lay the superimposed first generation tracings five at a time to try to discern the dark or median show-through line. As nothing of the kind ever appeared in superimposing the first sets of five tracings, Irina told me confidentially she tried superimposing ten at a time, which was about as many as the light box could successfully shine through. But she still wasn't getting a reasonably dark median line to trace for the second generation outline, and I assured her she never would unless all the drawings were carefully organized first as to similar types.

Irina went to complain to Dickinson about this, and he told her to do the work *however it was necessary to do it.* He was marvellous at old Army buck-passing phrases like that, in this case not involving killing anybody. As Irina and I were as thick as inkle-weavers together, Dickinson did allow, at her request, that I could help her with the organizing of the drawings, though you could see that it bothered him greatly that a non-medical male person like myself was going to be allowed to peer at all those pussies he had lovingly sketched in his youth, and for all I know blown kisses at them, each and every one. I certainly would have. I assured the feisty old doctor that I had nerves of steel, and that I was in any case accustomed to seeing the very same female organs in full, living color and from quite close up -- witness my book on *Oragenitalism* -- and did not expect to be overwhelmed by pencil drawings, be they never so many thousands.

I was wrong. They certainly did overwhelm me; and by the time the first rough organization of the materials had been made, I was considering entering a monastery for life. By the time I had the second and final division into vulvar and labial types done, I was continuously picking imaginary hairs out of my teeth, and kept repeating to myself compulsively Dowson's poem to Cynara, about flinging roses; roses riotously with the throng: "I am desolate, and sick of an old passion – Yes, Hungry for the lips of my desire!" You could say that again. My personal sex life was almost ruined, at a complete standstill, and to all intents & purposes non-existent. I don't know about Irina's. She was drunk most of the time, anyway.

After an entire day, for weeks on end, sorting out drawings of vulvas by the hundreds and thousands into six basic types – essentially by length from top to bottom, and by extension, shape and pigmentation of the fully spread inner lips of the labia minora – I simply could not go home at night and look a pussy in the eye. "I have been faithful to thee, Cynara! in my fashion." Oh man!! I also called for madder music and stronger wine, as Dowson recommends, but that didn't do me any good. I began to barricade myself away from my weekday and Sunday regular girlfriends, like the man going mad in Oliver Onion's story *The Beckoning Fair One*, who continuously hears a non-existent woman in the next room softly brushing her hair through the wall! As I had already been through that with Elaine's throat-clearing, pussy-hair was just too much. I couldn't take any more.

I realized finally that it had to be them or me, and told Irina that I had done all I possibly could to sort the ghost-ladies out, and was kissing their pussies goodbye. She would now have to continue alone on what she referred to irreverently as our expedition in search of the Great American Twat. I admit it – I had fallen unmanly by the wayside. Irina was a better man than I was, Gunga Din. My wife Judith says my problem was like reading too many cookbooks: eventually you don't want to eat anything at all. I wonder how Georges Simenon and Richard Burton solved that problem, after their first fifteen thousand women? Whores unquestionably have the same problem with pricks. My old standby *Ecclesiastes*, covers the subject pretty thoroughly in his fearful final chapter, on the desire that fails at dawn; but no one will find words of consolation there.

Our last colloquy, before I left Irina alone at our Barmecide feast of sexual parts on paper, said everything. Irina was just as disabused by then as I was, about the mock-scientification of what we are doing, and our being forced essentially into faking the drawings and figures –- in this case the purported anatomical averages –- in the name of science. For an eventual smooth dozen drawings that Dickinson then intended to publish as authentic human types in the next edition of *Human Sex Anatomy*, for which his publisher was now clamoring.

"If this is science," Irina told me disgustedly, "I'll eat it!" I just grinned at her. "Who wouldn't?" I asked.

By that time my friend Irina and I had in any case both decided, without saying too much about it, that neither of us could go on with the work much longer. It was too absurd to do, even for money. The whole idea of the tracings was essentially ridiculous, although the division of the vaginal specimens or drawings into broad types was certainly a reasonable activity. Otherwise I would not have stayed on the job even as long as I did. And I now quit, and went back to ghost-writing. And as I have a very low tolerance-point for pure bullshit jobs, I used to turn down at least as much ghost-writing as I accepted.

One doctor, for example, to whom Dickinson sent me on a hurry-up call for a jack-of-all-trades writer and researcher, wanted me to prove, by counting every tenth person in a biographical dictionary of doctors and adding up the years of his life (really subtracting, as I recollect) that doctors all live an average of five years longer than anybody else. His problem was that he was already at the age that so-called statistics say is the average male American age of death. As I remember, it was sixty-three years at that time, and *that was his age!*

This poor, uptight guy was so brainwashed by the phoney scientificism rife all around us, that he was now shitting green that he was about to die unless he could prove by even phonier statistics, that "average" doctors live an extra five years. But was he average? As he had already picked how many extra years the doctors like him were to get, by methods unexplained, I knew at once the conclusion my research would have to arrive at — or else I wouldn't get paid. I regretfully had to refuse the job, but had enough pity for him to explain to him in a few well-chosen lay sentences, which I trusted even the medical profession would understand, that the so-called average age of death wasn't really a death sentence, and that there was now another do-jigger, called extended life expectancy, which was still operating for him since, in fact, he was actually alive at the presumed death date. As it turned out, he lived to be over eighty years old – shitting green the whole while. If you call that living. Maybe I shouldn't mock. I expect I'll be pretty sore and scared when my time comes to die. It may be close. But I'm not going to lay down and die by statistics. I'll believe it when I see the pall-bearers. And even then — *Finnegans Wake!*

Back in her Garden of Precious Flowers, Irina was still having so much trouble finding the goddamned dark median show-through pussy line that I strongly suspect she was simply drawing her own favorite pussies on the eventual fourth and fifth generation tracings. We were, of course, supposed to keep track of everything in laboratory fashion, with exact records of the case history numbers used for each generation of drawings, so that other, later, future, better, wiser, stronger, less fucked-up artists and researchers would be able to check out whether we had found the show through line right. However, I am not temperamentally suited to the writing down of long lists of numbers, let alone to the fifth power of five, which is what the presumable ultimate average drawing of the Great American Twat would be based on. Irina was even less well-suited to the figure work. So it got overlooked.

It seemed there for a while as though history and science were never really going to know what the true average American female sexual part looked like. But then Irina got fired. I was told she got drunk once too often, in her little cubby-hole office – it seems to me that's the least anybody could do on a job like that – and may even have thrown up on the floor. Or else it was her dog that did it. She used to bring her pet schnauzer to work, after I was gone. You wouldn't think a former obstetrician would be squeamish about a thing like that, when you consider that having babies often tends to be somewhat heavy weather too, at every end. But good Dr. D. hit the roof, and fired Irina. The vaginal median work was turned over later to some more staid lady-artist types, and I believe was very successfully finished, if you still believe in that sort of thing. I don't.

Irina phoned me to say we would have to celebrate our escape from Dickinson's harem of preserved pussies, or at least her escape, and she invited me to come over to her studio for a celebration dinner that evening. She was all alone she said, so we could talk like human beings. Her drunken girlfriend had long since been replaced by another, and then others in their turn, and Irina was now between girlfriends, without any at all. I suspect that the same thing had happened to her on the job as happened to me: the cookbook syndrome – she couldn't eat a thing. And it was ruining her sex life. She was wise to get fired when she did. Otherwise she was ripe to end up in the same monastery with me.

As I was always carrying around with me in those days one of the big square envelopes in which some new-bought phonograph record was being protected between two one-foot squares of corrugated cardboard, everyone who knew me knew about my interest in recorded music. And Irina asked me to bring along some record that I thought was very beautiful as she had somehow fallen heir to a phonograph from her departing girlfriend. I can no longer remember exactly what record I brought along, but I have a persistent recollection that it may have been the "Fantasia on a Theme by Thomas Tallis" which Ralph Vaughan Williams arranged from the superbly beautiful Elizabethan originals, and which had just then been recorded for the first time when Vaughan Williams was already over seventy years old.

Despite her baritone voice, Irina was the wife-type in all her affairs with women, and she was a great cook. She had a small pork roast going in the oven when I got there – as we were both Jewish this seemed appropriate for a Freedom banquet – and was working on a fabulous sauce to be composed of sliced sautéed mushrooms and tiny little onions among other things. I sat down to slice the mushrooms, and Irina brought out a bottle of wine, on which we started without waiting for the first course. Or maybe the wine was the first course. She may even have had a headstart on me, from some preceding bottle, and began telling me, for the first time in all the years I had known her, something about her earlier life. I guess I led into it by telling her I was going to ask a ridiculous question, and then asking her simply why she was a lesbian.

"Damned if I know, Legman," she said heartily, in her deepest register, making my name sound like an animal's roar. "It's been the curse of my life."

"I don't mean that exactly," I said. "I mean, what do you think caused it? That's the part that interests me most in everything connected with sex."

"Oh, I can tell you that too," Irina said, her face clouding over. "I became a lesbian because I hated my father. He treated my mother like a swine." She then launched into the whole story, which occupied the whole dinner – of roast swine – and probably an hour more. I found it absolutely fascinating, though told entirely in most prejudicial way possible against her father. It just so happened, a long time before that, I had learned Irina's real name by accident, one year when I was helping her address by hand all her New Year's cards. Irina always sent out a fabulous number of these lonesome bottles into the sea, I guess to the whole roster of *Who's Who in Lesbian America and Abroad*, and no one person could make out that many hand-writ envelopes.

While resting my hand at a certain moment from the cramp of so much writing, I wandered around the apartment she had then, and was looking at the books on her shelves. Irina was one of those rare and truly blessèd female bibliophiles who love and collect books. In fact, at one time she planned to take up bookbinding, and I had to help her get hold of a turned-wood sewing frame and other paraphernalia from my own binder; but it took too much time away from her art work, and she gave it up. I picked up that day from her shelf a book about housewife prostitution called A Bed of Roses by the English feminist, Walter Lionel George, the first man to write a book in defence of women – instead of the usual attack – since August Bebel's *Woman and Socialism* in the 1880s. And I made some remark about George's sardonic "Bed of Roses" title, as being appropriate to all our lives.

That's just an old book of mine," Irina said, "It isn't very good." I remember that astounded me, because I had read the book too, and thought it better than most. I turned it over in my hands, and found inside the front cover a very nicely designed bookplate, though printed only in black & white from a zinc cut. The name enclosed in a frame at the foot was: Irene

Alicia Sachsen. I carried it over to Irina, and pointed to it without even realizing that it had to be her, and that Naxos therefore wasn't a Greek name at all, but just Sachsen backwards.

"Oh, my old bookplate!" she said. "That was before I knew how to draw."

"Who is Sachsen?" I asked stupidly. "Any relation to Leo Sachsen?" Leo Sachsen was someone I had often heard of when I was a kid.

"My father," she said shortly. And it had stopped there. This time she told me all the rest.

LEO SACHSEN was the great courtroom orator of the American radical movement at the turn of the century, and the only lawyer that movement had to compare with Clarence Darrow. Sachsen was the real oratorical successor to Colonel Robert Ingersoll, who had dedicated his gifts as a public speaker, for the last half of his life, to lecturing all over the country against "The Mistakes of Moses," and rather directly against religion, under the polite name of agnosticism or pretended know-nothingism. Darrow was a great lawyer, and had a tremendous courtroom presence, but he was not the kind of hypnotic orator that Ingersoll and Sachsen were, according to what one reads about them, with that strangely sexual sort of throbbing, intensely personal, and emotionally-charged voice that made audiences crumble to putty in their hands. And that in a day when public speakers, Chautauqua lecturers, crusading ministers and politicians, and half the other members of the bar were all striving for a powerful oratorical style. That was Irina's father, and it stunned me that she could state flatly that she hated him, and that he had treated her mother like a swine. It didn't seem possible.

What had really happened is part of the economic history of America that I suppose everybody knows. The Scottish-American steel-mill owner, Andrew Carnegie, and his steel-hard general manager Henry Clay Frick had forced a strike by the newly-created steel-workers' union in the early summer of 1892, at Homestead, Pennsylvania, by cutting wages. It was really a lockout, and the ever-ready Pinkerton Detective Agency brought in several hundred prepared strike-breakers on armored barges across the Monongahela River, like a regular army operation. The strikers were waiting for them, and attacked not only with clubs and guns, but also with homemade cannons – really the original bazookas, made out of steel tubes – and even with dynamite and burning oil. The entire militia was called out of course, by the government "to protect private property." Right in the middle of the excitement, the whole country was electrified by the news that the Anarchist leader, Alexander Berkman, who was at the same time the accredited lover of Emma Goldman, the goddess of the Anarchist movement, had managed to talk his way into Frick's office in Pittsburgh by pretending to be the owner of a strikebreaking agency, and had shot and stabbed Frick seriously but not fatally. Berkman was overpowered, and was found in jail to have two dynamite caps hidden inside his body, to commit suicide with if caught. Some say in his mouth; others say the reverse.

I heard this story when I was a kid in Scranton, swimming bare-ass naked in the falls under the Nay-Aug bridge, and I remember the long discussion us boys had as to how you would get the dynamite caps *out* of your ass when you needed them, without having them explode. This was not intended as humor. Who knew what similar heroism might be required of us if the coal mine strikes continued right on through the thirties, as they looked as though they might. Berkman was of course given a long jail sentence, and served nearly twenty years, during the course of which Carnegie and Frick hired a publicity man, as Rockefeller had done some years before, after a similar contretemps out west with militant labor. And they all had themselves very properly gold-plated and deified for publicity purposes as public benefactors – as founders of libraries, art galleries, and other items of public good, though you still very seldom see a steelworker or coal-miner in his blackened face and grimy overalls, wandering through the classic marble halls and corny rococo niches of the Frick Art Museum up on Fifth Avenue in New York, which was originally the neo-classic mansion of the master of the forge.

One of the young men electrified by the Homestead Strike and its sequels, in a way not so different from the young men and women who became Communists all over the world in the 1930s, in reply to menace of Hitler and Nazi Germany, was Leo Sachsen. Then a young Philadelphia lawyer, presumably destined for a fine and successful career, owing to his marvellous speaking voice and oratorical gifts, Sachsen dropped everything and rushed to offer his services to the lawyers defending the Anarchist, Alexander Berkman, who of course had no chance of avoiding having the book thrown at him and duly went to jail. Thereafter, Sachsen was one of the main Anarchist lawyers, and also defended Wobblies at the time of World War I. He was never disbarred for these activities, a constitutional legal nicety which was only finally dropped in the 1940s, but his career as a successful lawyer was of course ruined. He appeared in endless labor cases, where his incredible oratorical passion and sincerity nevertheless seldom won. This was a foregone conclusion. But he became famous as the Demosthenes of the poor, for his free consultations and successful defenses in the harassments and evictions of miners and steel-workers and their penniless families, inevitably following the strikes and lockouts for which Pennsylvania's enormous mineral wealth and ruthlessly exploitative mine and mill owners made that state a byword for decades.

As most people in non-mining states have no idea of what goes on, and went on, I might give one small but typical detail from my own hometown and family. During one of the protracted mining strikes in the 1930s, the hated Black Cops – this was Frick's invention, a private police force actually called the Coal and Iron Police, and even rougher than the Pinkerton men – invaded a whole area on the edge of our town where the Polish miners had their tawdry shack houses. The family of one of my sister's boyfriends were *sitting on wooden chairs on the porch, reading the funny papers,* when one of the mounted cops rode his horse right up onto the porch, crushing the miner's family against the wall, and stepping all over the father, who was also of course being truncheoned over the head meanwhile by the Black Cop, and whose back was broken. He was crippled for the rest of his life. That was the sort of case Leo Sachsen took, though by the 1930s he was already old and out of circulation.

How had a man like him succeeded in earning his family's hatred instead of their admiration? How had he treated his wife "like a swine"? Well, exactly those activities of Leo Sachsen that us kids were admiring and hoping one day to emulate, were considered by his wife, who came from a well-to-do family, as outrageously dragging herself and her family through the mire. As she saw it, he was also irresponsibly impoverishing them all, since his free legal defences and consultancies for the evicted strikers, who naturally could pay him nothing, left his own family's income practically at zero. He earned what he could defending small criminals and prostitutes, in the periods between strikes, since no respectable cases would ever be given to the defender of Anarchists, Wobblies, and wuss. It appears he also allowed his prostitute clients to pay him in trade, and even caught a disease from one of them; which I assume means that he did not get on sexually either with his wife, who felt that he had ruined his life.

Clearly Leo Sachsen had gained the love of thousands of poor miners, but had lost the love of his own wife & children. My father did the same thing, though by a slightly different method. Of course, I do not believe for an instant that this could have made the young Irene Alicia Sachsen into a Lesbian. Perhaps the angry and rejected wife who was her mother had some hand in turning her daughter's mind against the dedicated orator and unsuccessful humanitarian that thousands of other people adored and admired. That's the way these things usually work out. Though I admit it was not that way in my own family, where my mother always bent over backwards to defend my father for as many years as she could. Nor did any of my sisters become Lesbians.

By the time I'd heard Irina's version of this whole story, it was getting late, and we were finishing the next bottle of wine. I thought this would be a good moment to put on the phonograph records that I had brought, if only so as not to have dragged them uselessly across town and also to sort of clear the air of the violence and hatred, both outside and inside the families, that I remembered only too well from my own young life in a Pennsylvania mining town.

We sat quietly sipping our wine by candlelight, while Thomas Tallis' angelic music soared, and I was thinking the usual foolish thoughts about how everyone loves music because its intellectual content is ungraspable, and you're left with only the pure emotion of the composer. Whereas it's easy to hate any writer or speaker, because you know right away how insulting he has been. There are also people who can listen happily to the hour-long insult of pretended modern music, since Mahler and Anton Webern — all purposeful ugliness and ghastly noise — but who get up on their high horse if you're obliged to tell them their cultural fly is open. Or that their so-called music stinks like the unburied corpse it is.

My hostess Irina wandered about the apartment a bit, I suppose going to the bathroom, and came back and lit a stick of incense: one of my favorite hates. I like atmosphere, but am not attuned to the heavy 1920s studio type. Irina did not ever wear trousers – even lesbians didn't often do that in those days – but had now changed her dress for a dark-figured Chinese wrapper. I looked at her in some alarm as I saw her flitting about like this in the half-light, because even I could see that she had decided to turn the evening into a seduction. Of me. I would have to be careful in the future playing the "Fantasia on a Theme by Thomas Tallis." That polyphonic stuff is dynamite!

Irina once told me that she had been everywhere in the world and had slept with everything, and that her first sexual experience had been with the knobs on the back of a chair. So I knew she slept with men on occasion, as well as women. I could see that this was going to be one of those rare occasions. I felt like muttering, as girls had so often muttered to me, "But can't we just be friends — the way we've always been!" Irina was great, but she did not attract me as a woman. It's like electricity: it's either on or off. It's the worst kind of cliché, of course, to say you could have knocked me over with a feather, but honest, you could have knocked me over with a feather at the next remark or item on the agenda.

"Legman," said Irina suddenly, in her fine deep voice, of which I decided I now understood the origin, "how do you feel about buggering women?"

Some warning instinct told me that this was not a scientific inquiry, as mine had been, about the psychodynamic causes of Lesbianism, but was more in the nature of a practical question. Something like Garson Kanin's offhand replique, still famous in the annals of the American theatre among the great lines of extemporaneous additional dialogue, which he puts in the mouth of a rather bored young lady listening to an earnest young man of exactly the kind I then was: "Say, are you just one of them talkers, or would you be interested in a little *action*?" I recognize at once the cogency of the rectal argument — if you're planning to argue with me about assholes and other forms of birth control — that lesbians don't want to get pregnant, any more than any other unmarried women. In fact, it might even be very embarrassing for a lesbian, or emotionally confusing or humiliating, for her to have to go into a drugstore to buy cervical diaphragms and birth control jelly, and now the Pill and all that. After having already had to make her peace for years or decades with the depressing pointlessness for her, of buying sanitary napkins every month. I mean, what's the use of being a lesbian at all, if you still have to slop around with birth control? I understand that, and I also understand the peculiar wryness and illogical humor some people find in the phrase, "pregnant lesbians," though godnose plenty of lesbians do fraudulently marry and have children. I mean to say, I do understand, or think I understand, why Irina was asking me how I felt about buggering women. But the inquiry left me rather cold.

Next after the dream of every man, of a certain type, about being the proud owner of the Golden Penis that can make endless women and girls beg, and fall to their knees; also scream, climb up the walls, wave their silk-clad legs over their heads, and throw all their clothes out the window. That mythical Golden Penis can especially make "even the most frigid of women (including wives) have orgasm after orgasm; I suppose must come the matching fantasy or grand adolescent dream of being the man who can cure lesbians of their lesbianism, simply   by the application of that same auriferous phallic organ.

But as I had never really cured Irina's ex-girlfriend Susan Aguerra orally of anything in particular, let alone her lesbianism, in spite of three months of sixty-nining with her nightly all over the floor and walls of the apartment we had shared with Magda off Gramercy Park, I did not truly feel that it was going to be me that would be bringing Irina Naxos back to normality. Via the rectum. Rectal psychiatry forever! That might make a great sign-off for a soap-opera: "Will Irina Naxos be brought back to normality by the Golden Penis? – Tune in on this program again at the same time tomorrow . . . . And remember! *Tales of the Golden Penis* is brought to you by *CANTHARIDOL!!* The aphrodisiac of the *Stars!!!* Stiff, Strong, Unbending and Unwavering ingredients, that will make YOU Unforgettable, Unbreakable and Unbeatable! Including *YOHIMBINOID!!* The Miracle Rejuvenator Ingredient! Don't let your prick know anything about it. It doesn't have to. It knows. Golden, platinum, or just plain human clay, your prick generally knows better than you what you want – and don't want."

Irina and I were still friends later, after a suitable pause, but the subject of candle-lit buggery to Tudor music was never mentioned again. Well, you know what Marie-Antoinette said, "Let 'em eat pussy!" I did try buggery again with other women, mostly as birth-control, or because they asked for it, or said they were particularly addicted to it. I even tried it once in a classic sex sandwich with my friend Korzybski, him as the face-up bread on bottom, vaginally, and me as the face-down rectal bread on top, both of us sweating and sawing away like a couple of mad pelvic lumberjacks at that ecstatically moaning and thrashing girl. That time I wasn't impotent at all, but I've never wanted to try it again – except maybe in fantasy with me jealously as the meat in the middle, instead of the bread: Lucky Pierre! I also got into quite an argument about it with my best girl, when I refused it when once offered.

I could just see her in my mind, like the first girl thrashing about on her two men's pricks simultaneously, like a turkey-trussed corybant, and licking and slavering the other man's mouth with hers; clearly wishing that she had that third prick she needed there. For a woman it's different. I suppose: something her body naturally loves and her soul desires, to be totally penetrated and filled. And the rectal orgasm is certainly very powerful and wrenching. I've tried it myself, with a dildo (small size), and it's nothing to be sneezed at. But from a man's point of view, as top-sawyer I mean, when the vagina is yearning there only an inch away, it's like that line of refusal by Voltaire to Frederick the Great in the joke: "Not again, Fritz! Once a philosopher; twice a degenerate." It could happen to anybody.

CHAPTER 38

VIRGIN PUSHER

NOW THAT the bibliography of homosexual literature that I had been preparing for Will Finch was finished, as far as I could finish it then, Finch put the periodical article cards on deposit in the library of the New York Academy of Medicine, where Dr. Dickinson was a family friend and advisor. I believe these cards have since been transferred to the Institute of Sex Research in Bloomington Indiana, begun by Professor Alfred Kinsey, who was the real successor of Magnus Hirschfeld, something Finch was not in a position to become, as he would have liked. Kinsey had also not yet appeared on the scene at that time. Finch and I discussed lengthily what should really be done next to continue his attempt to create an atmosphere of tolerance for homosexuality in America with the relatively small amount of money, and even less influence at his disposal: simply his own not very large private fortune, which would fairly soon be gone at the rate he was living it up, and he knew this. I told him that an observing and sustaining action was all we could hope to accomplish; like the manuscript I'd written on *Homosexuals and Their Prostitutes*, and its graffiti collection, which backed up everything in the main manuscript to the hilt.

"But nothing that'll have any practical effect? Can we?" Finch observed, folding his incredibly long hands like Baudelaire's under his chin.

I told him my motto — I have a different one for every occasion, because nobody likes to hear you quote proverbs, but they do accept defiant mottos — Cyrano de Bergerac's stunningly gallant final line: *"I fight! I fight! Je sais bien que c'est inutile, mais c'est beaucoup plus beau quand c'est inutile!"*

"I must tell my brother that one," he laughed. Finch had a brother who was a professor of modern history at Yale, and always demanding practical results. He asked me if I'd consider writing any more books on the subject, but — not being Cyrano — I asked what the use was, since it was impossible even to get the one on homosexual prostitution published. And you'd think people would care about that. After all, it was their own sons by the tens of thousands, probably, who were prostituting themselves to homosexuals all over the country.

"Ah, yes, my dear," said Finch, "but that's *just* what they don't want to be told."

We agreed that it would be tactically wiser that any further studies of case-histories and all that, should be done, not by rough-&-ready me, but by people with properly acceptable scientific credentials, to lend an air of respectability to things. Like Dr. George W. Henry, to whose book of case-histories, *Sex Variants*, I had supplied under my own name a full-dress glossary of modern homosexual slang. None of the people who had helped Henry to form contacts, and find people who would give their histories in the homosexual world, such as my friend Irina Naxos, and Finch himself, had been happy about Henry's book, which they found unsympathetic and even mocking. I took it upon myself to transmit this criticism to Henry through one of his psychiatric lieutenants. They were horrified at my impudence, even though I pointed out to them that I myself had no feelings in the matter, not being homosexual, and was simply transmitting to them a message the homosexual community felt they might want to receive.

They wanted so little to receive it that when the post-Kinsey one-volume reprint of Henry's book appeared, my glossary was among the parts omitted. So also the photographic studies of homosexual body types in the original edition, which admittedly gave a negative finding — since there is no homosexual body type, homosexuality being caused strictly by psychological and environmental factors — but was nevertheless one of the most unusual and interesting sections of the book. The one-volume expurgated and abridged fake "New Freedom" edition was a total dud, and people are still searching year after year in the book trade for the original two volumes, which has become a rare and valuable set.

I suggested to Finch that it might be a good idea, instead of wasting any more of his fortune on my researches or on male prostitutes and wild entertainments for his homosexual friends, if he would invest some of his remaining money in a collection of books on homosexuality in various languages. I told him such a collection could not possible go down in value, and might increase greatly if he ever wanted to sell it later, when his inheritance would be gone. He said I was being a killjoy, but agreed I was right, and off we went searching for our first haul of books. Naturally we went to the Gotham Book Mart first, because *Wise Men Fish There*, but they had very little, except a lovely Carrington edition on fine paper, published in Paris about 1900, of the translation of the *Satyricon* of Petronius, falsely attributed to Oscar Wilde, and probably really the work of one Francis D. Byrne, Carrington's principal translator for Latin, Russian, and perhaps Arabic as well. It would have been Byrne who did Carrington's new and improved edition of the great Arabic love-book, al-Nafzawi's *Perfumed Garden*, but this too omits the long homosexual section which was finally translated into English a few years ago, and is very dull.

We had kept out the bibliography index-cards for books, as opposed to periodical articles, for this exact purpose, and they were our finding list. As I did not want to make any appearances in the Fourth Avenue second-hand book stores as yet, we concentrated our weekly search in the better bookstores on East 59th Street, and throughout midtown, also a few in Greenwich Village, for the homosexual fiction in particular. I told Finch he might find something more on Fourth Avenue, but he'd have to go there alone just then. He did not enjoy book scouting on Saturdays the way I did, though it was pleasant enough to do together. So we stayed above Fourteenth Street, and in not too long a time he had amassed a very creditable nuclear collection of books. There was no question of reading these books — they were being *collected*. Later they were all given to the Kinsey Library, an act of faith for future researchers' benefit perhaps. I did not buy or keep any of these books for myself except one, or rather two, and these were duplicate copies of those I bought for Finch. I couldn't resist these two items, as they were little masterpieces of unconscious humor, both by the same author, entitled *The Female Impersonators* and *The Autobiography of an Androgyne*, both published about 1920 in New York. The author's style was a joy, and read just like Mrs. Malaprop on a homosexual binge. I have no notes on this book now, but will never forget one passage beginning: "Oft have I desiderated feminine corporeality, and I opined the appellation *faëry* the most melodious that ever impinged upon my eardrums," or similar. The author was a true genius of overwriting and should have been composing Fourth of July speeches for southern orators.

Going around buying fine books with Finch eventually excited a yearning in me for my own long-lost Liggett Library of applied semi-erotica, on which I had spent all my pocket money and after-school earnings in the local chain drugstores when I was in high school, but had left it behind in two large packing crates in my family's cellar in Scranton, and had never seen again. Not to put too fine a point on it, oft would I desiderate to see those goddamned books, and I opined the appellation chump that which I deserved for leaving them in storage so long.

One night, leaving the public library, where I still always went immediately after finishing work at the Academy of Medicine, or book-scouting Saturdays with Finch, I walked west on 42nd Street beyond Broadway, in among the cheap movie-grind houses and the few leftover burlesque theatres that were still operating during the war, to my favorite spaghetti joint. Actually, the spaghetti there was pure poison, and very small portions too; but what I enjoyed was the superb wrist motion with which the night chef would spurt a small ladleful of mock-tomato sauce over each plate of spaghetti as it went by. He didn't ever turn the ladle over at all, but just snapped it forward with an upward hook, and the tomato red would splat all over the wilted noodles. I suppose it was sexual somehow, or it wouldn't have interested me, but I've never really been able to pin it down.

Anyhow, I loved watching it, and would take a seat near the front where I could see the chef do his act in the window, over the gas-rings and boilers filled with spaghetti. He was a real artist, though not in the same league, for total body English and lean choreographics, with the night-shift malted milkshake specialist, across the street at Grant's hot dog and ice cream soda emporium on the corner of Seventh Avenue. This malted milkshake man really belonged in the Russian ballet. There was never another like him. He was a landmark, and knew it. Never a wasted motion — he moved as beautifully as if he were fucking on ice-skates.

As I was sitting inhaling my spaghetti and watching the chef's wrist work with the *espada*, or tomato sauce ladle, who should barge in but Will Finch's educated hustler friends, both of whom had been my models for the body posture photography tryouts. I assumed they were stoking up to go to work on the corner of 42nd Street and Eighth Avenue nearby, which was known in the homosexual world as the Meat Market, and sometimes as The Bucket of Blood. This corner would be lined every night from nine p.m. onward with young hustlers or midnight cowboys holding up the walls of the drugstore there, lounging in figure-4 positions and waiting to be picked up by the homosexuals who prowled about studying the genital baskets outlined through the hustlers' tight blue jeans. This was the crude reality of midnight prick-peddling that the books Finch and I were buying were only bullshitting about in their literary and scientific euphemisms. Perhaps Steven Crane's lost manuscript novel of homosexual prostitution in the 1890s, *Flowers in Asphalt*, the sequel to his *Maggie: A Girl of the Streets*, would have told some of the truth, at least poetically, but the manuscript has long since disappeared. I once bearded old Miss Belle da Costa Greene, the elder Morgan's former mistress and later librarian, on the matter of this manuscript, which the Morgan Library was rumored to possess and keep hidden. She was furious at the suggestion of hidden books or manuscripts in her care, and snapped angrily, "All our holdings are catalogued!"

But she forgot to mention that at some time, many years previously, the younger J. Pierpont Morgan had decreed an *auto da fé* — according to what other librarians there admitted to me — and any "unseemly" materials they then had simply disappeared, leaving only Nicolas Blondeau's *Dictionnaire Érotique Latin-Français*, published by Liseux in the 1880s, which was presumably spared as being mostly in Latin. One hopes the hapless unseemlies were only sold off, and not burnt, and that if Crane's manuscript was among them there is still a faint hope that it will surface again one day. If it was as good as its sister Maggie — and it should have been better, since Crane was presumably homosexual, or he would never have written it — *Flowers in Asphalt* must have been a masterpiece.

Korzybski and his friend told me that they were going into a new line of business, which was apparently some type of black-marketeering, of block tin or other rare metals now worth fabulous prices in the war industries. Some ex-bootleggers in some mysterious locale upstate had cached away a stack of this at the end of Prohibition during the 1930s. Korzybski and his friend, known only as Jenk, were on the trail of this treasure trove, and swore me to secrecy. They were only hanging around Times Square this one last night to try to promote some loans — not blackmail, just loans from old friends — from some of the better-heeled homosexuals they expected would be at The Meat Market. They were going to need a truck to transport the block tin, and they had a small truck, but the truck needed repairs and a new set of tires all around, if possible. This would cost plenty, since tires were also a black market item then.

They were very excited as two young fellows searching for treasure should be, especially a treasure which they expected would get them both off Times Square and out of The Meat Market for good, and Jenk accidentally let fall the information that they would also need enough money for gasoline to get to Erie, Pennsylvania, and back. I suppose that was where the bootleggers had originally been centered, and brought the smuggled liquor across Lake Erie from Canada. And I suddenly had an inspiration. I told them I'd like to buy in on their caper, but not for any share of the eventual profits. I would stick around until the end of the evening, while they touched the rich homos for however much money they could get. Then I would put up however much was still lacking — if it was within my means — if they would stop by at my hometown of Scranton, an the way back from Erie , and pick up my two crates of books and deliver them to me in New York. They thought the idea was great, and agreed they would have lots of room, because they couldn't hope for a whole truckload of block tin, only a small amount. A truckload of block tin would be worth several hundred thousand dollars, and the underworld would undoubtedly highjack a haul like that.

"Well, what will you do if there *is* a lot?" I asked them.

"Our customer in Jersey would pay for that information," Korzybski told me, "but we wouldn't want to handle a real big load. Too dangerous."

"Sure," said Jenk, "They'd have some hoods knock us off."

I was sorry now that I had made my thoughtless offer, but I couldn't back down now. I was in the secret. Anyhow, treasure-troving is great fun, especially when you spend most of your time sedately in libraries. I figured I would be able to find out from them by phone, when they were starting back from Erie, whether they had a dangerously big load of just the reasonable nest-egg they were hoping for.

I don't know why it is, but practically nothing I ever plan ever turns out the way I plan it. That's the main problem I've always had with my sex life too. If anything, I had even worse luck in my new career in crime. Korzybski and Jenk did promote a surprising amount of money that night along Eighth Avenue, and if they twisted any arms for it they didn't tell me about that. We met every hour in front of the spaghetti joint to compare notes. I occupied myself copying down choice examples of what my friend Arthur Minton later called the Marlovian prose — referring to the Elizabethan playwright, Christopher Marlowe, of course — of the marquee signs and posters in front of the pathetic movie-grind theatres along West 42nd Street: "Titanic! — Stupendous! — Hair-Raising!! — Two Men Locked in a Death-Struggle on a Hurtling Locomotive!! — FOR THE LOVE OF AN EVIL WOMAN!!" They don't make marquee signs like that any more, either. It's a lost art.

By one a.m. the borrowings and pickings had slowed down. We hung around till nearly two, and then went into Grant's to count up the take. Crowded places are the best for discussing contraband topics, if you used moderately covert terms. Nothing is worse than trying to lay a plot in a quiet little joint, where everybody else is straining to catch your every word from behind the bar, on the staircase to the cellar, and godnose where else. They had netted nearly eighty dollars, which was more than they had expected. If I would put up twenty more, plus maybe extra gas from Scranton, I was in on the deal. I agreed. Korzybski would come to pick me up tomorrow morning, and I would stay home from work and get the twenty dollars out of the bank, so they could finish paying for the tires and get on the road.

When he arrived, at about ten-thirty, to pick up the money, Korzybski told me very apologetically that Jenk wanted me to go along with them both ways — I had planned to go with them just to Scranton, to visit my mother, and then wait for them to pick me up there on the way back. He found it hard to explain why Jenk wanted so much of my company. I finally understood when he said that he also thought I should come with them; they were worried about my knowing so much about their treasure hunt.

"It's for your own protection," Korzybski told me frankly. "If we got knocked off, or if they came after us and we got away, and you weren't with us — well, Jenk is a very suspicious guy. He might think it was your fault. He's been telling me all morning how sorry he is we cut you in at all."

I thought that over. "Ed," I said, "do you really think I have gang connections, and that I'm going to rat on you to The Mob? Why I don't even know who the hell The Mob is. It's just a phrase you see on theatre marquees to me."

"I know that," he said. "Anybody that has two crates of books wouldn't know his ass from third base about the rackets. I told Jenk that. But he still wants you to come along. And I think you'd better come."

I went. It was marvellous. The truck broke down at least four times before we even got to the Delaware Water Gap. I was positive it was the same truck my Armenian junkman friend had pressed into service that day when I went with him to retrieve my belongings from the Mulhollands' apartment. There was something about the way the motor fought back at you, and farted suddenly when you had to push the thing that made me sure it was Namoorian's old truck. As I was basically being kidnapped, I couldn't stay to visit with my mother very long, but she welcomed me with tears of happiness. She made the two boys come in and fed us chicken soup in the kitchen, just like old times. Fortunately my father wasn't home.

The two boys and I went down the cellar to study the crates we'd be picking up later. Just being down there in the dust and dark, with the light filtering in through the cobwebby window, and the pile of coal for the furnace, took me back instantly, infinitely far. There was the plastered-up hole between the laths in the walled-over window where I had bored the hole to try to watch the Spanish girl tenant taking a bath. There was the broken old sofa in the corner by the door, with the springs coming out through the canvas ticking where Merry and Sherry and I had thought we invented the sixty-nine. We *did* invent it too!

When we were back on the road — I was the navigator with a folded-out gas-station map on my knees: after all, I was a native Pennsylvanian, and neither Jenk nor Korzybski had ever even been in Pennsylvania before — I mentioned to Korzybski, who was driving, that I had invented the sixty-nine with two of my girlfriends when I was eleven years old. He thought that was great, and turned to tell Jenk about it in the back, nearly wrecking the truck as he turned.

"Hey, Jenk!" he shouted. "Legman here invented the sixty-nine."

"So why the hell didn't you patent it, jerk?" Jenk wanted to know.

"Don't you worry," I told him. "I've been kicking my ass ever since. The next thing I invent, I'm keeping it for myself."

The trip was entirely uneventful except for incredible problems with the truck, of which every part caused endless trouble except the magnificent new black-market tires. It was like that rare ballad concerning a wild midnight trip on "The Er-I-e

Canawl," on which I spent forty years trying to find the original bawdy text, and am still not sure I've got it. Do *you* know it? The block-tin was found, waiting quietly since Prohibition, in Erie, in uninspired wooden plumbing fixture boxes covered with dust and piled along the wall in a moving-van garage, presumably the former bootleggers' successors. There was nothing to pay or steal: the moving man was Jenk's uncle. It was his block-tin, as it turned out, and he would receive half the money. I was glad when we got started on the return trip. I have seldom seen anybody with such intensely penetrating and suspicious eyes as that uncle. I formed a prayer in my mind that Jenk would pay him promptly and in full. I could see that otherwise all our collective geese were cooked. We slept on the block-tin in the truck, beside the highway that night.

On the way back to Scranton the truck conked out again about a mile north out of Towanda, and we had to push it until we found a garage where they could repair it. Jenk wouldn't leave the truck; he was as nervous as a cat having kittens in a meat-grinder. But Korzybski and I bought some cheese and bread and tomatoes, and walked along by the Susquehanna River and ate lunch watching the water and the occasional scows floating by. It was a nice day, and I would get my books back. I was happy.

There was no further incident. The Mob didn't come out to highjack our block-tin. I am sure it got built into the critical parts of numerous airplanes eventually, and lots of German and Japanese women and innocent children were killed by bombs dropped from those airplanes who might still be alive today if it weren't for my twenty-dollar contribution. Maybe my block-tin went into the Enola Gay that dropped the Atom Bomb. That's how it is with corporate responsibility. When the next war comes, and the German and Japanese bombing planes come over and kill my wife and children — and me — I won't have any complaint coming, will I? Did you buy war bonds? You won't have any complaint either.

We got the crates of books out of the cellar in Scranton, and I banged the dust out of my and Merry and Sherry's old broken sofa with my hand, suddenly remembering how they had worn their hair in pigtails while they leapt all over my prick. Got to protect the young! My father was home this time, so I just said that Ed and Jenk were two boys helping move the crates. There was no chicken soup this time. My mother slipped me a chicken white meat sandwich from the last Sabbath chicken, and three thick slices of homemade cake. I hate the dry white meat – give me that tender, juicy dark meat of the upper thigh every time! I gave the sandwich to Korzybski and Ed to share later. The motor of the truck worked so much better since getting it repaired in Towanda that the fumes now made me sick, and I didn't even want my slice of homemade cake. I found it crushed in my jacket pocket two days later, and ate it then with delight. It was a mistresspiece: something wet and strange with ground-up nutmeats in it. A Hungarian recipe, surely. I wondered if my mother still made cabbage-and-apple strudel anymore, flinging the thin layers around through the air like bed sheets.

The block-tin was delivered out in Jersey somewhere. At my request — I explained that I was kind of carsick and needed to get my stomach right-side-up — they left me somewhere at a soda fountain while they went to drop off the tin. I preferred not to know where The Mob had its offices. I drank bubbly water and belched for a while, until the carsickness went away. On the way back through Hoboken to the Lackawanna Ferry, Jenk point to an enormous field of tall weeds we were passing, by the railroad tracks, with a solitary lunch wagon stationed on cement blocks along one edge.

"Tea," he said. "Marrywanna. Know anyone that smokes the stuff?"

MARIJUANA PLANTS

THE TWO successful treasure-seekers carried my crates of books up the stone porch steps into the hallway for me when I got home, with old Mr. Nossiter fussing around us and complaining how would anybody get by. I felt continuously sick to my stomach, and knew that I couldn't be toting the books up to my room that night. I told Mr. Nossiter that he would just have to lump it. Korzybski offered to help me, but I said I didn't feel up to doing anything that afternoon, and that it would be a long job. The next morning, to my surprise, he woke me up at eight-thirty. I was still in bed, which is unusual for me. Korzybski worked the whole morning with me, opening the nailed crates with a magnificent burglar-style crowbar he brought along, and charging up and down the three flights of steps all morning with me, carrying the books. I knew I had found a friend, and we stayed friends — with a couple of ups and downs — until I left America years later, and even afterward.

The books were a terrible disappointment to me, when I got them stacked up in my room and began looking them over. All the worst shit that the drugstore reprint and remainder counters had to offer at the lowest point of the Depression, when I was in high school, and New York publishers were dying off like flies. The only nice books were the strange, dusty old volumes of poetry, and historical romances by Robert Louis Stevenson and George Barr McCutcheon, that I'd have found in Stück's second-hand bookstore on Washington Avenue, when Tia and I would hide in the back stacks and kiss up against the bookshelves. Then we would come out, dutifully carrying some odd novel or little volume of poetry with red frames crossed at the corners of every page, and lay down twenty-five cents for it on Orvie Stück's desk. My uncle Joel would usually refuse the money.

"What's this," he would say, "rent? Here, keep it. We're saving money on coal, the way you two lovebirds heat up the place. So go and buy her a chocolate soda with it, sport!" And he would push the quarter back at me along the desk with his fingernail, over the thick glass covering the stamp sets for the young collectors. And I would buy Tia a chocolate soda, and hold hands with her under the counter.

The drugstore volumes that now infuriated me the most were the long set of reprints of what had been Horace Liveright's Black and Gold Library, mostly of semi-erotic classics, and which had been reissued after he went broke on a heavy bulking paper like the kind used for blotters. The texts and plates were the same – but the blotting paper and cheap getup were just intolerable to me now. I had two real volumes of the set, one of them being Pierre Louÿs' more-or-less complete works, Including *Aphrodite* and *Bilitis* and *King Pausole.* These shamed the reprints so badly that I decided that I'd sell off about half the books I had just brought home from Scranton after all those years in storage.

Some of them had my first bookplate in them: an innocent little rectangle of white, gummed paper the size of a calling card that Gertrude's father, who was a job printer, had knocked out for me in Old English type on his calling card press: It even had my long-lost middle initial E, for Eliezer, Moses' second son: Gershon E. Legman.

That was another one of the similarities between myself and Pierre Louÿs, of which there were many, I felt, except that he had been rich until the very end of his life, and I was always poor. He too only had a bookplate at the very beginning of his book-collecting, as a boy in school, and later had given up under the mass of books he bought, and simply rubber-stamped a facsimile of his fine large signature, always in purple ink, on the half-titles of his books. I was later to learn that he also spent years, quite aside from his secret and quite electrifying erotic manuscripts in both poetry and prose — on an international dictionary of sexual speech and a matching bibliography of erotic literature, exactly the projects that I was now on, at the same age as Louÿs had been when he started them. I laboriously turned up since then a few dozen of the thousands of manuscript cards on which he filed these materials, and the Paris bookseller Mme. Vidal Mégret had a large group of them for sale some years ago, but I could not afford the price. At least it's nice to know they have not been lost.

The one difference between us was Louÿs' almost total self-defeating masochism. Or maybe that was a similarity, but I was determined to fight it in myself. If I certainly defeated myself time after time in my career, at least I didn't do it quite so sweepingly in my private life. Louÿs had outrageously defeated himself in both, and for example refused to write or publish anything again, except for learned articles in bibliographical journals, for the last twenty years of his short life, after he found he had accidentally written a best-seller, *Aphrodite.* I suppose the real main difference is that Louÿs was totally oriented on literature, whereas I always felt that literature was only a popular, fictionalised form of the historical record, and that what had life and balls and the real electrical charge was folklore, when you got it unexpurgated and unprettified, and full of the sap of life, right from the spigot. Not the castrated stuff on the phoney folklore programs and records, and the commercialised fakelore festivals. "Now *don't* let's say any dirty words," one of these schlockmeisters once warned me, *"but keep it authentic!"*

I knew there was no chance of publishing the erotic folklore I was collecting. Jake Brussel might have done it, but he was in the can now, and the heat was on altogether because of the war. But I kept collecting, especially jokes and songs. It gave me a reason to hang around sometimes in barrooms and record stores. That was now almost the only contact I ever had with men; you couldn't talk with people in the libraries, except with the librarian at the information desk, and with the other readers in the men's room, as a matter of fact, you could learn quite a lot sometimes, about things you wouldn't expect to hear there. *The Latrine Gazette,* just like in the army. Well, one thing was sure; getting the books from Scranton had been a failure. But I was glad to have them, after I sorted out the trash and later sold or traded it off.

I found the pretty set of *Poetica Erotica* I had bought in Michigan, but of course that was all literary, and the few folksongs that T. R. Smith had slipped in were all historical, from *Pills to Purge Melancholy* mostly, and there were not five pages of modern bawdy songs. The rest he had saved to put in his anonymous *Immortalia*. Where was the matching set of *Eastern Love* that had brought about my down fall at Michigan? Gone. And so were most of the nicest books I had. I remembered now. — The local police were in cahoots somehow with one of the campus booksellers, and when I foolishly let fall the name of the set I had stolen the typewriter to copy, they called him in to my room while I was quarantined in the little student hospital, and seized whatever he told them was valuable. Meaning that he bought back from them later. A nice racket. And meanwhile I'm thrown out, and no way of complaining.

Thinking about it, and fuming about the beautiful books I had lost in that, my first seizure, I wrote a long letter about the operation of the censorship and the kickback customs seizures in America. I sent it to Alec Craig in England, who had asked me for a rundown on the American free speech situation during the war, for his little liberal politics and poetry mag, *Plan*. He published it too, but when I got twenty copies of it from him, by way of payment, I was afraid to circulate them. I had named too many real names, and it was clearly libel under American law. Just the two upper Park Avenue booksellers I had named would have had my ass in a sling in a hurry. They would deny everything of course, and probably had police protection.

I would have to be more prudent in the future, just as Dickinson was always telling me. Besides, why was I naming names? What kind of a fink was I? Well, I guess I had been angry, thinking about Jake in jail, while a real, hard-hearted crook like Abramson in Chicago did what he liked with police protection, and the same probably for his opposite numbers in New York. Well, that was the way things were set up. Not up to me to start blowing the whistle. I hadn't really thought about how it would look in print, or even that Craig would publish it word for word as I wrote it. Damn few editors or publishers in America had that kind of guts. At any rate, I never circulated the twenty copies of the magazine — not because of libel, but so as not to be an informer any worse than I already was.

I took a heavy pen, and black ink, and blanked out all the names and details I was sorry now I had given. I even turned over the paper and blanked out the same lines in black on the other side. No one would ever read it now. Unless they happened to be in England. I laughed bitterly all the time I was doing the blanking out, and even put on the phonograph of the record of Chopin's Funeral March., banged out in sombre octaves on the piano; and I laughed cacklingly in time to the heavy tread of the funeral *cortège*. This was the second time I had ever expurgated anything, though I suppose maybe it didn't count because it was only for libel, and even for honor, in a way. The first time had been worse: when I did the expurgated Fanny Hill for Jake sitting in the cellar of his summer rental at Coney Island in Brooklyn while the water on the floor rose. No honor there! Heigh-ho!! Nothing but the best for our boy! Sing it! — *Where. Will. We. All. Be! A. Hundred. Years. From. Now. PUSHIN' up the daisies! PUSHIN' up the daisies! Where. Will. We. All. Be! A. Hundred. Years. From. Now?*

THOSE DAYS were sunny and young, and every sin basically innocent. My own next prank was much more serious, and it's only due to my heavily overworked guardian angel that I didn't net a nice long jail sentence for it. My old friend from Scranton, John "Geewhiz" Brown, was in town briefly and looked me up. He was still working as a jazz saxophonist, and had never done anything at all with his literary ability. When I taxed him with this, he replied only with his usual half-smile, as always hiding the swivel tooth in front that so tortured him and destroyed his self-confidence. He was with another young-fellow-me-lad, not from Scranton, but from an even smaller hamlet nearby, called Archbald, out somewheres beyond Dunmore and Olyphant. I can't remember his name, and maybe it's just as well.

John Brown came into my room diffidently, as was his way, but his friend Archie, as I guess I'll call him, barged up the stairs and into the room and grabbed my armchair where he immediately started rolling himself a marijuana cigarette from makings his pockets were full of. As this was no different than lots of other jazz musicians I had seen, I said nothing, but did sidle over and opened the window, under the pretext of getting the typewriter chair for John to sit on, while I had to sit on the bed. I asked them what they'd like to hear and told them I had plenty of good jazz records, which was a lie, but I did have a wonderful jazz clarinet record called *Climbing and Screaming* which they admitted was very fine, and the other side even better: I think it was *Gravier Street*, or *Red Onion Blues*.

"Where do you get records like that?" Archie asked me. I told him there were lots of places around town, but especially the record shops on East 42nd Street, where all the musicians hung out. "I better get over there," he opined, lighting up his second or third stick of marijuana — but who's counting — "I'm running out of everything but papers."

"Are you kidding?" I said. "They don't sell that stuff there."

"Course not," he agreed cheerfully. "But I'll find some character hanging around that'll have an extra stick or two." And he puffed up with all the happy assurance of a man who knows where his safe supply is stashed out. He rolled all the rest of what he had in his pockets into little sticks and offered them generously to us. I believe my friend John may have lit up too, and I rather hesitantly took one. After coming on like a jazz buff, godnose why, I could hardly put on suddenly a holier-than-thou act like the girl with the two vaginas.

With John and Archie smoking, I felt constrained to light up, however, and wasted it purposely, by pretending to inhale but only holding the smoke in my mouth a long time with an avid expression, and then letting it curl out in proper form. No one was watching me. Even so, I began to feel sick just from all the fumes around me. They say intoxication makes people relax their inhibitions, and do the opposite of what they do all the time. Maybe that's why drinking always makes me silent and mysterious. But it didn't seem to work that way this time. John became twice as silent and withdrawn as he usually was. Archie became so totally expansive that he was sprawled all over the bed, having pushed me out of the way, while he explained us his dreams for starting a Jazz Foundation for young, white, and even colored musicians, at which the weekly paycheck would be in eight-ounce bags of the best Mexican marijuana.

In one of his lesser altitudes he began explaining where all the marijuana comes from in the United States, and why the quality is so poor. I suggested that maybe it was because the sellers were cutting the stuff with improperly cured cowdung, but he said it wasn't that.

"It's the birdcages," Archie explained, puffing and sucking away on the smoke. "The canaries don't wanna sing, only in the mating season. You know, when they're in heat. The only way you can get 'em to sing is with this special seedblock they sell — it's pressed hemp seeds in guck. The canaries love it, and they sing! Hoo-boy, do they sing!? And the little old ladies that own the birds" — delicate gesture here — "dump the crap out the window to clean out the birdcages. And so next to every house with a birdcage there's a field of hemp growing. And nobody knows what it is. And pretty soon the empty lots are full of it."

"I thought they grew it commercially in the south, for making rope," I said, enjoying the idea of the marijuana-crazed canaries singing their little hearts out in the off season.

"Yeah," Archie agreed, waving his arm, "but you never see that rope stuff further north than St. Louis. Johnny here saw a couple of miles of the stuff growing in Texas, didn't you Johnny?"

"Yeah," said John Brown vaguely, with his eyes shut, "miles of it!"

I waited for him to add "gee whiz!" but this time he didn't. As I had a record of canaries singing in my ten-inch albums of novelty records, I put that on for a joke, but the two of them began groaning that the high-pitched sounds hurt their ears. They were too high already. I put on another record of nightingales. They loved that. As I had slowed the speed button down, to try to tone down the nightingales' singing, everything was now too low, so I flipped the little aluminum disc on the spindle while the record ran. This checked the oscillations by appearing to stand still when the turntable speed was exactly seventy-eight revolutions per minute. But of course, only in electric light. The aluminum disc caught the reflection of the lamp bulb as it spun, and threw it up onto the ceiling as a swiftly turning patch of light. When I went to take the disc off, Archie asked me to put it back on. His head was going around, lurching in circles in time with it, watching it on the ceiling.

"That's beautiful, man," he said. "Leave it turn."

It was beautiful, and very hypnotic. I started telling them about Thomas Wilfrid's Clavilux color-organ, and the changing and surging up of colors and forms like waves of lava rising, while Wilfrid would play a record meanwhile of a Haydn quartet. Disney bloated that up terribly when he took it over for the opening of his *Fantasia*, in animated cartoon style, to the music of Bach's *Toccata and Fugue*. Wilfrid's Clavilux was much greater, and cleaner too. I put the Bach record on, in Stokowski's grand orchestral transcription, and both Archie and John nearly went out of their minds with happiness. Archie kept encouraging me to play it louder and louder, but I was afraid to do so. It would bring the landlord up, I knew.

"I thought smoking that stuff made you sensitive, and you only wanted the music low," I countered.

"Hell no!" said Archie, "I want it loud, like jazz. I just don't want it high." As I now knew he was full of shit, I put on "Climbing and Screaming" again, which was so high it was out of sight. They loved it. It was just canaries they didn't like, I guess. Archie wanted the address of Wilfrid's little auditorium in midtown, but I assured him they didn't even let people smoke ordinary cigarettes during the performance, so he lost interest.

By about five o'clock in the afternoon they had straightened out sufficiently to leave, and although I was glad to see my old friend Silent John, whom I had always liked and still liked, I was also glad to see them go. The room really stank. I opened both windows now, and even tried to circulate the air around and out by waving a couple of opened-out filing folders for fans. I was afraid to try to get a cross-draft with the door open, as old man Nossiter was wise to a lot of things, and this might be one of them, I thought. I couldn't get the place aired out, so I left the windows open and left. On the stairs I met Elaine coming up, and she told me she would have choir practice that night, which meant, in the chaste code we used, that she would be coming around to tap at my door about ten-thirty to make love. I did not feel in form, owing to the marijuana fumes, and told her that I had to go to a movie showing to write a review of it for an English magazine, but that when I got back I'd tap at *her* door if it wasn't too late.

It was lucky I'd done that, because when I did get back, who should be waiting for me on the outside steps but Archie. He had tried to find me again earlier, but Mr. Nossiter had told him I was out and refused of course to let him wait for me in my room, something I had always given strict orders about. I had lost too many nice books and things that way before I found out how dishonest some of your very best friends can be, if you don't watch them. I wish life weren't like that, but it is. He told me he had nowhere to sleep and no money, and it was obviously up to me to put him up overnight. I asked where John Brown was? Gone back to Scranton. I was really furious, but there was no help for it. The room was almost clear of the odor when we got there, but Archie had it all nauseatingly stunk up again five minutes after he arrived. I believe that goddam odor gets into anything made of cloth and sticks like lice.

He told me lots more stories in his happy stupor, in which I believe he continuously lived; and in particular explained to me all the various wild plants he and other kids in Archbald smoked. He knew and told me their exact common names, though of course not the Latin names, and I recognized half of them as being famous deadly poisons of the most dangerous kind. When I told him this he agreed lazily.

"Sure," he said, "but that's only if you eat them. We just smoke them. You never have anything worse than convulsions." He segued this information carelessly into a long tale of how three of his chums had died after accidentally smoking the wrong plant, which would never have happened to them if they had only continued with their usual favorites. Then he tried to borrow some money from me, against the morrow, when he would be going to the jazz record shops to try to find someone to sell him more tea. I told him I was broke, which was not far from the truth, and he grumbled and worried about this quite a bit, asking me how in the hell he was to get hold of the tea he needed if he didn't have any money? It was now selling for twenty-five cents a stick, which was twice the price of an entire pack of ordinary cheap cigarettes. I told him I was sorry. But . . .

It was this demonic suggestion, that There Is Money In Drugs, which began acting on my unfortunately too sober mind at that point. Meanwhile I did not give it a further thought. Archie fell asleep, and I decided there was nothing of mine he would steal – he certainly didn't read books, and old Mr. Nossiter would be there to stop him from sneaking off with my radio, I felt sure. So I slipped out, when he was snoring heavily enough, and tapped on Elaine's door. She let me in with her accustomed little grin and twinkling eyes, and I played caveman and immediately threw her on her bed and started kissing her breasts, as she was in a dressing gown which she helpfully let fall open. Just as we were getting things onto a higher plane, with all my clothes and shoes torn off and flung on the floor, we heard this long groaning snore coming through my wall, like a flight of pigs sawing their way out of the forest primeval.

"Who's that in your room?" Elaine quavered. "Is that a girl?"

"Quit 'cher kidding," I told her. "It sounds like the Mounted Police." Then I explained to her that I had an impecunious male guest staying over, to the accompaniment of more and more noisy snores and vocal gurblings, as Archie seemed to be arguing with himself. "I guess he talks in his sleep," I surmised weakly.

"But what ever are we going to do?" Elaine wanted to know. "We'll never be able to sleep with a noise like that."

"Certainly not. We're not going to sleep — we're going to make love all night," I averred.

But it didn't work out that way. Every time I would have her in position to slip it in, after waiting five minutes for the snores in the next room to subside, a new burst of anti-aircraft fire would break loose, and we would collapse in laughter, which we hoped would wake Archie up, but it never did. Finally we laughed ourselves to sleep in each other's arms, without ever having made love at all. We both had to sleep on our sides, with me curled up behind her like two spoons in a kitchen drawer, as there was no room on her narrow cot for us to sleep any other way. The minute Elaine was completely asleep the snores in the next room began to abate, so I began playing with her nipples and then with her pussy from behind, and she stirred in her sleep and canted back her heinie to help me get in.

"Are you asleep, honey?" I inquired.

"Oh yes," she murmured, "but do it anyhow. Just don't give me a baby." Then she fell asleep again. As I couldn't figure out any gentlemanly way of solving the problem this posed, I just lay inside her body for along time without moving, and finally sleep began coming over me too and I became soft, and I guess I slipped out. I fixed it into my mind, half-asleep as I was, that I should wake up very early and get out of her room, as, if Mrs. Nossiter found us together when she'd be making up the beds and cleaning the halls in the morning, it would cause trouble for Elaine. The Nossiters didn't much care what I did, or how many girls I brought up to my room, because I was a man. But if a girl roomer did it, she was a whore therefore, and they would throw her out. They had already put out a girl for no better reason the year before.

I got back to my room just in time. Archie was wide awake, and no longer under the influence of any drug. Except in the sense that he was clearly still thinking about his next marijuana fix, and had taken two full albums of twelve records each off my shelves – in fact all my best blues and jazz records – and had them on my chair, ready to go, when I walked in. I asked him, not altogether politely, what he planned to do with these two albums of highly saleable records, and then accompanied him and out the door. I also saw him as far as the corner, and pointed out the way to the subway. I wanted to be sure he left.

That was the last time I ever let a male friend sleep over in my room when I wasn't there, for many many years. And the next time I just as foolishly let down my defenses and allowed somebody else to do it, things worked out even worse. Either I have a lot

more phony friends than other people do —
something I have often suspected — or else honesty is
a pretty rare virtue, and H. L. Mencken was right:
"Conscience is the still small voice that tells you
someone may be looking." And if it comes to
apothegms, how about this one: *All men are enemies.* I
suppose it's caused unconsciously by competing for the
available food and cunt, but read it again: *All men are
enemies.*

IT TOOK me years to understand a couple of simple
things like that. Afterwards I wasn't so full of
broadminded tolerance, idealism, faith, hope, trust and
charity, live-and-let-live foolishness, and other liberal
bullshit as I was at the period I'm describing.
Meanwhile my excessive tolerance for everybody else's
follies, then and for a long time after, also allowed me
to be as foolish as I liked. That was the unspoken
bargain, of course. But alas, I didn't even know how to
go about being successfully the kind of damn fool I
yearned to be. Didn't know my ass from a gourd.
Curcurbitus vulgaris.

Here's what I did. After excogitating the matter
for about two weeks, I decided that Archie had
unwittingly given me a marvellous idea for how to buy
all the records, or at least all the blues and jazz records,
I would ever want, without it costing me a penny. *I*
would be the character hanging around the jazz record
shops, of which there were at least three or four

downtown, and nobody knows how many in Harlem. And it would be me that would have an extra stick of tea or two, for sale, when the jazzmen would come looking for it. Why not? Didn't I know where there was a whole mile-long field of the goddam stuff, out by the D. L. & W. railroad tracks in Hoboken, where Jenk had pointed it out to me that time? Well, there it was. I was in business. I certainly wouldn't be making any victims. Apparently everybody except me had been smoking the stuff for years.

Once I had this brilliant idea, I didn't even wait a day. I phoned up Dickinson's office and told them I had a bad case of the galloping mulligrubs, or something that didn't sound too serious, as I figured I would only need a day or two off. I emptied my two suitcases on the bed, and off I went to the Lackawanna Ferry slip on West Forty-Second Street, with my two empty suitcases, and on to Hoboken! Not even once during the beautiful ride across the Hudson, filled with tugs and barges and tankers chugging and tootling happily up and down the great, dirty river, did the thought occur to me that there might be any practical danger in what I was planning to do, or that there might well be a whole bookful of very active laws against it. Of course, I knew in a general sense that it was totally illegal to smoke anything except tobacco, or drink anything except hooch, because the government took a big rousing tax on those, so they were alright. Little did I know that there's also a tax on marijuana. Though perhaps not very high, it does the job. To the contrary, if I thought about the matter at all, I doubtless thought of myself as one of those patriots of the jazz music industry, comparable only to the Boston patriots of the famous Tea Party in 1776, who took matters into their own hands when faced with the iniquitous British government and its shameful tax on tea. Why not? Since tea was still what the jazzmen called the stuff they smoked.

It must have been the biggest haul since the Brinks job. Nobody paid the slightest attention to me. The field was right where I remembered it from my caper with Jenk and Korzybski and the tin, four blocks from the Lackawanna terminal in Hoboken. To prejudice the counterman in my favor, in the lonely lunch wagon parked alongside the breeze-blocks, I went in first and had a big tuna-fish sandwich and a cup of really bad coffee, and left him a nice tip. I then went out in the field nearby and started harvesting with my old Boy Scout knife with the six blades that I had prudently thought to bring along. I don't remember which blade of the Boy Scout knife works best for harvesting marijuana. It may be the ream-shaped one you use for making holes in leather to get your merit badge. Or else it's the hook-shaped one that you use to get the pebbles out of horses' hooves with, though that only counts for your daily good turn, but you can then untie the knot in your bandana. The only thing I'm sure of is that it's not the combined can-punch and bottle-top remover, better known as church key, because that's only good for opening beer. No merit badge for that.

After about an hour of working in the hot sun with my knife, I had both suitcases chockfull and bulging with pieces two feet long, and my hands and wrists and the cuffs of my shirt were black with resin. The laundryman was probably high for a week after he boiled up that shirt. The reason I cut pieces two feet long was because they would fit the easiest into the suitcases. I was not then aware that the active principle of the plant is in the flowering tops, and thought it was in the leaves, like tobacco. But I didn't want to stay out there in the field too long, and thought I would just take nice sized stemsful, and strip the leaves off at home.

It wasn't even that I was afraid of police interference — I swear, I hardly even thought about that. I just didn't want to attract too much attention to myself, in case some other hipster like Jenk might be passing by, and might understand what I was doing and then hijack MY field of hemp. After all, everybody knew that Jersey City was wide open under Mayor Hague, and there were more gangsters living the happy suburban life there than in Chicago and Florida combined. All the newspapers said so. But you never heard of any gangsters getting arrested, now that Prohibition was over.

When I was ready to leave, I picked up my two bulging suitcases, and walked back to the Lackawanna Ferry, where I paid my dime to get into the cavernous ferry slip, with its marvellous overhead ropes and bridges hanging and creaking like a particularly dark print in Piranesi's *Prisons of Rome* copperplates. I felt a little conspicuous with my hands so filthy black, but no one paid me the slightest mind. Next time I would come to do some harvesting, I would bring along a little bottle of rubbing alcohol or something, to get my hands clean with on leaving the field. I spent the rest of the day stripping the leaves off the stems, including the tops, which I figured I might as well throw in.

Then I took the stems out wrapped in newspaper, and put them in the garbage can of the Japanese restaurant on the corner that evening. Nobody would think about them twice there. If anybody noticed them at all, they'd figure it was okra pods from making soup, or kohlrabi stalks, or who-knows-what. Anyhow, my name wasn't on them.

On the way back to my room I bought a pack of ordinary cigarettes, to think over what I was going to do next. Rum & Maple brand: I liked the name. You couldn't get any of the standard brands, like Old Golds, because of the war. This was the first pack of cigarettes, for my own use, that I ever bought in my life. I was twenty-six years old. I didn't smoke, or drink anything stronger than wine. I even hated the taste of beer. Of such stuff are successful drug-peddlers made. G. Legman, Virgin Pusher.

The first thing I learned from the pack of Rum & Maples was that there was going to be a slight stage-wait. The tobacco in cigarettes had to be dry, and my newspaper-wrapped hemp leaves hidden in the suitcase under the bed were still very alive and damp. This was going to make things difficult. The next day I counted up my money, and phoned the Academy of Medicine to say that my galloping mulligrubs were much worse, and that I would probably be out for two weeks. Nobody gave a damn, of course. Medical research and the war effort would get along nicely without me. I went to the candy store on the corner and for ten cents got a very large pack of old newspapers; decided it would be too much, gave back half, and had a bottle of soda for the other nickel. Then I stayed in my room for two weeks with the door locked, drying out the hemp leaves on spread newspapers all over the bed and on my filing boxes, while listening happily to music on the phonograph and writing a book. It was going to be the history of sex censorship. I had a great title: *Taboo.*

When five o'clock came every day, and I could be expecting Elaine to tap on my door almost any time after that, I wrapped up the leaves again in their newspapers and slung them back under the bed in the suitcases, newspapers and all. When the two weeks were up, I decided that the leaves had to be dry enough now, and went out and got the best little Handy Marvel cigarette-rolling contraption they had in the cigar-stores, where everybody was buying them now, owing to cigarette restrictions during the war. They threw in two packs of rolling papers free with the machine. I rolled up the best cigarettes the machine would make, great big thick ones, after slicing up my leaves with a big scissors, which also turned black with resin almost at once. But I kept sharpening it with my knife, as I kept slicing, and making up my stock.

They looked like Havana cigarillos, except that they were white, and caused a sensation in the jazz record shop when I casually pulled one out there that evening, and pretended I was going to light it, explaining to the manager, Milt Gabler, what it was, since I thought I knew him pretty well. He grabbed me and started giving me the bum's rush to the door.

"What the hell is the matter with you, you crazy lunatic?!" he almost shrieked, but nevertheless in an undertone. "You want to get me arrested?"

"But look," I said indignantly. "There's plenty of musicians are really looking for this."

"Don't I know it!" he snarled. "But they're not going to find it in *my* store! Try my crummy competitors down the block."

Curiously enough, he was right. There was indeed a competing hole-in-the-wall jazz record shop not far away on Lexington Avenue, and this time I thought I would try being slightly less indiscreet. I took the manager into my confidence, while leaving my oversized cigarillos in my pocket, and asked him if he knew any musicians, maybe who would like to stock up on some very good, er, muggles just imported from Mexico? I had a friend who had two packs of them to get rid of.

This happy-go-lucky crook whom we will call Zorn, because that wasn't his name, but *Zorn* means wrath or anger in German, and that's close enough; well, he gave me one of the most peculiar looks I have ever had in my life. Thinking it over now, I suppose what it expressed was the question: "Can such things be?" or "Where did this lunatic fall from?" However, he allowed me to show him a sample of my merchandise, and told me that if he ran into anybody who was looking for something, he'd tell them that I was around. I started to leave, and he crossed his empty little shop and stopped me.

"Wait a minute," he said. "I'll tell you what. Just leave me a pack, and I'll give them to some right guys I know for samples."

"Not me!" I told him calmly. "No samples. How about we make a trade? You give me five dollars worth of records and I'll give you a pack – that's twenty. They're worth a quarter each."

He kept looking at me in that funny way. I decided he must be strabismic, like Jake Brussel, or something. "But what about my profit?" he asked. I now consider this the best line of the evening, by the way, but completely missed its superb crust at that time.

"Whaddya mean?" I asked. "What do you care if you make the profit on the records or anything else. It comes out the same for you, doesn't it?"

"Oh, yeah," he agreed slowly, as though a light was dawning, and took the packet that I slipped him. "Well just look around. Anything up to five dollars."

From then on, I believe I was considered the greatest benefactor that jazz music ever had, far beyond anything that Archie's pipedream of a Jazz Foundation could have been or done. Zorn would roll out the red carpet whenever he saw me, and was all oily smiles and palsiness. I couldn't help but have the feeling that he might not be totally sincere, but after all I had cleverly put him into the position — had I not? — where he was just as implicated as I was, so I knew at least he wasn't going to turn me over to the police. This went on for about two or three weeks, and I would drop by at least once a week, never telling him ahead what day I would come. I'd just take the IRT subway express down from the Academy of Medicine, after changing at 86th Street, and drop in on Zorn before walking over to the public library.

One night a man followed me after I left Zorn's. I couldn't mistake this, because as soon as we both got back around the corner onto East 42nd Street, he began calling, "Hey kid! Hey! Hey, wait a minute!"

I looked around and saw a typical jazz musician struggling along after me, toting an enormous cello on his back, in a black rubberized cloth cover. "Lissen," he said, very confidentially, "I wanna talk to you."

We went into the nearest cafeteria, and got two pieces of pie and coffee to give ourselves the right to be there. He slid the cello along on its back, right after our trays of food, and I was a bit staggered by his casualness about his instrument. He explained to me that he was Bop Biedermeyer, a name that I vaguely know from jazz record labels. It had clearly been taken by him to remind people of the earlier jazz musician, Bix Biederbecke. He was a slap-cellist, as other jazzmen play the slap-bass viol. His real first name, as I found out later, was Albert.

He was at that time the main marijuana dealer in jazz, and he was interested in highjacking my services away from Zorn. I assured him that I had a supply sufficient for both him and Zorn, but he was very anxious to cut Zorn out. He asked me if I realized how badly Zorn was rooking me on the price. I told him I thought a quarter a stick was the right price, but Biedermeyer was so zonked out on his own merchandise, no doubt, that he reminded me patiently of what I should have remembered myself: that marijuana sticks are generally slender little items hardly thicker than a kitchen match, and loosely packed into a hand-rolled cigarette paper with both ends poked in to keep the grains from falling out. My Handy Marvel rolling machine had run away with me.

"Your friend Zornie there, he told me, "he's got a kid in the cellar rolling four sticks outa each one of those Mexican Bombers you're flying in. That stuff is pure gold; don't you cut it at all?" Then, in another tone, "Listen! Why don't you wise up before somebody gets sore at you?"

"Are you going to get sore at me?" I asked, finally alert and tense.

"Naw," he said broadly. "I *like* you. But you're dumb, kid. Very dumb."

After that, I never went back to Zorn's, but would meet Biedermeyer in our cafeteria once a week. He paid me in cash, which made me feel a certain repugnance to myself, but I always religiously spent the money on phonograph records — classical, not jazz or blues — and felt that in that way I was only trading it for records, and was selling nothing. I went back one more time to the field in Hoboken, exactly as before. This time I had the impression that the counterman in the lunchwagon was looking at me somehow aslant or oddly, when I stopped in this time after I had made my harvest and had washed my hands with rubbing alcohol in the field. He served me and said nothing at all, but I was now suspicious of everybody since beginning my dealings with Biedermeyer, and never went back to the field again. I also told Mr. Bop, as he liked being called, that my line of supply to Mexico was now cut off, and that I might have some more material for him in two weeks, but it would be the last time, and would have to be in one big transaction. And that would be the last.

When we met again, two weeks later, I told him I had nothing with me, and I didn't. Clean as a whistle. We had to discuss price this time, I told him, and I recouped all my losses with Zorn by the time we finished bargaining. This was Mr. Bop's reward for having told me, like a Dutch uncle, what a dumb kid I was. We arranged to meet the next night, and he would have the money with him, but I told him I still wouldn't have anything with me. It would be in a lock box in Grand Central Station nearby, and when I got the money I would lead him to the box and give him the key. We met as planned the next night and he showed me the money under cover of the cafeteria table, but he wouldn't give it to me until I handed him the key. I explained to him that I'd give him the key at the box. We hurried along together, he with his inseparable cello on his back, yet even so walking faster than me.

Owing to my now intense suspiciousness and caution, I did not have the key on me at all when I came to meet him. Those keys were numbered and showed the location of the box. This way, if anything went wrong, or he narked on me, I was clean. I wouldn't know what anybody was talking about. I was a jazz lover, and wanted Mr. Bop's autograph. In actual fact, I had earlier in the evening left the key inside my floppy old briefcase full of books and papers, which I then asked the manager of my favorite bookstore in Grand Central Station to keep for me at his desk while I went to supper. The lock box was very close by.

When we opened the lock box, Mr. Bop assured himself very carefully that each of the packages in it really contained the contraband he was after. Despite his spaced-out air, he was as clever and cautious as they make 'em. If he had been as good a musician as he was a tea-merchant they'd have a bust of him in the Hall of

Fame today. He counted out my money right inside the box. It was a lot.

"Is that right, kid?" he asked. I agreed that it was right. To my surprise he then slammed the lock box shut again, and put in another coin. Nobody paid us the slightest attention, because of the cello, I guess. A hundred people must have passed us in the corridor there of Grand Central Station. We were evidently just musicians, and musicians are always fuddling around with their instruments.

"I'll have to come back for this tomorrow," he said. "There's too much to carry in my usual way."

"What's the usual way?" I asked. Actually, I didn't give a damn, but was just being polite. I was now out of the marijuana business forever.

He looked at me rather surprised. "You know me," he said with his usual disarming candor. "I keep it in the fiddle, on a string."

CHAPTER 39

SPANISH MISSAL

DOWNSTAIRS I could hear the phone ringing. It was very hot and I had the door of my room open to get a cross-current of air. Nobody else was home mornings, so they wouldn't complain about my typewriting and the phonograph music. It was Saturday anyhow. I could hear little Mr. Nossiter answering in his querulous old Jewish voice, two landings down. The phone was always too much for him. Then two rings; and two again. It was for me. "Legmunn!" he shouted. "Legmunn!" I galloped down the stairs.

"Darling!" It was Magdalen's voice. "I'm in town. I just must see you!"

"Me too!" I told her. Maybe not very inspired, but true. "Where are you?"

She was at the agency office she told me, and would be there until noon. Had just got in from Chicago that morning, and would be going back Monday. She needed a favor, a terribly big favor, and she knew I was the only person who could do it. "Anything I can," I told her.

Her father's birthday would be that week — I knew at once that meant she wouldn't really be going back to the Chicago office directly, at all, but would make one of her famous loops around, this time by Boston to see her family. That meant we would have the weekend together and part of the beginning of the coming week too. Better and better! Anyhow, it was her father's birthday and she wanted to give him a Spanish missal. He was Irish, of course, but had been stationed at Gibraltar when he was in the British Army years before, and loved reading Spanish. She had already given him a Bible in Spanish a year or two ago. Could I find a Spanish missal to match? She had to stay at the office to explain reports all morning; and didn't know where there were any Spanish bookstores anyhow. Tomorrow, Sunday, everything would be shut.

"I don't suppose they'd have Spanish books on Fourth Avenue, would they?" Magdalen ventured. "I could go there this afternoon."

"No, no," I told her. "They wouldn't have it. I know where to go. Just sit tight. I'll call you back when I've got it."

"Or just bring it," she said, and told me where she would be staying downtown on Horatio Street. "It's my sister Josette's apartment," she said. "She's in Florida with her husband." Well! That meant we really had it all set up for a weekend of wild, wet, artistic lovemaking.

A slice of unaccustomed Heaven was falling into my lap. I rushed back up the stairs to my big crowded room and shaved twice over in the little sink, happily accepting every scratch and scrape of the razor in the cold water. It would be worth it. A weekend with Magdalen! My god, how long had it been? Six months surely, on her last trip from Chicago. I went ski-jumping down the stairs whistling *"La ci darem la mano,"* and went immediately to the big Spanish record store, Castellanos-Molina, on West 72nd near Broadway, where Ferdinando, the clerk I bought my Flamenco records from, told me at once where to find Spanish religious books and perfumes. Just around the corner, as it happened, on a side street I had probably never gone down. Below Seventy-second on the West Side was a bad area, mostly whorehouses, horse-players and marijuana smokers, just like East Harlem. The drug-peddlers of hard stuff holed up there too, that supplied the Times Square vice area. So the West 60s were full of crooked shakedown cops — a good place to stay away from. I formulated a little prayer of gladness that my flier in the marijuana fields had ended without me seeing the inside of a jail. Never again, I said. Never. I meant it.

I found a beautiful Spanish missal for Magdalen's father, on cream-colored Bible paper and ridiculously heavily rubricated in red throughout to point up all the section titles and responsories and whatnot. What made it particularly strange and pretty was the binding which was composed of two slabs of curiously grained dark olive-wood with the edges all prettily bevelled and gilt. Maybe it was vulgar and naïve in a way, I admit, but a jewel, and not even terribly expensive. I wondered what it would cost to commission such a binding in America, even assuming you could get the olive wood here — surely five times as much. I got back with the missal, and phoned up

Magdalen at once at her office; it wasn't even eleven o'clock.

To my astonishment and intense irritation she wasn't very excited about the beautiful olive-wood Spanish missal at all. The Spanish Bible she had given her father was bound in white leather. Couldn't I get a missal in white leather to match? I was absolutely furious, but held it in. I would try, I told her. They would surely trade it for a white one, if they had it, I assured her. And if they didn't, I knew another Spanish bookstore — in Brooklyn, I said, pulling that one out of a hat, as I knew Castellanos-Molina had another store somewhere in Brooklyn. Would I really be an angel and go out to Brooklyn and try? Yes, I would be an angel. I tightened my lips and grimaced, feeling more like poor cuckolded Masetto than like Don Giovanni. *La ci darem la mano*, is it!?

"Don't you worry about a thing," I told Magdalen magnanimously. "Because if they haven't got it in Brooklyn, there's another place up by the Academy of Medicine in Harlem. I remember seeing it. Perfume and books."

I hung up the phone and went upstairs, threw the Spanish missal on the bed and got back to work on whatever I was typewriting; I can't remember what. Probably *Taboo*, my proposed bibliographical history of sex-censorship. When I figured Magdalen had enough time to get out of work and down to her sister's apartment, I went back down to the first floor and put a nickel in the phone.

"I'm out here on De Kalb Avenue in Brooklyn," I told her, not attempting any sound- effects. "They do have missals here, but they're all bound in black. Black leather mostly, or heavy silk."

"Oh, no, darling," she cried. "Not black! Is that really all there is?"

"That's it."

She allowed me to convince her that I should now take the BMT subway back to Manhattan, and then change to the IRT and get back to Spanish Harlem to try the perfume store there. No, they surely wouldn't be shut for lunch. Places like that, they always live in the back, anyhow; and they rush out if they hear the door open, with a napkin tucked into their vest. That reminded me: I was hungry. I went out and grabbed a sandwich, and came back and worked some more.

An hour later I phoned Magdalen again. No Spanish missals at all up here in Harlem, but they knew another place — their brother-in-law's on upper Broadway. I'd go there. Magdalen weakly tried to dissuade me, but I insisted. Conquistador me. Yes, this would be the last place I would try. No help for it. Yes, I was an angel. It was a pleasure. I'd take the bus over to Broadway, get the missal and then shoot right down the West Side to Horatio Street to her sister's apartment. And of course to her waiting arms.

"You're an absolute angel," Magdalen bubbled throatily. "I adore you."

But I was ruthless, and phoned back one more time, when I was almost ready to leave. Here I was, I explained, way up on Broadway somewhere past Columbia. Old Mr. Nossiter's door was open at the landing, and the radio was spilling out the usual confused gubbidge of music and voices. I trusted that sounded sufficiently like a Hispanic neighborhood over the phone, minus only the heavy perfumes and oily glop slicking down everybody's hair. Black missals here again, I reported. All black, and not even in soft leather, I embroidered my tale, and the missals, with sinister-looking big ornate crosses stamped in gold on the heavy black silk brocade front covers. I should have been composing propaganda truths for the Office of War Information or the Vatican. I was really in the vein that day, and spoke every lying word into the phone with a grinding movement of my jaws, my lips drawn tightly back over my front teeth in a happy death's head rictus, and an ugly shit-eating grin distorting my face. I was glad Magdalen couldn't see me.

I told her how I would have to go back to the first place near West 72nd and get the olive-wood missal, which in fact I still had, nicely wrapped on my bed upstairs. It was the best. Magdalen sounded very disappointed about the intended white Spanish missal, but a bit contrite too about sending me on such a wild-goose chase. Not at all, I assured her, grinning horribly at the telephone numbers scratched on the wall over the phone. It was a pleasure to be able to help. I went back up the stairs two at a time, glad I'd already shaved happily in cold water in preparation for making love to her. Chicago had obviously been bad for Magdalen's character.

Outside my window that darn old Artur Schnabel was practising again. Always the same Chopin warm-up and Beethoven Sonata movements, over and over. I wondered if I'd be able to keep it going that long. Seventy years old and never would or could stop. I felt kind of patronizingly sorry for him too: Schnabel was only a performer, after all, never a creator. And too serious a performer to ruin the concertos he played by sticking in out-of-kilter modern cadenzas composed by himself. The best and cleanest performer in the world — absolutely! But totally dependent on the great, bad, mad, sad creators like horrid old Beethoven. I wouldn't be able to spend that much of my life practising anything. About the equivalent, I told myself of spending one's entire time typewriting over and over forever: THE QUICK BROWN FOX JUMPS OVER THE LAZY DOG & JOVIAL BRAWNY SEX-GODS FLOCK UP TO QUIZ THEM. I'd give $9,876,543.21, to know the rest of that legend, dammit! But could I stand writing nothing but that every morning for the rest of my life till I was seventy? Never! Not for the whole ten million bucks — and no sense! I slung the old green cloth cover over the typewriter to keep out the dust and sun, slammed the window shut in case it rained while I was gone, grabbed the Spanish missal and left.

On the way to the subway I saw a big liquor store open, and got a nice bottle of port. Coffee was rationed, because it was imported, but you could always get all the hooch you wanted — it supported local American industry. Two doors beyond was a narrow little lingerie shop with a flossy window display. Fortunately I had taken twenty dollars out of the bank for over the holiday weekend. I bought Magdalen a pretty little chemise nightgown of imitation jersey silk. It wasn't blue, and cost practically everything I had left. "War restrictions," the young woman who waited on me said pertly, when I asked why it cost so much.

"Oh, yeah," I agreed. "I remember now. They're making all the parachutes out of the jersey silk pants, with a little blue rosette between the breasts." She wrapped up the chemise and handed it to me with my change in silver without a word. People who're gypping you always get very indignant when you complain.

In front of Schulte's cigar store at the corner of 72nd, where I crossed to the subway kiosk in the middle of Broadway, the rush-hour addicts were line up ten deep for rationed cigarettes. I'd already given my rationing coupons to the kid at Castellanos-Molina, who traded them for Flamenco records and Argentine *tangos canción* by Carlos Gardel, and would slip me my share on occasion. So I was a black marketeer too. The cigarette customers slunk away from Schulte's counter, each with two packs of Marvels, Sensations, Fleetwoods or the like. These were the third-line brands no one had ever heard of before the War, smelling to high heaven like the old-fashioned Fatimas and Sweet Caporals. And while no one really believed they were made of pure cow-dung and sawdust, they would bitterly say so, often. All the cigarette brands anybody really wanted, like Camels — definitely not made of pure camel dung instead — had "gone to war": only officers and war-profiteers and their whores could smoke them now. I'm telling you, friend, it was *agony* on the home front. We suffered!

Magdalen's advertising office had once run a competition for which I had sneaked in a Ballyhoo-style phoney advertisement which incredibly not only won the prize, but became a Madison Avenue joke, and Lucky Strike ended up using it for their "Do You

Inhale?" campaign. The ad showed a man and woman in bathing suits on the beach, the woman in the proper attitude of sub-total surrender on her back. The eventual ad-copy underneath read: "Do You Inhale? Lucky Strike is *clean and pure* . . . *kind to your delicate membranes!*" Somebody must've got a raise when they ran that one, but Mr. Anon, the Unsung Bard, was as usual left penniless at the post. Oh, well!! The best part of the joke for me was that in those days everybody said Lucky Strikes were the harshest cigarette on the market, and that if you smoked 'em long enough you'd surely end up with a hacking metallic cough. God knows what they'd do to any lady's delicate membranes. I guess the Cuban whores who would do their barroom trick for tips, of inhaling tobacco smoke with their vaginal muscles, and letting it curl out again in repeated puffs, were the only ones who really appreciated my ad.

SOMEWHERE on that subway ride downtown to Greenwich Village this whole chapter fell out of my conscious memory, right while I was living it. It's unusual for me to forget things — my curse. I know that surely means I was ashamed of it, but what part was I ashamed of? Surely not the simple Roland-for-an-Oliver telephone trick by which I refused to take seriously Magdalen's bossy and over-finicking nonsense about the little white Spanish missal. More likely I was ashamed of letting myself be bossed around by any woman even the little I was. Or that Magda assumed I could be.

My library researches in erotic songs & ballads had brought me by then to the really big folksong collections in French and English. I was slowly checking through the five fine quarto volumes of the great *Child Ballad Collection*, which have nothing to do with children but were kept on the open reading room shelves in the library, very near the counter and signal-board. There I had to wait each day for demanded books to come up from the subterranean stacks. And I would study over a page or two of Child's dense annotations every time while waiting. His Anglo-Scottish expurgated texts seemed contemptible to me, especially the presumably humorous ones about bickering husbands & wives, of which I had already collected unexpurgated texts "in the field," miles funnier, better and more real than the namby-pamby, iffledy-piffledy schoolmarm stuff that Professor Francis J. Child of Harvard and his successors Kittredge and Bronson ever allowed themselves to admit existed.

But what truly got to me about Child was the stupefyingly wide-ranging, monk-like thoroughness of the research in his enormous headnotes to each & every ballad, covering "congeners and collateral texts in half a dozen different Nordic and Latin-based languages, ploughing through the manuscripts and printed literature of half a thousand years. Francis J. Child, working without folktale indexes or any other such tools, since none then existed in the mid-19th

century, had done all his own tremendous research and done it forever, leaving damn little — and that, mostly thrice-threshed straw — for Professors Kittredge and Bronson and a few would-be other successors to glean up after him. Like Robert Briffault in the three great volumes of *The Mothers*, and its built-in bibliography covering more pages than the average novel; there was a hero and a heroic ideal for any researcher, on whatever large subject.

And reading along in the *Child Ballads* day by day, I had been stopped one day — sharp, hard, and most unexpectedly among the King Arthur and Robin Hood Ballads, all just old wild-west shoot'emup stuff but with longbows and armor instead of six-guns — by the ballad and legend of "Sir Gawain and the Green Knight." About the first of King Arthur's knights, who gets himself sent off by some clever queen and the hardcunted ladies of her court on a sleeveless errand and bootless adventure trying to solve the mystery of *what women really want.* A hard question men are still asking themselves, though no longer in verse nor even in music, as when Puccini made the same story into the viciously ugly plot of his last opera, *Turandot*, as late as the 1920s.

And what is the secret, finally? What is it Sir Gawain and Turandot find out that women really want? — Beauty? A good husband? Fine children? — Certainly all of those; but that is not the secret, and no secret at all. To find out the truth Gawain/Turandot of course has to meet up with a horrible old crone or female nark, who promises to unveil to him all the other women's deepest secret, which has endlessly escaped him through all the time and travail he is allowed for finding it, if he will "marry" her, which he desperately promises to do. Whereupon, after the paid-for lovemaking she apparently so badly needs, she naturally drops her evil enchantment the morning after and turns into a beautiful young bride — it says here — and tells him the secret. Which clever you have already guessed, to be sure. What women really want, his hag-bride confides to Sir Gawain, is MASTERY OVER MEN. Sounds familiar today, doesn't it, fellas?

So that's it — war! The War Between the Sexes that Aristophanes was already kicking about so bitterly in *Lysistrata, or the Women's Slave-Revolt* over two thousand years ago, and by the same methods of doghousing and pussywhipping the men. Now well escalated, in the consumerdom of the twentieth century, into men's pants and ludicrously broad-shouldered Harris tweed jackets for slave-revolt females, willing to confuse the pants for the penis. (And the padded shoulders with the testicles?) Also for reclamatory bitches and given-up-the-struggle lesbians and New-Chastity freaks and narcissists, terrified of human closeness and/or A.I.D.S., God's new viral Revenge Against the Frightful Sin of Lechery. Also tens of millions of just plain Janes going out helplessly with the fashionable tide, like lemmings, to emotional strangulation and dismal, lonely death. And that is what is called Mastery Over Men. Or in a single yearning word: *Power!* Well, maybe.

Of course, if women only wanted their way, no matter how unreasonably, it wouldn't be so bad. Men would eventually be able to figure out how to please them. But wanting mastery over men is entirely different than just wanting your way, in the same way that wanting mastery over women is entirely different from just wanting normally to fuck them until their ears fly off — or ours — which no reasonable person could object to.

Your hardcase mastery seeker isn't really looking for sex at all. Sex is merely the foreplay or afterlude to the real struggle: for domination of the other person, body & soul. As in Dominique Aury & Jean Paulhan's *Histoire d'O*, the cream of the degenerate French crop of the 1950s and a best-seller since, including comic-book and motion picture forms. Also Adrian Lyne's marvellously photographed but morally ghastly motion-picture continuation in the mid-80s, *Nine-and-a-Half Weeks*, in which the continually-grinning sadist saps all the will and self-esteem of his vulnerable female victim who loves him, until he has totally eaten out her soul and finally commands her to kill herself.

SITTING on the subway express, clattering downtown, I asked myself if I wasn't ashamed of having strung Magdalen along that way about the Spanish missals. No, I wasn't a bit ashamed. Besides, she didn't know the truth and wasn't being hurt a bit. I was just saving wear and tear on myself. I didn't feel like a better man, but I did feel as though I were getting a little smarter. Her new management job in Chicago was making her rather bossy. It seemed to me; a bit of an iron hand under all that silk jersey glove. Well, heigh-ho! People change. I was pretty sure she would still be the same Magdalen in bed. And naturally she was.

If only I could have remembered later the trick I learned that day, it would have saved me so much misery running around for years, trying to find ways of pleasing unpleasant *other* women, who did not intend to be pleased. As it was, I repressed the whole thing from memory — I guess I was more ashamed of it than I told myself — and only suddenly remembered it, in a big wailing flash, one day twenty years later, running exactly the same kind of sleeveless errand around town for some frigid bitch, but this time really running. And suddenly I stopped then, putting my shoe in a lump of dogshit on the curb as I came to a stop. And I leaned up against a tree, cleaning off my shoe with an empty cigarette pack I found on the ground, saying to myself over and over, "White Spanish missals! White Spanish missals!" And I began to laugh . . . and laugh . . . And yet I was not free.

Magdalen's sister Josette lived in a rather nondescript building on Horatio Street, but the apartment inside had been beautifully fixed up. Her husband was a jeweller's son who thought of himself as an art craftsman. He manufactured and sold massive silver rings, sometimes with turquoises set in them and always carefully stamped with his name inside. Actually he bought them ready-made from the Navajo Indian craftsmen out west through a local agent, and had only one workman, whose job was stamping his trade name inside with a little punch and hammer. Then he tripled or quadrupled the price, and sold them to the stores. You always have to have something to sell.

On the proceeds he and Magdalen's sister had this lovely apartment, a child they never saw because they kept it stuck away somewhere, and naturally they took a trip to Florida or Brazil every winter. They had never heard of the war; or rather, the war improved their business greatly because all the departing soldiers needed rings to give to the girls they left behind them, and the blue-green turquoises and silver bands made a sort of engagement ring without being the real thing, in case the soldier never came back. When the government then put restrictions on bullion silver for some purported "defense" reason, Josette's husband didn't give a damn. He just boiled up silver half-dollars and raised the price a bit. As I say, the hardships we suffered during the war in America! While, all unknown — except to millions of Germans and Poles with carefully shut eyes and clothespins on their noses — millions of Jews and others went up the massive cannibalistic chimneys of Auschwitz in smoke.

I heard about the brother-in-law after I gave Magdalen her Spanish missal bound in olive-wood slabs, which she agreed was very beautiful indeed. Not another word was said about the white leather binding originally demanded, or her notion of making up a Bible set bound in white. As I had sensed, at best it was merely a brainwave and of no importance. I also presented Magda the bottle of port, but kept the chemise nightgown hidden in my pocket in its paper bag — there were no gift wrappings during the war: they couldn't get the special metallic string.

Like the marvellous big sign in the Packard-Wilson ice cream stores: "PACKARD-WILSON GOES TO WAR!" Going on to explain that, to *Back the Attack*, and bring aid & comfort to Our Brave Boys, the usual fifty-six flavors of ice cream in the Packard-Wilson stores would now be reduced to only twenty-three, For The Duration! There would be no Banana-Almond Crunch, no Toasted Cocoanut Fudge, no Maple-Walnut Grenadine, and no other thirty missing flavors, For the Duration! Back the Attack! Our Brave Boys. You know what Sherman said, don't you? War is hell. Just Vanilla, Chocolate, Strawberry, Coffee, Butter Pecan, Pistachio and seventeen others, including that good one with the bits of chocolate and wild cherry in it.

Magdalen and I did not fall into bed together at once. I guess we were both shy about pretending that we were in a state of sexual starvation, since it surely wasn't true. Instead Magdalen bustled about and we raided her sister's icebox, turning up a big jar of fine rolled-up herrings with laurel leaves inside, and a loaf of Danish-style rye bread, as dark and wet as a half-petrified sponge but it went great with the herring. I refused to open the port to accompany that, so we had tasteless tea made with tea-bags instead. I idly tore open one of the bags to see why the tea was so bad. There was no tea at all inside: just some kind of dust. I suppose they swept it up off the floor, or shook out the last bags from India. Well, you know what Sherman said.

Magdalen wanted to know if I ever went to the bookstores on Fourth Avenue anymore; if Mahlon Blaine were still around — she was still flattered about his asking her to pose, and calling her a goddess built like a brick shithouse — if I knew Susan's new address; she had apparently disappeared. And, if yes, was Jake Brussel out of prison yet? The answer to everything was no, so we didn't go out at all. I found some paper monogrammed "J" in a drawer, and got Magdalen to tell me all the newest jokes from her office in Chicago, while I wrote them down. We agreed it was strange that intellectuals never know any songs, just endless dirty jokes and those godawful bawdy limericks, which we both agreed we hated.

Then we opened the port, and Magdalen dutifully sang me a song she said she had learned in high-school, about Lil who was a beauty, and lived in a house of ill-reputey. I wrote it down carefully, though I had already written it down from other people's singing at least three times before. Well, you had to take them all. You never knew, until you confronted them later, when you'd stumble across the best text, or the liveliest, or even the one that was perhaps the oldest strain. We put on the radio — good old WQXR never let us down for beautiful music, war or no war — and sat on the couch drinking up our port out of little glasses. I found it fabulous how long it was taking for us to be willing to start making love. There was an upright piano. I played chords for a while. We talked about how it happened that I loved music so much but had never learned to play.

"What's the matter with us, sweetheart?" I asked finally. "Why haven't we been kissing each other for an hour already?" I started studying her forehead ostentatiously, to see if my name was still invisibly written there, and rubbing my own.

"It's there alright," Magdalen told me with a faraway smile. "But I've been *very* unhappy in Chicago. I know you won't believe this, but I almost don't have any sex life at all — I truly don't! I can't stand the men! They're all cold bastards that want to roll me over, and pass me from hand to hand. I'm a boss too, now, and I suppose that's their way of cutting me down."

"With their pricks."

"No; well, maybe. But with their bankrolls too. They love to show off how much more money they can waste. Especially the big bosses. And meanwhile I know that it's all on expense accounts. Oh, they're so cheap, really, with all the showing off. Chicago is just ghastly. And the worst is, they're all *married!*"

The last moan made me laugh, which miffed her a bit. I said her complaint reminded me a little of Abie Kabibble's letter home from the German prison-camp: "The food here is absolute poison — and such *small portions!*"

Magdalen then knew another version of that, going the other way, where the prison-camp letter reads: "They treat us with every kindness here. Good food, soft beds, wonderful doctors, movies every Saturday night. — P.S. Meyer was shot for complaining." When I didn't take my little notebook and write that one down, Magdalen wanted to know why not. And I explained to her, which I thought all of my friends had long since understood, that I wasn't collecting anything but sex humor and folklore, with a scatological outhouse too, just by courtesy of falling under the same taboo. There were lots of other people to collect and publish so-called clean humor, I said. I was like that woman's poem on the Statue of Liberty; I was there to welcome only the rejected, "yearning to be free." I told her about my intended new book for Haldeman-Julius in the Midwest, a history of sex-censorship, to be called *Taboo*.

"But will he let you put in the examples of what's been banned?" Magdalen asked, hitting the heart of the problem on her first shot.

"That's what we shall see."

We were both silent for a minute. Magdalen was always worlds more practical than I ever was, and I knew she yearned to say something sensible and admonitory about me not yanking back my manuscript from the publisher this time at the first intolerable and intrusive hint of editorial expurgation or censorship. She did not entirely approve — none of the girls I knew ever really did — of my art of being so damned pure and intransigent that I had just about guaranteed myself failure in the world of commercial writing and publishing. No matter how hard and how often I promised myself to be sensible and pliable about my impossible details, "just this one time." But it never worked out that way. Somehow, I always ended up spitting in the editor's eye. Perhaps that was why Magda never really wanted us to get married. My image of myself was positively congealed as the new William Lloyd Garrison of freedom from censorship. The Total Abolitionist for sexual freedom! *"I am in earnest. I will not equivocate. I will not excuse. I will not retreat a single inch. AND I WILL BE HEARD!"*

No mistake about it. An uncompromising moral pose like that made for fine, rousing declamatory rhetoric, but it certainly ruined me as marriage material, the way girls and their mothers can always figure these things. Wouldn't ever support a wife & kids, for sure. Not that way.

"You ever coming back to New York?" I asked suddenly, perhaps with the odd thought of marriage in my mind. After all, I knew I'd never find anybody smarter and sexier than Magdalen, and certainly not combined. "You said you hate Chicago." I prodded.

"Well maybe," she agreed half-heartedly, "but not ever for the same company that I work for, and they're pushing me up fast." A pause. "It's like this," she went on all in a rush. "There's someone in the New York office that was writing me poison-pen letters. Anonymous. That's why I left when I had the chance. I can't ever go back there. I don't know who it is? What if he's waiting for me one night after work? With a knife?" Another pause. We stared at each other. "Here," Magdalen said, "I've got the last one somewhere in my purse."

She rumpled through the usual pile of paper and metal mysteries women keep in their purses, and handed me a filthy, crumpled typewritten sheet, underlined kookily here & there in red, and folded and refolded until it tore peculiarly in eight. I gave it a quick look. It said pre-psychotic sadist all over it, especially the opening words, and the blood-red lettering everywhere.

"But why didn't you throw away an awful thing like this?" I asked. "And why didn't you ever tell me?"

"I don't know. I threw away the earlier ones. There were a couple. Maybe I thought this time they could identify him by the typewriting or something. It's on our own office letterhead with the top torn off. It's scary, a thing like that. I found it in my desk drawer after that Christmas party last year. I must've said something about my 'nun's education.' I didn't tell you because it mentions you, or maybe Alex," she added. "Right in the first line. Where it calls me a 'kike'!"

Magdalen was a Boston Irish Catholic, as everyone knew. Here is the hate-letter. Very typical too. I've had more than one. Have you ever seen one? — or written one? This is what they're like: [transcriber's note: Spelling, etc. follows original document.]

YOU'RE A BITCH YOU GOOD FORNOTHING LOW DOWN JESUS LOVING KIKE <u>BASTARD</u>. You sactimonious ass kissing low down no good <u>muff dike</u> . Oh, if I only had the guts to kill you? Where is all the woe of the world but in my heart! Ten million women on this earth and I had to find you and fall in love with you. Where the hell was God and his humanity loving son Jesus? Up to no good, I'll wager. Out of all the motley different colore races of the earth I had to pick you to give myself to. Where's the justice in that? What the hell is this stinking sniveling talk about love? All this muck raking no good <u>farting</u> ass loving pederastic perverted stinking queasy gut spilling open loose mouthed slobbering slavering jabber about soul satisfying heart filling drivel? <u>Eonist</u>

priests have the right idea masturbating in their narrow cells beseeching their god to grant their wish to let their <u>virility</u> (this last word mockingly) grow till it can reach their mouths. I don't believe all this <u>foul-mouthed</u> chatter about their <u>affairs</u> with nuns. What saisfaction would they get out of <u>cuckolding</u> God? <u>Adorning</u> him with the mocking <u>horns</u> when they have it in their power to satisfy their own desires more cleanly than any Friday reminding, fast day reminding, <u>fish smelling fur</u> <u>adorned box</u> can do. Let they mealy mouthed nuns run away to their nunnery there to dream their own erotic phallic symboled dreams the size of the Empire State Blsg. Let them grunt in their hard cots as their vaginas expand tremulously under the onslaught.

"Everything!" I marveled, "Eonism and Ophelia's nunnery! I'm keeping this now, sweetheart," I said. "You've had it festering in you long enough." I folded it away (till now) and cast about for a change of pace. I figured we needed one. I took the little bag with the nightgown in it out of my pocket. "I couldn't get blue, Magda," I told her. "This one is cocoa-colored. I thought it would look lovely against your skin." I held it up against her throat, pushing down the bosom of her dress a little, to press the clinging jersey against the fine large swell of her breasts. Magdalen took both my ears in her hands like a jug; looking gravely into my eyes, and pushed my head down to kiss the deep furrow of her bosom. I turned my mouth first and bit both her hands lightly, to punish her for taking hold of my ears so unceremoniously. I don't like to be dominated by anybody, though I can stand it easier from a woman than from a man. Especially if we're essentially only playing at it. In serious lovemaking I always like to be the boss, unless the woman is lying over me: whether heads or tails. I guess I'm irredeemably like the guys in Chicago and other mammals.

"Famous punchlines," I told her. " — *Leggo my ears; I know my business.*"

Magdalen was already sliding way down on the couch, pulling up her skirt frankly and eagerly with both hands along her thighs. "Do *every*thing to me, darling," she coaxed me throatily. "I need it *so* much!" Magda was one of those wonderful unabashed women who don't hesitate a bit to express theatrically and in words — more often romantically expressed than dirty — what they feel in bed and want you to know they feel, no matter how corny it might sound. Corn has its place too. And it's very flattering to know or believe that you've moved a woman that much. Pride is a large part of the starch in any man's erection. As when a woman breathes out that fluttering groan of relief when she feels the hot old horn spoon sinking at last into her melting butter.

This time I understood from Magdalen's "do everything" that she very much wanted me to lick her first, as I always do anyway unless it's freezing cold and we have to stay under the covers. But this was the Fourth of July. I slid down to my knees on the floor and lifted both of her legs over my head and shoulders. Magdalen never wore any panties. Her long, moon-like thighs fell open like clouds answering to "Open Sesame!" before the Gates of Paradise. Her beautiful odor was rising from the altar of her open crotch, and curled invisibly up into the air around my face, driving me wild.

This time, after so long a separation, I didn't want to dive headfirst into her crotch at once. I wanted to take a long minute, or maybe two, in broad daylight as we still were, to savor and study with my eyes all her delicious pink tissues: the bulging labia minora that I spread open with my fingertips, burrowing with my nose under the delicately curling golden tendrils of her hair. Of all those young years I don't remember ever having experienced so deeply and beautifully the look and smell and finally the touch and taste of a woman's cunt as with Magdalen. Half the time you can't remember what any given woman's genitals looked or felt or tasted like at all, because you were in such a hurry to dive in.

When I finally gave up looking and bent that last inch forward to taste her, deep and full at the opening of her vagina, Magdalen's sweet, acrid juices had already come down, as ravishing and floodlike as ever I remembered. I spent a very long time mouthing and sucking her long, full, pinkish-purple cunt-lips and tiny clitoris.

"Oh, I had to have it!" she groaned or rather grated, in shameless melodrama at the first touch of my tongue, her voice way down and throaty in her deepest register. "I *had* to have it!"

I smiled to myself at the incipient ecstasy in her voice. Well, you've got it now, honey, I said to myself. And I resolved she'd have to pry me off that fountain of ambrosia with a crowbar if she wanted to get fucked too. "Let me not to the marriage of true minds admit impediment . . ."

Some men say that they can't bear to suck a woman that they know has other lovers. Too afraid of meeting the other man's penis in the woman's body. Pierre Louÿs has a remark to make on the subject in his elegantly droll way, in *Trois Filles de Leur Mère*. But I don't feel that way about it — I mean, not unless it's just an hour later, and the woman hasn't had a chance to wash, or something like that. I'm just as nervous about having another man in bed with a woman and me as anybody else; and no normal man wants to think of himself as meeting up with vestiges of another man in the woman's body. But most girls do a lot of washing nowadays. Too much, really, and wash away all their own lovely odor. Also I have never heard a woman claim she wouldn't suck a man because he had fucked another woman, though they do complain about the other woman's odor. I mean, if it was recently. People who are jealous about sex partners way in your remote past are too painful to live with. Your remote past does not mean last week or after a cocktail party yesterday. Infidelities like that hurt real bad. It takes more than bubble-bath to wash that away. And what about the germs?

Magdalen began to moan, and put both her feet with the soles on my shoulders to open herself out even more to my mouth. I began thumbing her too, at the same time inside, front & back in the bowling-hold, shaking my whole hand intensely, but she groaned and pushed me away when I tried to pull her down with me on the carpet.

"Please take me off to bed, darling," she pleaded. "I want it to last forever this time. We'll only be cold on the floor."

We tottered into the bedroom together, our arms around each other. I grabbed the nightgown off the table as we went along, but Magdalen couldn't be bothered to put it on after we had stripped. Naked was infinitely better. Instead, she tied it around my upper arm for a chevalier's token, pushed her lovely breasts into my face, and fell backwards on the bed. Well, as they say in the expurgated magazine stories, I can't remember the rest. I know it was lovely, but what happened in the next two hours has passed completely out of my memory. I guess what happened later drove all the usual beauties and delights out of my mind. Not that there was really anything wrong with it later. It was just — so unexpected.

After we had made love for a long while we found we were hungry. The herring roll'emups had been cute, but really only an appetizer. We dressed and went out to walk around a while, and then found the little Spanish restaurant nearby that Susan had originally introduced us to now over two years ago. It was early and we had to wait a long time. We talked a lot, before and during supper, and when we got back to the apartment we talked a lot more. That was one of the nicest things about Magdalen: you could talk to her, because she was really extremely brainy and informed and didn't spoil it by being unreasonable and oblique the way women often are in conversation. Men too.

When we had talked for hours maybe, and the port was long since gone, we undressed at both sides of the bed like a plain married couple, and she put on the new little nightgown this time, which we named Daughter-of-Blue-Nightgown, because it was brown. The radio was playing Wagner, which was very unusual and even courageous in war-time — all orchestral. It was a Toscanini program, and I suppose that was how they got away with it.

"Would you promise not to be shocked, if I told you something?" Magdalen asked, not getting into the bed but sitting wiggling her toes at her side of the coverlet, and looking up at me with her gray-green eyes.

"Nope," I said cheerfully. "No promises. Don't tell me you want me to beat you now to excite you, because I won't do it. Get a machine"

"Well," she said slowly, "it's funny you should say that. You know, I learned about this in your book." I did not answer. I could see it coming.

MAGDALEN got up and went over to her open suitcase on a chair, reached under the froth of petticoats and brought out a small, stout cardboard box of a kind I recognized instantly. The Revenge of the Vibrating Dildo!

"I know what it is," I said. "Why will it shock me?"

"Because I'm addicted to it now," Magdalen told me, opening the box and taking out a very professional looking scalp massage vibrator, the kind I knew well, that goes over the back of the hand, held there with two light triple-coil straps. The long electrical cord fell loose and trailed on the floor. But no dildo, to compete with; just the vibrator and the human hand.

"Well, I'm glad to see the Oster people make the cord white now," I said, a little at a loss. "When I wrote about it in *Ora* the cord was always black, and it looked like a torture device." A pause, both of us silent. "Are we really going to take that thing into bed with us?"

"I'm addicted," Magdalen told me. "I really am."

"Oh, come on!" I laughed. "Two hours ago you seemed perfectly happy without it."

"Yes," she admitted, "but there's getting to be a world of difference for me. Please darling! Be foolish with me. We'll only be young once."

"Goddamit!" I cried, "I'll stand behind anything I write in my books. Gimme that goddam thing!" I felt unreasonably hurt in my pride, I must say.

I strode around the bed, stark naked as I was, took the vibrator from her hand and squatted down by the bed-table to plug it into the wall with the lamp. Fortunately there was a double plug, so the light didn't go out first, but the vibrator's switch was on and the instant I plugged it in it began leaping in my hand, and buzzing like a horde of wild Indonesian goofer-bugs. And much too loud!

"How do you shut this fucking thing off!?" I shouted, almost flinging it in the air. It was naturally mounted off-center to make it vibrate, and that made it noisy too. Just an engineering problem.

Magdalen seized it and threw off the little toggle-switch, and we both rolled on the bed screaming with laughter and practically in tears.

"Well, it's the Twentieth Century," I prophesied. "A hundred years from now they'll come in sets of two machines — male & female. You clip 'em together and turn 'em on, and throw them on the bed and tiptoe away. They won't bother with people anymore at all."

"Isn't it ghastly?" Magdalen wailed. "Here I am, twenty-three years old, and I sit around evenings all alone, playing with myself like a high school girl."

"Yes," I said in astonishment. "And all the time I thought you were helling it up with all the big butter & egg accounts from Minneapolis!" I put my arms around her and began kissing her eyes and blowing the soft blonde hair away from her forehead. She responded by toying with my ears.

"That's what everybody thinks," Magdalen said. "But now you know the truth. And it's habit forming! I'm really half-crazy about it. I sit up most of the night reading romantic novels with one hand and keeping that thing going with the other!" I observed that she didn't say she read pornography.

"What do you do if you want an apple?" I asked. I attached it over the back of my right hand, pushing my fingers and wrist through the coil straps. I clenched my fist. "Maybe I could just beat it to death," I suggested, lifting it over my head. "Like the snake that it is!"

"All right," Magdalen agreed. "In the morning. But turn it on first now."

I wished fleetingly that I were a smoker, so I could light a Murad and be nonchalant, the way the ads always said. Well, I decided, needs must when the Devil drives. It was probably true that Magdalen had learned about it in my book, of which I had given her the very first copy, inscribed like the crimson foulard scarf with a 69 in a circle on the flyleaf: *"Plus ça change, plus c'est la même chose"* — The more it changes, the less it changes — a line Alphonse Karr once complained was all anyone ever remembered out of all the books he wrote. I had the same experience too, years later. If I'm ever immortal it will be for just four words I once dropped into an address I was giving at a university library in Ohio — just as an aside — to underline a point about children's sexuality: *Make love, not war.* That's four words less than Karr. And now I was going to be immortalized as the inventor of the vibrating dildo. Strapped over the back of my hand, with me as attached dildo!

Actually, it was absolutely marvellous, though as always I refused to touch Magdalen with it as long as the light was on and I could visibly see it, or that disgusting long cord either. Couldn't these things be run by radio or remote control, or batteries or something, and get rid of the cord? Well, I supposed the batteries wouldn't be strong enough, though as it turned out what was really wrong was that sometimes the damn thing was *too* strong. I would write a letter to the Midwest manufacturer, and tell them to fit a cheap little rheostat into the switch, so you could slow the damned thing down to a caressing purr when that was what you wanted, instead of that steady over-rapid buzz. Elementary, my dear Watson! Too exciting as a steady diet.

I ran it all over Magdalen's body, teasing her with it, down behind her ears and the sides of her neck and breasts. I didn't touch it to the center of her breasts; I could see it would shake them up too much. In the dark, the thing gave off eerie sparks through the little ventilator slots. Of course, I talk about "it," but it was really I who was touching her — my fingers, never the machine itself strapped to the back of my hand: the machine only transmitted its vibration to my fingertips. A person would have to be pretty crude to press a vibrating machine directly to the woman's flesh. Couldn't pretend that was human contact; could you? So why the hell had I invented the goddam vibrating dildo? All Fortunato's fault! I ran my fingers down Magdalen's thighs and turning at her knees, came up again on the inner flanks, round and round. But when at last I got to her pubic hair I trailed up the side, and pretended I was going to go on up again over her belly instead.

She lifted her hips into the air, squirming slowly in circles and begging me wordlessly with her body to stop teasing her. I moved my hand in circles too, around & around her silky mound, and finally let my vibrating center fingers slide down through the hair, parting her crack and pressing down on her clitoris, one finger right on it and the other two pressing together its shaft and the top of the inner lips so they would quiver too. Magdalen immediately began to come, but then she was always very easy to make come. It swept by, and I thought I would continue, but she begged me quietly to stop.

"I can't!," I whispered, trying to joke. "It's habit-forming!"

But I tried to be kind to her too, and figured out at once a way to reduce the violence of the vibration, by laying down my other hand first against her pussy, and touching my vibrating hand to the other hand and not to her. I found I could even twist two fingers together and touch my vibrating hand to only the top finger: this reduced what she felt to just a ripple of vibration, and I was able to touch her clitoris again that way almost at once. A person wants to be stroked to ecstasy, yes. But nobody really wants to have their orgasms ripped out of them against their will, like ploughing a cork out of a recalcitrant wine-bottle. All that crude stuff was behind me now.

We also used the vibrator while making love, in what had always been our favorite position, with Magdalen lying on her back, and me on my side under her uplifted knees, our opposite legs twisting together in charming ways. I didn't invent this. It must be pretty ancient: the Mexicans call it *las tijéras*, the scissors. This left her whole body open to my caresses, from her face to her pussy, though it was not possible to kiss her mouth that way. And as I was not slung up over her, tensely suspended on my knees and elbows as usual, that made it possible for me to last a long long time before I would come too.

Magdalen's orgasm came over her repetitively now, as I kept my vibrating fingers at her clitoris and sometimes around under at her anus. I was kind of jealous too, as I had to be watching myself and holding back all the time. I wished we had left the light on so I could see her ecstatic face. But I could feel the arching gratitude of her body, and hear her panting and sobbing out words of helpless love; and that made me feel proud nevertheless. Like years before, when it all was new. And I was Man and his Machine! I would pose for that statue — vibrator and all — in the morning.

The only thing that bothered me, finally, was my new method of reducing the power of the vibration. Since I had to keep both hands together at Magdalen's crotch to do it, one over the other, I couldn't caress her breasts and nipples at the same time nor anything else. It made me feel like a Turkish bath masseur, minus only the towel temporarily knotted around my hips. And also I had to caress her then with my left hand and not with my right, because I had strapped the darn motor on my right hand to start with, and one strap pulled up tight over my wrist. As a lover, I'm right-handed. Only a detail, perhaps, but often it bothered me a lot. I surely wish I were one of those rare red-headed, left-handed, ambidextrous, athletic geniuses like Swinburne and Mark Twain who have it over everybody else, but I'm not. Nary a red hair. And not six-fingered, neither.

I suppose it's a big secret, but I'm willing to tell it for all the other Plain Joe, home-economy, family brand fuckers like myself — right-handed and single-pricked, which means most of us — that there are certain things it isn't so easy for a man to relearn in bed. When you've finally mastered the midnight art of twiddling a woman's clitoris artistically with your right hand, at just that tender-to-mock-brutal and slow-to-rapid *accelerando diabolico* that does her job, it isn't easy to change over to your left hand on the spur of the moment owing to some strained logistics of your body position, and still bring her to orgasm creditably. So there; now you know. Gimme that old *lang syne*, and let me use the hand I'm used to using, even if it means unexpectedly having to charge around the bed naked to the other side!

I realize I'm taking a mere crude, mechanistic, performance-oriented approach to what should be all deep emotion and that fine fucking rhapsody of totally unthinking D. H. Lawrence erotic Togetherness, which is sure to succeed for both parties. But lemme tell you, friend, even the most sentimental woman, who is sure to maintain that sex & love are very different things, is fairly likely to arrive after a sensible amount of foreplay on both your parts — if I've said that right — where what she wants and needs is not some further romantic flight of her or your emotions, however loving, but a nice stiff handsbreadth of hot prick stretching open the hungry tissues at the mouth of her cunt. Likewise some high class *doigté* at her clitoris and maybe even a touch at her tail vent betweentimes, to arrive at that one, plain, thundering, or at lest fluttering orgasm. Which all the romantic poetry in the world that you can recite, however sincerely, will have a damn hard time doing.

I know some women can come just watching Rhett Butler stagger up the staircase to their bedroom with Scarlett O'Bitch panting in his arms for that ultimate kiss; but unless you plan to spend most of your erotic life munching popcorn-for-two in front of a television screen, you'll do better to trust at least in part to your and her crude physical instincts instead of the totally imaginary and emotional.

In that area of crude practicality, no one wants to end up straining and hanging on desperately; her with agonized fingers clawing overhead and you with clenched teeth, cursing your sex partner silently, while your unaccustomed wrist aches as though it's going to fall off. *And here it is, four a.m., and she hasn't come yet!* As for me, I realized now I should have learned to play the piano or cello — extended finger trills especially — when I had the chance. I would certainly write to the Oster company now, to put that sensitivity rheostat into the vibrator switch: marked *Slow, Fast,* and *Hang On!*

When I really pressed down with my vibrating hand, wringing Magdalen out in orgasm after orgasm, while her body bucked and twisted, and finally swayed, shivered and went limp. Exactly like an engine stopping. Poor fool! — and she thought she was enjoying herself! Not like me, her *cavalier servant,* twisted up there on my side, servicing her doughtily and thinking my deep philosophical thoughts meanwhile about the sexual peculiarities of humanity. Well, it was certainly better than counting to a thousand by sexes, to hold off my orgasm. I clipped the body of her clitoris between my thumb and vibrating fingers. Really had nothing to do but to steer the damned vibrator with my by-now half-palsied wrist, and carve another notch on the motor-axle each extra time Magdalen came, weeping and moaning with joy.

Maybe Oster could build me a special model with a pistol-grip too. For us Texas millionaires. I'd have to be careful, or Magdalen would be wiping my feet with her hair, pretty soon now, like the Gospel says, just out of gratitude. But what if Oster mounted it on a bicycle frame, and then cut out the middle-man — me — altogether? Well, that's the way it is with those dangerous miscegenational marriages of Man & Machine. How does the song go? — *Fuck 'Em All!*

Where was my Man & Superman pose now, with vibrator wings on hand & foot, as just a few years before when I'd first used the vibrator on the sad, tall brunette, Eleanor, I think her name was, and all the other girls I knew since then? Where indeed? The damnable thing began to intrigue me. I made a few violent pro-humanistic speeches against the machine to Magdalen at midnight, full of noble avaunts and imprecations — wish I could remember them — but continued experimenting, like Alfred Jarry's half-mechanical fucking-machine man, *The Supermale.* If the basic individual non-biological purpose of sex was orgasm, then this was obviously the best answer, as you could force an orgasm this way out of even the most frigid bitch — which was certainly not Magdalen nor her problem.

There were certain technical problems, however. It wasn't easy to use it while licking her cunt, with either me above it, or it above me, as there simply was not enough room in the human crotch, however receptive. I mean it was possible, but not comfortable, except in a sixty-nine. Also, I didn't like having my face and ears that close to the buzzing machine. The whizzing sparks I could see through the ventilator slots and the vague smell of heated oil as the motor churned on and on, likewise bothered me a bit. I wondered if a person's hair and eyebrows could catch on fire from those sparks. Probably not, but what a way to go!

I began to feel like Dr. and Mrs. Frankenstein making Monster Love. If we had a baby as a result of that night, would it be born with ratchet-wheel balls and a bamboo-and-ivory slide rule instead of a prick, plunging up & down with a whirring noise? Or if it were a girl, would it be a mechanical hula-dancer, like Maelzel's mechanical chess-player, or the mechanical soprano in *The Tales of Hoffman*, continually running down? Lotsa problems. Phooey!

Magdalen was nowhere near as squeamish as I was, and it was her glory to be able to turn off her intellect in bed as I could not. When eventually she felt me draw out, because I knew I would be coming soon from the transmitted vibration, she whispered, "Let me now." But with all the tohu-bohu of turning off the motor, and having her slip it on the back of her hand instead of mine, and then turn it on again, and especially sorting out that goddam cord from among our entangled legs, it made me lose my hardon — predictably enough. Magdalen put her vibrating fingers deep beneath my balls, which she clutched lightly at the same time, and pressed hard upward against me there at the back door. Then she sank her lips down on me as I stiffened, and neither her mouth nor her fingers ever stopped moving, though at entirely different speeds, till I had come, and very violently too.

I realized that Magdalen knew a lot more about that contraption than I did. I had done virtually nothing but trail my vibrating fingers over her consenting anatomy. She had used her vibrating hand, instead, as though there were no churning motor strapped to the back of it at all, pressing and kneading and shaking and spider-clawing the base of my prick and everywhere in my crotch and beneath my balls at the same time. And then, as my orgasm approached in great whooping leaps, insinuating her vibrating middle finger twistingly into my rump. I had a crazy image as I came of Magdalen as a long-haired Kanaka yo-yo champion, demonstrating the delicate points of the art of captive top spinning, and me as the whirling yo-yo top. I came the way it only says in books, and fell asleep almost instantly, murmuring, "Boys, don't forget to cut the motor when you crash!" And I held up two flaccid fingers as I conked out, in Winston Churchill's V-sign, representing either *Victory!* or *Fuck You!* – depending which side you look at it from.

MISSAL WITH OLIVE WOOD COVERS

THE NEXT morning when I woke up, Magdalen was sitting up in bed in the rumpled little brown nightgown, listening to music and admiring the Spanish missal, running her fingers over it sensually. Since neither of us could read Spanish, she had to satisfy herself stroking the polished olive-wood sides and rubbing them against her cheek. For my part I was remembering back to our previous encounter with The Machine in bed, with Fortunato's prototype small-size vibrating dildo that time — so long ago, it seemed — in Washington. That hadn't shattered me anywhere near the way this had, even though it had seemed more perverted at the time, what with Magdalen even buggering me with the damn thing at the end. The vibrator on the back of the hand was just more *human*, I decided. That's why it did so much better a job. When Magdalen saw I was awake she gave me an extremely roguish smile.

"Well?" she asked. "Be honest."

"You know me," I said, wondering where I could get a drink of water, or better some orange juice to cut all the fuzz in my mouth. "Honesty is my worst fault. All I can say is, Scotland lost a great bagpiper when you decided to become an advertising executive. You've got your own style."

"Bagpipes are Irish too," she assured me, smiling. "The Scotch stole them from us."

I went out to the kitchen and found a bottle of ginger ale in the refrigerator, also a cut- open lemon. I made up two glasses and brought them back to bed. It was ambrosial: the little bubbles felt like cool kisses going all the way down the back and inside of my throat. I told Magdalen this, and she pushed me against the pillows and took great mouthfuls of lemon ambrosia and trickled them into my mouth with hers. One thing led to another, and when she had me reaching up with my mouth in O-shapes, mutely begging for more kisses, she stopped and tantalized me. I kept hold of both her breasts, with my hands pushing them together.

"Well?" she said smiling, and quoted from my midnight peroration: *"Damnable intrusion of The Machine into human love:'* Have you changed your mind?"

"No! Wholly damnable," I insisted. "And they better put me in the same corner of Hell with you, when we both get there, or I'll pull all the little Devils out on strike. Anyhow, it couldn't ever be habit-forming," I averred, knowing damn well I was lying. "It's a question of character. A dog can lick its balls with its tongue, but you never see a dog sucking itself off all day, do you?" Magdalen got out of bed.

"That's because you haven't written any book for dogs yet, darling," she observed magnanimously, lifting one of her buttocks toward me grandly for a kiss. Magdalen put on bedroom slippers and an apron, nothing more, and made me the classic nourishing morning-after breakfast of a slab of Virginia ham and scrambled eggs. She admitted she had gone out and stocked the refrigerator while waiting for me the afternoon before. I felt a sudden surge of shame about my Spanish missal telephone caper. I made her promise me that if she took her vibrating motor back to Chicago with her — "Why? Do you want it?" — "No, of course not! I wouldn't have anybody to use it on!" — she would phone me up and reverse the charges while the motor ran, so I could whisper love-words in her ear.

"We'd never be able to afford it," she objected. "Sometimes I go on past midnight with it. Twice I fell asleep with it turned on. It hypnotizes me."

"Only you, darling," I lied gallantly. "Only you!" We kissed for a while, by way of dessert, as she had forgotten any fruit except the lemons.

I warned Magdalen seriously, if she was really that addicted to the back-of-the-hand vibrator, at least to remember never to take it with her to the bathtub. "You don't want to die electrocuted, do you?" I added, trying to feed that very intensely into her memory banks. I wondered whether I should have mentioned it at all. I told Magdalen about one of the cranks I had met, when working as amanuensis and front-office troubleshooter for Dr. Dickinson. This guy wasn't really crazy, but there was no way to help him. There was no money and no real organization for sex studies in America then, except the chunk that Noah Slee, Margaret Sanger's husband, ante'd up every year for her birth control propaganda.

Aside from my crank's sexual schemes, which were all homosexual in fact, under a "big brother" disguise or neurotic bent, his main idea was that there should be a twenty-four-hour phone number you could call if you felt an urge to commit suicide. And a defrocked or out-of-work minister like himself, or a priest or rabbi, or psychiatrist, or some other authority figure of friend of humanity or nourishing mother would say soothing things to you — I suppose until the police or firemen could arrive with the butterfly net. The idea wasn't really bad at all, I thought, except where to get the twenty-four-hour people to sit by the phone. There should be a similar service, I suggested to Magdalen, for lonely girls with vibrating machines and horny bachelors who couldn't sleep, to whisper hot promises and exciting remarks into their ears by phone, and keep them from going mad those lonesome nights in their rumpled beds.

"I know you think you're joking," Magdalen wailed, "But you're not. There are times when I don't know which of those two services I really want the most."

She stayed over for two more days, and didn't leave for Boston till Tuesday night. Her father's fiftieth birthday party was to be the next day. We had of course stolen the two days that she planned to stay in Boston. Magdalen protested weakly, in bed, while making next-morning plans, that she should really be visiting with her father and family, and not lolling in bed with me — and the vibrator. Naturally I quoted her own Scripture back at her, opening the olive-wood missal and tapping significantly on the rubricated page, while I intoned in best Holiness church style: "Waallll, it says here in the Good Book, on page sixty-seven, 'Be foolish with me, darling: we'll only be young once.'." And we were. Only once. Only once!

For some reason, surely the imminence of seeing her father again, Magdalen suddenly began telling me that morning, for the first time in all the years we had known each other, about her father and herself and her sister, and how for years he had seethed with obvious lust for them, but had held himself in with an iron hand and got drunk all the time instead. I wondered if that was the explanation of all Irish drunkenness: instead of incest?

"And did you seethe for him too?" I asked. Magdalen bit me.

Monday morning early I phoned the railroad station, and pitilessly changed her sleeper reservation for Tuesday night. By Monday afternoon, being pretty nearly fucked out, I thought I should give Magdalen some advice. Good advice: the hardest kind to take. Mostly about the vibrator. I figured I'd better set the stage a little, so I waited till we stopped chasing each other around the apartment and fucking on all the furniture, and got dressed to go out and eat. We were famished and had eaten up everything in the refrigerator for breakfast.

We decided not to go back to Susan's little Spanish restaurant, because we agreed that the food there had been so hot both our assholes were still burning. Mexican heartburn. Going to Marcia's chili joint down on Sixth Avenue across from the women's jail would be even worse, rectally, and that was the only decent place open so early in the afternoon. I had an inspiration. We would go to Alex's Ptomaine Ptrap, and eat *boeuf Stroganoff* with Alex's thumb in it.

I knew Magdalen would love Alex, who was small, middle-aged, noisy, completely extroverted, and an old-line professional Russian, with an accent you could eat with *borscht Smetany*. He had a large triangular corner place originally, at the eastern tip of Sheridan Square, but was forced out by rent rises and apartment house speculation and now had only a tiny hole in the wall, below street level, just east of Sixth Avenue on Ninth Street. To get in you now had to clamber sideways down a short, almost vertical flight of wooden cellar steps. When Alex saw Magdalen's long legs and fluffy petticoat coming down the wooden staircase, he let out a wild whoop of appreciation.

"Such legs!" he shouted. "Such legs! Migod, such legs!! Around your neck you should only have legs like that, you wise-guy, you!" he cursed me happily as we came in. Magdalen was beaming.

"Thank you, Alex," I said. "But we're here for something Russian to eat now. Is that all right? We'll only stay till sunset."

There was a narrow counter, three stools, and a wooden kitchen chair; that was all. And in the back of the counter a broken-down stove and a few enormous pans. And a door-frame leading only to an icebox and sink. Alex squeezed out from behind the counter and sat down on the stools with us. I introduced the two of them formally, and stood back while he went into his standard act. There was a chunk of brown bread in a basket on the counter, and Magdalen and I munched on that while Alex pretended to be taking our order but actually expounding at great length his theory of the universe, and especially all about sexy girls whom I didn't deserve, but presumably he did. We finally coaxed him back behind the counter where he started preparing the Stroganoff, and slicing mushrooms with an enormous kitchen knife.

"So what did you do with that last brunette?" he demanded, finally deigning to pay me some attention. "You jealous?" he asked Magdalen aside.

"Horribly jealous," she assured him. "Tell me all the dirt, and I'll knife him when we get back home."

"No, no! Knife him now!" Alex encouraged her. "I'll give you a knife. You gotta understand these American intelligentsia. It's all *balls* with them. A little talk: You wanna go see the movies at the New School? And zup!! Opp goes the petticoat!" He leaned halfway over the counter at this point, to take another appreciative look at Magdalen's legs and petticoat.

"*Such* legs!" he groaned, and turned back to start mixing the slices of the Stroganoff furiously, with Smetanya yoghurt sauce. Alex also confided to us that he didn't use real steak, but a secret shoulder-cut just as good. I don't know its name in English — he wouldn't tell us — but in French it's called the *paleron*. I can still afford that. Until the rich snobs hear about it. Cheapskates!

Eventually I remembered who the brunette was that Alex was talking about. That would be Jake Brussels' daughter, Eva, who had been with us the first time he brought me to Alex's place on Sheridan Square. We talked about Jake, and how he was in jail for a book he had published. For words, not acts.

"You wrote the book, hah?" Alex accused me at once. "And Jack goes to the can? Just like in Roshia! All the books you go to Siberia for, except the telephone book. And even that, they lock up your whole family on suspicion for it."

He was talking about Imperial Russia, of course. Alex had left at the outbreak of the Revolution, the year I was born, when he was only a youngster himself. I assured him the censorship hadn't really been so bad under the Czar. In fact, there was even a censor-free period, I said, just before the end of the Romanoff dynasty, for ten years between the two Revolutions, when they were publishing erotica openly in Russia.

"Hoo! Hah!!" Alex shouted. "What do you know about it? They even had a paper ikon with the Czarina and all the high-class court prostitutes kneeling stark naked in front of Raspootine, praying to his pecker. Right to Siberia if they caught you with it!"

"Was that the Russian Orthodox religion?" Magdalen asked with a big smile.

"It's the orthodox religion everyplace!" he snarled, and dished out our Stroganoff which was exquisite, flinging extra yoghurt sauce on it like a boiling orgasm. Alex then charged us a dollar, for both of us, and stated he was throwing in our wine because Magda was so beautiful and blonde and had such long legs. He didn't have a liquor license but served wine anyhow. Free. Only to friends, which included all blondes with long legs, so the wine was legal, he decided.

I was thinking, for my part, that I'd give its weight in gold — but literally; how much can a sheet of paper weigh? — for a copy of that paper ikon. Just on a wild shot I asked Alex if by any chance he still had one in the clothing-wrapped bindle he'd have brought with him from Russia, but of course he didn't. I wonder if one still exists? The last one anybody ever reproduced was in Leo Schidrowitz' Sex Research Institute in Vienna of which I failed to save the library for a lousy couple of thousand bucks, when Hitler's S.S. motorcyclist death-squads were taking over Austria, because Dr. Dickinson was too cheap and blind to understand its value.

And now? Well, there are 79 copies of Shakespeare's First Folio in the Folger Library in Washington, if you happen to need that many, and nobody ever can or will; also 58 Second Folios, 24 Third Folios, and 36 Fourth Folios, all but the First of 1623 being basically worthless textually; plus over two hundred Shakespeare quartos, though he hardly wrote forty plays. These are all exact and authentic figures.

How's that for wholly mad, insane collectomania and conspewkious consumption on the part of Henry Clay Folger, President of Standard Oil? But not a single hand-colored Rasputin pecker-ikon available anywhere in the world today, and whither have they flown? The butterfly ephemera of folklore, lost in the night of time. I do what I can, but it ain't much.

When we left Alex's, I offered to show Magda where his old restaurant had been, at the easternmost tip of Sheridan Square only a couple of blocks away. Just there on West fourth we ran into my engineer-bookseller whoremonger Irish friend, Tim Trace, who was also suitably appreciative of Magda's sexy beauty. We stood talking awhile, mostly about how hard small apartments were to find because of the influx of well-paid people into New York during the war. As he left us Tim pointed across the street, at an antique shop with a big telescope mounted outside on a tripod, and said, "Get a load of that before you go."

We ankled across the street and I peered idly into the eyepiece of the telescope, which was obviously out in the street for people to look through, to attract buyers. To my astonishment, what I saw at the other end was a stark naked woman lying on her back with her head twisted up in a scarf and her pussy-hair shining in the afternoon sun. I was so sure it was a fake that I jumped around to the other end of the telescope, where I expected to see the legart picture pasted inside the lens cap, or I don't know what. There was nothing there. The whole thing was real. I went back around to the eyepiece and took another look, and then invited Magda to look too. She looked, and turned away rather puzzled.

"It's a woman taking a sunbath," she said with a so-what air.

I ducked into the antique shop, where a tall Englishman, the proprietor, was leaning against a counter full of bric-a-brac watching us silently.

"That woman is my mother!" I told him, in pretended agitation. That broke up his lofty, Limey air, as I thought it might.

"Oh, no, it isn't," he said with the beginning of a smile.

"Is that telescope for sale?"

"Not yet."

We left it at that, but the mystery of how it was possible for him to have discovered such a view bothered me. Up practically on the roof, in among all those high buildings on the other side of Seventh Avenue. I asked Magda what she thought.

"It's probably his wife," she said, matter-of-factly. "And he just wants a lot of other men to see her naked." We walked on a minute. "I ran into a couple like that in Chicago," Magdalen added. "I was introduced to them in the bookstore of that man you went to get Miller's money from."

"Ben Abramson. You go to his store?"

"You have to. It's the only really good bookstore in town. Everything else is just department store lending-libraries."

She told me about the various wife-trading couples and orgiasts Abramson had introduced her to. Some of them also showed stag movies at their homes to get the parties started.

"So you went?"

"A couple of times, yes."

"I thought you said orgies were unsanitary."

She reached over and plucked me by the earlobe as we walked along toward Josette's apartment and the big bed. "That was before you and Susan gave me the taste for it," she chided me. "You know, you're such a hypocrite!"

"Well, I like women to be purer than men," I insisted shamelessly. "It makes them so much more interesting to rape. Don't you try to give some new virginity to every new man?"

"Yes, but it's awfully hard to do. Just the same old virginity ———"

"——— All darned with pink wool? ———"

"Yes, and ribbons. It's what I've got to offer. Are you bored with me already?"

"Never!"

We walked home to the apartment arm-in-arm. Somehow, I never got around to giving Magdalen the planned avuncular advice about her vibrator that night. We were too busy looking for new and untouched virginities in each other. And were trying to create our own Russian Orthodox ikons, with her pretending my bollocks were the Holy Grail, and kissing and sucking them. It takes the Irish to be really sacrilegious. The Spanish too. Tuesday afternoon though, only a few hours before she left, I did manage to get us into a position to do some serious talking. I was totally fucked out after only three nights with a juicy blonde and a vibrating motor — that's our improved version of a Jug of Wine, a Loaf of Bread, and Thou — and I was feeling somehow depressed and very wise.

"Honeybunch," I told Magdalen, "it's time for us to talk seriously."

"I know," she said. "Anytime you call me 'honeybunch' instead of 'sweetheart,' things are going to be very severe. You're going to take my machine away from me because it's bad for me. And I'm going to have to buy a new one the minute I get back to Chicago."

"No," I told her, "It's worse than that. I don't want you to go back to Chicago at all."

Well, that was it! If I had wanted to be happy in my life, instead of driven and miserable, as I was, *that was the crucial moment.* Maybe of Magdalen's life too. The last chance, really. The boat was pulling out for both of us. Time & tide. But I didn't realize that until years later, when it was far too late. Big talker that I was, I didn't know enough then simply to add: "— So let's get married now, and stay together and be happy."

And that's what would have happened. And we would have torn up her train ticket back to Chicago, and lived happily ever after. I'm sure of it. For once in my life I even had plenty of money — dirty-earned, rotten money, the worst: unworthy, dishonest, ghost-writer money. But instead I let Magdalen go. Not only that, but she needed me then. Here I had already dedicated myself for year, and later for decades more, to giving girls the midnight orgasms they needed, at the expense of mine if necessary. But when the nicest woman I knew needed something more than that, there was nobody home where I lived. Nobody home and nothing doing.

I knew Magdalen was having one-night stands with other men in Chicago. Probably lots of them. She had said as much. And besides, her sureness that I'd have changed my mind about the vibrator, the first morning after, meant plainly that she already knew precisely how it acted on a man. But that didn't matter. I wasn't seriously jealous. How could I be? Wasn't I creaming my way through plenty of other girls' crotches too? Midnights in New York ripping up the sheets.

Well, why not? Nobody was falling in love with me, nor me with anyone. Maybe that was why I didn't marry Magdalen. It was the perfect match, but neither of us really loved the other and we knew it well. What had come closest to touching me was her unspoken cry of despair: that she was hooked on a vibrator, instead in love with any man. So I not only failed of common sense, but of gallantry too. That was always the most visible part of the hidden iceberg of my unconscious inferiority feelings: that I *needed to be needed* by a woman.

As to being hooked, now I tried to tell Magdalen that it wasn't true. She wasn't hooked. She was only using the vibrator rationally, of course a lot, because woman can stand incredibly large amounts of fucking — plain or fancy — not like us men. But if she imagined, that she was using it because she wasn't having enough dates with the kind of men she really liked, I told her, that was where she was making her mistake. It was the other way around: She was *throwing away her sexual tension* on a meaningless whirl with a hand-held machine. Therefore, and very probably for that reason and no other, she was surely not meeting the men who did present themselves, with all the erotic magic and aura she'd be giving off if she really needed them to the bottom of her womb, as when we two had met.

"I'll bet you don't even slide down in the chair at cocktail parties, anymore," I accused her, "and wave your knees around." Fat chance! She could no more stop giving all the men a free show than she could stop breathing.

"But you don't understand," Magdalen wailed. "All those men are *married!*" Hint; hint-hint hint-hint. But I heard nothing. I was talking too loud.

"No, look," I told her. "Seriously. This is what you ought to do. You don't have to throw away the machine. Just forget the machine! I'll forgive you if you sleep with the whole fire-brigade, but it's got to be living men."

What a blunder! Now that I know better, I'd never say that to any woman again. What Magdalen wanted to hear wasn't that; but that I'd beat the living shit out of her if she even looked at another man! That I loved her, and wanted her, and that she was *mine!* But the real trouble was, I knew I just didn't love Magdalen — not the way that makes your heart beat fast — and I guess I was still waiting to find that kind of love. The real thing. They say middle-aged men and widowers and Englishmen and all that, understand philosophically about making a happy life with any woman. You simply get on nicely with her in parlor, bedroom & bath, and know the wisdom of not demanding more, when you have all that, though no real love. I didn't know anything about that flaccid kind of wisdom then and didn't want to. Too proud for that. I tried another tack.

"Chicago is bad for you," I told Magdalen with a big frown. "We both know it. The only time I was ever there was that one day I went to see that crook

Abramson about *Tropic of Cancer*, for Miller's royalties. You could smell how cold and mean the town was. I swore to myself that I'd never live there on a bet. It's the place that's killing you; you've got to get away."

She nodded. "You know," I went on, "the last time I saw Susan she told me your company was willing to send you to San Francisco. Why don't you take them up on it? Everybody says that San Francisco is a wonderful place: it's small, it's warm-hearted, and everybody's on the bounce. And there's country all around. I've never been there, but that's what people have told me: that San Francisco and Vancouver are the only two really civilized places west of Philadelphia and the Hudson River." I paused. Might as well, since I'd already admitted I didn't know what I was talking about. "If I ever figure out a way to make a living, I'm going to live in one of those towns. Will you be waiting when I get there?"

"Who knows?" Magdalen said, looking out the window. "Maybe. It's a pretty long train-ride."

I only saw Magdalen once after that. Our magic always held out, for each other, but we were already racing apart at the speed of light. Like two heavenly bodies — anyhow, hers — that can rendezvous once and once only, all except comets, somewhere in the overpopulated sky, prisoners of inexorable mathematical laws, and then whirl apart like clockwork automata into spiral eternity. And no way back.

The next week, when I got paid, I bought another vibrator for myself, the same brand and best model that they had. I'd owned one long before, in fact several, and had left the first one with Dr. Fortunato when we were working on the prototypes for the vibrating dildoes which were the *wrong* idea. Anyhow, I always thought so, though plenty of women have told me that they love something that goes inside and vibrates there next to the perineum too. Something admittedly no man can do, which is maybe why I'm prejudiced against my own idea. But the vibrator that straps over the back of the hand and leaves the fingers free to do the vibrating — outside the woman's vulva or in her vagina or anus, as you please — that certainly was the *right* idea.

There were supposed to be war shortages just then, but I found a vibrator on the back shelves of my favorite phonograph and appliance shop near Radio City. As I say, the electric cord was black. It should have been white, so as not to show so spookily against the bedsheets in the dark. I learned a lot more about the vibrator and its uses than I'd written in *Oragenitalism.* After that I bought many others, always the same heavy professional model, which was the only one that could really go the course for even as much as an hour. I gave them away as the best possible parting gift to all the women in my life. Only one of my legal wives ever refused it — she was doing her venomous bitch act that last day. I believe I still have one today, but I seldom use it. Maybe I should, even though I admit I'm afraid of the competition in a long relationship with one woman.

When I moved to France I found that the current here is 220 volts instead of 110 as in America, and most of the European and Japanese vibrators available as barbers' supplies and in the sex shops more recently are just rattletraps anyhow: the worst kind of Mickey Mouse schlock. Not the sort of thing to bring home to you wife or even to take on a long weekend with a nice decent girl. They're the ones who are most grateful when they find out how much higher a heaven of ecstasy the vibrator AND YOU can force them to than they've ever reached before, let alone time after time.

I suppose I could import another Oster heavy-duty model from America and stick a voltage converter-coil under the bed, quietly converting while the vibrator hums and buzzes, and shoots off those oily sparks inside – while I make total romantic love, romantically. But in a way, I'm afraid. I know now that when I do that, there isn't going to be any road back. After that, a machine is going to be my bedroom partner for life.

Well, why not? I'm certainly typing this on a machine. And the music of Mozart and Vivaldi in the background of my love-making certainly comes out of a machine, though I admit it doesn't touch the woman's body. But then neither does the hand strap vibrator. So heigh-ho, what's all this squeamishness? I dunno. I suppose it's only a rationalization of my fear of being outdone by The Machine, but, you know, even though the vibrator is the greatest thing in the world on the human clitoris except the tongue, or inside the human vagina except the penis, as women all admit — it's cruel somehow too. I can see it as overwhelming the woman every time, and over-demanding on both the woman and the man. I can go it, but I'm terrifically jealous of the vibrator, and I admit it.

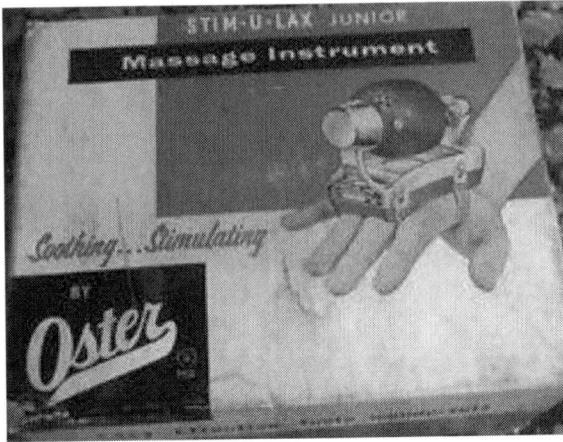

Aside from being visibly habit-forming for the women, the damn thing has always made me feel a little ridiculous, like a one-man band, every time I've used it. That cord in bed always bothered me too, but I suppose batteries can solve that at least for the simple flashlight-dildo types. And you can't combine a vibrator very well with fellation: a lot of women are shy or scared of putting their faces down that close to the sparks inside. Well, there's no halting progress, is there? And the women certainly adore it. Maybe the Oster people will bring out a 220-volt model for Europe. I must remember to write to them about that three-speed rheostat: Fast, Slow, and Romantic. That's the model I'll be holding in my hand when I pose for my heroic statue cut in eternal stone by Gutzon Borglum Jr. in the South Dakota hills, right in front of that other nature-faker and hunter of mammals, Theodore Roosevelt.

❧

CHAPTER 40

THE DEVIL'S ADVOCATE

MAGDALEN was gone. My imaginary anabasis through darkest Brooklyn and parts west, searching for the elusive white Spanish missal, had excited an overpowering urge in me to go back to the old second-hand bookshops on lower Fourth Avenue, which I missed very much. It wasn't just the book-hunting Saturday afternoons that I missed. Of all the cultural activities I could afford to engage in, book-hunting was the one which cost the least money — if you kept your head, which I admit I couldn't always do — and where you were sure to meet the largest number of congenial girls and young women who were particularly susceptible to my particular line of seductory conversation. In other words, I went back to book-hunting for girls not books. There were lots to be found of both. One of those down east dialect humorists remarks somewhere to the effect that "Many a man marries in haste thinking that girls will be scarce next year, and lives to wonder how *the supply does hold out.*"

The bogy of the postal inspectors still being on the lookout for me had ceased to scare me, or maybe I wanted the girls I knew were endlessly ankling into old bookstores looking for odd volumes and unattached men, more than I wanted to be safe. If the heat wasn't off me now — but I was pretty sure it was — it never would be, and I couldn't be skulking about for a whole lifetime, moustache and all, on the lam. Also, I wanted to spend on books some of my ill-gotten profits earned in the tea trade, though that's not what happened. I wasn't lacking in news of Jake Brussel, which Joe Kling and other outlying booksellers in Greenwich Village and the East Side had given me all along. But anyone I asked about him now on Fourth Avenue always had something to say, much of it obviously fantastic. One piece of news that didn't sit too well was given me by a novelty-shop proprietor named Henry Klein.

He was a sort of honorary bookseller, because among the schlock novelty items he generally sold in large, temporarily vacant stores here & there all over town, were often a few books and pamphlets. This time he had a handful of the long out-of-circulation issues of the rare and wonderful slang–and–scandal tabloid sex newspaper of the 1930s, *Broadway Brevities*, of which I had the only almost-complete set in existence, but lacking two issues: Volume XI, number 7, and Volume XII, number 10, both dated about 1934. As the magazine had ceased publication for several long intervals during the worst Depression years, while searching for new angels and capital, I always assumed these two issues had never really been published, and were simply overlooked in the numbering on starting up again after a pause. Well, here in the little bin of back-issue magazines of a humorous kind that Henry Klein was offering were a few *Broadway Brevities*, just five or six. And looking them over mechanically, I found to my astonishment one of my long-missing numbers! Of course, now I'm hooked for life, and will never again sleep quietly in the belief that the *other* really never did appear. I'm only missing one number now, and *I've GOT to find it!*

The paragraph you've just read gives the key and the crucial difference between the compulsive, neurotic collector I still was then, and the cultivated booklover I hope I may one day become. Soon. Your standard compulsive collector is driven entirely by anxiety. Knowledge — *possession* — is power! He or she is almost exclusively interested in getting it ALL, or as close as humanly possible to all. Or at the very least a damn good big selection, of some peculiar group of associated objects that, for some generally inexplicable reason, is considered worth collecting, usually irrespective of what their intrinsic merit or worth may be.

And money is no object — not ever! Often, in addition, the collected objects are of such a nature that it's essentially ludicrous to collect them at all, such as old cancelled postage stamps, or galvanized iron tractor seats. I saw a photograph recently of a Hobby Lobby Swap Festival in America showing a collector of just such cast-iron tractor seats. He was displaying on the wall his two hundred *duplicate* tractor seats, which he had come there to swap for other models he did not yet possess.

But even when there's some purported sense of social value to the collection, as with books or art or nude photos, or even old gold coins, which can at least always be boiled down and resold for their metal value, the desire of the tyro or the neurotic collector is generally for long or especially unbroken series: of one author's or artist's complete works, of one printer's or photographer's total output of books or nudes, of one Japanese craftsman's lifetime range of decorative swords or even sword guards, or snuff boxes or spinning tops or old phonographs or early automobiles. Or perhaps even of all the books in the world on some particular subject or interest, such as sex or some lesser subject.

This mere bookish form of the disease is known as bibliography when one collects, not even the books themselves, but simply their names or titles, on little slips of paper or cardboard — now computers — or the names of all the models or types of prehistoric potsherds found in some small geographical area, or sylvan butterflies, or grebes' eggs, or twelve-rayed cockle-shells, or full-dress suits of blue filigreed armor and swords, which begins to come a bit close — does it not? — to the collecting of galvanized iron tractor seats moulded to fit the driver's arse. Or its equally common companion collection, of foot-long pieces of hundreds of different models of ugly barbed wire, tacked to strips of painted plywood board.

The final position of total neurotic collapse on the part of the compulsive collector-maniac of this type would be, or have been, in my case, if I were willing to sell or auction off the one hundred and eighteen issues I already possess of this idiotic sex-tabloid, *Broadway Brevities*, in order to raise the money necessary to buy the two missing numbers, assuming they could still ever be found at all. Mad collectors have been known to pull switches exactly like that. Look, *you* don't happen to have those two issues of *Broadway Brevities*, do you?

Price no object! We can weigh them off against gold-dust, if you like. I'm no fool, mind you. I realize that recent ephemera like that are far rarer than old Gutenberg Bibles, which are even more unreadable now. My phone number is France 33-93-42-02-53. You can call me any hour of the day or night, and reverse the charges. *Just get me those two missing issues!* [Transciber's note: This is no longer current, alas!]

I admit I didn't go so far, yet, as to sell off my collections to buy more, but things very similar to that happen all the time. Nothing is more common than the old case-hardened trivia collector who has sold or traded off one early collection of the drivel he collects, and who is presently engaged in amassing another collection, usually quite similar and seldom as good. Until we arrive finally at the totally lunatic or bibliomaniacal type, of which the English book-collector in the early nineteenth century, Sir Thomas Phillips — and, even better, Richard Heber, the elder brother of a bishop — was the classic case and perfect example forever.

Heber simply bought books, on unrelated subjects, until his house was totally full of books and could hold no more. He then locked up the house, bought another house, and filled that with books too. And so on. He never visited his preceding houses full of books, nor read the books; nor would he allow anyone else to do so. When he died he had ten or a dozen such houses full of unread books, and the subsequent auction sales took years. No one has ever been able to make any sense whatever out of the catalogue.

We all agree, certainly, that Richard Heber was a pathetic case, and probably half-mad. I certainly have to agree. In the attic above my head, as I sit here typewriting these lines at the age of sixty-nine, there are some four to five thousand very fine and laboriously selected books, still in the roped-up yellow cardboard and wooden cases in which they were packed when I left America for France thirty-five years ago, and which have never been unpacked since. I've been far too busy — buying more books, many of them duplicates of books I know I POSSESS!!!! They're somewhere in those unopened cases, but I just didn't have the time to start opening them with a crowbar and searching for the books when the long-awaited moment came that I needed them, to look something up for my work. Poor, poor mad Richard Heber. *N'est-ce pas?*

What am I to say? Nothing. The French fabulist, Jean de la Fontaine already said it all perfectly, in the elegant, periodic accents of classical French: *"Loin d'épuiser une matière, sachez n'en cueillir que la fleur* — Far from exhausting your subject-matter, learn to pluck only its flower." If I'd had the sense to print that on my bookplate all those years ago, I wouldn't have to ridicule myself today. While the second-hand booksellers charmingly give big bags of cookies to my children. — Just passing by in Europe on a Sunday outing. How's your health? Had any more heart attacks? — And the erotica collectors send boxes of candy and phonographs records to my wife. They'll be there to seduce her later on, if they can. Now, instead, I'm taking a line from the Ecclesiast for my bookplate: *Hodie mihi* − *cras tibi*. Mine today − yours tomorrow. Brothers and sisters, remember me with a smile.

WELL THEN, so I handed Henry Klein a dollar to pay for his six issues of *Broadway Brevities* at fifteen cents apiece, five of which I knew positively were duplicates of some I already had. But I'd give those away to friends or trade them off. No sense leaving them there for the junk buyers in the schlock-shop, who wouldn't have any idea of their rarity, and would just pick them up idly for their bawdy jokes, and then use them to line the garbage can with that evening. I assumed Klein would hand me back my dime in change, but instead he pocketed the dollar and folded his arms.

"I'll give you a break," he said. "Take another quarter's worth for the dime – anything you like." I took two pocket combs with a rubber band around them, and a tiny vial of perfume for Elaine.

"What do you hear from Jake Brussel, Henry?" I asked. "When is he getting out?"

"Who the hell knows?" he replied. "That's another fifty cents for the perfume. That wife of his, Minna, was in here just a couple of days ago. Claims I owe her money for some books."

"So what did you say?"

"What did I say?! I don't owe nobody any money. I always pay cash. I told her to go piss up a rope. And you know what she did? She walked out right in the middle of the store, and she opens up in a big yenta voice: 'Ladies and Gentlemen! Don't buy anything in this store! This man owes my husband hundreds of dollars for books and he won't pay. My husband is in jail, and my children don't have what to eat! Please boycott this store!' *That's* what she did."

"And what did you do, Henry?

"What did I do? I grabbed her and kicked her out of the store. That's what I did. I said, 'What are you hollering about, you crazy clitoris?! I don't owe you no money! Get outa here before I call a cop!' And she won't budge. She stands in the door, and she says, 'So call a cop! I'm gonna take you to court. You're not honest. Ladies and Gentlemen! My children don't have what to eat! Please boycott this store!' You ever hear anything like it in your life?"

"No," I said. "I never heard anything like it."

I didn't have to wonder who was telling the truth. If Minna Brussel had just wanted to put the arm on somebody, she wouldn't have picked a hard case like Henry. She'd have picketed Tiffany's, Ladies and Gentlemen! I decided I would go looking for Mahlon Blaine and find out where Minna was living now with the kids. But I couldn't find Blaine either. The silent elevator-man in the old loft building on West Third Street across from New York University told me they'd been out of there years since. "The cops came," he said. "They took away everything in trucks." I knew that already and got away fast. I wanted to find Minna and maybe help her, but I wasn't interested in going to jail.

I already knew they had left the house at the corner of Grove and Hudson, just opposite Maya Deren's place. But I went there anyhow. I would ask Maya Deren if maybe she knew where they had gone. Only her husband Alex Hammid was home, but she came in right after. We got into a long discussion of their avant garde films. They had only finished one so far, but I said I thought it was great: *Meshes of the Afternoon*. It stank. Hammid was the photographer. Formerly Hackenschmied, he was a German modernist of the real old intense *Cabinet of Dr. Caligari* school. It was his photography that was great. Maya was the star, of course, with her terrific little *zaftig* body and her elflike, sort of Chinese face, always pouting. Anyhow, they didn't know where the Brussels had gone. They said they'd give me a pass for a private showing of their new art film in progress. It would be called *At Land*, about Maya as a sort of Candide fish cast ashore.

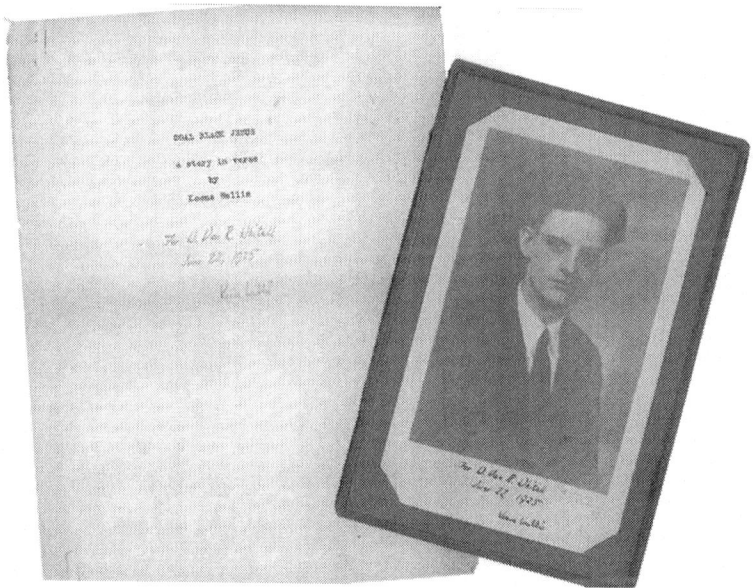

KEENE WALLIS WHEN YOUNG

Keene Wallis was my best bet. I should have thought of him first, but I didn't know where he lived either. He always said he lived in Paradise Alley, but I knew that wasn't its real name. It was somewhere in the bowels of Alphabet City, the worst slum on the East Side, of lettered endless streets called Avenue A, Avenue B, and so forth, beyond St. Mark's Place. Just as I crossed Fourth Avenue going east, under the high blank brick wall that was the backside of the big old opera house on Fourteenth Street, I bumped into Sugarman slouching along with his red nose and empty coat sleeve.

Abe Sugarman was a book scout, and people said he was a very good one. Mostly he ran books for one homosexual bookseller at the Pegasus bookshop, whose catalogues were always a riot. Sugarman had had tuberculosis and lost one arm, and now he was that then-almost-unknown thing, a Jewish *shikker*. He got drunk all the time to forget his troubles, and would drink up all the money he earned book-scouting. If I had his troubles, I'd be drunk all the time too. Anyhow, he didn't look a bit drunk. I asked him where Paradise Alley was.

"Why? You wanna move in? I can get you a room. I know the super." He told me where it was. "Be sure to tell the super I sent you. Just say Sugarman sent you."

Paradise Alley was really called something else, as I had guessed, and it was pretty bad. A true slum. Dirty, gone-to-ruin, sour. A miserable little back-wash, and smelled pretty high, too. Keene had been right to call it Paradise Alley. Just the odor of undumped chamber pots of shit, here & there by the peeling wooden doors and the grimy old low red brick walls, made it unmistakably Heaven for whatever damned souls had to live there. Keene was one of them. He was home. Appropriately, he was busy translating Dante's *Divine Comedy*, using a nineteenth-century American translation as a pony, to save looking up the archaic Italian words in the dictionary. It was by Bayard Taylor, and I asked Keene whether that wasn't who had translated Goethe's *Faust* too.

"Yes!" Keene said, in his fanatically slow and over-accented way. "He translated *every*thing. And *badly*. Because everything had to be translated into *verse*."

"I didn't know you were against verse, Keene," I said. With Keene you always had to stick to his subject and his hobbyhorse gait. You could never rush or panic him. Keene was an old time Wobbly, back from the days of World War I, and he was now a fiercely devoted rank-&-file recruiting member of the Communist Party. What counted was results. You must never rush. You had to be patient, and convince everybody of everything. Slowly.

"Poetry is *mira*culous!" he assured me. "Everybody *loves* poetry. But only if they *sing* it. Nobody will buy a book of poetry *today*. Hardy's *'Dynasts'* knocked the public on the *head*. The publishers *only* put them out *now* for *prestige*. Poets have *always* had to publish their *own* poetry. *For* each other: The Little Mags That *Died* To Make Verse *Free!*"

"That's a great line, Keene," I told him. "Can I quote it?"

"It's *not mine*. Maxwell Bodenheim."

I tried to veer the subject around to Jake Brussel, but poetry now interested Keene a lot more. He began telling me about how it was in the late 'Teens and early

'Twenties, when Greenwich Village got the reputation it's coasted on for decades since. He stunned me by mentioning that Brussel, whom he always called Jack, had been one of the lovers of Edna St.Vincent Millay in those days.

"Oh, I can't believe it!" I told him. "Jack is so gross. I love him, but he is the perfect vulgarian. Edna St.Vincent Millay is the greatest American poet since Whitman."

"Well, that's *true*," he admitted. "But she slept with *every*body. That was her *revenge* against *all* of us, and against God, for not making her a *man* instead." And he quoted:

" 'I might as well be easing you, as lie alone in bed . . .

Boys and girls that lie, whispering in the hedges,
Do not let me die; mix me in your pledges.'

That was *another* one of her *prob*lems," Keene pursued. "She *wanted* to be *immortal.*"

"Why is that wrong?" I asked. "It didn't hurt Dante any, to be immortal."

"*Ger*shon," he said, terribly sincerely, "immortality is *not* a *whore*. She *gives* herself to whom she *wants*. *No* one can *rape* immortality."

That was the trouble with the best sellers too, we agreed. Then we got off onto Dante again, and Keene explained that his new translation of the Divine Comedy was *absolutely necessary*, to put things back into *proportion*. "In *most* people's minds," he said — my mind, probably — "Dante's *great* poem is about Hell." I admitted it.

"Well, it *isn't!*" Keene stated triumphantly. "But that's *just* the way people *are*. They take the greatest *poem* ever written to express the *love* of *Humanity*, and they make it into a trip to *Hell!*"

I asked him where Minna Brussel was living, and told him I had heard she was having a bad time, and wanted to give her some money. I told him I had earned a little extra — I didn't say how I had earned it, pushing marijuana — and that I felt I owed something to Jake. I told Keene how Jake had come the night of his arrest, in the snow, to warn me to get out of town. And how grateful I was for that.

"Yes!" Keene said, stretching his mouth into a grotesque mask. "*Some*one was just *telling* me. He's very *gross*. He's the *perfect* vulgarian."

I looked into his long, cadaverous face and bad, yellowing teeth. "I'm very ashamed, Keene," I said. "I'd better start reading Dante, about human love. So tell me where Minna is. I want to share what I've got with her."

"*No*," he said. "I *won't*. And I'll tell you *why*."

He told me that Minna was very angry with me, and had felt all the time that if Jake hadn't shielded me he might have got a lighter sentence. If I turned up now, Keene warned me, *somebody* might be liable to turn me in.

"But it wouldn't shorten Jack's sentence now, if they pulled me in," I expostulated.

"Of *course* not," Keene agreed. "Prosecutors *like* to prosecute. And they have *records* to show at the *end* of the *year*. *Two* stiffs in the *can* is a better record than *one* stiff in the *can*. It doesn't *matter* how long they're in *for*. You just stay *away* from Minna."

What we finally decided was that I would give Keene the money, and he would give it to Minna. He didn't know where I lived, and he didn't *want* to know. And I wasn't to know where Minna lived, either. The money would arrive at its destination. I knew that, all right — Keene was the heart & soul of honor — but it bothered me that he was so sure that she would turn me in.

"I can't believe it!" I argued, the next day when I brought Keene the money to Paradise Alley, and counted it out in his hand, as Mr. Bop had counted it out for me: six hundred dollars. "I'd think Minna would be grateful. She told Harry Klein the kids don't have what to eat."

"Oh, *they* have what to *eat*," Keene assured me. "But only *just*." He looked at the stack of money with pursed lips, and then tapped the bills together in a neat pile – it was all in twenties – and slipped it into an old red manila manuscript envelope with his translation of Dante, tied round with a string. I figured I'd better leave, so he could take the money over without me. We shook hands as Keene opened the door out into Paradise Alley.

"If I were *you*," he said, "I wouldn't *count* too much on people being grateful."

He was right too. A couple of years later, when Jake was out of jail, and I was again in & out of their house all the time, now an apartment on West 3rd Street, very near Sixth Avenue, I found it surprising that no one ever mentioned the money again. I mean, not to express gratitude or anything like that, but just to mention it somehow in passing. I asked Keene about that, discreetly. He explained to me elaborately, as always, that the money had never arrived at its destination. Someone must have seen us counting it out, in his squalid little street-level room in Paradise Alley, and they broke in that night and stole it. Keene had been badly beaten up in the process.

I expressed my commiseration. I've been beaten too, and know how it feels. Was there any chance, I asked of finding out who it was?

"It was *something* about *drugs!*" Keene told me, pursing his lips, and with a two-handed gesture of asseveration, as though pushing something away. This seemed to me so overdone that I was instantly certain that what had really happened to the money was what I might have expected. And that Keene had been beaten up as the result of one of his attempted homosexual seductions. In other words, someone had fag-rolled him — for my money. Observing the leery look in my eye, perhaps, he added that the worst of it was they also took away his translation of Dante's *Divine Comedy*, which was in the same red manila envelope. He had to do it all over again.

I told him I was very sorry he had lost his translation of Dante because of me, but Keene assured me that the new version was much better than his first draft had been. As I felt a little bitter about the whole thing, I couldn't forbear to add that maybe they ought to change the name of Paradise Alley to Purgatory Alley.

"Well, that's *just* what Dante *means!*" Keene said, his old eyes shining. "But *backwards*. He wants to change the name of *Purgatory* to *Paradise*." And he quoted, not from Dante but from his oracle and guide Virgil: "If I can't reach *Heaven*, I must move *Hell!*"

That was Freud's motto too, on the title page of his first book.

AFTER a lot of moral wrestling with myself, like the patriarch Jacob with the angelic hit-man in the night, I decided the only practical thing to do was to get back to writing pornography. Old Johnson out in Oklahoma would be tired of Henry Miller's horseshit by now, assuming that Miller had ever done any manuscripts for him in the first place. No millionaire was going to be able to stand Miller's anti-patriotic soundtrack very long, no matter how much he beat on his literary chest and pretended to be the new Walt Whitman and Emerson combined. All from Brooklyn! Anyhow, Whitman had only been able to get away with his act by announcing that he was two-hundred percent American. If Miller had done any porno manuscripts, I hoped to god he had had the sense to hold out for a hundred dollars, the way I told Anaïs Nin. Those old, 1938 Depression-days low prices were now just a forgotten bad dream.

I went up Fifth Avenue to Johnny Furness the Agent's office. First shock. He wasn't there any more. His office on the fifth floor was now a typing service: two middle-aged female buzzards who stated they had never heard of him. True or false, that was all the answer I could get. I knew phoning Rudy Bernays directly would be the sure way to get a nasty turn-down, which would queer things probably forever.

The only way was to find Slapsie Maxie, and to start back with him the way I had at the beginning. I wondered if he still carried around his little leather-cased packet of visiting cards marked: "MAX FREEMAN – LITERARY AGENT," with no address, only a phone number. Well, no sense looking for him in the bookshops on Fourth Avenue near where he lived. You never saw Slapsie Maxie wandering around; he was much too odd and furtive for that. I'd have to go over to the perfectly middle-class apartment house he lived in, just east of Union Square, still unmarried and living with his mother even though he was over forty now. His mother was glad to have his company; she was a widow and had nothing but her two sons, one of whom had married and moved away long ago.

I phoned ahead from a candy-store on the corner downstairs. You had to do that or risk panicking Maxie. He was home and said sure to come up. The card over the doorbell still read: GROBE – FREEMAN. I hadn't remembered how big and sunny his mother's apartment was. Maybe this living with your mother had something to be said for it. I was remembering how my own mother had wisely refused me any such privilege — not even for me to live in the little two-room apartment downstairs in the back; not if it meant her paying my bills for the next three years. Or thirty? I guess she was right.

Maxie had a couple of books around, but none of the handsome ones I had seen there the time before except a broken copy of *La Tarantula* with the back held together with strips of court-plaster — his favorite? — which I certainly didn't want, doubtless covered with his jism-stains inside. He assumed I was there to buy books, but I now had no money left for that sort of thing. Least of all for pornography which I could never read anyhow, and had only ever bought out of crude collectomania. Maxie said I could have any book I wanted in his suitcase for ten dollars, or three for twenty-five, or even seven for fifty dollars, if I were flush. The same deal Jake Brussel had been offering the doctors. He said he would throw in a deck of pornographic playing-cards from Mexico and a double-header dildo — "from Japan, before the war" — if I took a hundred dollars' worth. To put me in appetite, I guess, he extracted the long double rubber dildo from a very shiny bright brown leather briefcase he now sported, and sort of snapped it in the air a few times with a toothy, totally phony grin. He really grossed me out. It was an art. Slapsie Maxie, the sublime vulgarian — gold tooth and all.

I mentioned that his books used to be five dollars, not ten. He disagreed. Sure, some were ten! Always. Anyhow, times had changed now because of all the soldiers. There were army officers now, and petty officers off ships, all the time. They were crazy to get hot books. He guaranteed he'd have all his stock sold within a day or two. He didn't even have to take the books out to peddle. The soldiers & sailors would come to him now. They had money. Plenty. I could believe it. So I'd better grab the stuff, he said, thoughtlessly snapping the double dildo again. The greasy-looking thin thing looked like a long, droopy, milk-rubber cucumber. I felt sorry for any two whoors that would have to stick the ends of that thing into themselves to excite some voyeuristic army officer covered with furlough money. I told Maxie I was a little short of money myself; in fact, that was why I had come to see him. Was the Syndicate still running, — you know, for the manuscripts? I had been working on some honeys recently, that his client would really like to buy. In fact, it would be a long series. Probably run for a year or more, like the old times.

"Oh yeah," Maxie said vaguely. "Sure. My client is always lookin' for good manuscripts. He's workin' exclusively through me now. Ya got 'em wit ya?"

No, I explained. I had only worked up the outlines so far. I naturally wouldn't do the writing before I saw him and got the go-ahead, that the Syndicate was still in operation.

"Yeah, sure," he said. "You call me tonight if ya want. But not after nine o'clock. I'll tell ya what he says."

"Don't tell him it's me," I cautioned him. "I've got a book coming out soon with a big publisher, and I want to keep my name out of this."

Slapsie Maxie gave me a big, conspiratorial grimace and hand-signal, to indicate that he understood professional niceties like that. I let Maxie be as mysterious as he liked. He put on his topcoat with the velvet collar, even though it was midsummer, and accompanied me out as he always did. Since my experience with Archie staying overnight in my room, I understood why. Maxie took me to the corner. He wanted to be sure that I wasn't hanging around to trail him after I was supposed to be gone. He was slap-happy, all right, but terribly shrewd and cautious too.

As we parted, I'd had time to think things over abut prices, and I told Maxie it was very important he should see his client and get the go-ahead before I would start writing. Because times had changed for me too, and I now wanted a hundred dollars a manuscript. No fifty bucks apiece anymore.

"Hey!" he expostulated. "I can't get you a hundred bucks!"

"All right," I said. "I'm not mad. Just ask your client first. I'll phone you tomorrow morning. If he says no — no harm done. But I'm not working for fifty bucks a shot anymore. Besides," I added, giving him an overdone shrewd wink, "it's better for you too. You're the agent, aren't you? When my price is double, your commission is double. Just tell him so. But remember — *he's* paying you; I'm not."

I left Maxie on the street corner, at his request, even though we were both going uptown, thinking how exactly this dumpy little man in his absurd velvet-collared topcoat in July looked just like Peter Lorre as the demented child-murderer in Fritz Lang's movie, *M*. Just the wrong person for the job he was in.

When I called the next day, he told me the deal was on. The client would pay what I wanted, but had refused to give Maxie double his former fee, so I'd have to pay five extra dollars out of my hundred. I grumbled a little but agreed. I knew he was lying, of course. Then I sat down immediately to start knocking out an erotic manuscript, but nothing came. It was just like constipation: tough shit. The more I pushed and strained, the more unpleasant I felt. And nothing came. I got up and took a drink of water from the tap in my corner sink. I studied the little oblong program leaflet they used to send from WQXR, and checked off the music I wanted to be sure not to miss for a whole week ahead. I changed my typewriter ribbon by turning it upside down, like turning your shirt inside-out when you haven't any money for the laundry. The way the ribbon-jigger doesn't keep flashing up in front of your eyes, when you use the bottom half of the ribbon. I counted out two hundred sheets of paper, white and yellow — that included for the carbon copy too, so as not to give the bastards even a page too many. Then I started on the manuscript again. It came a little, but it was hard sledding.

I stopped and listened to Artur Schnabel practicing Beethoven's *Appassionato Sonata* across the back garden. He still lived on West 75th Street, just facing my room in back, but on the ground floor. When he started working on a piece for his next concert, you had to give up listening to it seriously for the next two years, because you were going to hear every ten-bar section of it played separately several hundred times, over and over, for months. That son-of-a-bitch never seemed to be blocked, did he? But of course he was only playing somebody else's music. No trick to that. Beethoven was blocked for the whole last twenty years of his life, wasn't he now? And deaf, too. Just a blank, for fifteen years between his two last symphonies. Never wrote anything the whole time but the Choral Symphony and those god-awful last piano sonatas, and the final string quartets even worse.

This melancholy thought cheered me up somehow. Better him than me, I guess. I decided to see if I was really blocked, and got out the unfinished manuscript of *Taboo*, my history of sex-censorship, and worked the rest of the day on that very happily. So I was only blocked writing erotica. Something had to be

done about that. I'd also have to recount the blank
paper in the stack, as I now wouldn't have the exact
count for the erotic manuscript which I'd entitled
Horny Heaven. I was only up to page 8 on that, and just
getting into the first erotic scene. That was where I had
blocked. I really hated writing the stuff now. Before it
hadn't been this hard. I wondered fleetingly how Anaïs
Nin was doing. Was she killing her art with the hack
stuff too, as I'd cruelly recommended to her?

As it was Sunday, I knew there wouldn't be any
choir practice for Elaine. I knocked at her door and
asked her if she'd like to go out to dinner, and take in a
movie. Poor dumb chick, I seldom took her out. I was
too selfish. Egoistic. I preferred to save my money,
what there was of it, and spend it on books. Anyhow,
I'd tell myself, it's the sex part that means the most to
Elaine and me. But of course, it wasn't true. It was
merely sex for me, but girls always managed to slip
some kind of romance into love-making, unless they
were just whores, or else they wouldn't do it at all.
They always have to have some kind of belief about it,
even if it's nonsense, above the bellybutton, or they
don't have many orgasms, or none at all, below the
bellybutton.

We went out. We had a good time, as it's called.
The movie wasn't too bad, and we both laughed a lot.
Elaine was very perky and willing when we got home
and went to bed, and this time I put my mind carefully
and cannily to work noticing and remembering
everything we were doing in bed. I purposely varied
the erotic menu wildly. Next morning I would stay
home from the Academy and write it all up from
memory. At five pages typed up in an hour, in three

days I'd have the whole hundred pages done. No rewriting, of course. You never rewrote anything, working for the Syndicate. However it came out was good enough. The customer never complained.

In the morning I found that I had totally forgotten absolutely everything we had done in bed. But by contrast, I could remember the entire plot and all the gags in the crappy movie we had seen, word for word. Poetic justice. Well, *needs must when the Devil drives*; that's my motto. I got to work and wrote up the whole movie from memory, in a steamy erotic version that would have to be Horny Heaven. And little by little, as I wrote, I began to remember what Elaine and I had done the night before. But it didn't fit the plot too well, which was all about getting laid in speeding sports cars, and that sort of snob exotica. So in the end I had to leave Elaine out.

I went back and redid the first two pages of the eight I had originally typed up before I felt blocked. This reset the scene and changed the title to The Belly Button. Of course with a play on words, meaning this was the clitoris. It was now about a girl who could only have an orgasm in motion, in cars. Rolley-coasters were her favorite, but two-up on a galloping horse with the Hungarian Gypsy riding-master on her millionaire father's Connecticut estate was acceptable in a pinch. I figured I couldn't pervert the customer's mind very badly with that. Poor old coot.

I wondered if he masturbated all alone in his office, doubtless with starched cuffs and discreet gold cuff-links. Maybe he had a prim-looking girl secretary — to fool his wife. That secretary unquestionably had to be the world's greatest fellatrice, and a volcano of passion when she took off her eyeglasses and her pleated serge skirt and shirtwaist. Girls with eyeglasses, especially librarians, they can fool you sometimes. Wow! And she would bring him each new manuscript as it arrived in the mail, or more likely by air express, and present it to him on one knee, maybe both, unbuttoning her shirtwaist as she did so, to let her, full voluptuous bosom pour out — practically to the floor, no doubt. Hmmm, maybe that would be a plot I could use for the next manuscript? No; Johnson would know he was being kidded, and would phone Bernays to get rid of the crude new writer.

I was determined to make some money now, and knock out a manuscript a week, just as I had done a few years before, after my jobs in the theatre and all that came to an end. I'd work out something with Dickinson, so I could show up only half weeks at the Academy of Medicine. The reference books I needed on my book *Taboo* were all down at the public library, anyhow. Maybe I'd just work there half days. And I'd hightail it home and get typing every afternoon. No, it was better to work in the mornings, typewriting. You were fresher and made less typing errors.

The main thing was to get out a manuscript a week, and get that hundred dollars, now down to ninety-five because of Slapsie Maxie. I wasn't getting any advance at all on *Taboo* from Haldeman-Julius, and I'd have to live somehow while I'd be researching and writing it. Also I was tired of never having any money to buy books with, or anything else. Having that marijuana money temporarily in the bank had given me the taste for knowing where your next foolish expenditure is coming from, something I hadn't known in years. So I had thrown away that money on a foolish gesture. I'd make more. I had laboriously fought Dickinson up from twenty to twenty-five and now thirty dollars a week since beginning on his project, and I knew that comedy Scot would never go a penny higher. It wasn't in his nature. Well, that just paid my living expenses. If I wanted any more money, it had to come from somewhere else. I got down to work. I had to.

BY THE THIRD week everything began to fall apart. I wasn't blocked anymore — never had been; just the usual difficulty getting going — but it started raining knives & forks point downward on my plan for making money. The first thing that happened hadn't really happened *yet*, but I knew it would cause an explosion in the Syndicate very soon. My friend John "Gee-whiz" Brown had given me Bob Sewell's new address in New York, but I hadn't looked him up yet. I was too busy then in the tea business. One evening I had free now, and I went over to Bob's new address to drop in and pick up again. I had no phone number for him.

I suppose the thought in my mind was, that if I did go into block I'd do what I had done the other time, when I couldn't go on writing erotic manuscripts. I'd turn the job over to Sewall, to keep the contact until I got back into the vein, just as I had when I couldn't do more than one imitation of The Oxford Thesis on Love. Imitating or even translating someone else's book and style is not a steady diet for me. But Sewall not only didn't seem to mind; he thrived on it. It saved him all the trouble of creating plots and characters. The same as when I had plagiarized the movie I had seen with Elaine, to get started on The Belly Button. I couldn't throw any stones.

The first crack out of the box, as I remember, Sewall told me his wife Alice was going to have a baby. Being the kind of suspicious bastard I am, though not really cynical yet, I wondered if he was really the father. But I said nothing; Sewall was already sentimentalizing about names for the baby. Getting married and having babies was very important then; it kept your draft status inactive during the war. That's what caused the baby-boom ecologists now worry about. Unmarried men like me had to think of something else. Bob's wife was living with his family in Scranton until the baby would be born, and he too was looking around for ways of making money. Herman Miller, the little bookseller in the Chanin Building arcade at 42nd Street had a mimeograph machine in a back alcove behind the screen for his catalogues. Sewall was typing up three of his manuscripts done for the Syndicate, but single-spaced this time, from the carbon copies, to make a book Miller would issue by mimeograph. They would split the profits.

"For Christ's sake!" I exploded, "that'll ruin the whole thing! The client has booksellers scouting him books on both coasts. He'll see it a week after it's out and know we kept carbon copies. He'll hit the roof!"

"So what?" Sewall shrugged. "We're not working for him anymore."

"Well maybe *you're* not, but I am! And I need the money."

Sewall needed the money too. For his wife and the coming baby. I couldn't argue with that. We decided that the client — I always called him that; never told anybody his real name — would just have to be sore at whoever he thought had written that manuscript. But that wouldn't necessarily include me. Or would it? I'd have to take the chance. I couldn't stop Sewall anyhow. I had kept carbon copies too, of all my manuscripts, though in the end I never did anything with them but trade them with Rubin Bresler for some important items and sexological rariora, like one of the only two known copies of Swinburne's flagellant poems, *The Whippingham Papers*, that I figured were paradoxically better worth saving from the forgetfulness of time than my own perfectly normal erotic manuscripts, when I was cataloguing the Havelock Ellis library for Bresler. He sold all my manuscripts to Louis Shomer later and a few of them got published that way, in printed form. I wish they hadn't. They were really pretty bad. One miserable item was called *South of the Border*, I think. Not my title, and printed really crappily. Another one printed up was my imitation of *The Oxford Thesis on Love*, as *The Oxford Professor*, along with Sewall's later continuations too.

Well, in for a penny, in for a pound, they say. Sewall was having trouble, with the stencil typing because he wasn't used to long hours of typing anymore. He had been working as a bartender or something, in Scranton. He had a true loser's talent for taking very peculiar jobs. After an hour of two of typing he'd start making scads of mistakes on the stencils and spend the rest of the day floating in smelly correction fluid. As usual, Miller the bookseller in the Chanin Building was in a hurry for the job, but nevertheless he had to give Sewall back a whole slew of stencils that had so many corrections on them that they couldn't be used. Sewall asked me if I'd help with the typing and I agreed. We'd split the money sixty-forty. I had just finished an erotic manuscript, and figured what the hell. My book *Taboo* was progressing, but was still mostly in the research stage.

Of course, I hadn't made any money yet on the erotic manuscripts I was writing, of which I had now done three. It was like this. Every time I'd arrive for my ninety-five dollars, foxy little Slapsie Maxie would pull out his brief-bag and the battered suitcase, now full again with beautifully printed underground erotica of the 1930s. Instead of getting a single dime out of him, twice I ended up owing Maxie money. I'm no match even for a guaranteed cretin if he has interesting books.

Still, we were both satisfied. At Maxie's price of seven ten-dollar books for fifty dollars, I was more than getting back on each hundred the five dollars he was holding out. That was the arithmetic of bargain lots. To him, of course, it was even sweeter, because he was probably making a hundred percent profit on each of the books anyway, or more. The net result was that I had picked up over fifty quite interesting erotica, including a few small items he threw in, as always. Maxie now had no books left in his brief bag, and I had no money. I had bought all his stock of erotic books by writing three similar books. Not bad, I figured. It wasn't what I had planned, but I couldn't complain.

Money just goes for expenses when you have it: in your mouth, out your asshole. If you *buy* something instead — it doesn't matter what: books records, flower bulbs, a little shack in ruins somewhere in the backwoods and a piece of land to go with it — you end up with something real and for good. You don't just flush it away. There speaks the true anal-retentive collector maniac, I know, but it's also perfectly true. You know it too.

That extra five-dollar holdout on my manuscripts always rankled me a bit, but it was eventually wholly amortized owing to Slapsie Maxie's complicated discount scale. At seven books for fifty dollars, the hundred dollars for each manuscript gave me the right to pick fourteen books. But since I was now to get only ninety-five dollars, that meant only thirteen books and the odd change in cash. Maxie really hated to part with any cash, and I pretended to be unwilling to accept so unlucky a number of books as thirteen. So we met in the middle, and in the end I got fourteen books each time. Big deal. As I say, they must have cost him very little. He also had the shrewdness of many small dealers, always throwing in little sweeteners each time.

The only real regret I had was that I hadn't been there to buy all these erotic books ten years earlier, when they were first published, and when I would surely have been able to get a line on who was publishing them. This way, ten years late, I was never able to find out for sure. You could always tell Sam Roth's cheap typography, but some of the other books were so handsomely designed they were obviously the work of one or more of the big limited editions publishers, or more likely of their printers. Several or even all of these publishers were involved, I feel sure, because they had all been hit very hard by the Depression, when buying luxury books was one of the items everybody scuttled first.

Meanwhile all the limited editions houses had been openly publishing whatever semi-erotica they could get away with all along, for instance Horace Liveright, and Covici-Friede, and lots of others too. When the real pinch of the Depression came, between 1932 and the couple of years following, it seemed logical that the big semi-erotica publishers — and even more logically the small ones — would try to slip something stronger through, something they were sure of selling privately even when money was getting scarce. Governments may rise and fall, but sex goes on forever.

Macy-Masius certainly did publish erotic items, at high prices, and had done so even before the Depression. Jacob Baker, the head of a very big book-distributing firm, told me a number of years later how he had handled the whole edition of the bawdy folksong collection *Immortalia*, issued secretly by Macy-Masius in 1928 with the false date of 1927 on the title page to lull the police into overlooking it. Roth and other clandestine publishers later published this too. It had been edited anonymously by Thomas R. Smith, the elegant and learnèd chief editor for Liveright, as a supplement to his anthology *Poetica Erotica*.

In his charming autobiography, *The Mechanical Angel*, Donald Friede, the money-backer for Horace

Liveright and later Pascal Covici, both highly successful publishers before the Depression, tell how in order to survive in 1932 their firm began producing cheap novels to order, to fit snappy titles dreamed up before the books were even written. He cites: *Speakeasy Girl*, *Bachelor's Wife*, *Boy Crazy*, *Her Body Speaks*, *The Sportsman on the Sofa*, and *Alimony Jail*. I have never run into a single one of these titles. Other publishers evidently went a lot farther, with secretly published items. Maybe his firm did too, and the titles Friede gives here are purposely phony.

There were also all the usual underground publishers then, like Sam Roth. His books were always very cheaply but pretentiously done, in a typographical style you couldn't mistake, from the first off-center half-title onward, once you'd seen a few of his front or "cover" items. In fact, few of the publishers could disguise their special typographical styles, but a certain amount of bibliographical caution is necessary there. The printers were just as hard-up as the publishers, and each printer obviously worked for more than one publisher, and probably in very similar typographical style.

Well, it was all a mystery, and will probably stay that way now. Nobody writes their memoirs anymore, except theatre people and politicians. Posing egomaniacs to the last! But the erotic books do still exist, a couple of copies of each of them, anyhow. Amazing how they disappear. That's another mystery. Where have they gone? Are they read to death? Maybe the collector's widows all burn them after they die, at the demand of shocked father-confessors. A lot of books have gone that way. But surely not all the collectors are Roman Catholics. There are lots of questions in studying erotica, but not many answers. The farther back you go in time, over the centuries, the harder it gets to find any answers at all. It's hard enough just from the accidental attrition of lost evidence and general disinterest. With so-called pornographica you're also up against purposeful concealment most of the time, especially by the shame-faced authors and publishers.

The question that always interested me most was not who the publishers were. For that there are at least the typographical clues if you can manage to decipher them. But who were the writers? All these books had authors, after all, from the fanciest *de luxe* items to the cheapest pocket reader, marked "Havana, Cuba : Price, Ten Dollars," but really costing only twenty-five or fifty cents or whatever the slum-shop operator could get from his usually pretty young customers, whose erotic education this very often was.

In France, when the big publishing depression had come in the 1890s, simultaneously with the beginnings of the sexual explosion in literature and in open social life, many of the best French authors and poets wrote the flood of erotic novels published then "under the mantle." This continued as the private output of practically all the French luxury publishers, and especially the semi-luxe and fake-luxe publishers, right through the rich years of the 1920s and since. The situation must have been the same in America. But there's no way now of matching up the names of the writers with their books, especially not in France. Pascal Pia tells the most, in his bibliography of French erotica, *Les Livres de l'Enfer*, but even he admitted to me that he felt "we must leave something for the Ph.D.s (*agrégés*) of the future."

I was told several times that Maxwell Bodenheim had written really erotic books, not just his public teaser-items like *Replenishing Jessica*, in the years when he was down on his luck. This finally got so bad that you would see him peddling his autographed poems to tourists like me in Greenwich Village restaurants as low as half-a-dollar apiece. Bodenheim was, in absolute perfection, the typical Bohemian of that period, with soft slouch hat and cloak — the works. His onetime collaborator, Ben Hecht, who went on to become a rich Hollywood writer, wrote Bodenheim up as he was then, in the 1920s, under the name of *Count Hippolyte Bruga*. He seems a likely enough candidate for erotic authorship.

I have the definite impression it was really mostly the dead-broke youngsters in the writing field, again like me, and not the dead-drunk oldsters who wrote most of the erotic books, and for very little money too. That was certainly my case and that of several other young writers I knew, like Tony Gudaitis and the *Snappy Stories* crew of hacks. As later with the youngish Olympia group working for Maurice Girodias, also Pauvert and Losfeld, when I got to Paris and knew most of them. Anaïs Nin's expatriate New York erotica-writing group was similar, all working for the same Oklahoma millionaire and his bi-weekly aphrodisiac reading.

One of the few purposeful self-unveilings of erotic authorship, and even there under a further pseudonym, was by the Hollywood writer and biographer, Gene Fowler, author of a scandal murder-mystery he wrote under the pseudonym of "Herbert Kerkow" in the 1930s, *The Fateful Star Murder*, on the newspaper sensation of the period, the death of a beautiful young call-girl, Starr Faithfull. He carefully drags into this irrelevant references to his own erotic novelette *The Demi-Wang*, by "Peter Long," which is probably the most amusing manuscript ever hacked for the Syndicate, and surely the most curious item, for its strange verbalizing and neologizing style — similar to that of Aleister Crowley in his *Snowdrops* — of anything published in the whole undercover period. There is another similar item, certainly also from Fowler's hand, entitled *Nirvana*, by "Dr. Desernet." Both these books were reprinted briefly during the New Freedom publishing upsurge in erotica during the late 1960s and '70s in America, in the cheapest and tawdriest form, clearly still as aphrodisiacal tools and nothing more. Mafia-backed pornographic videotapes will eventually replace these now, as t.v. illiteracy takes over, and still with a minimum of art and authenticity in the production of three out of every four tapes. And sometimes it's just the best artist and the most artistic item — as with Swinburne or his imitator Crowley — where the actual erotic subject-matter is the most repellently perverted. In fact, that's the whole recent history and tragedy of violence in the movies and t.v.

Poets, because of the refined and constricting rules of their art, seem particularly prone to private erotic excesses in verse. Shakespeare is certainly the most famous name here, since much of his contemporary reputation was as an erotic poet, not as a mere playwright for the *hoi polloi*. Witness his boilingly erotic *Sonnets*, published secretly and against his will from an unauthorized manuscript copy, two-thirds latent homosexual adoration of his patron, and the last third vicious sardonics at the expense of the poetastering "Dark Lady," Emilia Bassano Lanier, who had replaced him in his patron's emotional life.

Private erotic and scatological poetry is very common among the best literary men in all countries and centuries, especially in France and beginning almost a century before Shakespeare with Ronsard. In France, as in the Levant, poetry is thought of as a sort of ecstatic madness like love, after all, and the poetic form is considered to excuse any impropriety. The finest religious poets England ever had, Donne and Herrick, were better at erotic poetry — written in their youth, no doubt — than any other kind. Herrick alternates his lovingly fetishistic droolings over women's underwear and breasts with outrageously violent and obscene attacks on probably the same women, but now referred to as witches and hags: the perfect standard alternation of roles in sado-masochists, here strictly at the verbal level.

In America, Eugene Field, otherwise known as the poet of childhood, is the most famous name that comes to mind here among true poets or even occasional rhymesters. Practically all his erotic output is included in his very rare erotic miscellany, *The Stag Party*, published while he was a newspaperman in Chicago about 1890. He narrowly escaped going to jail for this according to manuscript notes in one of the three known copies, and was only saved owing to his newspaper editor's political pull. Field also wrote the one best-known American erotic novelette, *Only a Boy*, which he also published in *The Stag Party*. In the 1920s,

Gene Fowler and his Hollywood sidekick Don Marquis wrote a certain amount of erotic verse too, like Fowler's topical ballad, "Anne Cooper Hewitt, or The Sterilized Heiress," but only Marquis' bitter "Ode to Hollywood" was ever then committed to private print.

As is very well known, Mark Twain delighted in presenting his various erotica in prose & verse to all his close friends and his rich and influential patrons, but the public was not allowed to know to know a word about this during his lifetime. When the scandal of his penchant for very young girls in his old age became public during his last Caribbean vacation, Twain was privately allowed to die under "heavy sedation" — I'd call that plain murder — on being doped to the gills and rushed back to America on the next naphtha launch in disgrace by way of hushing things up. Mr. Clemens was "indisposed." After having been caught, presumably in the bushes in the Bahamas having a bit of huffmagundie with his favorite teenage bathing-beauty, with whom he had posed for an extant picture in a bathing suit, Twain must have wanted to die. But it's still murder. He didn't die just because it was the year of Halley's Comet, under which he had also been born.

Nobody ever talks about Twain's final disgrace — and compare Charlie Chaplin's practical crucifixion under the Mann Act, even worse — and Twain's unexplained death under sedation. Why do I have to tell you all this? I guess more time will have to elapse before the old-timers who know are willing to talk, if they haven't died off meanwhile. Maybe the next time Halley's Comet comes back. You're not supposed to murder national monuments.

I've never made a secret of the erotic manuscripts I wrote in my early twenties for the Syndicate, as I have just described. Many other writers, some of them a good deal older and probably better than me, also wrote for this millionaire client, then and earlier. All of us knew we were prostituting our minds and being used as sexual tools and aphrodisiacs. That includes Anaïs Nin whose erotica were true art. Your brain is part of your body too, just as much as your asshole, and sometimes you have to prostitute one to feed the other. Meanwhile, as to all the other unknown names and dates and places and the simple facts, it's that thousand-year-old Chinese proverb credited to Lao-Tzu: *Those who know do not say, And those who say do not know.*

THE MIMEOGRAPHED item by my phony friend Sewall was to be called "The Devil's Advocate," in order to feature the initials "D.A.," since the secret erotic villain turns out to be none other than the crusading District Attorney. What never set so well with me about this story was that this character also runs his own flagellation farm, and keeps a small branding-iron in his briefcase with which to brand his secret mark, of a scorpion as I remember well, on his girlfriends' left buttock or underbelly the morning after. A bit more obvious than just taking their pictures nude, wouldn't you say?

I hate, and have always hated and despised flagellation and everything connected with it, including the people who write it and read it and dream about it and make pictures about it and write gloating letters about it to the newspapers and to each other. I think it would be wonderful if they could all be automatically attached to their own fantasy machines and beaten to death — as long as they wouldn't enjoy that too much. After all, the machine might grab them, by accident, when they were in their masochist phase instead of getting them when they were acting out their advertised sadism. It sometimes alternates, you know, like electricity.

So I asked Sewall about this shit. The very first rule that had been laid down for all of us by Slapsie Maxie, years before, straight from the client, was: *No flagellation!* Which I always felt did him honor. Well, Sewall told me, once in a while he would slip in a little in his manuscripts, had never had a complaint sent down through channels from the client till the very end, so he kept it up. This *Devil's Advocate* was the item that got him fired. Even so, it never went as far as the Marquis de Sade's grimmer stuff, like cutting up women in chunks and eating them with Worcestershire sauce, but it was pretty bad. One Edward Plunkett, who wrote under the name of Lord Dunsany, has a presumably delightful murder-mystery story exactly like that, called "Three Bottles of Relish" — thus including the Worcestershire sauce too, which is how I fished it up, you see — where the man actually eats his wife's corpse to get rid of the evidence after he murders her. This story is a big favorite in all the anthologies of horror. As Santa Claus says, *Ho, ho, ho!*

Sewall and I arranged that I'd come back the next week of mornings and do three hours of typing on the stencils each day, to help him out. I told him I couldn't do anymore than that, because reading carbon copies hurts my eyes, which I've always overworked. Besides people are generally very cheap or forgetful about changing their carbon paper often enough or even once in a while, and the damn things are usually illegible, so what good are they? Also, as I pointed out to Sewall, I had my own work to do for the rest of the day afterward. He gave me a very odd look, at that, which said more clearly than words that after he'd do three hours of work on any writing job in any one day, he'd consider that he'd done a full day's work. That may be why he never got anywhere as a writer, which is a job that takes a lot of sweaty-ass sitting, if you want to do it seriously.

It's funny how people realize perfectly well that you have to work a full day slicing meat if you're a butcher, or practicing scales if you're a pianist, or evicting sick and dying people if you're a banker, or tharbing fnark-a-twarks if you're a fnark-a-twark tharber by profession and the suckers are buying them. But who nevertheless imagine that the writing racket consists, or should consist — as in Hemingway's books — of lightly tickling the sensitive keys of an electronic typewriter with a patchouli-flavored peacock's penis for about an hour or so per day, or an hour and a half maximum. And then sitting around guzzling hooch in bars, shooting off to nowhere in particular in expensive red sports cars, and finally doubling back and laying one's underpaid secretary on a turkey-red couch or in a credit-card motel with heated swimming pool the rest of the day, in search of Inspiration.

The last part or activity depends of course, on how much whiskey a man slops up each day as his normal portion. With enough of that inside, you're not much danger to any young attractive woman — check out the Porter's soliloquy in *Macbeth* — and can only talk big, brag, and make promises. While hoping that the young lady is an honorary member of the AIDS-intimidated New Chastity freaks, and will fight you off with a pained expression on her map if you make the ritual pass at her.

As far as getting any literary work done is concerned, that's not in the area of action at all; more like the relaxation or Warrior's Repose. You have to make sure you've done some fighting first, before you go looking for slave-maidens to rape or be raped by — depending on how Newly Chaste they are or how tired and tuckered out you. Hypothetical writers who just can't get around to writing anything because sitting on anything but a bar-stool takes the crease out of their pants, are like the mock ski-athletes at winter resorts who spend the whole time in the well-heated lodge in snazzy après-ski costumes lapping up liquor and promoting their next lay among the female non-skiers of exactly the same type. They should watch the output of effort of some poor, heavily overworked and over-rushed Kelly Girl temporary typist, blinding herself all day long on computer-setting publicity prospectuses for fnark-a-twark tharbing or other vitally important stuff. Or knocking out template addresses by the tens of thousands for form-letters to marshal the

Forces of Right for Media Morality, to prevent literary semen though never objecting to blood.

Well, a writer — and for that matter a plumber — who plans or hopes to get anywhere at all in that chosen profession has to work all day, every day (including Sundays) about twice as hard as a Kelly Girl typist, and often for less money. In his spare time he can then do his research, and perhaps even glance at the reviews of his competitors' latest books and other trivial pursuits, preferably while sitting on the toilet. Otherwise he might just as well keep flabbily tharbing his fnark-a-twark, or else marry rich. Or both. I could say a lot more about it, but that'll have to hold you for starters. You hear?!

I hadn't typed off a page of carbon-copy on Sewall's *Devil's Advocate* when I ran into a marijuana-smoking scene. Well, there it was. The stuff was rare then, in fact, but very very frequent in the minds of jazz hangers-on like John "Geewhiz" Brown and Archie, and Bob Sewall. That was the milieu I met them in originally, in Scranton, with John playing saxophone in a tiny bar in Dunmore, Saturday nights, while he was still in high school.

A few pages further along the various sadisms and flagellations started, and there I drew the line. I simply left that shit out, as I typed. I just don't like sullying my fingertips in women's blood. Maybe a maidenhead once in a while, if I accidentally *hafta*; but not purposely whipping or branding some girl's ass. Try it out on yourself first, before you come back and start bullshitting me how thrilling it is — on somebody else's, or even on your own ass. So, I just left all that out, and sometimes replaced it with a bunch of better-written material that I made up quietly as I typed along.

Naturally, I didn't bother to get into any argument about this with Sewall. "Sir, I shall not degrade myself to, etc., etc." The most intelligent course, and the most useful to humanity, if you want to know the truth, seemed to me that I should simply and silently expurgate, expunge, edulcorate, deterge, decrassify, and defecate — especially defecate — and altogether Bowdlerize and castrate all the fuck'n sadistic and flagellational parts as I typed them. And that is exactly what I did. If you don't agree with me, come around any time and tell me so, and I'll be glad to kick your ass raw. (Since that's what you like.) You can have a high-colonic enema too, for the same price: it's part of the same rotten perv. I felt just as happy and smug about what I was doing then, and still do — *my rotten perversion* — as I had felt humiliated and shamed typing up an expurgated text of Cleland's *Fanny Hill* in Jake Brussel's cellar on Long Island years before, where the parts I was perforce leaving out were simply the *normal perv.*

Ever since Hitler and the Nazis — and I don't just mean after everybody found out about the German concentration camps and the death furnaces, but for a whole decade before — I had totally lost my dewy-eyed liberal notions about free speech for the other side, if I ever had them. When you have an enemy, CRUSH your enemy! Or he will crush you. That's how a man has to think. That's also what Hitler taught everybody who didn't secretly want him to win. Those mental crips and weaklings who nattered on about listening to the other person's point of view, in the face of so obviously a mortal threat, were in fact those who secretly *did* want the Nazis to win. And they would have won too, if Marshal Zhukov and the Red Army hadn't stopped them at Stalingrad. Three immortal words: Crush your enemy! If you haven't got the guts for that, and merely turn away or cop out, you won't be able to do much good either for those you think you love but don't have the strength to protect.

Think about that the next time you hear someone start parcelling out that tired nonsense about "Everybody has a right to his opinion," which then always ends up with that even tireder freaky old nonsense about "I am opposed to your opinion, but will fight to the death for your right to express it." That really means that you're *not* opposed to his opinion. You just haven't got the balls to admit it. Who started that silly stuff? Was it really John Stuart Mill in *On Liberty,* where he says that stifling any opinion is worse than the opinion itself? He'd have changed his mind about that, fast, if he were a Jew in Auschwitz, where the furnaces were running full blast *that very week,* while I was expurgating out Bob Sewall's branding irons for girls' bellies. Does that make everything clear?

Be that as it may, I simply did not consider it my duty to humanity to do any charity typing of sadistic passages, so that Robert Sewall and his wife Alice and baby-to-come — *Goo, goo, goo,* fellow sadists — could have some money, and I did not do so. It just didn't seem logical to me to be reading those weeks in the newspapers, as we were, how the combined American, British and Canadian armies had now invaded Sicily from their vacation in North Africa, with two thousand ships full of soldiers and guns and tanks, and Lucky Luciano and the Mafia waiting to welcome them, in order to attack "the soft underbelly of Europe," we were told, for the purpose of getting *into position* to launch a further, later, someday, theoretical and total attack that would wipe the Nazi Jew-torturers off the earth. And yet, at the same time, for me to sit placidly at a typewriter on New York's blighted west side, typing up mimeograph stencils for the publishing of gloating passages intended to describe whipping women's bodies, and branding them with a hot iron with the sign of the Scorpion on their soft underbelly or thigh. Meaning on the cunt — that ancient expurgation-by-metonymy of *Genesis* 24: *omphallos* for *phallos*, bellybutton for prick — as the Marquis de Sade didn't hesitate to come right out and say, but not friend Sewall. It's not always easy to have the courage of one's fantasy perversions. That must be why Sade is the black priest or demigod of so many would-be worshippers-of-evil, because evil is in (always) and goodness is square.

Make no mistake about it, I realized very well that in merely expurgating out or rewriting into innocuity the worst parts of Sewall's manuscript, instead of just flinging the whole thing into the incinerator unit, I was being cowardly and absurd. Like the man whose wife is being raped by the highwayman, and who satisfies himself that he is protecting her by secretly pulling out his pocketknife and stabbing the highwayman's saddle. I did what I could, or, the way I thought of it then, I would *not* do the parts that I saw perfectly well were rotten and wrong. Obviously I shouldn't have helped at all on that project, or should have tried to stop it in some more effective way. I would never make a mistake like that again. I also resented that scorpion stuff a little, because I was born under the astrological sign of the scorpion myself, and Sewall wasn't, and I was tired of being kidded about it.

Sewall naturally didn't bother to read the stencils over, nor the mimeographed book when Herman, the bookseller in the arcade, got it out. But that miserable son-of-a-bitch, Bob Mexico, whom I had introduced to Sewall years before and who still saw him occasionally, unfortunately had read — at proud author Sewall's offering and urging — the whole carbon manuscript once already. He adored the flagellational and branding-of-women parts, or at any rate he adored them after first reading about these sadistic delights in Sewall's *Devil's Advocate* manuscript. Mexico then attempted to try it all out on his wife Gerry, who divorced him for it. I'd known Mexico for nearly six years then, and had never even once heard him mention the subject of flagellation. Now he talked about nothing else, and how great it was, especially for the victim — which wasn't going to be him. He even wrote poems about it, and gave me copies, which I threw away.

It seems that Mexico was sitting around one day reading the mimeographed D.A. again about a year after it was published — shows you the kind of guy he was, reading erotica instead of doing it; not like you and me — and was very puzzled by not finding the flagellation bits that had so pleased him earlier in the carbon copy of the manuscript. He came charging up to Sewall's room to announce his frightful discovery, and to complain about where were the wonderful flag passages now missing in the mimeographed edition? Missing! That rotten bastard Legman had pulled the Gypsy switch!! The two of them put their collective head together and figured it all out by paralleling the two texts. What a job for a Hinman collator!

The next time I dropped in at Sewall's room, the two of them ploughed into me. What kind of a bastard was I? A rat, that's what! I like fighting for what I believe in — it's exhilarating. The only kind of sadism you never have to feel too much guilt about is beating the shit out of (other) sadists. Some people have told me that Freud wouldn't agree with me here, but I think he would. Who knows? Anyhow, it's me that has to live in my skin, not Freud. He had troubles of his own, worrying about being Jewish; something that never bothered me for a minute.

"What the hell was the big idea ruining the book?" Sewall wanted to know. He ran one hand nervously through his blond hair.

"I didn't ruin it," I said very calmly, studying my fingernails. "I improved it. I just left out all that degenerate shit. You can't expect me to type that — branding scorpions on girls' twats. What next? Come on, Alice," I said to his wife who was now living with him. "Pull up your dress and show us your scorpion!" Actually, I couldn't remember what I left out, except that it was all flag and the like, and I hadn't wanted to type it. Still don't. Besides I added in more good erotic stuff than the crap I left out — much more. Some people are never satisfied.

Everybody looked at me in disgust, except maybe Alice.

"That was a novel, you know," Sewall said; "not my autobiography." He sucked hard on his inevitable cigarette.

My reply was a loud razzberry, with a well-vibrating tongue, followed by the loud, clear, neo-critical mass-observation statement of principal: *"Horse.....shit!"*

"What kind of a liberal are you anyway?" Mexico wanted to know. The poor slob was ignorant of the fact — along with many others — that "liberal" is fightin' words where I come from. "Don't you believe what Voltaire said? – *'I object to what you say, but I'll fight to the death for your right to say it'.*"

"In a pig's ass I'll fight for your right to say it!" I told them. "That's one thing Hitler taught us pisswash liberals, isn't it? Besides Voltaire never said it a damn bit. Somebody named Mrs. Tallentyre admitted in a letter to *The Times* just a couple of years ago that she faked the whole thing. It's very good Voltaire, but he didn't write it — *she* did."

They were all sure I was making that up on the spur of the moment, but it was true. Some nerve, eh? That's historians for you. I think Harry Weinberger tells all about it in *Liberty of the Press*. So why are people always picking on us autobiographers? Anyhow, if Mrs. Tallentyre can fabricate a Voltaire quotation and half the idiots in the world parrot her forgery, exactly why can't I forge shamelessly inauthentic normal passages in Robert Sewall's deathless sado-porno? You know, throw in some Redeeming Sexual Significance, as it were.

But my two sado-masochistic cronies weren't to be satisfied by mere logical tergiversations like that, and kept muttering about how I was contradicting myself all the time, and how would I like it if somebody took away *my* freedom of the press permit, *and* my freedom of speech for the mere and boring normality I kept trying to peddle. I took a broad view and let them rave. Sewall didn't seem to be half so exercised, as author, about my crime, as Mexico was — the mere voyeuristic audience. Whoever said the perversion is habit-forming wasn't just talking. Those poor perverted fuckers really need it, and the job of any intelligent human society is to see that they don't get it. Like any other dangerous habit-forming drugs.

"I don't want free speech for anybody but me," I assured them, with my least ingratiating candor "Savonarola – that's me! Anyhow, who cares about free speech? You certainly don't: you want what you want when you want it, and so do I. I claim the right to be exactly the same kind of rotten sadistic pervert that you'd love to be. So now you've got *my* scorpion burned on the underbelly of *your* book. How does it feel?"

Sewall laughed his twisted, half-strangulated laugh. Mex screamed something: one of his florid mock-Mexican imprecations.

I didn't see any of them for quite a long while afterward, certainly not until after the baby was born. But the Gruesome Twosome of the two Bobs, Sewall and Mexico, had the last laugh on me a year or two later. The bookseller in the Chanin building ran out of copies; *The Devil's Advocate* was a terrific success among his hard businessmen customers upstairs and across the street in the Chrysler Building where he'd meanwhile moved. But when he went to run off more copies he found that his carefully preserved stencils laid away between newspaper sheets on a shelf were too rumpled to use, and he asked Sewall to make another set.

Sewall said maybe yes and maybe no. But he had learned something from having been paid off the first time with just a few free copies to give away on his own, and a hearty handshake. That is to say, a poke in the ass with a sharp stick. So this time he and Mexico cut and ran off the new stencils themselves on a rented mimeograph machine — the Eager-Beaver Perverts Squad — possibly with Alice Sewall helping them. And they put back in all the flagellation scenes I had expurgated out, while leaving my additions in; and, as I remember, an extra few paeans to marijuana too.

They now changed the title to *The Sign of the Scorpion*, and made the same bookseller pay through the nose for the copies he wanted. That's only a figure of speech, of course. I doubt if Herman paid five dollars apiece for them. The retail price was ten. Anyhow, there was only one solitary delivery made — a trick I'd taught them — so the bookseller couldn't buy two copies only, and then use them to pirate his own edition of the de-expurgated flagellant text. Years later I believe one or both texts were reprinted by California schlocksters and by Barney Rossett's Grove Press. He had a young book-scout working for him in the 'sixties, named Jeffrey Rund, who was particularly interested in flaj and later republished some of Irving Klaw's horror picture-books with introductions by himself and some matching flagellation comic-books. I assume it was Rund who found Rosset the copy he used. Birds of a feather. . .

So, that's how it was. As I say, I always felt a lot worse over having expurgated the sex scenes for an edition of Cleland's *Fanny Hill* for Jake Brussel to publish, some years before when I was living on his charity in his dismal, rat-infested, flooded-out cellar in Sheepshead Bay. By contrast, expurgating some of the sadism out of the *Devil's Advocate* made me feel great. How not? Over the years, certain foolish young people of all sexes, flagellation enthusiasts and total free-speech advocates, have tried to make me feel like a new Daniele da Volterra about this — Painting pants on the tremendous naked figures of his master Michelangelo's "Last Judgment" in the Sistine Chapel to please a prudish pope. I will admit that with all its faults Sewall's book is probably the best piece of erotica published in America, anyhow in its erotic passages, if you exclude Henry Miller and Anaïs Nin. That still leaves an insuperable distance between him — or all of us — and Michelangelo. This is *my* last judgment.

Paint me with shears in one hand, if you wish, cutting out the sadistic parts of the literature and art and folklore of the world, and sticking in a bouquet of coupled pricks and cunts to replace them, putting the sex back in. *La Corona dei Cazzi*. Let love & sex drive out cruelty and death. Make love, not war! The *Song of Songs* says it better than I ever could: *"Love is strong as death."* And while you're looking in the *Bible*, check out *2 Timothy 4* too — "Preach the Word; be instant in season, out of season; reprove, rebuke, exhort with all longsuffering and doctrine. . . For the time of my departure is at hand. I have fought a good fight. I have finished my course. I have kept the faith." And *damn The Devil's Advocate.*

IN THOSE DAYS, when the time came to do the
title page stencil on a private mimeographed item, we
naturally put on a false date of a year or two before, as
was standard, to throw the police and the feds off the
track. That gave it the air of an old book, already out
for some time and therefore not worth chasing.
Anyhow we hoped so. On this one I also gave, as
author's name, "Wood C. Lamont," or something like
that, just for fun, to imply that the author was the
minor Southern poet, Clement Wood, who one of my
original contacts with the syndicate, Jack Hanley, told
me had already hacked quite a number of manuscripts
for it. To which Slapsie Maxie Grobe added, when I
casually dropped Wood's name, to ask about him, that
Wood had been the only person except Tiffany Thayer
who ever who give more than one hundred exact pages
in the manuscripts. He would get interested in the
erotic story he was writing, and would run on often ten
or twenty pages more to finish off the story as he
thought it should be finished, and for the same money.
Wood was rich, of course. a dilettante — banking
family. Well, I hated him, but underneath he was a pro.

    I only met Wood once about a year later. Once
was enough. Sam Roth mentioned to me one day,
when I was at his office for a ghost-job I was doing,
that Clement Wood was in town temporarily. He was

staying at a residential hotel near Gramercy Park with his wife Gloria Goddard, who was also a poet, although not in the same class as her husband. I had wanted to meet Wood for a long time, because Roth had told me he was a limerick fancier and creator, and published his own limericks privately This meant they were bawdy, and I wanted to see them. I asked Roth to phone up Wood and tell him I had a book that was being falsely attributed to him, with his name on the title page, and all, and what about that? Roth built me up over the phone with his usual insincere verbiage, as "my young literary advisor," and so forth, which was intended to apprise Wood that I was Roth's current ghostwriter, just as Wood had earlier been for years.

He was very excited to learn about a book being falsely ascribed to him, and I shouted to Roth so that Wood could hear it over the phone, "Tell him it's an erotic book!" Of course Wood asked if I could come over at once and show him a copy. I went. I happened to have a slight cold that day, just the usual spring-&-fall, or Mike & Ike snuffles when the weather changes rapidly, and I stopped before ringing the apartment doorbell, when I got upstairs to their floor, and got out a handkerchief to blow my nose. To my surprise, the door was pulled open instantly, before I rang, by a man of medium height with nothing to distinguish him from anyone else except an intense, rapid way of glancing which one associates with criminals and hunters.

"Mr. Wood," I asked, finishing wiping my nose. "I'm Legman. I'm afraid I have a cold today, but it's not very serious."

"Ahh!!" he cried in a loud, harsh voice, flinging the door wide open, and announcing to someone inside: "Mr. Legman – *and his cold!*"

I see, I said to myself. A real schmuck. Big inferiority complex there. If he can't cut me down before I even get in the door, I'm too much of a threat. His poetry is probably pretty bad too. I had never read any of it. Sitting on the sofa, with her ankles but not her knees crossed, as young ladies were taught to do before the 1920s, and actresses are still sometimes expected to do in the theatre so the audience can't see up their dresses, sat a rather plain, plumpish woman of what seemed to be early middle age. This would be his wife, Gloria Goddard, who according to what Wood was always writing about her with the utmost fulsomeness was a combination, never before seen on earth, of Minerva for wisdom, Diana for inspiration, and Venus for all the rest. Other than that, she seemed to be cast in the exact same mould as her husband, except without the same vulturine look. He would have made a great advertising man — no shame about peddling his crummy shtick.

I handed him the wrapped-up copy of *The Devil's Advocate* I had brought, and he flipped it open instantly to the title page where the author was given as Wood C. Lamont. He held it out silently for his wife to see, and then started flipping the pages with intense attention.

"That's surely supposed to be you, isn't it?" I asked innocently, as if I didn't know. No answer. "I don't suppose it's by Corliss Lamont's younger brother."

"One question, Mr. Legman," he said severely. "Is this book written by you?"

"Absolutely not!" I told him. "Though I do know who wrote it. But I'm not at liberty to tell you. I can write much better than that."

He went over and sat down in an armchair and started reading it here & there, while I made small talk with Gloria Goddard, hoping to be impressed by her qualities as Minerva, Diana, or at least Venus. But I felt no charge. Wood made a sudden wild ejaculation (vocal), and started tapping on the book with one angry fingertip.

"Look at this!" he cried. "Look! – 'behinder'! There is no such word as 'behinder.' The word is 'behind'! Ass! Buttocks! Bottom! But never behinder!"

I assured him again that no one really suspected him of writing the book, and that I knew the real author. He seemed mollified, though still a bit shaken that anyone would take his name in vain, and use a word like "behinder" in his disguise; and asked if the book was a present for him. Naturally I told him that the book was his if he wanted it, which he surely did. Then we got onto the subject of limericks, of which I told him I had quite a collection and was looking to enlarge it. He immediately jumped up and rummaging through some large envelopes on his desk, pulled out not one, but two copies of a little paperbound pamphlet, which he presented to me in return for the book. It was entitled *The Facts of Life – In Limericks: Erotologically Classified.* The author's name was given as "Richard Offenbach Harder," which was of course to be read as "Dick Often-back etc." There was no place or date of publication given. I looked through it politely, and on the first page I opened to, the following unusual sequence which I had never before seen in any printed collection of erotic limericks, struck me between the eyes: [with the apologies of the transcriber!]

My wife is an amorous soul
On fire for an African's pole
She told a coon chauffeur
That he was her gopher –
And say, did he go for her hole!

As he creamed my wife's cunt, the coon said,
"I could fuck this until I was dead!"
As he plugged up her trough
I jerked myself off;
"If that's how you feel, go ahead!"

I came back as if from far away, to find this Clement Wood person speaking to me. He was telling me proudly that he had printed up this little collection, mostly of his own original limericks, to be sure, just recently at his country home at Delanson in upstate New York. He also invited me to come up there for a weekend.

"If you know some charming young lady you'd care to bring along," he finished, as significantly as humanly possible without simply hitting me over the head with a club.

Would-be wife-traders and swingers of this type weren't as common in those days as they are now

[1975-1980]. At any rate, they didn't go around flashing their meat quite as much as they do under the present dispensation. Though even today you seldom have a limerick sequence of that much candor accidentally handed to you as introduction to the sex-party pitch. I wondered how a poetic purist like himself, who got so upset about "behinder," could rhyme "trough" with "off" in his limerick sequence in his wife's honor, but decided to say nothing about it. Doubtless a southernism. Instead I allowed as how I was married to my work, and knew no one but the usual tramps.

"Oh, we're not snobs; are we Gloria?" he said broadly.

I told him I also didn't have a car — nor a Negro chauffeur, for that matter, but I didn't mention that — and he assured me that all the busses and trains out of Albany came close by. I was to phone him as soon as we, meaning the hypothetical charming young lady and myself, arrived at the station, and he'd pick us up somehow. He gave me in addition a little leaflet or magazinelet, of which I have forgotten the title. It was also published by himself and was devoted to local news and high-jinks on his plantation, but written in somewhat covert terms. One item concerned a girl visitor who had been flung into the Bozenkill River and dragged out with her clothes all dripping. True fun and games.

In case I still didn't get the idea, he finally gave me another of his privately printed items which I believe was called "The Bold Ballad of Bozenkill," which made everything only too clear. I wondered where he got the money to print up all this poor white

trash. At premium prices, after all, when you consider
the laws they had against it at that time, of which all
printers were damn well aware, even upstate. I decided
he must have money in his family. Later I found out
they were bankers. He also couldn't ever have bought
a country estate by writing poetry, even about the
South.

As I left, Wood had the nerve to call out after
me, "Now don't forget! The most *charming* young lady
you know!" What a bunch of brainwashed chumps he
must use for friends, I thought. As I always used to
wear a big dark grey Borsalino felt hat in those days, I
tipped my hat politely to Gloria Goddard, and gave the
Soaring Eagle of Southern regional Poetry, her
husband, a formal half-bow and quarter smile which I
had learned in a Groucho Marx movie, where Groucho
is pretending to be the Duke of Ruritania. Exit Mr.
Legman, and his cold.

By the way, anybody who thinks the limerick
sequence I've just quoted from this repulsive prick is a
bit crude, is recommended to take a look at the other
one I'm not quoting here;, by the same master-er-ah-
hand, which I've given in full — it's nine stanzas long
— in *The New Limerick*, No.738, under the title "Wife-
Trading from A to Z." Taken from a somewhat later
collection of originals by Clement Wood, this self-
evident sick fantasy ends with the belovèd wife finally
being strangled, at the poet-husband's own request, by
a burglar named "Willy O'Bangellar" (to rhyme with
mangle her and *strangle her*, of course).

I believe this is at least the runner-up for the title
of "The World's Worst Limerick," and not for its
subject-matter only. The next ten nearest contenders

for the title are all by the ineffable Aleister Crowley, orgiast and occult sociopath of exactly the same type — but wuss! Especially in his attempts at would-be humorous erotic poetry & prose, such as *Léa Sublime* and *Snowdrops From a Curate's Garden* — of which the title is the only good joke — both several times reprinted recently for an audience unknown. Maybe they do have occult meaning, as purported. As sex, they are merely and intentionally nauseating. Funny they're not.

I KNOW it looks as though I met an awful lot of no-goodnicks in those years in New York, and I certainly did. But there were also a few casuals — lunchcounter-men, booksellers, and people you often wouldn't suspect — who would take a fatherly interest in me and try to save me, generally on the basis of doing a *mitzvah* or good deed for an obviously errant Jewish boy. Both of my uncles in the theatre were certainly motivated that way, since we had no close family ties. Alex, the *borscht* and *stroganoff* king, in his tiny Russian restaurant in Greenwich village, was another of these, but his basic well-meaning was generally lost in a flood of rough, pretended insults and aggressive kidding. Unbeknownst to me, the erotica publisher and pirate Sam Roth also thought I was good stuff, worth saving, and even included me in his fantasies of a dream-family, presumably as son-in-law, during his frequent periods in jail. But as his affection to me always showed itself strictly in the form of literary exploitation, I never realized how well he actually liked me, and would have been horrified if I had, since I hated him as an anti-Semite.

Two well-wishers I got on with best were both little restaurant owners, as it happens almost facing each other across Columbus Avenue near my room. The one on the west side of the avenue was Greek, wonderfully extroverted and lively, who always had a big ham cooking in baked beans in his stove in a great greasy black cauldron. I'd come in mornings, on my way to the library or some job before taking the subway, and Steve would slice me off a great slab of the baked ham, and whip me up some scrambled eggs with it, in butter as I insisted always. Not because I objected to the taste of cooking fat, but because of the awful smell after it had been used at least ten times before for frying doughnuts and whatnot.

Like all the Greeks I ever met, Steve had only one topic that interested him, and that was Greece. He saw the War, then at its most desperate moment, strictly from the point of view of whether any battle or political incident being discussed would be good or bad for Greece. There was a certain logic to this, like the little tailor in Scranton who wanted to know only one thing about his son's interest in Communism: "Is it good for the Jews?"

But Steve took his patriotism too far — also like all the Greeks I ever met — and could get very nasty and pestiferous on the subject, and at a moment's notice. Eventually I stopped going to his little restaurant anymore, when one morning I said that the situation looked very bad in the German attack on Russia, and Steve so far misunderstood my position that he answered crustily, dusting off the counter near me with a dirty napkin: "You know what I think? I think you want Hitler to win!" That finished our friendship, probably on both sides.

The man in the lunch-counter on the east side of Columbus was entirely different and almost taciturn with other customers. He was a middle-aged Russian Jew, and had the standard narrow delicatessen, with a square gas-plate of hot-dogs frying themselves to a crisp in the window. All the standard Jewish delicatessen sandwiches were served at the four little tables lined up against the wall inside: corned-beef, hot pastrami, and tongue, all with plenty of dill pickles, mustard, and sour rye bread. Like Steve across the street, he kept a specialty baking in an oven somewhere in the back, in this case roast beef, really *gedampfte brust*, heavy with a strip of fat around the outer edge in the same way as the pastrami, which I always ripped away before I began eating. Fat meats like that always made me feel a little sick, a weakness that eventually developed twice into a full-fledged gall bladder crisis without my even realizing what I had done or eaten wrong.

His name was Gordin, and he had another white-aproned partner even more taciturn than himself, known only as Lou, who used to save all the rye-bread crusts and bologna ends for me and give them to me in a bag for a dime when I came in late at night, coming home from the library. I liked these because I liked the crunchiness of the crust better than the softness of the mid-loaf bread, but both men assumed I had no money

— usually true — and would occasionally slip a big, delicious turkey neck into the bag of bread, and shoo me out with it, sometimes adding, "Here, take a pickle too!" All for the same dime. And I would climb up to my third-floor back and feast while listening to music on the phonograph, carefully handling records by the edges, and one wary midfinger pressing on the center label, so as not to grease up the grooves with the turkey neck or bologna ends.

Gordin loved music, and immediately recognized the occasional square envelope I would tote home as a phonograph record. He was contemptuous of everything except Russian music, all of which he adored, especially the big, planturous late-nineteenth century orchestrators like Rimsky-Korsakoff and Tchaikowsky. When I had to admit one night that the record I was bringing home was a Mozart symphony, he nearly lost my friendship forever, as I had lost Steve's across the street, by informing me that "Mozart was just light stuff — you know, dinner music!"

I thought I was going to beat him to death, then and there, but began laughing instead when he followed up by suggesting that I should take the Mozart symphony back and trade it for Mussorgsky's *Pictures at an Exhibition*. "That's *music!*" he told me; and invited me up to his house when the delicatessen would close, to hear his record of it and meet his wife and his teenage daughter. I went, and loved his record, which he played loud enough to tear down the walls and bring the police, though nothing happened. It was just an ornery little flat, a couple of subway jumps up into the Bronx, and Gordin sat there in the diminutive parlor on an overstuffed sofa with his hands crossed on his chest, basking in the final tremendous bells and glories of "The Great Gate at Kiev." To him that expressed the Russia he had left behind him years before. When I told him that Mussorgsky had written the piece only for the piano, and that we were really listening to an orchestration by Ravel, he assured me that Ravel was unquestionably Russian too.

I was never invited back to Gordin's home, however, to hear any more music, because in the meanwhile I mentioned to him one day that I was going to be a semen donor at one of the university hospitals around town, in order to earn enough extra money to buy the Glyndebourne recording of Mozart's *Don Giovanni*. He wrinkled up his forehead very hard at this information, which I guess somehow closed me off as a son-in-law candidate. But I mistook his evident perturbation as musical disapproval, and assured him that *Don Giovanni* was the greatest piece of music ever written in the world, and that if necessary I'd pay for it not just in semen but in blood! That made things even worse.

His silent partner, Lou, particularly enjoyed Gordin's discomfiture, and opened up a little bit more with me after that. He was himself a singer, and used to practice with the church choir on Central Park West, though only for their concerts. They were unaware that he was Jewish, and probably wouldn't have cared if they knew. I heard him sing there several times, and he had a splendid voice. In an expansive moment he told me once how, as a boy in Russia, when the great, swelling choir music would come rolling out of the Orthodox cathedrals in the three-fold litany, *Hospody pomilui! — Oh God, save our souls! —* he and the other bad little boys skulking outside would parody this as *Moyu sraka v tvoyu rylui! – My shitty ass in your snout!* — to the same powerful polyphonic tones. Cholera, and the diarrhea of which one died when one caught it, had become the century-long reality in epidemic after epidemic in Russia during the nineteenth century; and shitty asses were hardly more than conversational small change to little Russian boys then. My own life was almost equally simple: I typed my erotic manuscripts, went to the library, studied, ate, slept — sometimes with a girl — and listened to music. If *Moyu sraka v tvoyu rylui!* Wasn't exactly my motto, the Elizabethan equivalent was closer to me then, and expressed my real emotion: *A fig for Fortune!*

After the incident of the semen donation for *Don Giovanni,* nothing I ever did pleased Gordin anymore. That included all my friends, particularly Bob Mexico and Bob Sewall, who came into the delicatessen with me one day for lunch when we were on our way downtown, and looking for flamenco records in the Spanish store on 72nd Street. Gordin detested Sewall on sight because of his blond hair, which he identified of course as Russian, though Sewall's family was actually Dutch. Mexico was his usual impossible self, and easy to hate. He insisted on ordering a complex bologna omelette at the busy lunch hour, while Sewall and I had boiled franks; and he then elaborately spent five minutes letting his omelette get ice-cold before he would eat it, picking out imaginary bologna-casings which he claimed had been left in. He may even have been right.

The next night when I came in alone, Gordin attacked instantly with his opinion of my friends. As usual when he was excited, his accent became thick enough to cut with a spade. He naturally swept away my half-hearted defense concerning the bologna-strings.

"That's a lot of bologna!" he announced with a grimace. "What for are you roshing around with a couple krubby bums like that?"

I explained that Mexico was a pest, all right, but that Sewall had certain redeeming characteristics, and was a good writer.

"Who, the blond one?" Gordin demanded. "Writer-schmiter! They're both the same. One farts and the other stinks."

❧

CHAPTER 41

RUM-SOAKED CROOKS

WHEN I had my next erotic manuscript ready, the one on which I was to start making money, since Slapsie Maxie had no more books left to sell me instead of payment, I discovered that he had disappeared. Just off the face of the earth. When I phoned him, his mother began to cry and talked nonsense. When I went to his house, first she wouldn't let me in, and cried some more, and then told me to come back at noon. When I came back at noon, there was a man there, Maxie's older brother, who told me curtly that Maxie had gone on a vacation to Florida. When I asked when he'd be back, the brother turned away and slammed the door in my face. It didn't take much brains to figure out that Slapsie Maxie was in jail. I got away from there fast.

An inner voice warned me that I'd be better off not going near the Fourth Avenue bookstores, looking for information, and so instead I continued east. On the north side of Fourteenth Street, between Second and Third Avenue, there was a little book and magazine shop run by a rather nice guy named Ed Lipton. He never had any books I wanted, just second-hand magazines, but he knew lots of songs, poems, and odd bits of sexual folklore — all of which latter he believed in sincerely — and would help me to write it all down from his dictation without impatience. He had no idea of what had happened to Slapsie Maxie, whom he knew of course, but told me he would ask Sugarman the next time he saw him. Sugarman always knew everything.

"I have to know soon," I told Lipton, and he told me Sugarman's address, which was not in Paradise Alley, but close to it. Sugarman wasn't there, and two kids hanging around the hall where the mailboxes were told me he didn't live there anymore. I remembered how he had told me that time I was looking for Keene that he knew the super in Paradise Alley, so I tried there. The super had no idea where Sugarman lived, but told me where the beer-joint was where he usually hung out. I found him there, staring moodily over his ravaged nose and nursing a drink. I sat down with him and asked if I could buy him a sandwich. The oldtime free lunches in the bars had long since disappeared, since Repeal, but they would still make you a damn fine meat sandwich with pickles and whatnot. Sugarman refused the sandwich at first — I could see he was afraid it would cut the effect of his drink — but I assured him we'd drink up again afterward, so he slouched over to the counter with me and we both had a roast beef sandwich. I figured sandwiches were all he could eat with one arm.

"What's up?" he asked.

"I'm trying to find out what happened to Slapsie Maxie Grobe."

"He's in the can. He won't be getting out soon."

"That's what I figured," I said. "What did they get him for?"

"They didn't get him." Sugarman told me. "He walked right into it. He's really crazy, that guy."

It appears that Slapsie Maxie had been walking down the street a few days before when he passed a schoolhouse with all the kids playing outside at recess. Just as he passed, the bell rang, and all the kids disappeared inside in a flash. Maxie must have decided that they ran away because they saw him coming, so he went into the school to explain to the principal that he was absolutely harmless to children, despite a previous charge of molesting, on which he had been released, for lack of evidence. He had told me this story a number of times. He was innocent.

He never even got as far as the principal's office. One of the women teachers saw this pudgy little apparition in the empty school hall, with his velvet-collared topcoat, and looking exactly like Peter Lorre as the child-murderer in *M*, and she instantly pulled the fire-alarm! All the students and teachers came pouring out of their rooms, marching in perfect order, with Slapsie Maxie standing there in the middle of the hall, unable to explain to anyone what he was doing there. The teachers all surrounded him, knocked off his hat and started pulling his hair. The principal called the police. And Slapsie Maxie disappeared in the black Maria, just as Sugarman came ambling by and heard the whole story, including Maxie's explanation of the whole pathetic error, which he was repeating like a crazed animal at the top of his voice to everyone as the police dragged him away in handcuffs.

"You actually saw it?" I asked, amazed that I had fallen in this way on an eye-witness. Asking Lipton had been an inspiration.

"Oh yeah," Sugarman said. "Maxie didn't look so good. Those schoolteachers musta worked on 'im a little before the cops got there. Dames can get real dangerous when they're scared somebody's gonna do something to kids."

"What do you think will happen to him?" I asked.

"I dunno. He didn't really do anything, but they'll keep him for observation. If they psych 'im they don't *ever* have to let him out."

I bought Sugarman a drink, though I hated to do it, and left.

"Ain't you drinkin'?" he called after me.

"No, I'm on the waterwagon," I said, tapping my stomach. "Ulcers."

If I didn't really have ulcers yet, I obviously soon would. Well, at least it hadn't been an obscenity bust. There was no real danger to anybody except poor Maxie. I thought things over and decided I'd just have to deliver the manuscript directly to Rudy Bernays, though I knew he wouldn't like that. He thought of himself as having a complete cover, in acting always through a runner like Maxie. I figured I'd better not go to his office directly — as he might panic. I phoned, and reminded him who I was and that we had met a few years before.

"What do you want?" he said, very crisp and tense.

"Well, a mutual friend of ours named Max Grobe is sick. And he was planning to come and see you, about a manuscript of mine, and — "

"I don't know what you're talking about," he snapped.

"But Mr. Bernays," I said. "We know each other. I'm a friend of Roy Melisander Johnson, of Oklahoma City. Don't you remember? He gave me an introduction to you."

Silence at the other end of the phone.

"Hello?" I said, thinking he had rung off.

"I can't see you," Bernays snapped again. "Get in touch with my literary agent, Johnny Furness. He's on Madison Avenue."

When I got to Furness' office, Bernays had obviously called him already. He handed me a hundred dollars in cash in exchange for the manuscript, which he half pulled out of its envelope and riffled the tops of the pages to make sure of what it was. Then he told me shortly that no more manuscripts would be wanted. The client was no longer interested. I knew that I had made a mistake calling Bernays, but I didn't know what else to do. It would have been even worse if I got in touch with Johnson directly. He might have panicked completely, and closed the whole Syndicate down, or continued only with manuscripts from the West Coast. Well, that was it. I had made a hundred dollars, and there wouldn't be any more.

Troubles never come singly. Not mine, anyhow. Two days later Dr. Dickinson had a slight heart attack, and diagnosed himself as needing a long rest. He used to sleep odd moments in the little triangular room at one end of his big studio, which was really the closed-off stage entrance to the auditorium on the other side of the wall. But recently he hadn't been doing this, because the lovely little flat pocket watch he had, with a tiny alarm built into it, had fallen and broken, and he hadn't been taking his naps as usual. He was afraid of missing his appointments, and it hurt his dignity when one of the lady artists had to wake him up in the middle of the day. The alarm-watch kept his secret. At the age of seventy-eight Dickinson couldn't admit that he was getting old. So he had had a heart attack, from fatigue, and the project was put on ice until he would get back. The entire staff was on leave — indefinitely. Meaning that if Dickinson got better we would have our jobs back, and if not, not. Meanwhile there would be no change in the draft status of the men on the project. We were on leave. Without a salary, of course.

I was glad that Dickinson had survived his attack, because in a lot of ways I liked and admired him. But I knew that when a man of his age has one heart attack he's going to have another. He was tiny and wiry. I had no idea what his blood pressure might be, but I was pretty sure it wasn't high. No, it was obvious. He was wearing out. I'll bet that insane brandy-and-aspirin regimen of his years back hadn't improved his health either. Some people are enormously smart for other people, but goddamned dumb for themselves. I'm one of them.

When the hundred dollars would be gone, for the final manuscript, I would be broke. I had nothing left in the bank. All the money I had made in the tea trade at first, from Zorn, I had spent as I got it. The money from Mr. Bop — well, I didn't regret the gesture, but that was gone too. And the three hundred dollars shy for the first three manuscripts I had left in Slapsie Maxie's paws, for deluxe erotica of the 1930s. I was that classical piece of cultural bric-a-brac, the dead-broke bibliophile.

Well, I said to myself, everybody is making money in the war industries. I better get into a war industry. What can I do? They're not going to want my kind of writing. I supposed I could get some sort of librarian job, but it would be at a pretty low level, probably just cataloguing, as I had no library degree, or any other for that matter. Besides, I could spend weeks trying to find a library that had such an opening, assuming there was one in New York at all. By then even my last hundred would be gone. No, I had to have a job *right now*.

I guess I must have looked worried or absorbed that night when Elaine tapped on my door. I told her my boss was sick, and my job had closed down. I also admitted my money would run out soon.

"I've been saving my money," she said. "I'll loan you some if you need it till you get another job."

"Oh no!" I told her. "What do you think I am?"

"I guess you're my boyfriend," she said, with a little odd smile. "You're certainly the best friend I have."

I kissed her, but that didn't change much. We went down to eat supper together, and Elaine insisted firmly that we would be going Dutch from then on. Except at Thanksgiving, of course.

"All right," I told her. "But that means separate checks. I won't have a woman waving five-dollar bills at my knees under the table, like a Times Square pimp."

She put a finger against my lips. "You're too educated a man to talk like that," she chided me gently. I could see that Elaine would make a sweet little wife for some guy. I felt ashamed to have been taking up so many months of her time, just for a steady lay on the other side of the wall.

The next day I phoned Bob Mexico. "Listen, you bastard," I told him, "I lost my job."

"Drop dead," he replied in his usual friendly fashion, perhaps even a bit less friendly since our argument over my expurgating Sewall's flagellation manuscript. "I'm not lending you any money."

"I don't want any money," I rejoined. "I need a job. You said they were hiring people out at some Army camp near where your parents live. Where is it?"

"Somerville," he told me. "You won't like it."

"How much do they pay?" I asked.

"I don't know. You won't like it. They paid me forty a week and I didn't like it. Listen, buzz off, will you? I got a job to finish."

Mexico worked on odd literary jobs, and tried to write, but had never been able to sell anything. When all else failed, he typed up Spanish biographies for one of those endless biographical directories that are really disguised vanity publications — the same job he had when I met him. I didn't envy him that kind of work, and wondered how bad Somerville must be, if doing Spanish biographies at so much money per column-inch seemed preferable. I bought a sandwich in a delicatessen, and stuck it in my pocket, in case I got stranded all day somewhere out in the boondocks and no way of getting anything to eat, and swung onto the first train going in the direction of New Brunswick and Bound Brook.

Somerville was close to New York, out in New Jersey just beyond the suburban line. If I got a job there, I'd be able to commute, which was God's mercy.

I certainly didn't want to move to Jersey. When I got there, I just asked around, and found myself very rapidly in a hiring office. They asked me only one question when they found out I wasn't a carpenter: "Can you typewrite?" The answer being yes, I was hired. Forty a week, just as Mexico said. They were enlarging an Army camp, and the employer was the contractor, not the Army. The job did not involve any typewriting whatsoever, and there was only one typewriter in the entire office, a sort of large, buzzing beehive. About forty people were skidding around meaninglessly in it, matching up receiving lists for lumber and similar items with bills for same, then stapling both together and tossing them in a wire basket. Every hour a girl came around and took the basket away, and that was the end of it. I presume the basket went to a similar office somewhere, where another forty people would be skidding around making out checks to pay the bills. She left an empty basket behind, which we then filled up with stapled sets of receiving lists and invoices. It was brilliant work, especially for a speed typist like me.

After a week, one of the girls in the filing vault stayed out sick. The office-manager, a young man named Bellinger to whom I sometimes talked in the field cafeteria at lunch, unless there were other bosses present, when protocol forbade him to talk to clerks, told me to take the job with the files, which it turned out was the heart-&-soul of the whole office's activity. Because it was there that the invoices were found — or often not found — that matched the receiving lists the field checkers sent in. Most of the lumber came from one west coast company named Weyerhauser but

213

would be sent and billed from any of about a hundred small foresting sub-companies, each with a different name. This often made it almost impossible to find the invoice, lost in the files under the sub-company names, when the receiving list simply showed the lumber as having come from Weyerhauser. The office-manager had read me at once as an intellectual, and figured I could no doubt navigate this tremendously taxing work of filing and sorting invoices, which I felt certain a chimpanzee could be trained to do in about an hour.

Actually, it was a great improvement on the killing drudgery of the week before, of checking the receiving lists, and remultiplying all lumber measurements on the adding machines of which there was one on every desk. The filing vault was lit by two overhead electric lights, but there was only an hour's work there every morning, putting away the day's invoices alphabetically after they were brought in the inevitable wire basket by another girl. This girl was a silent Italian beauty, who appeared only that once every day, and never said anything except a quiet "You're welcome," when I would thank her formally in my most throbbing voice as she handed me the wire basket. She looked like the Madonna with the same sad smile; Dante and Beatrice had nothing on us when it came to restrained glances. The rest of the day I spent in a sunny outer office matching up the paperwork.

Though the office was full of girls and young married women, the only other one that was at all interesting to me was the solitary typist who did the interoffice memos for Bellinger. She was obviously Jewish, though I can't explain how I knew this, as she had no exceptional nose or other Jewish features, and her name was non-committal. Nevertheless, I knew it, and took to sitting with her in the field cafeteria at lunch, where she always sat alone, which seemed to me like a signal: "Calling C-Q. Come on, anybody!" Though none of the other men seemed interested in taking her up on it. She told me her name was Jeanette Milton.

She was quite good-looking, though very heavily made up, and the girl who worked with me in the file told me that Jeanette spent twenty minutes or more every morning in the ladies' room applying all her various levels of makeup, eye-shadow, temple creams, and whatnot. Plus re-doing her hair. The effect was good but very theatrical. However, Jeanette's outstanding feature — that's evidently the only phrase I can use — was her bosom, which was cinched-in cruelly tightly into a sort of binocular framework underneath the tight-fitting sweaters she always wore. The effect was of two loaded howitzers, pointing in different directions and ready to fire!

Jeanette told me, at our continuing lunches, that she was from New York City, but had a little furnished apartment here in Somerville, so as not to have to commute. She made her own supper and read magazines in the evening, or sometimes went to the local movie, which showed all last year's pictures and never anything new, and then went to bed. Her reason for telling me all this was only too evident, as also her complaints about what a ghastly dead place Somerville, which she referred to as Slumberville. But I didn't want to get involved with her too amorously, which would have been about as difficult as forcing as hot-dog bun on a starving bear. Since she lived in the town, it would mean sleeping over with her, after which I could see we would be practically living together for the duration of the job and/or war. I *had* to get back to New York every night, but not because I thought Elaine was any better in bed than Jeanette would be. In fact, the poor girl reminded me of a caged female rabbit in heat, and you could see that once let loose her passions would practically chew a man up alive, like the riptide and the whirlpools off the volcanic island of Stromboli. It was just the death I was hoping for, and I wasn't in the slightest afraid of her, but I still didn't want to take up with Jeanette. I wanted to get back to New York every night, because I *needed* the music waiting for me on my phonograph. The stupid work I was doing made me as dependent as a drug-addict on the music I would listen to at night, which was the only thing that happened to me in any day that any longer had any real meaning. And a fig for the vulgar error that music has no graspable meaning! I would sometimes try to read a book too, but it would fall from my hands, as my eyes were tired. The music filled me and held me up, and when it got late I would wind the alarm-clock and tumble into bed, generally with Elaine. By now the landlady, Mrs. Nossiter understood very well that we slept together, since Elaine's bed was very often not mussed in the morning. But, since we were both paying roomers, the rest was our own affair. Especially since Elaine never saw any other man, nor brought anyone else to the house.

In the morning, very early, I would turn off the alarm-clock before it rang, and wake her up, often by slipping down in the bed and licking her pussy if her position allowed it. And, if not, by pulling on the hairs gently with my teeth till she spread her legs, almost in her sleep. This was for reciprocity, because we always ended our lovemaking the night before orally, and also I had often noticed that the more unhappy I was, the more interested I was in cunnilinctus for my own pleasure. Whereas I would forget about it, for long periods, except to please or excite the girl, when things were going right. I recognized that cunnilinctus was a sort of nursing at a new and more deliciously located mother's breast, but I couldn't see anything wrong with that.

Then I would have to dress and leave to catch my train to Bound Brook, and I would re-set the alarm-clock to wake Elaine an hour later. It was autumn now, but not too cold, and I would leave her spread open on the bed where I had been licking her, with her nightgown pushed up and her crotch all shining in the first light of morning, and her breasts softly rising and falling under the cloth as she went back to sleep. It was pretty hard to leave her that way, but the first few times I had tried continuing logically with making love to her for a morning pick-me-up, I was always late for work. This meant a severe reprimand, as the whole office was waiting for their bloody invoices, while the other girl dished them out frantically.

On the train early every morning I would see the Madonna-like Italian girl, who also commuted from New York, where she unquestionably lived with one of those leftover medieval Italian families where a woman's life means to shut up, get married, and have babies. I would always get in at the front end of the car where I saw her getting on, and would walk along the aisle looking for a seat until I saw her. I would give her a polite but very warm smile, as I passed, which she always returned though not as warmly. After about two weeks of this, I felt the proprieties had been satisfied, and simply sat down with her every morning without asking, just cocking my head to one side with my smile, as though inquiring if the seat were free. I had to speak to her first, of course, but she answered in her lovely quiet voice. I told her how odd I found it that we met each other at work every day, the first thing every morning, and yet never said anything to each other but "Thank you," and "You're welcome."

"What else is there to say?" she asked, with her sad Madonna smile.

"Oh, there's everything to say!" I told her. "We could begin by finding out each other's names, couldn't we?"

"I have a funny name," she said with an even sadder smile.

"Well, so do I. My name is Gershon Legman. That's out of the *Bible*, you know. It's pretty funny, isn't it? Now, what's yours?"

She told me her name was Celeste Maria Notturno, which she pronounced almost as though it were English, especially pronouncing the '-turn' as in "Turn again Dick Whittington, thrice Lord Mayor of London!" I seized my opportunity.

"Celeste Marie Notturno!" I repeated, giving every part of the name its full Italian value. "Why do you say it's funny!? That is the most beautiful name I have ever heard in my life, or ever expect to!" Every word of which was true. Her last name, in particular, when pronounced rightly, came out like dreams of liquid beauty.

"That's because you say it right," she admitted. "Most people call me 'Nodderno!'."

"Oh!!" I said, "what a crime! I'm going to meet you on this train every morning from now on, and say to you, *'I wish you a good morning, Celeste Maria Notturno – Celestial Maria of the Night'*."

She looked me full in the face then, and I could see that her eyes were brimming with sudden tears. "Don't say that to me," she told me; "it'll just make me cry. You can call me Maria."

"No, I won't do it," I told her. "I want to say your name! You can cry if you like. It really and truly is the most beautiful name, probably in the world. I'm not just saying that to flatter you."

She turned and stared out the window without speaking to me the whole rest of the short trip to Bound Brook. When we got off the train, where there was a company bus that took us out to the staging-area, she turned to me and gave me her Madonna smile.

"Thank you," she said. "Thank you very much." I could see I had made her day. I could also see that I'd better not be so effusive with her in future, because she couldn't take it. She was obviously very depressed — more the Madonna at the tomb, I realized now, than nursing Her Child. As her remark about her "funny name" showed, this was unquestionably about feeling like an indigestible dago, foreigner, spaghetti, salami, wop. Though I never felt racially inferior myself, I knew the feeling from often having been told about it: imagining oneself a mocky, kike, hebe, yid, dirty Jew, cutcock. And a few rougher ones I'll omit.

Maria and I were friends, but of course nothing ever came of it, nor did I ever try to push the relationship in any way. Not with a Sicilian girl who-lives-at-home. We met every morning on the train, for all the remaining months I was on that job, and spoke quietly about minor nothings or the latest war news, from Sicily and Italy, since her family were Sicilians. Often as I would be talking to her in the early hours of the morning, while the train clicked on, I would think to myself that here my mustache was filled with another girl's pussy-juice, Elaine's, and wondered if Maria recognized the odor. I also wondered why I always tried to complicate my life with more than one woman at a time, when essentially I am not now and never was more virile than anybody else, and one passionate woman can more than satisfy me.

Well, it was a mystery. Man, the Hunter. I dunno. One thing I was sure of is that virility isn't in your prick. It's in your head. And if it *isn't* in your head, it's not in your prick either. I was like the man in the vaudeville skit I saw many years later in Paris, representing the peasant just come to the great city from Auvergne or Gascony, who brought down the house by just standing and scratching his head, and musing in an accent so thick I could hardly understand it: "My trouble is, there's two million beautiful women in Paris, and I've only got *one prick!*"

Early one afternoon, a nasty-looking little guy that I had never seen before suddenly stuck his head into my file room and asked me for a certain company's folder. I went to get it, but didn't do it fast enough to suit him and he snapped at me, "All right, hurry it up!"

"Take it easy boss," I said, in my most dulcet mock Uncle Tom tones. "I'm hurrying as fast as I can. These files are in pretty bad order. People come in here every day and take things themselves, and the worst is they put them back wrong."

"You heard me," he rapped out; "hurry it up! I don't want to hear your complaints."

I put down the file I was bringing him, on the inside table, and just looked at him. "You know," I said, "I don't much like being talked to like that for a lousy forty bucks a week. And I have to waste eight bucks of that commuting from New York." I then gave him a big phony smile, and handed him his file with a flourish.

He gave me a look that was supposed to stab me through, and whirled and strode over to the office-manager Bellinger, turning and pointing at me with a beetling glare. I reached into the drawer of the table and took out a book I had brought with me to read at lunch. I could see what was about to happen, and I had only one thought in my mind: "How can I get to say goodbye to Maria?"

Bellinger walked over to me slowly when the little beetle-man had left. He looked me up and down with his lips pursed.

"I had you pegged for an intelligent guy," he said in wonderment. "How could you talk to the Big Boss like that? Do you know you're fired?"

"Sure I know," I said. "It was a pleasure. Do I get two weeks pay instead of notice?"

"Yes," Bellinger said with a sigh, pursing his lips again. "You'll go and pick up your pay right now. Just wait for the guards."

"Goodbye, Mr. Bellinger," I said to him. "I enjoyed working for you." It was a lie, but I figured I might as well sow what doubt I could in his mind about the rightness of yessing the Big Boss.

"You're a funny guy," he said. "You're either going to go far, or they'll hang you. Or both."

I went over and said goodbye to the typist, Jeanette, and shook her hand, overlooking her rather horror-stricken air, and waved a casual farewell to a couple of male cronies of mine that I had gotten to know vaguely. I didn't exactly know what Bellinger had meant about the guards, but soon found out. Two armed guards in civilian clothes suddenly appeared, with large blue-number buttons where those of us lowly clerks were merely black and white, and escorted me out. It appears that when you get fired off an Army contract job, they make sure you leave quietly and don't sabotage the whole staging-area with dynamite or some other bagatelle. They must have had a few sad experiences before they made that rule.

The two guards were crude-looking brutes, so instead of cringing in dulcet tones, I said to them in a crisp voice as we marched down the hall out of earshot of the office: "Mr. Bellinger wants me to return this account book to the lady in the invoice department."

"What's her name?" one of them said to me, in a totally flat, goonlike voice. "We'll give it to 'er."

"I don't know her name," I said, "I only know her by sight. This is a government document, and I *have* to give it back."

"Ya wanna get cher pay, don't cha?" the other goon asked.

"I can't get my pay as long as I haven't returned these documents," I said severely. "Please take me to the invoice department first." I hoped they wouldn't look at the book. It was a little Modern Library edition of one of Anatole France's novels, *The Red Lily*, I think.

They escorted me to the invoice department, where to my surprise I found Celeste Maria at the desk of a filing vault exactly similar to the one I had just been presiding over. It must have been the symmetrically matching wing of the building. I had never known. I handed her the book very formally.

"Goodbye, Miss Notturno," I said, pronouncing it like the poem it was. "I'm leaving the government service now. This is for you." I shook hands with her, taking hold of her elbow with my other hand, so as to make the most physical contact possible, despite the two watching guards. I was glad they were so poorly trained. I'm sure it was against the regulations to allow a possible saboteur like discharged-me to go around saying goodbye to the other, as yet unimpeachable employees. Who knows how I might pollute them. Maybe I was the first person ever to be fired from an office job there. The guards' shoes looked as though they did most of their guarding and escorting out on the staging area. Those Swedish-American carpenters were famous for not taking any back-sass from overseers. Me neither.

I got my pay and came back to New York. As I had a weekly train-ticket, however, I simply went out all the remaining mornings of the week and sat with Celeste Maria on the train-ride anyhow, and then took the next train back. I should have thought of that earlier, before making a fuss about saying goodbye to her in the office. She was very surprised to see me on the train, but I assured her I had come to live up to my promise to say *"I wish you a very good morning, Celeste Maria Notturno."* every day. She smiled a real smile this time and asked me if I wanted my book back. I told her no; it was really for her. I was sure she would like it. The last morning on my train-ticket, when we got off in New Jersey. I told Celeste Maria it really was goodbye this time.

"I think I should kiss you goodbye," I added boldly. "We've been very good friends, and for a long time too."

"You can kiss me," she said very quietly. "But wait until those people get on the bus."

I gave her a real kiss, and held her till it made her flush. She struggled away a little, and gave me a look like a frightened doe. I wondered how Joseph the Carpenter felt on his wedding night?

"Goodbye, Celestial Mary of the Night," I called after her softly. And the little bus chugged away with her. End of story.

❧

MY FRIEND Tim Trace, who was an engineer in the process of becoming a bookseller — not a frequent trajectory in either field — told me that they were hiring in the offices at another staging area up at Orangeburg, New York, up the Judson River beyond Poughkeepsie, but on the other side of the river. He gave me a note to someone there, but I couldn't find the person. It didn't really matter, as they were evidently willing to hire any warm body that had a head. You didn't have to have either two feet or two arms, and some of the other clerks didn't. One of them was in a wheelchair.

This contractor was also enlarging a big Army camp, and now that the invasion of Europe was actually starting, all such projects were obviously not going to last an indefinite time. They were usually contractors on the standard government cost-plus basis, of five per cent profit on whatever they spent, so it was to their interest to spend as much money as possible. The purchasing offices were always carefully watched by the Army, so the only good way of increasing expenses was by featherbedding shamelessly on the matter of employees taken on. It was the personnel department that made the profit. To give you some idea, at the project in Somerville, which was of exactly the same kind, and building the same sort of barracks out of the same sort of materials, one girl and myself took care of the entire file, A to Z, of the vendors' invoices, while the clerks in the office did the checking of the receiving lists, mostly for lumber and pipe

At Orangeburg, in an office at least twice as large, and covering a whole floor of a large wooden building, each clerk was given *one* and only one filing folder to deal with, representing one vendor's invoices and receiving lists. The files each contained sometimes only two pieces of paper, perhaps two invoices waiting for receiving lists not present yet, or sometimes the reverse. Occasionally the single filing folder dealt out to a clerk in the morning was entirely empty for days at a time, when the clerk would have unwisely put an invoice through for payment. The boredom and fluff-duffing was absolutely gruelling. If we had been allowed to read newspapers, the job could have been endured, but that was entirely forbidden. Some of the clerks would bring cut-out crossword puzzles from newspapers and do them all day inside their solitary filing folder. Others made idle tick-tack-toes on bits of paper. Everybody talked all the time, in undertones, to the clerks sitting next to them — on backless benches. There were too many people in the office to bother with chairs for them all. There were also two bosses in this one large room: a head boss who did nothing, and a sub-boss who helped him.

I was ready to kill myself trying to find things to do. One day I redesigned the rather crappy receiving list form, that the lumber had to be figured on, and took my design, all carefully hand ruled and lettered — it took me hours — down to the duplicating room, and lallygagged with the girls there while they ran me off a thousand. I came back and gave them to the sub-boss, who seemed tremendously grateful for something to do, and went around magistrally handing each clerk ten copies. He then sent me back to run off a thousand more, so he could have a stack of them on his desk. I felt like Gutenberg inventing Mah-Jong, or whatever it was Gutenberg invented.

Aside from the truly killing boredom, the one worst thing on the job was the air. You would think that there in the Shawangunk Mountains, which is their real name, those Red Indians long since kicked out would have laid down a nice supply of good air, and I suppose they had. But the contractor's offices were heated with some type of radiant oil heaters, and as it was now getting to be late autumn, and getting cold, the place stank to high heaven, and was always very stuffy and unbreathable. The only thing you could say for it was that it was like an Alpine peak of purity compared to the air in the dirty bus we had to take at the George Washington Bridge early every morning before it was light. Many of the plumbers on this project were New York Italians, and they almost all smoked the twisted, ugly-looking Wolf Heart Cheroots, also known as rum-soaked crooks, and apparently made out of wrung-out yak dung dipped in Brazilian arrowhead poison to make sure the victim was totally paralyzed. Now I am not a very good traveller anyhow, and prone to car-sickness. But I want you to know that even when a dozen Italian plumbers would all light up simultaneously these truly horrible torture devices the instant the bus started across the bridge, I would hang on somehow, anyhow, by unloosening my belt, self-delusion, Yoga, the Boy Scout Oath, or anything else I could think of, to keep from throwing up all over the place for the whole three-quarter hour trip, which would only have added one more, though comparatively mild ester to the stink. The logical solution would have been, of course, to open a window. But this was completely forbidden by the Italian passengers. The one or two times I tried opening my window on the bus about a one-inch crack, when I felt that I was really *in extremis* and just wanted one last small breath of fresh air before I died, a half a dozen large, burly Italian plumbers all leapt on me and slammed the window shut over my protests and if necessary, on my clawing fingers, with shouts of: "No drafts! No drafts! We don' wan' no drafts!"

How could there be a draft with only one window open, I never did figure out. Many years later, an old Italian lady immigrant to Canada on a boat, from whom I was collecting South Italian gestures and proverbs, explained the mystery to me. At the conscious level it is, in truth, a matter of drafts. Cold air is naturally bad for the health. The proverb goes: *"Aera di finestra, colpo di arbalesta!* — The air from a window is like the shot of a crossbow!" The reference to the arbalest gives you some idea of how old this proverb may be. But that's only the top, or polite level of the thing. The crucial point, which has always been the most mysterious to me, was that it was only the night air that was dangerous. Night air, you see, is filled with endless demons and other fallen household gods, all of whom had a thousand names in ancient Italy, before they were rather shakily converted into a thousand benevolent Christian saints devoted to the same areas of human health and disease. Our bus would leave from the George Washington Bridge at the last hour of the night. Just as we would be pulling up into Orangeburg on the creaky old bus, which of course had all its own gasoline motor odors too, to add to the mixture, the enormous sun would start rising, red and magnificent, over the other side of the Hudson. At which point all the Italian plumbers would leap at the windows and flip them open wide, shouting cheerful remarks about "Sure stinks in here! Gotta get these windows open!" and the like. The proverb is: *"The rising sun makes all demons flee."* And they would generally look at me, cowering with my face ashen by the unopened crack of my window, as though I had probably farted the place up myself. It would have taken a whole performing troupe of palm-eared Indian elephants, exclusively nourished on garlic, to fart up anything even similar to what we lived through on that bus. I would cut my way out through the fumes of the Wolf cheroots with my pocket knife, and stagger up the stairs to my job. The rising sun makes all demons flee.

One morning, when the sun didn't rise at all! — the sky was overcast — I arrived at the job still very nauseous, because the windows had never been opened on the bus at all, not even at the last minute. No sun. I had long since finagled a seat near the window on our billing group's bench, where I would keep the window a discreet pencil's-breadth open all the time, and this particular morning I must have sucked up my pencil's-worth of air more noisily than usual, or pressed my head groggily against the windowpane. I was really feeling pretty bad, and the natural sink of the oil fumes in the big office wasn't helping my leftover case of Wolf Heart Cheroot poisoning. Anyhow, two billing clerks at another table saw me, and realized the crime I must have committed. They dashed over and slammed my window shut, explaining to me loudly that I had no right to be freezing people out. Neither of them were Italians. The sun was now up. How is that to be explained *now*? And what good is all that primary folklore and etymology stuff, when you come right up against the nitty-gritty of human neurosis? No damn good at all.

But this time I had had enough, and was prepared to get fired, as at Somerville. I stood up and dragged myself over to, not the sub-boss this time, but the real boss, who was openly doing a very large crossword puzzle on his desk, nor did he try to hide it as I approached. I asked him in a rather weak voice whether it was true that it was forbidden to open the windows?

"What!?" he shouted, leaping into the air. He was a fiery little Irishman of the fieriest type. "The place stinks in here!" he screamed. And he precipitated himself on two or three windows nearby, and nearly ruptured himself throwing them open. He then strode down to the end of the office, where there was a big door out onto a balcony entrance never used, probably intended as a fire-escape, and pulled open the double doors there too. He stood there about five minutes, sucking in the air, and finally began doing chest-exercises with his bent arms, something like rowing a boat. He then very ostentatiously looked at his watch, and when passing the sub-boss' desk, on the way back to his crossword puzzle, he announced, succinctly: "From now on, door and two windows open for five minutes at ten o'clock! Same in the afternoon at three. We're all likely to be found dead here of carbon monoxide poisoning!"

I expected to be lynched for having openly caused this horrible invasion of fresh air onto the premises, but to my surprise everybody seemed to get used to it very fast, and some even loved it. They just hadn't been as sick as I was, and ready to risk everything to get it fixed. The rule is: Never make your enemy desperate. He's like an animal. You must always leave him a way out, and not cut off his escape. If those two slobs had only left my pencil's breadth of air, I would never have exposed them to the horrors of having the office aired out twice a day with that magnificent Shawangunk Mountain air.

After a while some of the clerks even stood up at ten o'clock and at three, and stretched their legs, while the boss took up his station at the open door, as he did from then on. A few of the more obvious ass-kissers even began doing the same boat-rowing chest exercises as the boss did. One of these new and dedicated boat-rowers was precisely the clerk who had shouted at me that I had no right to be freezing people out. How about that? Bad conscience, maybe. Proverb: Go with a winner. Why get left at the post? Or, as Benjamin Franklin never said, "If you can't lick 'em, kiss ass and join!" There was a movement for a while, to have this fine sentiment engraved on the back of the Great Seal of the United States, as the National Motto, but it got beaten at the second reading in the Senate, owing to an argument over whether 'ass' should not, in fact, be spelled 'arse.' Better luck next time.

Only a few mornings later, when it was eleven o'clock, I was astonished to see the crippled clerk in the wheelchair suddenly wheel his chair away from the end of the table where he worked, and cry out in a somehow strangled voice, like a rabbit being killed by a weasel, *"Everybody up!!"* I thought this was going a little far, as the exercises when the windows and door were opened were entirely voluntary. But everybody in the office except him — perhaps eighty men — all suddenly stood up, leaving their solitary filing folders forgotten on the tables. I suddenly remembered that it was Armistice Day, November 11th, and stood up too.

Later, I remembered the story of the event, the Armistice in World War I had been set for the eleventh hour of the eleventh day of the eleventh month: as significant a gesture as has ever been made in world history, with its obvious and intentional reference to "the eleventh hour," meaning the last chance. And yet not one numerologist, star-gazer, horoscope-caster, or other horse-crap caster in the world had guessed it. I was told that the man in the wheel-chair had worked it out with the boss that we should all stand up for a tribute of one minute — it ain't much — to the memory of the dead in World War I. He was a crippled veteran of that war. I will never forget his intense, strangled, almost weeping cry: *"Everybody up!!"*

❦

WHEN THANKSGIVING came, Elaine Fenner, my little telephone operator steady girl hadn't forgotten, and neither had I, that we were going out to Thanksgiving dinner together. As we both had the day off, I arranged two plates for us, and a nice table too, by a window, in a better restaurant than we had ever been to together, and where I knew we wouldn't be pushed around by any phony sprayed-on atmosphere. We went in the afternoon, rather than in the evening, as it turned out that was the way things had been done in both our families.

Elaine had been preparing for days ahead, and turned up in my room in a lovely new dress she had bought, on which I complimented her deeply, because it did look very well on her, and brought out all her petite femininity in the nicest, simplest way. I had a big corsage of small red roses to surprise her, which I'd bought the night before and kept in the Nossiter's refrigerator overnight. Mr. and Mrs. Nossiter took the occasion to speak to me, when I came to get the flowers, about a subject that obviously perturbed them.

"You shall not minding if I'm asking you a question?" old Mr. Nossiter began, as I thanked them for keeping the roses for me and turned to go back upstairs.

"Sure, what is it?" I said.

His wife and he looked at each other a few times, very significantly. "It's none of my business, you know?" he pursued. "I'm old enough to be like your father, maybe your grandfather — "

"Oh, Hymie!" his wife broke in. "So ask him!"

"You should lemme alone, please?" he said to her sharply. I was getting mystified. "I mean, a boy like you, with his *tallis 'n' tefillin* right on the dresser; you gonna marry this *schiksa?*"

"What *schiksa?*"

"You know what *schiksa* — Miss Fenner. You happen to know she sings in the choir in that church right up the street? You wouldn't be putting on *tallis 'n' tefillin* very long after you'll marrying such a *schiksa*. My own brother's grandson, God forbid, it's the same story."

"I'm surprised at you, Mr. Nossiter," I said. "How come you're so prejudiced against *goyim?* And today, on Thanksgiving too. Where the hell would us Jews be if we were still in Europe and not in America? I'll tell you where we'd be — we'd be in Hell! We hate Hitler 'cause he's an anti-Semite, and now you want me to be an anti-*Goy*ite, is that it?" He just looked at me with a shrug, and sighed, as though to say *"Oy, veh!"*

"I told you, Hymie," said Mrs. Nossiter triumphantly. "He's gonna marry her. And what about that Nice Jewish Girl, Alma, that used to come and see you? You got rid of her for a *schiksa?"*

I was stupefied by their parental concern about me, and thought I should be gentle with them.

"Look," I said, "I'm only taking her out for Thanksgiving dinner. I can't take a horse, can I? Does that oblige me to marry her?"

"Humph!" Mrs. Nossiter sniffed. "That Alma, she don't eat no Thanksgiving dinner? She's on a diet?"

"Lissen to me, sonny," Mr. Nossiter said, putting his hand on his heart. "I'm talking to you like your father would. Lissen! It says in the book that the lion is gonna lay down with the lamb. Sure — but it don't say when. You lay down with the lion today; only the lion gets up. You're gone. Even if you're there, you're gone. You're not a Jew anymore."

"I'm not such a very good Jew as it is, Mr. Nossiter," I said.

"I know, I know," he agreed. "You never go to shul. Nidder do I. That ain't it. At least your children should be Jews?"

I wanted to get away. I realized they were just two old idiots trying to do the right thing by a Nice Jewish Boy going wrong. But I didn't want to hear anymore of it. I excused myself and said I'd have to be leaving soon for the restaurant. I started up the stairs with my roses, and Mrs. Nossiter let fly her final shaft, with both her hands on her hips, up the stairwell after me.

"So if you're so crazy about her, why don't you move her in with you? We wouldn't stop you. Why should she wasting her money on a bed she never sleeps in?"

I didn't tell Elaine about any of this, but just pinned the roses on her bodice, with two kisses to match, and escorted her down the stairs. When we passed the Nossiters' door it was significantly shut. I was just as glad. The Thanksgiving dinner was a great success. The whole kit and kaboodle: turkey, white meat and brown — actually they were both brown, but I got a thigh — apple and raisin dressing, and little glass dishes of cranberry sauce, mine in the form of a diamond, and Elaine's in the form of a heart. We exchanged bites. The restaurant had wine, and we had a whole bottle of New York State wine, which was extremely good though a bit sweet for me. Fortunately, the wine was cold enough to cover the sweetness. Elaine loved it. I kept her in stitches with some of my old, less vulgar comedy routines. I even stole Charlie Chaplin's ballet with the forks and the two rolls from *The Gold Rush*. I tried to keep Elaine's mind very much in New York City, but at the moment they brought us plum pudding and vanilla ice cream with tiny dots in it for dessert, she began playing with the ice cream with her spoon, and sighed a little.

"I wonder what time it is in Ohio, now," she said. "I mean, I'm just wondering."

"We're an hour ahead of your family," I told her. "They're probably wondering the same thing about you. Would you like to phone them? That'd be my Thanksgiving present to you, if you want."

The poor thing was all torn two ways at the thought.

"You ought to forgive them," I pursued. "Christian charity, you know." The Nossiters' sound track, but in disguise.

"I *do* forgive them," she said, "but they don't forgive *me*. I already wrote to them twice this year, and they never answered. You don't understand my parents. They only loved me when I did everything exactly the way they said. When I did something else, and it went wrong, they were through with me. They don't think I'm their daughter anymore."

I didn't know what to say. Here was the little lioness-cub and she couldn't lie down with the lion either. Elaine told me the latest news from her work. At the beginning of the year her training would be over, and the telephone company was going to transfer her to Philadelphia. She didn't have to go, but it was a much better job, and she'd be paid considerably more. I told her to grab the chance, and pointed out how I was slaving at doing nothing at the war camp until I was ready to scream, and for very little more money than she would be getting in Philadelphia. Besides, I wasn't really getting more money, because I had to spend it on transportation — and what transportation!

I didn't insist on the bus-ride details this time: I didn't want to spoil our Thanksgiving dinner. Philadelphia was really a nice town, I told her. My sister had lived there for years. It was old and intimate, and not at all like New York. She'd meet people there she would like. The one thing I told her to be sure of, was to find the biggest church in Philadelphia where they had choir concerts and all that, and to sign up. They'd like her voice. And she should do it right away, as soon as she got there. That way she'd meet people right from the beginning, and not be lonesome.

"But not all the churches are as liberal as the Unitarians," Elaine objected. "Maybe they won't take me. I'm a Methodist, you know."

"Oh, that's just names, I said. "It's all the same God, isn't it? When Christians pray to 'our Father who art in Heaven,' that's Jehovah, isn't it? It certainly isn't Jesus. So it's the Jewish God. He isn't so particular. There's room for you."

"Well, 'our Father' is really Jesus too, in a way," Elaine began explaining painfully, but I cut her off.

"Oh, who cares about all that theology, really?" I asked. "The main thing is that people shouldn't be too cruel to each other, isn't it? It's all in the Sermon on the Mount. I was taught the same thing, word for word, when I was a kid, every Saturday afternoon. Only they called it The Wisdom of the Fathers, and said it was Rabbi Hillel and not Jesus. He was a Rabbi too. Everybody was Jewish then. Don't let our cheap imitators confuse you now, with all that junk about Methodists and Episcopalians, and High Church and Low Church and Medium Church. Like business competitors. I used to like the Holiness people best, anyhow. They're wild. I'd sneak away when my parents didn't know, and go to their singing services. They'd jump up and howl, and carry on, and faint right on the floor, and roll around. It was great theatre. Some of them were faking it, of course."

Elaine was looking at me in amazement, and a little shocked too. I didn't mind. I suddenly thought of my best syncretic card. "You're singing Bach now, aren't you?" I went on. "Did you know that Bach wrote the biggest Catholic Mass there ever was — it's the biggest, most glorious piece of music for human voices that was probably ever written in the world. If you ever get a chance to sing in it, grab it! You'll think you're in Heaven. A Catholic Mass! Well, Bach was a Protestant. So there you are!

We talked about her choir singing. The performance of Bach's "Passion of Our Lord According to St. Matthew" would be in just a few weeks now, before Christmas. I promised her I'd sit in the first row this time, or as close to the front as I could get. I explained to her that I hadn't sat at the back during rehearsals out of religious shyness, but so as not to embarrass her, perhaps.

"I'll stare at you the whole time now," I promised. "And each time the chorus stops singing and you rest, just look at me, and I'll blow kisses to you."

"Oh, don't do that," Elaine smiled. "I'll forget my words!"

"All right," I said, "I'll kiss you now." And I reached across the table and kissed her on the mouth, enjoying her embarrassment. The waitresses didn't pay us any attention, but the other diners did. Well, they could kiss each other too.

Elaine's new dress was the one she would be wearing when she sang in the Passion. She was in the chorus of sopranos. Everybody had been pleased with her singing. She'd be in the front row of the chorus because she was so small. And the singing meant so much to her. It had been such a wonderful idea I had given her. She was so grateful. She didn't know how she could ever thank me. If she went to Philadelphia she would never forget me. I choked a little on my ice-cream, and washed it down with what was left of my wine.

"Well," I warned her, "just don't tell anybody all the secrets I taught you. Let them discover it themselves. Some people shock easy."

"Oh, don't I know it!" Elaine said.

There was still some wine in the bottle, so I poured us two last glasses and offered a toast. "Here's to your lovely voice," I toasted. "May it always sing in beauty a song of love!" Now why in Hell did I say that?!

Elaine looked up at me under her lids with eyes as big as saucers, and drank. I drank too. If I had a big, expensive movie camera here, I'd pull away and upward now, very high, to make the man and woman look very very tiny, down somewhere there below. Two little people, barely existing along in mean and nasty jobs, each on the margins of a tremendously big, uninterested city. Offering each other a little mockery of love, for comfort, through the wall.

CHAPTER 42

WATER BOY

MY DOWNFALL on the job was caused by a mountain named High Tor, which I never saw, nor ever even was sure I got the story right. When the time came, I was deeply glad to leave the job, which was the most unpleasant and humiliating I ever had in my life, because there was nothing whatsoever to do except to sit around wasting time in order to make five per cent cost-plus for the employer who had overhired a ludicrously large office staff. There were also no women in the office where I worked, just eighty other men. The few women there were seemed to be kept all in the payroll department and the duplicating room, with of course the usual secretaries for the higher-ups. One never saw them except distantly, during the lunch hour.

I tried to make friends with some of the men, but it was hard. The best success I had was with marginals, in age or nationality, like an elderly man named Bert Timpson who had a marvellous stock of bawdy songs and recitations from upstate New York, and a thin, beak-nosed Egyptian, Izmir Shadoof, who seemed to be the most intelligent man in the office, and was used as a trouble-shooter by the boss. He always had plenty to do, and I envied him. At lunch he would tell me stories about life in urban Egypt, which he made sound like a couple of big, overcrowded, dirty cities, about like Memphis, Tennessee. He also was very good on bawdry, but mostly in the form of jokes, riddles, and any other type of wordplay. Typically intellectual approach, rather than the situational songs and rhymed tales that old Bert Timpson adored spieling off. When Timpson sank to mere jokes, they always had a pronounced castratory tone, or would actually be about castration by sharks, railroad trains, etc., so I did my best to keep him on songs.

There was an adding machine on each table for refiguring the lumber deliveries, and I had sort of taken possession of it, as the other clerks preferred figuring the lumber by hand. It took up more time and helped them to pass the empty hours. The adding machine was of the old-fashioned type with ten or twelve vertical banks of numbers from 1 to 9 and zero. To add on it you just punched the numbers in the various columns, but multiplication was harder. You had to hold your fingers in all sorts of claw shapes, to touch each of the figures of one multiplier, and then bang out the other multiplying number, backwards, from right to left, and the correct number of times, moving your claw-held fingers one column to the left at each figure.

It was awkward learning to do it, which may really be why the other clerks didn't use the machine, but I found it fun to learn, and got quite proficient at it after a while. I would never have figured out how to do it, but a girl from the payroll office showed me how, one day when the sub-boss sent me there with some messages about a correction in one of the pay envelopes. After the receiving list I had redesigned and duplicated, I was his teacher's pet, and he sent me on errands all over the place, which made the day a lot easier for me to live through. Sometimes I even went out into the raw torn-up muddy fields of the staging area, looking for information for the sub-boss. It was great.

Naturally, I figured out all my lumber-invoices in about the first half-hour on the adding-machine each day; so to keep it going all the rest of the day I would dream up mathematical problems to solve, as lengthy and laborious as possible. I began on the classical problem about the Hindu prime-minister who invented the game of chess and wanted to be rewarded with one grain of rice on the first of the sixty-four squares, two grains on the second square, four on the next, then eight, sixteen, and so forth. Ripley's *Believe It Or Not* had said it would take the entire population of the world working on adding machines X number of years to figure out how many grains of rice this wily prime-minister would get when he hit the sixty-fourth square, so I thought it would keep me occupied for a while. However, I ran out of interest in it at the twenty-fifth square, when I was still in the relatively low hundreds of millions.

This got me onto the subjects of squares, cubes and all that, and I banged those out happily on my adding machine for quite a while, also discovering that the eventual final differences between the consecutive squares or cubes are always the same repeating numbers. This was the same discovery that led an English mathematician, Charles Babbage, in the nineteenth century to swindle the British government into advancing him thousands of pounds to build on this principle, an enormous calculating machine that would not work, because the numbers ran too high for manual operation, exactly as with the problems of the Hindu chess-board. The poor guy went out of his mind, and became so sensitive to noise that he spent the rest of his life prosecuting street-vendors in London for crying their wares in the street. He is now the demi-god of the modern electronic calculating machine buffs, as it was his work with the repeating differences of squares, cubes, and some higher powers, that are the basic theory of the modern computer. I never got that far. I got fired too soon.

However, it did lead me to the discovery of what I have modestly named "Legman's Law," which is perhaps the briefest and most useless of all mathematical formulæ. This is saying quite a bit, as almost all of pure mathematics is entirely useless, unless you can get someone to figure out a practical application for it, as did Leonardo Pisano Fibonacci, the thirteenth century Italian mathematician who brought the Arabic figures to Europe, and also convinced God to use Fibonacci's Law or Series when creating the universe. As usual, he forgot to patent it, and died in poverty. I am dedicating Legman's Law to the science fiction readers of the world, as they are the only ones who are able to use it: *To determine the number of plane surfaces of a cube* (tesseract) *of* n *dimensions.* The formula — my masterpiece — is *n!* (*n* factorial). This means that a cube of the usual three dimensions has *3!* surfaces (that's 1 x 2 x 3 = 6); a cube or tesseract of four dimensions has *4!* surfaces, which translated into vulgar numbers equals twenty-four surfaces; a tesseract of five dimensions has *5!* surfaces, which is a hundred and twenty; of six dimensions has *6!* surfaces, or seven hundred and twenty; and so forth. In this way, whenever you find yourself stranded in a science fiction story, all you have to do is count the surfaces of the nearest tesseract and apply LEGMAN'S LAW, and you know where you are. If it has five thousand and forty surfaces, you're in the seventh dimension. If it has forty thousand, three hundred and twenty surfaces, you're in the eighth dimension. What could be simpler? Nobody goes into the mere fourth dimension anymore. It's not *in*. And, as I say, this is not patented, and not copyrighted. My gift to humanity. The attentive reader will have noticed that this is not my only invention, but the other probably had more practical applications.

How I got to High Tor is closely connected. One day when I was out on the staging area, running some errand for the sub-boss, I struck up an acquaintance with a field guard, a pipe-smoking Irishman of the classic type, who told me cheerfully that "Oll Oirishmen look like chimpanzees, an' think like *gods!*" With that for starters, I knew I had found the friend I was looking for, and used to clump out happily into the mud of the staging area every lunch-hour to listen to his charm. Although I'll give this from here on without tiresome respelling, his accent was so thick you could spread it on bread and have enough left over to grease up a wagon-axle.

His name was Kendrick McMurrough, and he was a retired Boston policeman, who had taken the job at Orangeburg to increase his retirement nest-egg. He was always good-humored, and seemed to spend most of his life packing his pipe with his baby finger, and tapping it out again, after smoking it briefly. The one thing that could ever rile him was thinking about Oliver Cromwell's massacres of the Catholics in Ireland in the mid-seventeenth century, and the Battle of the Boyne. This took place in 1690, but McMurrough was still sore about it, and assured me that so were all true Irishmen. I could well believe it. The Jews are still sore about the destruction of the Temple at Jerusalem in 69A.D. and the dispersion of the Jews all over the world after the revolt of Simon Bar-Kochba in 135, and have a holiday of mourning for it every year.

McMurrough took a very broad view of human frailty, especially that of women, whom he considered to be the weaker vessel, but to be handled with tenderness. He told me that he had never roughed up the whoors, as he always pronounced it, when required to arrest them in the line of his duties in Boston. But he had also never succumbed to their blandishments, even when they would on occasion pull their skirts right up to their necks to show him what he was missing.

"Ah, sights like that'll make a man go blind," he told me, " — and it's worth it!" He added that he never really understood why he had street orders to arrest "those poor gorls" to keep them off the streets. "It's not as though they wore hurting anybody, y'know," he observed. This was my first encounter with the new legal concept of victimless crime, something the *Talmud* and those Goyishe Talmudists — and Blackstone were always hell-bent on studying. McMurrough also noted that the whores' customers were almost never horny adolescents, as people otherwise liked to suppose would rape some delighted spinster, but were mostly married men, looking to get their thirst straightened out "Saturday nights," before they had to take the rest of their pay envelopes home to their frigid wives.

At a lesser level of human interest he pointed out that the field checkers were all a lot of dirty crooks, and mostly Eyetalians too. He did not like Italians, and considered them treacherous, even among themselves. I told him about the rum-soaked Wolf Heart cheroots every morning on the bus, and how hard they made life for me. He puffed a gust of pipe smoke delicately in the other direction before answering.

"Those poor fellers'll smoke things a self-respecting dog wouldn't turn around twice and shit on," he agreed.

The field checkers' main dishonesty was that they were apparently all in cahoots with the truck drivers who delivered great loads of crushed stone and gravel for smoothing out and enlarging the staging area, so that it would not be total mud during the Army maneuvers of men and machines. The way it worked, McMurrough told me, was that the truck drivers were supposed to have a receiving slip signed for every truckload of gravel, so that it could be billed later by the quarrying company. The receiving slips, which were numbered, came in little pads of fifty that each truck driver carried. When he would arrive to unload his gravel, the truck driver would hand the field checker the pad to sign. Inside the cover of the pad, which contained fifty slips, would be a folded twenty dollar bill. The checker then went into the field shit-house while the truck was unloading, signed up the whole padful of fifty slips, and pocketed the twenty dollars. This went on all day, every day, as a steady stream of trucks arrived and left, like a great lumbering snake, bringing the crushed stone.

After that, when the filing folder I would be dealt out in the morning by the ambulant file clerk happened to be for one of the quarrying companies supplying stone and gravel to the staging area, I would often wonder, while passing it through for payment, if the amount of stone being billed and paid for had really been delivered, or, as McMurrough claimed, was only one-fiftieth stone and forty-nine fiftieths graft. The amounts of money involved in the bills were often extremely large, and it seemed incredible that so much crushed stone could be used in merely one camp. I got to work on my trusty adding machine, and figured out rapidly, after checking out the square surface in miles of New York State in my trusty Webster's Collegiate Dictionary, Fifth Edition which I kept on my desk, in the Pronouncing Gazetteer section in the back of the book, that just one single grouped invoice for stone that had come through for payment one day, for several hundred thousand dollars, involved sufficient crushed stone to bury the entire state of New York under a layer of the stuff one inch thick.

I wondered whether McMurrough had perhaps made a mistake, and there were a hundred receiving slips, and not fifty, in each pad being signed up fraudulently by the checkers out in the philosophical quiet and perfumed calm of the field shit-houses. Anyhow, this invoice confused me very much, and I thought there must be some error connected with it. As I needed to get some more receiving slips for the sub-boss from the filing vault, I carried the invoice into the vault in its folder, and owing to some clumsy gesture while talking to the vault-clerk I accidentally dropped it down in back of a couple of vertical filing cabinets where I strongly feared it would never be found again until after the war, if then.

Of course, it was evidently an absurd gesture, and useless, since a duplicate invoice would normally be sent after thirty or sixty days had passed without any action from the disbursement division at the camp. In so thinking, I counted without the impatience of the quarrying contractor to get his money. Somewhere in the back of my head I had a vague recollection, also that a bunch of red-necked intellectuals living thereabouts, or across the river in New York, had been making a stink about the razing by stone contractors of a beautiful and isolated mountain called High Tor, somewhere nearby. This was uncommon in those days, and red-necks and other undesirables were prone to get angry about it. Since that time, with improved methods and larger mammoth steam-shovels, people have become accustomed to mountains disappearing. A friend of mine living near Pittsburgh came back from his summer vacation a few years ago, and found that the entire mountain view in front of his house had disappeared. When I asked him what he had done about it, he said they had almost finished paying off the mortgage on their home, so he and his wife had no choice but to stay. His wife had a nervous breakdown because of it, but she was a little better now and he was taking care of her at home. Without the view.

Some weeks later, about eleven in the morning, there suddenly erupted into our peaceful office, just revived and renewed by our fresh-air breathing exercises at ten o'clock, a strange apparition, raising a hell of a stink and pounding on the desks of the sub-boss and the boss, and shouting in a loud voice about why the hell hadn't they been paid?! It was a red-faced man in, I would say, his early forties, dressed rather inappropriately in hunting clothes. And when I say hunting clothes, I don't mean an old brown corduroy jacket and pants, with canvas shoes. I mean the complete and authentic set of spanking new fox-hunting togs, with knee britches, riding boots, and even a small derby hat attached to the flare-waisted jacket of this getup by means of a black cord ending in the lapel buttonhole. This apparition, who was very angry indeed, was the owner of a local stone-crushing firm; perhaps, as I saw it in my mind, the very one that had ground up High Tor into gravel and delivered it to the camp, whether or not on the fifty-for-one basis already described, I certainly couldn't say. I couldn't prove a thing, and neither could they. Nobody knew what had become of the invoice, or why it hadn't been paid.

All the clerks, including myself, were fascinated by this red-faced stranger in the strange fox-hunting clothes, who, I remember, shouted among other things, "Don't gimme that! I delivered that invoice to this building *my self!*" Eventually the boss and the sub-boss got him mollified and he left, I presume in the direction of the disbursing office. We all discussed this strange event until noon and at lunch-time, and in one of these discussions I made the perhaps foolish remark that I had been figuring things out on the adding machine and that the amount of gravel already delivered to the staging area was sufficient to bury the entire state of New York under a layer one inch thick.

Saying this was an error on my part. The conversation was reported to the sub-boss by one of the staff ass-kissers and spies. I don't know which one; there were quite a few, most of whom did the standing up rowing exercises at ten o'clock now every day, in imitation of the boss. Suspicion fastened on me for the regrettable loss of this important invoice, from an important vendor, for these obviously important hundreds of thousands of dollars. I wondered vaguely, why, with all that money, he couldn't just buy a fox in a pet-shop and cut it up into steaks to feed his guests, without all that galloping around in funny hunting togs in the middle of a war, with the soldiers in the camp — not in hunting togs of the same type — gawping at them. I was interrogated by the sub-boss on the subject of the missing invoice, but I had completely forgotten about my maladroitness in the filing vault and denied everything. Nevertheless I was under a very dark cloud.

The next morning, while I was peacefully figuring out some Weyerhauser lumber receiving slips on my trusty adding machine, I was suddenly conscious of someone standing in back of me. It was the sub-boss with a very large artificial smile on his puss.

"You're pretty handy with that machine," he remarked, with what seemed to me excessive enthusiasm, since I was only doing my work — the little of it that there was. "They need somebody to help out in the payroll department. We're transferring you."

Five minutes late I was set up with an exactly similar machine, in the middle of a private harem containing about thirty girls sitting on stools. All working at high speed like semi-insane beavers, also at adding machines, at towering stacks of time-clock cards, obviously one for every employee on the staging area, including me. (But not for long.) The straw boss in this computational sweat-shop, who was a man, shoved me a stack of time-clock cards and told me to add up the hours and mark the total for each week on a sheet. After about two hours of this, my eyes were dancing, my chest was feeling caved-in and my back was aching from the peculiar stance I had to take on the backless stool, and the seat of my pants was covered with sweat and sticking to the stool. After the *dolce farniente* of the billing department for the months I had been there, I was not ready for this sudden leap into the intense and unremitting galley-slave labor of the payroll sheets, though it might have been vaguely fun to do for about twenty minutes — in every month. I looked with mounting respect at the frail little women all around me, twisting like Turkish dervishes on their stools as they knocked the work out, hour after hour without seeming to notice. Obviously a hitherto-undiscovered race of upstate New York superwomen, all with double-jointed fingers.

When lunchtime came, I slid off my stool and stood up, twisting my shoulders in a sort of hula dance to try to get them vertical again. I realized I was suffering from culture shock, and wondered why I had been beefing all these weeks about not having enough work to do? Well, if I wanted an egg in my beer, I had it now. One of the superwomen who had been sitting near me stopped to speak to me, and I observed that from close she really looked more like a moderately young housewife who had perhaps taken the job to eke out the allotment from a husband in the army. She asked me why I was using the adding machine in such a peculiar way, and told me it was much harder the way I was doing it. I hadn't known what I was doing was peculiar, and asked her what the right way was.

She showed me in half an instant that you don't reach for piano octaves all over the keyboard when doing this type of repetitive stuff. Instead of hitting the nine key, you hit the three-key three times, fast. Four is two times two — that's that new thing they have. Five is three and two. Six is two threes. And so forth. You never have to go higher than three or four. In other words you become a sort of human binary calculating machine, with the compass of your hand-motions kept very close to your chest to save fatigue. I thanked her very much for taking pity on a greenhorn such as I was, though I didn't use those precise words. In the afternoon I started with the new system, which was a lot easier, but the job was still really gruelling. And so interesting!! I wondered how long you had to do it before they carted you off in the funny-wagon.

I was sitting there with my stack of time-clock cards, going like the wind now: three-three-three! Two-times-two! Four-and-three! Two-two-two! — no, wait a minute, six was two-times-three; you didn't have to do two-two-two. And I was calling off the numbers to myself as I translated into binary finger-punches in the system of mechanical-voiced pronunciation Elaine had told me she was required to use as a telephone operator: sev-*venn!* ei-*yut!* ni-*yun!* Somehow it took me back to the days when I was harvesting ragweed for my poor, hay-fevered father, hour after hour, and picking slate out of coal, bent over the conveyor belt in the Myrtle Street Colliery after school. In a few more days of it, I could see, my mind would probably go back even further, to a century I hadn't lived, the way you saw in the woodcuts in histories of mining, where bare-breasted women with tump-line around their foreheads were crawling on all fours, dragging carts of coal along in underground seams too low to bring in a mule. Maybe that's where that song came from: *"My sweetheart's a mule in the mines . . . ."*

At four o'clock the straw-boss and watched me working for a minute. "You can't do this work," he said, flatly.

"Not without going insane by the end of the week," I agreed cheerfully.

"You want to pick up your pay?" he asked. "You won't get any severance. Don't insist on it, or I'll have to mark the card 'Incompetence.' This way you're not being fired."

I understood. After I had picked up my pay, I had to go back to the billing office to get my coat. The sub-boss was staring at me with unconcealed hate and triumph. The ass-kisser who had originally slammed the window down when I opened it was also watching me, with a hyena-like shit-eating grin. I knew now which spy had turned me in.

WHEN I phoned Dr. Dickinson's office the next day, as I had been doing every week no matter where I was, the secretary told me he was still convalescing from his heart attack, and no one knew when the project would start up again. The artists were all gone except Belskie, I think, who was not on our project but worked on contract for the National Committee for Maternal Health, all alone in the big studio, on the sculptured anatomical models. I called Tim Trace, too, but he didn't have any other ideas as to staging areas that might be hiring in the offices. I decided I would take a chance and go out to Somerville, New Jersey, again.

Talking to old Ken McMurrough out in ploughed-up fields, with the grand backdrop of the Catskill Mountains behind, had excited a taste in me that I had nearly forgotten since I was a kid in Scranton at the top of the Poconos, for hills and the out-of-doors and especially for green trees. I would stay away from the business office, of course, where I'd been fired, and would try out for a job in the field offices which all the camps had scattered over the staging areas. I purposely took the early train I used to take before, and tramped it from one end to the other looking for Celeste Maria Notturno. But she wasn't on the train. It's always like that.

At the hiring office they still asked me only one question: "Can you typewrite?" I told them yes, and that I had a lot of experience in field offices at Orangeburg, so I was immediately sent out to a cruddy little shack in the fields. It had a pot-bellied stove and a counter with a swinging half-door in the middle, to divide the office part from the trampling horde of laborers, mostly Negroes and Italians, and the inevitable Swedish-American carpenters. Everybody was getting hired, fucked and fired so fast it made your head spin, and I was typing like a madman, filling out hiring forms and termination forms, which were known to all the men, — not as humor, but quite innocently, it appeared — as exterminations.

"Whaddya want?" I would say to a laborer who would come in when I was holding the fort at the staggered lunch-hour.

"I wanna get exterminated," he would tell me. And I would duly make out his extermination sheet, and clip it to his time-clock card so he could go to the payroll office and get his pay. All the Negroes and Italians believed they would get two weeks' extra pay when they quit, and I had to explain endlessly that they only got that if they were fired. Sometimes they would ask me what the best means of getting fired was, privately, you understand. I finally had to make up a standard response.

"Well, one carpenter tried to get fired by shitting in the field-boss' hat," I would explain. "But the field boss was bigger than him, and pushed the hat on over his head. How big is your field boss?" That usually closed the subject.

As there were of course no women allowed out in the field offices, I moseyed over to the main cafeteria one day, near the large symmetrical office building, and looked around for Jeanette Milton, the smouldering volcanic sex-job I had not forgotten. Though I had been a bit shy of her hardly restrained, unsatisfied passion and binocular bosom the last time I worked there, this time I was looking for a woman in my life. Elaine had been gone over a month, and I was too knocked-out each night when I would get back in the dark on the bus from Orangeburg, to go out trying to find a new girlfriend in the logical places I'd have to haunt: the evening plays and concerts at the Hunter College Auditorium, and the Museum of Modern Art, and the lectures at the New School, and all that old standard route. Also, I was getting too old for such kid stuff, I felt. College girls were never very interesting, and always said exactly the same things during each season. Then the next season they all said exactly the same things again, though the soundtrack would have changed. Their clothes were exactly the same way. It was as though they had been stamped out with cookie cutters.

The girl I really wanted was Celeste Maria, but she was never on the train anymore, either morning or evening, so I knew she had disappeared forever out of my life. I hoped Anatole France's *Red Lily* had stirred her up a little. She was ready. A woman once told me that pornography never excited her, anymore than reading about how pigs are slaughtered in the stockyards made her hungry; but that Anatole France's delicately allusive bedroom scenes made her deliciously nervous and willing. Well, sex is all in your head. For men too. Why else is it that a man can see a girl pull up her skirt part way, to fix her garter, and then goes around and wants to bite her on the neck?

I settled for Jeanette, whom I finally did find in the cafeteria, the third time I went there. She still lived in Slumberville, still hated it, and was bringing a sandwich for her lunch now, usually, to stay in the warm office, instead of clumping out in the cold, rainy weather to the cafeteria. She asked me how I had the nerve to come back to Somerville after having been escorted out by two guards? I told her that it didn't take all that much nerve: I wasn't a saboteur or a German spy. I had simply been fired for telling the Big Boss to shit in his hat, and pull it down over his ears and call it curls.

"Is *that* what you told him?" she boggled. "We were all wondering. My *God!* You really have a nerve!"

I basked modestly in her admiration, and asked her what was showing at the Slumberville movies that evening. I said I'd like to take her out.

"Do you live here too now?" she asked eagerly.

"No," I told her. "I commute to New York. But I'll just get a later train back." We both understood what that meant. But it was polite. The way you have to be, at first, with girls. She gave me her address, and I met her after work that evening at her house. I didn't want to queer the deal by embarrassing her about being seen with me on the company bus. So I told her I got off work later than she did and took the bus on its second swing around, with the workmen, instead of with the office smoothies.

To my surprise she made me a lovely supper. She had very little on hand, and had not had the time to get to the local market, she apologized. But she made little croquettes out of canned salmon and chopped celery, which were delicious, and served them up with reheated canned peas which tasted exactly like eating small chunks of water-logged cork. Then she started coffee going through a not-very complex device consisting of a large paper cone set into an enormous funnel, which was the latest *in* thing, and for which she told me she had paid a young fortune.

Somebody is always making money off whatever is *in*. That's who manipulates the fads, of course, but the suckers always buy. It's hypnosis, like with women and whatever the latest fashions may be. Poor things, they're always demanding equality with men, but don't realize they'll never get it as long as the men know they can get women to throw away all their last year's clothes and buy a complete new wardrobe, twice as ugly, just with a full-page ad. Often on some male sucker's money. Who wants to be equal with brainwashed female sheep like that? The solution the advertisers and fad-pluggers and millionaire politicians seem to be trying for, with the coffee dripolators and all that gadgety propaganda shit, is to make the men as easy to push around mentally as the women are, and then both women and men will be equal together – at the bottom of the heap.

Jeanette's making dinner for me was just her way of being pleasant, and attractive too. Jewish girls are always thinking, in the back of their heads, about maybe you're going to marry them. So she was showing me what an effective little wife she could be. Sometimes I think all girls are that way, but Jewish girls are terribly conscious of it, even when the basic subject in hand is self-evidently sex and not marriage. Well, they must feel there's some connection between the two.

We looked over the newspaper she had bought on the way home, and studied all the movie advertisements. They were pretty grim, we both agreed, and she suggested we stay in, instead, and play

Scrabble, or something similar. She had a board. She kept serving me coffee, and apologized for having nothing else. It might keep me awake, she said, but I assured her I didn't care.

"I'm not planning to get much sleep tonight," I said boldly, standing up and walking around behind her chair. I reached in under her arms and took those incredible binocular bubs in both my hands, tipping her back toward me and kissing her hair. She drew in an enormous breath, which added about four sizes to her bosom measurement, and murmured "Oh, yes!" in exactly that totally and gutturally insinuating tone that Mae West always used in her movies. Also giving her shoulders a sort of corkscrew twist that prophesied well for her abilities in bed.

We never got to the bed. She dragged me over to the small sofa, on which there wasn't really room, switching out the lights as we modulated in that direction. We started kissing and clinging and squirming until we ended up on the floor. I pulled down a sofa cushion and tried to get her skirt up, but she stopped me and tried to press her knees together, which surprised me. If this girl turned out to be a cockteaser, I would have to reread the book.

"I'm having my period," she murmured. "Do you care?"

"Not a damn bit!" I assured her. "Just get out of that saddle before I tear it off with my teeth."

She disappeared for a moment in the direction of the bathroom, and then called me from the darkened bedroom a few moments later. I stumbled in, in the dark, and fell into her wide-open arms and legs. She had laid a bath towel across the bed under her, or maybe two, and clearly knew what she was doing, because I saw it crumpled in the bathroom the next morning, and it looked like I had murdered her. She was willing to die. She was just as passionate as I had pegged her to be the hour I first saw her, and kept moaning, "Oh, why did we wait so long? Why did we wait so long?" which was what I was finally wondering too. I made love to her once in what she clearly thought was the proper position, because she had been waiting for me spread open on her back. I wanted to hold back but couldn't – it was too long between times – and let myself go when I couldn't hold on any more. Jeanette had already come, but almost silently. All her theatrical sighs and studied statements fell away when the paroxysm came over her, and it allowed her to stop talking and be real. I rolled off beside her and covered the small of my back with the pillow, as I saw it would be impossible to find the thrown off covers without a fuss. But it was too cold, and I began reaching around with my foot to see if I could snag a coverlet or something.

"What is it, darling?" Jeanette murmured, stirring finally.

"I'm cold."

"Oh! Let me cover you!" She leapt up, picking up the bath towel we had lain on and stuffing it up between her legs, and dashed around the bed to cover me tenderly with a big fluffy comforter of down. I could already hear the rabbi pronouncing the words, *"Behold, thou art made sacred to me, according to the laws of God and Israel.* – Put the ring on her finger." Some girls really move too fast from mistresshood to motherhood, and a guy gets scared. But I let her mother me, and when she came back to bed, I showed her another, better position, in which I could get my hand on her pussy and my fingers at her clitoris while we made love again. She had no juiciness now, because her blood had made her sticky instead, so I had to keep licking my fingers to keep it wet. I know it's against Jewish religion to swallow blood, but you have to be willing to risk Hell to reach Heaven. Wasn't that what Dante said to Virgil, or how did it go?

After that I stayed over every other night with Jeanette, and she would bring me a sandwich each alternate day at the cafeteria. I would buy all the food in the local markets after work, and bring it along with me. I explained that this was my share, and that she was doing enough cooking the stuff and keeping the apartment nice for us. Naturally I didn't mention the rent she was unquestionably paying, because I was paying a rent too, though not there, and the less discussion there is of money in a cooking-and-sleeping affair like that, the more charming I find things stay. I also like meat suppers when I can get them, especially chops. Most people are trained to prefer steaks, which cost twice as much and don't taste a damn bit better. Also steaks were not always easy to get then during the war, and there were meat-stamps and rationing, and all that. But the ration was more than anybody really needed, and so you could buy extra stamps from other people, or trade them privately for shoe-stamps and suchlike. War or no war, Jeanette and I didn't lack for chops and fried chicken, and eggs for breakfast; not to mention the fish croquettes and packaged soup. Did you? She even baked me a cake once — pure white flour with chocolate icing. It certainly wasn't anything like the great Hungarian exotica my mother always whumped up in the way of cakes, but I had to admit it was pretty good for an unmarried young woman, working in an office all day, and making love all night like there was no tomorrow. Besides, it's the sentiment that counts. I recognized that Jeanette's cake, aside from all marital advertising purposes, perhaps unconscious, was to thank me for the sexual satisfaction she very badly needed. I needed it too, and we practically wore out her vaginal diaphragm, waltzing and trampolining together up there in the cervical vault at ten p.m., just like proper married folk.

This seems to be a big secret, but I'm going to tell it. Like most so-called experienced American girls I ever met – and European girls even more so, be it said – this girl was not accustomed to having orgasm regularly when making love, nor to having it very deep when she did, as she admitted to me. And she imagined I was some kind of sexual superman because I didn't make love to her with my cotton picking hands in my pockets, and tried to see to it that she came too. Yes, and just about every time. Put your hand on your heart and say the same. Sometimes I wondered what would happen if women in general, found out what they were missing? Or maybe they knew, but didn't know how to or couldn't convince their men how relatively simple it is to fix it. Jeanette didn't care very much about oral sex, though she was willing enough to do anything I asked or wanted, as long as it was only an *hors d'œuvre*. For the main dish she really wanted and needed to be ploughed with her legs up over my shoulders, and the more violently the better. The *Kama Sutra* says that plump women are generally like that.

Jeanette wasn't particularly plump, but I guessed she would be later. The *Kama Sutra* must know. Think about these things, will you?

For us there wasn't any later, because the job didn't last. When spring came they had hired enough people for the construction job, and if one of their field offices stayed open for sustained firings and hirings, it wasn't the one I was working in. When it came time to exterminate myself, I realized that I was loath to go back to New York and look for jobs there. I was getting seduced by Jeanette's regular home-cooking, and steady midnight enthusiasm. As I did get back to New York every other night, I wasn't even lacking for music, and had also bought her a good little radio on which we were able to get WQXR, which always had something decent in the way of music, and not too much gubbledy talk.

This was the first time I had had a taste of real home life since I had left home to go to college nearly ten years before. My three months with the Spanish artist, Susan Aguerra, didn't count, because we had been more like roommates, really, than lovers, no matter what we did in bed, and we mostly ate out, as neither of us really knew how to cook. I was becoming a family man without knowing it, just the way the wise old mommas that taught girls like Jeanette Milton how to get a man, must have been explaining it to them. This marriage thing has been working for tens of thousands of years, since Eden. It's not perfect, by a long shot, but it must have something. Anyhow, I didn't want to leave New Jersey, and asked the field boss if he thought there was any kind of job I could transfer to on the staging area. I knew I could never get successfully rehired in the offices, though I didn't tell him why.

"Only thing I can tell you," he said, "is to get in with some of the carpenters or plumbers." But the plumbers wouldn't take you at all unless you were an Italian, or a union member they couldn't refuse. And the carpenters made things even harder, by simply demanding that you bring along a wooden toolchest you had built yourself, with your tools in it. With one glance at your toolchest they knew if you were real or a faker. If I had wanted to chance it, I suppose I could have bought a black-market toolchest, or had one built for me, but how would I keep the pretense going after that? Carpentry isn't just a matter of sawing wood and hammering nails. The public doesn't know that, but carpenters do. At the first assemblage I'd try to prepare, they'd have me run off the staging area.

I tried to get placed as a helper, to the plumbers maybe; but the few jobs like that were already filled by their own young sons whenever there was an opening, and the carpenters didn't have helpers. In the end, the only job I could get, to stay on at all, was that of water-boy. The first time I went out, wandering over the staging area, with that heavy can of water on my back, the straps cutting into me, and all the laborers shouting and cursing at me —just like in the song —I began to understand something about the difference between being a vain and unemployable intellectual, and being something socially useful like a carpenter with a handmade toolchest slung over his back. What the hell did they care whether they were in Sweden or America? Everybody needs a carpenter or a stone mason. That too has been going on a long time.

Every profession has its secrets, and being a water boy is no exception. It was my good fortune that the secret was explained to me the first day by one of the other water boys. Most of them were up to ten years younger than me, which also made me feel rather contemptuous of myself. The field boss had arranged for me not to be terminated as working for his office, so I was still on the payroll as a typist at forty dollars a week, instead of at a regular water-boy's wage. But that didn't cheer me up much. Sometimes it isn't just the money that counts. Maybe always. This other water-boy saw me filling my can up after lunch, after having struggled with it all morning, and he held up his hand in the Stop! gesture. He waited until the other water boys had moved on in their directions before continuing.

"Listen," he said. "Whaddya wanna kill yourself for, toting that heavy can around all day?"

"It's a man-killer all right," I agreed, "but what am I going to do?"

"There's a secret to this job," he said.

""What is it?" I had already been warned not to hide out and fall asleep, as the workmen would treat me rough if they found me. "If you mean to shag off, I was told I better not do that."

"No, don't do that," he agreed. "If them plumbers catch you they'll take your pants down and paint your whang green. They put a carrot up one kid's ass. He looked like a nigger wench being run out of town." That was South Jersey talk.

"So what's the secret? I asked him.

He looked both ways before he told me. "Don't fill up the can. You just keep coming back and filling it up half full.

After that life was a lot easier for me. Or would have been easier if I hadn't somehow earned the enmity of a young fellow who helped the field sawyer at his portable sawmill. The field sawyer was a cheerful, careful cuss. But somehow, this kid hated me for some reason. I had never even spoken to him. Maybe it was because he saw me reading a book every day at lunch hour, sitting up against the shade of the sawmill shack, the days I didn't go in to the cafeteria to eat with Jeanette. One day he even said to me when I was refilling the field-sawyer's bottle with water, "I betcha you think you're better than me."

"Who, me?" I said. "I'm the water-boy." That was my answer to anything anybody said to me. But it didn't satisfy him. He continued to try to pick a fight and pester me every day. The sawyer let me leave my book in his tool locker, and one day the helper stole it. I never saw it again. Just a Modern Library book, but it was irritating to lose it. Encouraged by this success, he found my sweater in the grass one Monday morning near the sawmill, where I had taken it off and stashed it when the morning sun got too hot, and he stole that too. He must have been spying on me, to have known where it was.

I like sweaters, and always wear them, even in the summertime. This one was really warm, made of gray heavy wool. The nicest thing about it was the zipper at the front of the neck, which meant you could close it in the early morning when it was very cool, and then zip open the collar as it got warmer. Even the zipper was good, the best I ever saw; much better than the usual Talons in America or Éclairs in France. It was called Jewel, as I remember, and the stitching partly covered the metal parts so you could hardly see the teeth. It had the most beautiful action, as though on ball-bearings. None of the other zippers came within miles of the Jewel. I never saw another, except on that sweater. Well, when the sawmill helper stole that, I wasn't going to take it lying down. The book hadn't mattered —I could get more. But I wanted my sweater back, and I told the sawyer that I knew the kid had taken it, and I was going to complain to the field boss about him if I didn't get it back by evening, when I would need it again. It was lunchtime then.

The sawyer must have told the kid what had to be what, because the next time I passed with my can on my back, the kid thumbed his nose at me with both hands, and shook his fist at me. I didn't give a damn about all that, as long as I got my gray zipper sweater back. I wasn't very far away, and had stopped to give a laborer a drink, pouring the water out of the little side-spigot into one of the stack of paper cups I carried on top of the can, when there was a lot of shouting at the sawmill. Then we saw the sawyer running full speed down the truck path. In a few minutes a truck came tearing back, and the sawyer jumped out followed by a doctor in a white coat; the ambulance was parked right by the sawmill.

"What's happening down there, water-boy?" the laborers asked me. They couldn't leave their jobs, but I was free to wander where I liked. I went back to the sawmill to see what was what. It was clear that somebody was pretty badly hurt. But I couldn't see anything. The sawyer was alone, and starting up the saw when I got there. The ambulance was pulling away. Suddenly the ambulance stopped, and the doctor came racing back.

"Hey!" he shouted to the sawyer. "Where the hell is it? Where's the hand?"

He reached down on the ground near the saw, and picked up a cut-off human hand all covered with blood and sawdust sticking to it. He folded it into the skirt of his white coat and rushed back to the ambulance which then tore off down the field.

"What happened?" I babbled to the sawyer, as if I didn't know! He pointed to the ground again, where now I saw my gray sweater all mangled and torn in the blood-stained sawdust.

"Kid tried to cut it in half on the saw," he said. "Musta got tangled in it. Can't be too careful around these goddam saws. Not anything to fuck around with, if you don't know what you're doing."

He engaged a piece of wood in the saw, and started working again. I felt very peculiar, and suddenly realized I was going to throw up. I stumbled behind the sawmill shack and began retching, totally and completely. I must have thrown up everything I'd eaten for a week before, and felt like I was turning myself inside out, and I was retching stuff that wasn't even food. I slid my arms out of the straps of the water-can, feeling pretty weak, and left it there on the ground.

I walked back down the truck path to where the company bus stop was. I didn't go to the field office. I didn't want any pay. It was Monday, anyway. I just wanted to get the hell out of that staging area. Forever.

I started walking out the gate, and showed my number-button to the guards for the last time. There was no bus service at that hour. Walking toward the town I thumbed a ride with an automobile going in that direction. I let myself into Jeanette's apartment with my key, and drank a couple of glasses of water, and laid down on the bed and fell asleep.

Jeanette woke me up when she got home. I refused any supper except some soup, and told her I was sick, which she could see anyhow. I told her I had quit the job, and would not be coming back. My health wasn't too good. I didn't tell her anything about the sweater, at all. She gave me her family's address in New York, and promised she would write to me, which she did for quite a while afterward, heading her letters "News From Slumberville." That night she very much wanted me to make love to her, to say goodbye, but I was unable to do it. Then she wanted to cradle me in her arms, but instead I put her head on my shoulder and held her quietly that way until she fell asleep. In the morning we said goodbye.

G. LEGMAN 1943

JULIA 1940

G. LEGMAN 1943

MATILDA, GERSHON, DAISY, EMIL, JULIA, &
COOKIE JUNE CA. 1942

CHAPTER 43

SHAKESPEARE'S SILENCE

THE NEWS was good that spring. The British and American armies in Italy finally broke through the stalemate that was so humiliating to read about later in the absurdly crowing football-style headlines: *"Our Boys Gain Fifty Yards On the Plains of Ravenna."* By the middle of May the main German defense at Cassino was broken through, between Naples and Rome, and Italy was essentially out of the war. However, the Germans engaged an impeccable delaying action, and held their line right across northern Italy from Leghorn and Florence to Ancona, until the day they learned that Hitler was dead and Berlin taken, ten months later. Then they all surrendered. Meanwhile, the "soft underbelly" of Europe held. But in those ten months the war was won elsewhere.

At the beginning of June 1944 the Anglo-American invasion of France so long promised and so shamefully delayed since the rout at Dunkerque, finally began the pincers movement which meant the end of Nazi Germany, when two hundred and fifteen Russian divisions swept past through Poland and reached Berlin by midwinter. The Anglo-American striking force on the western front was only a quarter or one fifth as large: forty divisions, facing sixty-five divisions under Von Rundstedt. The tide had turned at the defense of Stalingrad, when the Germans had already driven inward a thousand miles beyond the German border. The entire Red Army under Zhukov was given one order only by Stalin: "Stop the *Nyemtzki* there, or we die."

Everything was in motion in America. People were continuously coming and going, especially young people in the armed services and defense plants. That included women too, who were of course replacing the men in the factories, but were also trying wordlessly to get as close as they could to where the men were. All the trains and busses — and some of the planes, were filled with young people shuttling and being shuttled around. That's part of the nature of war, which has been scientifically defined as *A destructive process in which rich old men send young men off to die, to make the rich old men richer.* This time the war was evidently justified, and more than that, essential. But it was still the young men who did the dying. And helpless, innocent civilians of all ages.

Long-range rocket missiles and the airplane have improved the science of war a great deal since the machine-gun in the 1860s. Now the young, and even some of the not-so-young, are allowed to die right where they are, instead of having to rush about so much to die. The war is brought to them wherever they are. The bombs are transported to the people, instead of transporting young people to battlefields full of showering bombs. It's a great improvement, and more democratic, and now there's also lots of extra money by the billions to be made in the rocket- and bomb-building and transporting business. While the rich & powerful now arrange to hide in locked and guarded caverns under mountains, with a tutti-frutti of military decorations pinned to their chests, while they push the necessary large red buttons to kill everybody else. A true science. During World Wars I and II there was still quite a bit of regrettable non-logistic movement, herds of young people being sent this way and that, to & from the current killing sites. Very disorderly. Like a large, badly-disorganized butcher-shop. Some say that's all it was.

In between battles, some of the young men are regularly allowed to rush home for brief intervals, to fuck the women left behind, so cannon-fodder, or rather bomb-bait will not be lacking for the next war soon to follow. To follow, that is, in twenty or thirty years, when the resultant kids are worth killing. You make more money and get more points in the history books for killing them when they're bigger. On the other hand, no one refuses any longer to kill women & children in their sleep, and by the tens and hundreds of thousands, as a patriotic duty. Duty calls: Kill them kids! Women and children first.

But really, young men are still the preferred kill, perhaps because the old men are jealous of their sexual potency and inevitable opportunities. Many old men are like that: when their pricks won't stand up anymore, they like to mow the young men down. Or even killing birds and animals will do. If they can no longer create life, they will create death. If you have a strong stomach, read the history of Aztec Mexico, which was a civilization dedicated in that way to death. Just like ours. That's the rule: *Old men, who know they must die soon, like to kill young men.*

The system is good, and has been working successfully for tens of thousands of years. No one ever complains — anyhow, not loud enough to change anything. They're too busy making money and going bowling. Or watching horror-movies and prize-fights on prime-time television, to maintain the peace of the world. Those who manage to survive get old and rich themselves, comparatively, and then send the next generation of their own children off to die, waving before them the banners of God, King, Country, Standard Oil, and most recently American Telephone & Telegraph. Each of these banners has had its centuries. And the rain it raineth every day. The twenty-first century will have its killing banner too. We don't know what it is yet. They haven't told us. They'll tell your children when the moment comes. But some of the disgusting bullshit you've already been trained to mouth is assuredly the wire on which the banner will be hung. Stay plugged in. Keep buying. Keep talking. The rain it raineth every day.

I used to meet all sorts & conditions of people very briefly then. Not just women. Some just that once, and some would turn up again on & off for years afterward in my life. Some were even turning up from years before. Like my friend Mel Cantor, who had first introduced me to, and then stolen back, the first girl I ever truly loved. Mel arrived in a very peculiar uniform. He was now an American army officer, but was for some reason wearing a French beret — but only indoors. He took it off when he was in the street.

I think he felt he was expressing in that way his solidarity with the Free French, who were a largely non-existent, non-fighting force dreamed up by a tank commander, General Charles De Gaulle, who after having fought the Germans briefly and been beaten at their first attack, spent the rest of the war in the best restaurants on Greek Street in London, writing fiery messages and directives of hope, faith and patriotism which were dropped by Allied aviators on the now-enslaved French population he had left behind. Mel truly thought De Gaulle was grand. I asked Mel about my lost love, Tia, of course, but he either couldn't or wouldn't give me any details.

With Mel was Elena, the never-to-be-forgotten sex dynamo of Ann Arbor, Michigan, now nearly ten years before, whom Mel had stolen from her husband and stuck with all this time. He had, however, gallantly allowed her to remain married all these same years to her original husband, who supported her unknowingly in whatever city Mel was, where she was always taking more and more advanced courses in philosophy or whatever her incredible soundtrack was by then. Mel had unquestionably enjoyed as much of her highly charged sexual offering and Oedipal fun as he either needed or wanted. He had now smartened up in his peculiar uniform, and was anxious to move on to someone else. As it happened — either on that move or the next — to a fairly rich heiress he now thought he had a chance to marry. He didn't tell Elena this, and although he didn't tell it frankly to me either, until later, he left me to understand that he was delivering the package — Elena — to my door, and that anything I wanted to do with it or her from then on was my business, not his. As Elena had been well into her thirties when we originally met her, and was now within sighting distance of the menopause, she seemed a bit old for me for me at my then age of twenty-seven. For him too. His leave now being over, Mel went back on duty, leaving Elena to me, forever.

I treated her as kindly as I could, and took her out to dinner several times, as I was now working again. The entire meal was in every case spent on her explaining and recounting to me lengthily all the intimate details of her liaison with Mel, since before the beginning, when she had already become disenchanted with her legal husband, now visiting Professor of Minor

Mathematical Functions at the University of Pittsburgh. I never did figure out why she thought I cared about all that complicated soap-opera crap. Maybe she thought it was seductive. More probably the poor thing didn't even know I was alive, and just needed somebody to tell her troubles to. She realized, of course, that Mel was ditching her, but couldn't admit it to herself yet. Or that her over-fruity sex magic just wasn't working.

One thing I avoided completely, though I was tempted to try it just once, was ever going to bed with her. I never even did more than kiss her hand, which I felt I owed to her European background. I saw that Mel had neatly picked me for the fall-guy, or sloppy seconds Leporello, on the basis of our former friendship. And I was even willing to let Elena cry on my shoulder briefly while Mel scurried on to his next erotico-financial arrangement. But I was certainly not going to let any emotionally wrecked and stranded sex-faker like that poor, frantic female passion-flower louse up my life. Elena had alienated her husband, and was now loosing her lover, and she was visibly ready to clamp on for dear life to whatever convenient chump would come next. It wasn't going to be me. Let her go back to her masochistic husband, I told myself — and her.

Meanwhile, I had really underestimated the crust of that guy Mel. As the heiress he was now softening up lived out of town, Mel was entertaining himself in New York, on his protracted leaves, with a *goyishe* young lady or White Anglo-Saxon Shicksa named Athena Besterman, whom he had picked up in the Museum of Modern Art to be sure. That's where we all went, ostensibly for the old Charlie Chaplin movies. Athena was more complex than she seemed, but to the external eye she looked like a cold-hearted, well-dressed college cupcake, or piece of goyishe ass, probably of good family. Mel was clearly resting up from Elena's still bubbling sexual Vesuvius in Athena's cooler embrace. While poor Elena was suffering the Hell of erotic withdrawal symptoms from her supply not only of stiff prick but of nourishing romantic illusions.

Mel introduced me to Athena, to be sure, picking a day when he was pretty sure that Elena wouldn't ketch us all, and I got the impression that he was intensely proud of having graduated at last from Jewish girls to his first authentically Christian *shicksa*. I found this strange, and yearned to tell him that there were two million Christian females in the city of New York alone, so it was not really such a remarkable trick as he seemed to imagine, to find a congenial soul amongst them. Why was he introducing us, I wondered. But I held my peace and said nothing, and played the part of the dumb, friendly pal that I thought was required of me. Mel had changed. He had hardened considerably. He was now full of empty, sentimental self-importance and was also oddly close-mouthed, like an underworld character planning a caper, or a theatrical producer looking to milk some generous money-angel and preparing to lay a really massive egg. The bouncy young world-changer who had been my friend was now among the missing.

It turned out I was not far wrong in my unvoiced suspicions. Mel was introducing Athena to me for the same reason he had *schlepped* Elena along. Namely, I was to get her off his neck too, under the now-standard pretense of taking care of the little woman while our heroic warrior was off fighting the war, like De Gaulle in London chop-houses. Actually, Mel was clearing the decks for action with his heiress, and wanted to come to her free & unencumbered. I mean, he didn't say so, but I could see he was worried about his prospective bride's butler bringing her in on a silver salver, one morning before the wedding was safely over, the usual anonymous letter in a large, angular feminine handwriting, signed *"One of the Former Victims of Your Fiancé."* That would be Elena's work, naturally. I couldn't see that Miss Besterman would do anything very dangerous, or even gave much of a damn about Mel personally. This raised her considerably in my estimation, though she was a rather thin girl with nondescript hair but plenty of brains. Basically a one-night-stand college type.

To tell the truth, I was getting kind of sore about Mel using me for an erotic trashbox, or snapper-up of sloppy seconds. I had only seen Mozart's Don Giovanni once, owing to high price of good seats and the atrocious badness of the cheap seats I could afford at the Metropolitan

Opera. But I still had a very clear memory of that long scene, done in masked disguise, in which Don Juan simply turns over to his valet, Leporello, the noblewoman and/or wife-of-his-bosom he is now tired of, and tells him pretty plainly to keep her busy for an hour or two, "courting" her — and even shows him how — while Don G. goes on to seduce his next tootsy, a chambermaid.

Mozart's librettist, Lorenzo Da Ponte, who was originally a Jewish tailor's son really named Emanuel Conegliano, had made himself a specialist in glozing over essentially scabrous situations like this one. At the opening of the opera, he pulls off the not inconsiderable feat of having the young soprano whom Don Juan has just raped before the curtain rises — a trick repeated in Richard Strauss' *Rosenkavalier* later, and how's that for sly? — describe to her chump of a fiancé the entire rape scene, ending with her father's murder, as he was trying to protect his daughter's lost honor, in a duel with that practised cock-and-swordsman Don Juan. All this she describes without ever mentioning even once that she has been raped, or similar; and also omitting to explain at all how the hell Don Juan got into her boudoir at midnight *in the first place.* She alleges that she thought it was the fiancé chump himself, climbing in her window for a sex sample. Her later great "Vendetta" aria, however, demanding vengeance for her seduction and her father's murder, is one of the most chilling in Mozart's whole opera repertory.

I think what bothered me the most was the implication that I was to play the valet Leporello to Mel's Don Juan, and tidy up his abandoned females — presumably picking up seconds with my prick, if I have to be franker about it than Da Ponte was — so that they Will Not Make A Fuss. Now that I began to think of it, was it possible that Mel even thought of himself as doing exactly that, and nothing else, when he had sort of bequeathed to me originally the one true love of my 'teens, Tia French!? Why, I'd kill the bastard! I'd tear him limb from limb! My Tia!? Sloppy seconds?! Where is he?! Well, he was off to War. My revenge would have to wait for his next leave, of which he somehow got marvellously many. He must have known where the general buried the body. No denying it, Mel was a smart cookie when it came to looking out for Number One. As for all the other people in his life — well, they were Number Two.

THAT WAS about the mood I was in when I found myself angled into taking out Athena Besterman for the first time, after Mel left. One thing I told myself was that I was positively going to lay her *the first night*, just like a college boy. If only to start getting some anatomical return on all this bereaved widow consoling I was doing for the well-established Spanish firm of Don Juan Cantor & Cia. Nothing could have been simpler. Although the last time I had seen Mel and Athena together, they were necking and embracing all over an armchair while I was presumably talking to them, I don't believe she ever mentioned him again more than once, when I came to pick her up.

I invited her to my room to hear my high-fidelity phonograph — which has it over the formerly-used Rops etchings and Persian hooked rugs in bachelor apartments, like the proverbial tent, believe me. Also, it's a lot harder for a girl to holler Rape! in your room than in hers. I knew Athena wouldn't do anything of the kind, but Mozart's soprano, or rather her father, was still on my mind. I kind of felt sorry for him. There are girls like that, you know, that like to get men fighting over them. I suppose they're really trying to match out the contenders for putative fatherhood of their eventual pups, to improve the breed genetically, as it were. But it's also possible that they're just cheap little female sadists, for whom watching men half-kill each other takes the place of sex. Or excites them to it. If you're the sort of slob that goes to bull-fights or prize-fights, you probably know that there are even more men like that than there are women. In fact, if you go there, you're probably one of them yourself.

Athena seconded my every initiative, as we sat on my bed listening to music, and I began to feel rather ashamed of my college boy insistence of laying her the first night. She was obviously no rape-crier, and was ready and willing to make love, and would probably take pride in doing it very competently. I thought I would slow down the pace, therefore, and pointed out we hadn't even eaten supper yet, which she found very droll. We went out and found a Chinese restaurant, and as it was then getting late after we had eaten, we wandered through Central Park and found a high, isolated rock-formation not too far away, on which we figured silently to be safe from peepers and other dangerous creeps.

"Open yourself up to the moon," I said pressing Athena's knees apart, when we got to the top of the rock and sat down. She was not wearing any panties, and we both stared pleasurably at her pussy shining in the moonlight with her legs spread wide. I touched her crack with one exploratory finger, showing her my mouth simultaneously in a promissory kiss.

"Let me see you too," she whispered, and took my prick & balls out, cupping them and pressing them to look at me erect and pearling in the moonlight. She bent forward and touched her tongue to my tip, to take off the pearl.

"Athena," I said diplomatically, as I thought I saw a movement somewhere down beyond our rock formation, "we won't be comfortable here at all. Let's go to your apartment and sleep in each other's arms all night."

"Oh yes!" she breathed Athena was very intense and serious about certain things and wanted to be passionate — very sincerely too, I believe. But she had a way of speaking about sex and during sex that reminded me awfully of the intellectually overwrought heroines in the novels of Thomas Hardy and Arnold Bennett, especially as satirized forever in Stella Benson's *Cold Comfort Farm*. Or more closely in one of Max Beerbaum's parodies under the name of "Euphemia Clashthought." Actually, that's rather unfair to Athena, but there's a definite resemblance. I want to be fair to her, because I owe her a lot.

That time, I steered Athena out of the park fast, in case the movement I saw in the dark meant we were being targeted by sex-peepers or other dangerous night elements. We took the subway back down to the Village, and isn't it a pleasure to read a book or see a movie where the impecunious young couple doesn't grab a fifteen-dollar taxi every ten minutes? Athena was staying on Greenwich Avenue in the apartment of some friends who were away. We were alone in the apartment, and made love very pleasantly all night and in various ways. Athena told me she was wearing a diaphragm and that we "didn't have to worry." I don't know how to say this without ungallantry, but she was somehow not very exciting to me. There was a lack of erotic tension about her lovemaking, perhaps owing to the diaphragm and the lack of danger, and a sort of studied theatrical quality to it, that made me feel very casual and artificial too. Athena knew everything and did everything, but it didn't jell. Of course, we didn't love each other either. That counts too, you know. But I'm pretty sure it was the diaphragm: no spice of danger for her? I don't know.

In the morning I could hear her bathing, and wandered into the bathroom which she had left open, to watch her. Athena washed all her body very carefully, and I came over and helped her soap her breasts for fun. Then she stood up, and with a somehow defiant air, and started washing her pussy, back to front, with a big loofa sponge. I wondered if maybe the reason she hadn't excited me was because she was too clean? The next guy would have the same trouble too, after so thorough a bath. Is it possible to be too clean? I guess it is. I think a girl should have a real marked pussy-smell. Some men claim not to like it, but every other male mammal follows the female by means of her vaginal spoor, so I don't see how we could possibly be different. In fact, most mammals have to lick the female's genitals, and really lap up that target odor before they can get excited enough to mount her or plough up against her. Even whales. I must be partly mammal.

We made breakfast, with a charmingly broken toaster where the toast kept falling in and burning. I love burnt toast! As long as it isn't really charred black. While I was burning the toast satisfactorily, Athena decided for some reason to explain to me how many lovers she had had since entering college. She mentioned all their first names — only — and counted in part on her fingers. Like cutting notches on guns. I was only the twelfth.

"Oh!" I said, very disappointed. "And thirteen is my lucky number. Couldn't I go round the corner, and come back after your next lover leaves?"

I imagined Athena saw she was making a mistake, if that was supposed to excite me in any sense, because she stopped. However, I then accompanied her uptown, again on the subway, as we were both going to 42nd Street, me to the Public Library, and Athena to do some shopping. We got on at the big Village station at West 4th, and as the train pulled away, a young man hailed Athena and they talked awhile. She introduced me vaguely, and when he got off after only a few stops, she gave me a strange, triumphant stare and said, "Number Eight!" And for this you need a college education?

After that, I didn't like Athena anymore, though I saw her again a few times. I was glad she hadn't asked me for my signet ring, or a tuft of my pubic hair. I haven't got a signet ring, anyhow. She must have been partly a witch, I now believe. That would explain her cold ass. They say witches have this compulsion to count things. Like office sadists making long, numbered lists and complex outlines and underlining things. If a witch chases you, all you have to do is empty a paper of pins or a box of matches across her path. Her inner witchiness forces her to stop and pick up and count every single one of them, and that gives you your chance to get away. So always carry pins or matches in big cities. You hear!? Athena was pretty certainly a witch. I'm not really for burning witches, you understand, but I also don't feel like getting burnt. Anyhow, the next time I saw her something happened which made me so furious that there was no chance of our going on together very long.

She came to my room this time to listen to music, and stayed over with me all night. In the morning I told her to stay in bed, and I'd go down and get us some Danish pastry at the bakery, and some oranges, and smuggle it all in and we'd have breakfast in bed. It wouldn't match the burnt toast and coffee we'd had at her place, but it would be nice. When I got back my door was wide open and Athena was standing there with my worn out blue bathrobe wrapped around her. She wasn't alone. Old Mr. Nossiter was kneeling on the floor by the hand basin in the corner, trying to fix something, and pestiferating fluently in Yiddish, a language I don't understand. But I did catch something, basically in German, about a black year, and everybody catching cholera if only God willed.

Athena had decided to take a finger-bidet, on taking her diaphragm out, and hoisted herself up to sit on the hand basin in the corner, which immediately tore loose from the wall and fell on the floor. She had the sense to get the faucet turned off somehow – it was apparently geysering in the air – and she then put on my bathrobe and went down to find the landlord so they could figure out what to do next. He was turning off some lower-down extra stopcock with a pair of pliers when I walked in, and was kneeling in the puddle on the floor.

Being in a total fury I put on my best air of glacial calm, crossed my arms, and suggested to Mr. Nossiter in a controlled and refined voice that we should let the young lady get dressed, whereupon the two of us would go out to breakfast, and perhaps he could get a plumber to fix the basin, which I would of course pay for. I then shoved him out of the room by main force — he wanted to stay and ask or be told for the fourth time just *why* Athena had wanted to sit on the sink — and I stood looking out the window while she got dressed behind me. If ever I wanted Artur Schnabel to start playing some scales across the back garden, this was the time, but there was nary a toot out of him. I kept my air of phoney calm all the way to the subway. Athena was very contrite.

"I know you're just furious," she said. "It was very stupid of me. That little man was so funny, wasn't he?"

"Like a crutch."

"Are you going to be mad at me forever now," Athena asked; "or will I be seeing you again?"

If it were on a vaudeville stage, I admitted to myself, I'd have found a slapstick scene like that pretty funny. So why was I so unreasonably angry about it? What did poor, prejudiced little

Mr. Nossiter matter in my life? I made a date with Athena to see her at the end of the week. Meanwhile she was going back for a few days to Connecticut where she lived, because the people whose apartment she was staying in were now coming home. The next time I saw her she'd be at another address. She'd phone me. She wouldn't be coming to West 76th Street. We'd be able to go to her place.

The new place was somewhere else in the Village, but not in the old part. It was in a modern apartment building, where a girlfriend of hers was simultaneously receiving her soldier boyfriend, who was on leave but hadn't arrived yet. While Athena and I sat in the cozy little parlor waiting for the soldier boyfriend to arrive, the girlfriend busied herself in her bedroom at the other end of the apartment, getting primped up. She was very sweet and sad-looking, and I had a fleeting and doubtless unworthy wish that I could trade with the soldier, sight-unseen. Athena wanted to know if I'd mind coming back there later, even though the other couple would be at the other end of the hall. She had evidently decided that I was peculiarly sensitive, since the comedy of the broken washbasin and finger-bidet. She was right, too, but I wasn't going to admit it.

"Not at all," I told her. "I used to live with two girls at once. Anyhow, all the weekends for a year."

"Did you really live with them?" she asked, intrigued.

"Yes," I said, "we all slept together in one bed. The other girl was a Lesbian. It's very interesting philosophically. Mathematically too. But I wouldn't do it again." I only added that last, which wasn't true, because she had such an intensely interested air. I recognized the symptom. Athena was a philosopher too. She had majored in Greek philosophy at Barnard, although maybe they didn't mention three-in-a-bed gymnastics in the usual textbook. Still, the Greeks had a word for everything — about sex, several hundred words — so they must have done it too. Isn't Lesbian a Greek word? How about pederasty? — clitoris? — orgasm? — all Greek. And philosophical? — Oh my!

After the four of us had dinner and came back, the sad-looking girl served us one fast nightcap in the parlor, and then she and her soldier practically raced down the hall together, waving us goodnight. They seemed to be in love with each other, and not at all happy about the long separations between his leaves. I know Juliet says to Romeo that parting is such sweet sorrow, but she's wrong. That's another one of those things that's more poetry than truth.

Athena and I settled down to some powerful necking on the sofa. I've often wondered why girls like kissing so much, but they do. Some of them can stand literal hours of it, where a man wants to start driving into their vagina after only a couple of kisses and some good tit-squeezing. I always had to hold myself back when I got in with one of those real dedicated kissers, and the only way I ever found to abbreviate it was to get my hand into her crotch at the same time. Lesbians must get part of their fame as long-drawn-out lovers — and much better than men at it, admittedly — from the fact that they're women too and adore lengthy preliminaries before lunging for the crotch. This eventually makes your normal woman willing to move on more often than not from some part of the kissing frenzy and the long, languorous tongue-sucking and spit-swapping, and either put the tongue elsewhere or just plain accept the shaft. But I still don't understand it too well. I know it has something to do with the connection and psychological development between the oral and genital stages, which I ought to be an expert about; but I always somehow loose track of my Freudian page-references when I'm actually there with a woman's more and more naked body flowering open under my lips and hands.

We pulled all the sofa pillows down onto the floor, and continued there, while the radio played some lovely music I did not know, all surging violins and throbbing heavier strings. And then a long, intimate, twining duet between strings and flute. This one time I was praying inside that the announcer would interrupt and tell up what the piece was, but it was their "Music to Love By" program of discreetly unannounced classics at ten or eleven p.m. and he never said a mumberling word. It's just my private Lost Chord. I know it wasn't the Mozart Sinfonia Concertante. Years later I ran into the Triple

Concerto for Strings, Flute and Orchestra, by Bach, which I suspect was it — it's Number 1044 in the Bach listings — but I can't be sure.

Anyhow, I listened to it as in a dream, kissing and fingering Athena the whole while, as though she were the cello and I were the bow, and she became so hot that I took fire myself, when I could sense all her deepest female odors rising. I felt a little ashamed too — I realized I had not prepared her long enough the other times, and that is why she had been so antiseptic. Now she was burning, and begging for it with her body, one leg thrown over my hip and the other stretched wide the other way. In the half-dark I could see her like a big, upside-down letter Y. But I pitilessly played every note of the music on her body, and only finally rolled over, under her uplifted leg, and insinuated my prick into her as teasingly slowly as I could, when the music ended and became something else. It's the Lost Chord.

Somewhere, though, the beautiful music did not soothe this savage breast or beast in me, and I made love to Athena as though I were revenging myself on her for some unknown slight. I turned her every which way, and rammed her most of the night; and first she was ravished and then she was ravaged and begged me to stop, but I wouldn't. I did not come very often, and did not want to. I just wanted to keep driving and pillaging at her, and lifting her legs and bending her up like a wishbone while I kept ploughing and plunging into her and sinking my prick angrily deep, with a sound like the *chunk* of chopping down a tree as our pubic hair and share-bones struck together time after time. Finally, while we were making some square-dancing cross jostle from one position to another, and I was slapping Athena lightly and silently on the ass to direct her motions, her diaphragm got displaced and bothered me when I went in again. So I just reached in with two crooked fingers and snatched it out. I had thought Athena was floating away somewhere on a cloud of oversatisfied passion, but she was suddenly complete conscious again, and panicked when she felt me taking out her diaphragm. Now she really tried to fight me away.

"Don't worry about it," I grunted. "I'm buggering you this time." And that was what I did. And to my surprise, as I sank my prick like a poisoned tusk *à la* Norman Mailer into the tissues of her ass, which were fortunately so lubricated with sweat on the outside that I didn't tear either of us too badly, I could hear as though it were an inner voice trilling inside me, in a rough but constricted tone I knew was not my own: *"Busting the goddam sink!!"* And I knew then that I hated her, and that it was all just pelvic revenge, for that totally unimportant affront to my dignity.

In the morning the other girl and her soldier did not make an appearance. They had a double bed to sleep in, and we had only the cushionless sofa and the floor, where we did sleep tangled till morning, with some small throw I pulled over us for a cover. Athena went out into the kitchenette and brought me back toast with marmelade. I dressed munching it, and told her I'd be glad to wait while she made us a real breakfast, if there were any eggs.

"Yes," she agreed. "You deserve a real breakfast." While we ate, Athena kept staring off absently to one side, as though she weren't quite awake yet, or were trying to remember something. Of course I offered her a silver penny for her thoughts. And she answered, with obvious sincerity but in her most perfect Euphemia Clashthought tone: "I was just remembering a certain blessèd rock in Central Park." Then, almost without a pause, "You do really need two women, don't you?"

I could see I was just being flattered, but I loved it. I could also see sadly how enormously differently Athena had understood and experienced the night before from what I knew it had really been. We were living out the story of the giant Marseilles dockworker who hates his wife because she's a sloppy housekeeper, and decides to kill her by making love to her till she's totally passed out on the bed. When he comes home the next day, instead of finding her dead, she's preparing a chicken dinner for him, dressed only in high heels, two hair-combs, and a tiny apron, and the house is spotlessly clean. "What's going on?!" he asks. "Well," she says, wriggling her buttocks provocatively from side to side, "you treat me right, and I'll treat you right."

But Athena was not as dumb as she looked. That's just a phrase: she didn't look dumb at all, and wasn't. A little later, also apropos of nothing, she added, "we're really worlds apart, aren't we? I have a friend I want you to get to know, named Beverley. I went to college with her. She's been in Mexico until now. You'll love Beverley. She's just like you."

A FEW days later, when I came home from the library late, my throat felt dry and I wanted something with bubbles in it — maybe Seven-Up, a lemon soda I'd begun drinking in summer. All the cola drinks had so much caffeine in them that they kept me awake and peeing the whole first half of the night. I took a dollar out of my wallet, which I left in the drawer, and ran downstairs to the candy story on Columbus Avenue. As I was turning south now, I saw the moon, which had been in back of me when I came home from the subway at 72nd Street. It tempted me and I began walking. I was still working weekends on *Taboo*, and I like to compose walking, though I generally loose half of it by the time I get back to where there's a pencil & paper. I walked up to the park entrance and went in. Nobody would peep on me tonight, as I was alone. And I wouldn't peep on anyone else, either. Let 'em have their fun! Hard enough to find a bit of green to make love on in New York, as it is.

As I was walking along somewhere by the band-shell, two park cops, but dressed in brown instead of blue, stopped me. It was good to see some cops in the park at night, I figured, and answered their questions cheerfully. Why was I in the park at that hour, and so forth? Their last question stumped me, though: "Where's your draft card?" I had left it at home in my wallet.

"All right, mack," one of them said to me; "come along with us."

They took me to a small, long stone building almost unnoticeable along the edge of the crosstown artery passing through the park. It was apparently the office of the air-raid and blackout wardens. New York naturally hadn't ever been air-raided, but there had been lots of propaganda fun all through the war, with blackout regulations, and officious wardens with armbands. These two characters, whom I had taken for cops, were really blackout wardens. They told me I would have to wait there for the F.B.I. to come and get me for not having a draft card.

"I do have a draft card," I assured them again. "But I left it in my wallet at home when I came out for a walk."

"Well, we're not going looking for it," one of them said nastily. "So just shut up and wait here." Obviously they liked to show their authority when they were on their home grounds.

They walked over and began interrogating another young man, who had similarly been brought in. There were altogether only four of us, two of them hardly more than boys. One of them made some answer the wardens didn't care for, and to my astonishment one of the wardens grabbed a small black rubber club — very small and odd-looking — out of his back pocket , and struck the boy across the side of the neck with it in a sudden evil stroke. The boy staggered back, but caught himself against the wall, and tried to put on a sneering, contemptuous grin, as though to say he hadn't been hurt.

His defiance seemed to infuriate the two wardens, and now both of them leapt at him with their small black clubs, and started battering him over the head with them in a perfect hail of violent blows. In a moment the kid was rolling on the floor. One of the wardens then bent over him and gave him an extra, particularly hard slam on the head with his little club. The boy did not move. They left him there, and one of the wardens went over to write something down on the sheets of paper they had been filling out, concerning each of us, on the desk. Doubtless to add the remark that this poor kid had been "Resisting Arrest," or "Fell Against Door." The other warden stood looking at the rest of us draft-cardless prisoners, his mouth twitching slightly.

"Anybody else wanna argue with this sap?" he inquired darkly, giving his little black rubber club a whirl like an Irish cop. None of us spoke or moved. Welcome to our air-raid shelter.

Then the F.B.I. came, which really meant just an ordinary paddy-wagon that took us somewhere downtown to F.B.I. headquarters. We sat on benches in a hall with a wire grating closing it off, and a guard sitting outside. We sat there all night. In the morning early the F.B.I. arrived. Two rather beefy individuals eventually took me into an office with them, and got my name and address, paying no attention whatever to all the same information on the sheet in front of them, which the wardens had made out and sent along with me. One of them made a phone call, while continuously staring at me as he phoned, as if he was sure I was going to pull a knife or jump out of the window, or I don't know what. He said my name & address into the phone, and was evidently told my draft status. "Uh-huh," he said, and wrote it down.

I gave him a small, very discreet smile, assuming I would now go home. Instead he pulled out a new sheet of paper, and started filling it out in much greater detail, asking me a whole mess of futile questions. I answered all of them with helpfulness and alacrity. It seemed possible that he too might have a little rubber sap — guaranteed to leave no inconvenient marks and draw no blood — in his back pocket. I didn't care to find out. His questions also rather surprised me, since he now was aware that I had properly fulfilled all the draft regulations. Did I smoke? — No. Did I drink? — No. — Did I smoke marijuana? — Never. — What were my politics? — Democrat. — Church affiliation? I thought this had a charming democratic sound, instead of crudely "Race?" or "Religion?" as in Germany. — "Jewish," I replied.

He gave me rather a sour look at that, and turned to look briefly at the girl typist who had come in and was sitting at her desk.

"Come 'mere," he said to me. He got up and led me out into the hall, and shut the door. "You a masturbator?" he asked in a heavy undertone.

"Well not in recent years," I replied, a little stunned at the care the F.B.I. was taking about my moral status.

I was then let go. When I asked if he could give me some sort of temporary document, in case I was picked up again while going home to get my draft card, he just smiled nastily.

"Nah. If they pick you up again," he said, "we'll see you again."

Nobody picked me up again. I tried to think it all over on the subway ride uptown, and walking along the parkside home. I couldn't arrive at any decision. It had been a strange, ugly night and morning, though very banal perhaps. I thought most about what the Negro boxer, Joe Louis, had been reported in the press as saying, when a disguised pro-German group trying to split the Negro loyalty for obvious purposes, but under some pro-Negro pretense, had asked him to join their organization. "There's lots of things wrong with America," Louis said, "but Mr. Hitler ain't going to fix 'em."

Another night, as I walked west on 42nd Street to the subway at Eighth Avenue on leaving the library, studying the strange, half-criminal pullulation that got worse and worse as one went west, I ran into a stocky little book scout I knew, named Seymour Hacker, whom I remembered seeing several times a few years before on Fourth Avenue downtown. He would find junk books contributed to the Salvation Army on the Bowery, and push them up to Fourth Avenue in a pushcart to sell at some small profit there in job lots. He was in a blue uniform now, and told me he was in the merchant marine, just back from Europe. This was the biggest moment of the Lend-Lease supplies to England and Russia, and the backing up of the convoys now by other ships and naval destroyers meant there was no longer much danger of being sunk by German submarine wolf-packs. But the pay was still wonderfully high, as it had been at the beginning, when thousands of sailors and merchant-mariners had been sent to the bottom for shark-food by the torpedoes, or been coolly machine-gunned in their lifeboats by the submarine captains surfacing to have the good German carnival fun of picking off the helpless men like salt fish in a herring-barrel with the deck cannons.

There were now also lots of opportunities for an alert naval officer to pick up some cushy slices of side-money at the European end. The Allied convoys were bringing in enormous logistic supplies — especially of cigarettes, Hacker said with his hard little tooth-baring laugh — to *back the attack*. That was the current propaganda slogan, meaning the mock-military tug-o'-war and graceful ballet entertainments from El-Alamein to Bizerte and back, with the German troops under Rommel in North Africa, guaranteed not to have any effect whatsoever on the war in Europe while the main German army bled the Russians to death, as promised for decades in Hitler's *Mein Kampf*, while Churchill smiled and held up two plump fingers for the news cameras in the V-for-Victory gesture to the opening notes of Beethoven's Fifth.

Like everything about Churchill, this gesture had two sides. It meant *Victory!* the way the public saw it from the front, and *Fuck you!* The way the Russians saw it from the fingernail side in back. Those endless four notes, *Pom-pom-pom-POMMMM!!* — of "Destiny knocking on the door" in every newsreel — only meant victory from the propaganda or front side. From the back, or Potemkin-village side, those same four notes meant the nice long three-year stage wait. From Dunkerque till the landings on the beaches in France, while Hitler hammered the pre-destined nails into Communist Russia's coffin. *Pom-pom-pom-POMMMM!!*

And now the billion-dollar convoys of supplies were preparing to back up the carefully delayed but eventually necessary Allied landings in southern Italy and in France. Hacker and I had a soda together standing at the counter at

Grant's and we watched the marvellous ballet motions of the nightman who specialized in making malted milkshakes. It was better theatre than Rommel.

Hacker told me about some of his experiences in Europe, especially in Naples, as I remember, where you had to guard the ship day and night after docking, or the Neapolitans would steal everything on board. There was a joke or rumor that they had dismantled an entire battleship, while the sailors were ashore, whooring it up and drunk, and then sold all the parts back to the U. S. Navy for repairs on other ships. He was full of great stories, and we wandered around for a long while talking. I asked him if he missed his bookscouting, and he told me with a laugh that there were no books in America *at all*. Europe was the place for books.

Afterward, Hacker took me to his place though the hour was very late. He had something to show me, he said, that would make me laugh. He was staying with his mother, he said, in an apartment building near Grammercy Park, very close to Magdalen's old apartment where I had lived those months with Susan. Hacker told me it was his family's place — he lived nowhere now, as he was mostly on the ships. What he wanted to show me was a tiny little crudely-tinted photograph, in a cheap metal filigree frame, showing an incredibly fat old prostitute sitting in a chair with one leg flung happily out to the side, to show her tired-looking crotch. He found this in Europe somewhere and considered it excruciatingly funny, and had brought me all the way from Times Square to show it to me; so I tried to squeeze out a laugh but couldn't. It was one of the most pathetic photos I had ever seen.

"It doesn't make me laugh," I told him. "It makes me cry."

"Which is the same thing," Hacker finished, laughing, and showing his top teeth in an aggressively chilling way. I didn't see him again after that until a year or two later, when the war was over.

ATHENA phoned me up to invite me to a little party, where she wanted me to meet the girl she had told me about, named Beverley Keith.

"It won't really be a party at all," she said. "Just four people." And she gave me the address, on Grove Street in the Village, just west of Seventh Avenue. I wondered if *four people* meant that she was now up to Lover Number Thirteen — lucky fellow — and that I would be Beverley's blind date, or what?

It turned out that I was still Number Twelve, and that the other fellow was Beverley's informal boyfriend. He was quite interesting to talk to, and was working on some kind of project at Columbia. He was a mathematician, but not the cold kind — very interested in the philosophical aspects of physics and the remotest history of the planetary system. We talked about Fibonacci, and I told him about Legman's Law for finding the number of surfaces of a tesseract of any number of dimensions. We both laughed over this, and its only practical applications, but could not explain to Athena why it was funny when she asked.

Beverley sat quietly and said nothing. She brought a few little plates of cookies and things, which she set down near everybody, and munched some cookies herself. She was small and slight, with dark brown hair, and a strange soulful face. She looked about like the pictures the papers had been full of at the time of the invasion of Italy, showing beggar children and street-thieves pretending to be shoe-shine boys, all with enormous staring eyes, very hungry. Beverley had those same eyes.

The apartment was upper middle-class, and nicely furnished with antiques. It was her mother's apartment, it appeared. Her mother was away for a month. Beverley had been living in Mexico for two years and had just come back. She said we could have coffee, or cocoa if we wanted. In Mexico people drank a lot of cocoa and had a special way of making it. I chose cocoa, and went out in the kitchenette to watch her make it in the special way. She had a strange long Mexican wooden spoon, that was more like a top ending at the bottom in a sort of engraved hollow egg, which she whirled between her palms as the cocoa heated, to make it froth. I asked her how it was different from an egg-beater, and if it made the cocoa better.

"No," Beverley said, "it's not better. But it's more beautiful."

After about an hour, the mathematician boyfriend said he had to leave, because they were very strict about keeping regular hours on his project at Columbia. I didn't see any way of staying on after he would be gone, and did not really want to sleep with Athena again. I had assumed the set-up was to be the same as with the earlier sad-looking girl and her soldier boyfriend, but clearly that wasn't it at all since the other man was leaving. Athena urged me to stay a while longer, but there didn't seem to be any point. Anyhow, I wanted to talk more to this mathematician, on the way to the subway. He was already waiting for the elevator. I shook hands with both women, and thanked Beverley for the cocoa. When she turned back down the hall to the parlor, Athena brushed against me and pushed her face up to mine for a kiss.

"I want to see you again," she said.

The elevator arrived, and I left with the mathematician. We got interested in something we were arguing about, and decided to walk up to Fourteenth Street to get the subway express, instead of taking the local there at Sheridan Square. We still hadn't solved things when we got to Fourteenth Street, so we continued up to the next express stop, which I think was at Twenty-third Street. And so on the Thirty-

Fourth, Forty-Second, Fifty-Ninth, and then we walked up along the park side as far as the Planetarium and the Museum of Natural History, which was already two blocks past where I lived. I told him he'd have to turn west now, to Broadway, to get his subway, and we said goodnight. It had been a very interesting conversation, and I hoped privately that I would meet him again. I never did. I know it's my own fault, but I've never had many men friends, and practically none whom I liked or respected.

ATHENA called me again early in the morning. "Beverley has something very interesting she brought from Mexico," she said. "How about coming to supper with us tonight?" I said I'd come. It wasn't really much fun spending all my evenings in the Public Library, and I figured, what the hell? I assumed vaguely that Athena had some idea of setting up a trio evening and that Beverley was probably some former half-lesbian partner from her college days. Athena had certainly been intrigued by my telling her about the trio ménage I'd lived in with Magda and Susan. I'd said I'd never do it again, but nobody ever knows, when it comes to sex.

Old Mr. Nossiter had been puttering around on the stair-landing while I was on the phone. When I hung up he crossed his arms and looked at me sharply, plucking an imaginary little beard.

"That's the same guyl that broke the sink, ain't it?" he asked, having recognized the voice when he answered the phone. I admitted that's who it was. "Some *shicksas* you know!" he said, with an imploring gesture of his eyes toward heaven. Rather than continue taking the comedy of the finger-bidet and broken sink tragically, I preferred to tease him about it.

"So you see," I told him, "there's different kinds of *shicksas*. Miss Fenner wasn't so bad, was she? Maybe I should have married her."

"Don't marry no shicksas!" he warned me in terror, but hopelessly. "A young boy like you with all those books!" He went back into his apartment, where I could see old Mrs. Nossiter reading the newspaper sitting on a small sofa set in the exact center of the room. He was already telling her that the *sink-breakner* girl had phoned and would doubtless be arriving in the night to strike again. I didn't disillusion him. Let 'em stew!

The interesting thing Beverley had brought back from Mexico turned out to be a very small packet, made of a folded-up sheet of airmail paper, containing about half a dozen marijuana cigarettes. This surprised me greatly, as she seemed to me the exact opposite of the kind of person who would smoke tea. It turned out she never had. She had been living in Oaxaca with an Indian family — not out in the brush or anything quaint, but in a small town apartment, actually half of a frame house. They liked her and she liked them. When she left, one of the daughters gave her the packet, more as a joke than anything else. Beverley said that marijuana was not considered disgraceful in Mexico, and all the children sang a little song about it, concerning a cockroach that's so konked-out from smoking it he can't walk straight.

"Everybody sings it," she said. "That and *Guadalajara*."

She spoke, as always, slowly and in a rather low voice, and even my untrained eye had already noticed that she was deeply depressed. Now that I thought about it, she had reason to be depressed if her boyfriend preferred to walk halfway across New York talking cosmological mathematics with me, instead of staying overnight with her.

After supper was cleared away, which was not any exotic Mexican food but a tiny pork roast that Athena had brought and served, we sat and listened to music on the radio. We also ate up a box of little round chocolate-covered mints I brought as my contribution to the evening. When the mints were gone, we had Mexican cocoa, and I tried to learn to work the wooden spindle spoon that was to froth it up, but didn't get it working very well. No froth. After the cocoa was drunk up Athena proposed that we should all smoke the marijuana. I said I had tried it before and it wasn't very interesting. I didn't want to admit that it always made me throw up, and therefore had very little effect on me. But Athena's eyes were shining, and I could see it was her idea of a real thrill she had somehow missed at college. Beverley expressed no opinion.

Athena was telling me over the cocoa about some of the droll aspects of Barnard College, at Columbia, where both she and Beverley had gone. Once a year, in the spring, they had Greek games, a sort of private college Olympics. But not really athletic in nature. More artistic and idealistic. The whole class, or as many of the girls who could be convinced to partake, would dance in patterns to flute music, in flowing Greek gowns, very transparent " — But with nice solid panties underneath?" I interrupted, already mocking. "Isadora Duncan never wore panties."

"Oh, yes, panties," Athena admitted. "Very much so. We were forbidden to smoke in the halls, too. Weren't we, Bev?"

Beverley agreed with a nod. She was smoking an ordinary cigarette with her cocoa. She had not ever taken any part in the games or any other college activities except going to classes, which she said were all very dull except Greek primitive philosophy. Athena told me the rest about the Greek games, which were irreverently known to the girls as the Trash-Can Races, because the grand climax consisted of a group of large galvanized tin trash-cans hand painted with Greek fret designs and mounted on wheels to represent chariots, being dragged across the stage — really the gymnasium, which is a left-over Greek idea too, isn't it? Most of the girls would do the pulling, while selected others, dressed in Greek gowns of a slightly different color, with fillets holding back their hair, and ribbons crossed tightly over their breasts, would stand in the trash-can chariots holding reins made of ribbons, and drive their college-girl steeds in the direction of a large, hidden, offstage ventilating fan, set up vertically like an airplane propeller, which would blow everyone's Greek gowns backward to give the effect of speed.

BARNARD GREEK GAMES

"Did you sing meanwhile?" I asked. "That's all that's missing." Oh yes, they did sort of sing; wordless surgings of shapeless melody like Debussy's *Nuages* and *Sirènes*. Only the girls who pulled the chariots sang or chanted. The girls who drove the chariots didn't sing, but held the reins in one hand, and held the other clenched upward behind their heads, leaning backward slightly in a Greek attitude representing speed, or pride, or I don't know what. Athena had been one of the drivers, of course. I could just see her, with the ribbon fillets in her hair streaming back in the wind of the ventilating fan, as her face proudly lifted in her purest Euphemia Clashthought expression.

Then she came back to the matter of the marijuana cigarettes. She really wanted to smoke them. They had wise women in Greece, didn't they, called pythonesses, who inhaled the toxic vapors over volcanic rifts in caves, and went into trances and could foretell the future. Athena know all about this, and opined she'd like to become a pythoness too. I just knew she was a witch. Marijuana would do it, wouldn't it? she asked. I told her I doubted it, but said that if they wanted to smoke the stuff I would take one too, and stand by to make sure they didn't do anything foolish.

"Do people do foolish things when they smoke this," Athena asked, rather eagerly. "I thought they just had visions."

"I should think becoming a pythoness is pretty foolish," I ventured. "Why do you want to foretell the future?" I told them they would have to inhale very deeply, and hold the smoke down a while to get any effects. I carefully did not do so, but just stood by at the window pretending to smoke my stick, while they lit up and puffed and sucked away assiduously on the couch.

It seemed to have no effect on Beverley, who I realized was already a hardened tobacco smoker. And at her age too! Athena started floating off almost at once, and kept coming back to her stick with very deliberate motions of her hand and mouth, to inhale more. She dinched the stick, and I lit another for her. The refined oral sexuality of smoking became clearer and clearer at every puff she took, with her mouth forming first into a sucking kiss and then into greedy not-very-mock fellation. Between puffs she held a refined half-smile unchanging on her face. I was embarrassed to see her mask so lop-sided, and wondered what was happening to her behind that frozen smile.

How far back would she go, I wondered, just on two sticks of marijuana, as ontogeny would repeat phylogeny? Miss Clashthought turning first into a Vestal Virgin, no doubt. The fake smile was the Virgin part, and the greedy sucking would be the after-hour lesbian orgies in the temple. Or maybe that was the main thing the temple was for. And then where to? Back to the angry Elektra, surely. But not Clytemnestra, the murderess-mother that Elektra kills, I hoped. And then? I knew Athena was deeper than she looked. How prehistoric would she get? But she surprised me with her next gesture.

Slowly rising from the couch, and carefully laying down her still smoking stick in the ashtray, Athena floated past me as I stood by the window, and to the telephone, her half-smile beautiful on her face. She dialled and waited. So did I.

"Hello?" she said. "Police? This man has given us drugs to smoke, and now he's trying to rape my best friend."

I didn't wait to hear her give the latitude & longitude, but dived for the phone base and clicked the cradle off.

"Hello?" Athena was still saying. "Hello?" Then seeing me close to her, holding down the phone, she raised the telephone receiver high, like Queen Victoria posing as Empress of India and Pythoness of Greece, and brought it down with a hell of a slam on what should have been my head — but I ducked. She did get me on the shoulder, which hurt for several months afterward. I remember thinking as it connected, "Thank God it's my left shoulder! It won't ruin my sex life." I'm right-handed. If she'd got me on the head she'd probably of killed me.

I got a good grip on her with my right arm and sat her down. "Take it easy, Athena," I said caressingly. "Things are not what they seem." I don't know why, but I wasn't a bit mad at her, as I had been over the broken sink. I guess you forgive people easier for unveiling their layers deeper down. The further down and the further back you get, the less it's anybody's fault.

Beverley was not particularly under the influence, and helped me calm her. Then Beverley went and made coffee, which I hoped would bring everybody's heads back where they should be. I was so perfectly calm and collected myself that I totally overlooked the burning marijuana stick, which had fallen to the floor in the struggle and was starting a fire in the carpet. But I caught that in time, and stamped it out. After we had coffee and calmed down a while, nobody seemed to remember anything. I told them both to go to sleep in the bedroom at the other end of the hall, and I vigilled on the sofa in the parlor, by the phone. I didn't sleep too soundly the rest of the night. Something told me Athena might wake up and try to phone the police again. I don't really mind pythonesses foretelling the future. It's that snakey part that bothers me. Nothing is anybody's fault, of course, but I knew for sure that I'd never piss up her ass again if she was dying of thirst. Some *shicksas* I know!

This little incident bothered me for quite a long time. It nagged me because I couldn't really understand it. Even if I had planned to see Athena anymore, I wouldn't have bothered to try to find out how she explained it. She had stated her case. It must certainly have had several levels. The obvious one is impossible: that I had been so aggressively virile with her at our last encounter that she was sure that I was going to rape them both. Or her best friend rather than her — thus jealousy too. That would be flattering to believe, but I don't believe it.

The next level down, or up, satisfied me for a long time: that she had wanted to set up a trio orgy, and then panicked for some reason. Well, it seems positive to me that she wanted to set up a trio. She had given me half a dozen hints, all of which I've carefully dredged up from memory, and tried to put life on their bones in the preceding pages in proper form. Then why did she panic? She was a girl with a string of lovers on her trophy belt, and she owned two diaphragms — that's one for Sundays, I guess. Could she really begrudge her best friend a little bit of sexual attention too?

In the end that was all too simplistic because it didn't answer the real question: Why was she phoning the police for help? What was the danger she thought she faced from me? The answer only came clear to me a number of years later, when my best friend in Paris, Jeff, tried several times to set up exactly parallel situations which would have logistically ended with the two of us in bed with one girl or another, always picked for her total pansexuality. And to her we were to make love at various ends, obviously staring deep into each other's eyes meanwhile. In other words, Jeff and I were to make love to each other, in a cryptic homosexual way, using the girl's torso as sexual stalking-horse — a sort of yard-long, quasi-human fornication sleeve, at the two ends of which Jeff and I would be shooting our unconsciously homosexual sperm at each other. But, would it be unconscious?

I understood this type of situation perfectly, and always refused it, sometimes rather desperately, as will be seen. It just never occurred to me at first that Athena might be an unconscious lesbian too, at her moments. And that in finally setting up an erotic trio with the best friend she had loved a long time, the part reserved for me — proud, powerful, superphallic me, with half a yard of foreskin hanging well below my knee! — was merely that of a fucking-stick, or ancient Grecian double-headed dildo, for two ashcan-racing Vestal Virgins to make use of in their corybantic mood.

Never! Everybody knew that if you were in bed with two girls or ten, they were all there for you, and you used them as you wished. Cock-a-doodle-doo!! You were not there for them, let alone to be the mere diddle-stick of their lesbian cohabitation, owing to some little anatomical problem of linking that you were stupidly outfitted to solve. My vanity as a man did not allow me at first to see how similarly Athena was setting me up to the way Jeff later tried to set up his little Indonesian girlfriend in Paris, who just wanted to give her friends pleasure, and then the horrid beautiful German girl who said she wanted to make up for what the Germans had done to the Jews by her more-than-total sexual subservience, which her *Hitler-Jugend* training had in fact taught her would be "defiling her blood."

And then, the first time, when the whole thing had been arranged just the way Athena — let us say unconsciously — wanted it, with the packet of Mexican marijuana accidentally on hand, to make it that much easier for her to cop out on any moral responsibility she still might feel, it nevertheless was not possible for her to let the truth of what she wanted come up out of her pythonic depths and face her, fang-naked: that she wanted a lesbian affair, or at least a taste of one. And that I was simply to be Dumb Juan, the ball-bearing anchorman, who would sort of lie brawly in the middle, to support the squirming, sperming triangle on his pecker-head, while the feminine vectors kissed. Or whatever else they might want to do. Well, why not? Pretty ancient stuff, that. But Athena had looked hard at me in her daze of almost self-recognition, and decided that it was me, not her, who was the Paradisiacal snake, and intrusive penis. And so she pulled the alarm switch and phoned the cops, to prevent me from "raping her best friend."

As to Beverley and me, even at best Athena's pythonic prognostication proved wrong. Beverley was surely not like me at all. In fact, we were as different as day & night, except that we were both somehow total outcasts and non-partakers at the world's feast. Meaning, I guess, that people assumed our cue was to try to solace each other. Which we did. As to loving her, I was never really able to love Beverley as I would have wanted to, and I tried very hard. What's the use of that? You can't force it. Love is total. If you don't feel it, why lie? It's very much like shooting a gun: there's no sense saying you've pulled the trigger only nine-tenths of the way, or ninety-nine hundredths, or even nine million, nine hundred and ninety-nine ten-millionths. If you can't pull it *all the way*, and especially that damnable, impossible, unavailable last ten-millionth that makes the sudden blistering electrical flame flash out and envelope you, then you're not in love at all. You can call it affection, closeness, fondness, Togetherness — anything you can bear to call it, even a "meaningful relationship." And of course it can be lots of sex. But it can't be love.

THE ONLY steady work I was able to find, after hitting rock bottom as a water-boy, was book cataloguing, which must be the bottom of the intellectual professions, I would think, though few other people agree. I've done a lot of it. You copy down on a small oblong piece of cardboard what it says on the title page of a book, or a thousand books, also marking down very precisely the number printed on the last numbered page. That's essentially all there is to it, and if your employer — head librarian, bookseller or collector — should catch you lingering over or, God forbid, actually *reading* any of the pages between the title page and that last fateful numbered page, you're likely to be fired very soon for soldiering on the job. If you add to your cardboard index-cards any random notes or details as to what the book is all about, or concerning the author or what century or literary current he belonged to or fought, your enlarged activity is usually referred to elegantly as bibliography. This for some reason pays even less than book cataloguing, so most cataloguers carefully avoid it. It takes a little more trouble, and as I admit, for some invisible reason diminishes your income, but it's really the only part of the work that's any fun at all, or was to me.

Oh, yes. You also have to arrange all the hundreds or thousands of small pieces of cardboard you then end up with in alphabetical order, usually by the authors' last names as in a telephone directory. This is work for intellectual giants. It can also now be done automatically by computers, if you're plugged in to all the necessary and very expensive machines, which not all of us are. I made my living at this kind of work for years in America, with a pad of index-cards, whenever I couldn't find any ghost-writing to do, another anonymous and ancillary literary profession usually considered one step up from the bottom. The presumed bottom being the writing of pulp-magazine stories and pornography, the first of which I unsuccessfully tried and the second of which I did.

As to my signed and serious books, it may surprise the reader to learn that I never made even the barest living, or in fact any reasonable amount of cash money, out of a single one of the books I wrote or edited, during the first twenty years after their publication. Very few authors ever do, despite or perhaps because of the heartbreakingly brief period of newspaper or other media publicity given to any book — even to bestsellers, which seldom last more than a few months — by the canny publishers. These gentry have, after all, many other books on their lists to publicize too, and generally claim or pretend to spend five or even ten percent of every book's retail price on publicity for it.

I don't know for sure about other author's books, though I have some well-informed suspicions, but *none of my books have been advertised in the public prints or media at all.* Not one, and not once. All my publishers without exception have been either too cheap or too impoverished — or maybe too ashamed — to advertise my books, though they do sometimes carry them in their house catalogues for a brief period. Some of these poor fellows have been millionaires. How many millionaire authors are there?

The average yearly income of professional writers in America — and it's less in Britain, where the intellectual competition is very much fiercer owing to less cash flow — has been coldly assessed by the Department of Labor as significantly less than that of non-union plasterers. As to the best-selling authors you hear about, and the highly-profitable movie-rights deals they make, any author's chances of writing a best-seller and selling it to the movies thereafter are a great deal less than what insurance company statisticians feel is your chance of being hit by lightning. Think it over. I have.

Meanwhile, a lowly book cataloguer or ghost-writer, *if* he can find steady work, is engaged in a reasonable and mathematically rational profession that will support him very nicely. The problem is getting the steady work. This I was never able to do, and still can't unless I want to catalogue my own library, now numbering 24,000 beautiful books mostly in English and French, at a salary of $0.00 per week, month and year, something I'm still planning to do. Or I may have to exploit my wife to do it — she's a trained librarian — at the same astronomical wage. Years of work there.

On one of my regular phone calls to the Academy of Medicine, to find out if any of Dr. Dickinson's research projects would be taking up again, and if so when, the secretary told me that a Dr. Benjamin on Park Avenue, to whom I'd been recommended by Dickinson over a year before, had called to ask where he could find me. He had a cataloguing job to do. I was shaved and moderately respectable-looking and there before noon. Dr. Benjamin was able to see me briefly after his last morning appointment, just before going to lunch. I would like to be able to say that I impressed him so much with my unusual knowledge of European sexological books, bibliophily, and paramedical subjects generally, that he invited me to lunch with him at the Waldorf-Astoria, but that's not exactly what happened.

Dr. Harry Benjamin was a European sexologist who transferred to America at a time when sexology was not yet understood to exist as a proper profession, though the extermination of rats and roaches has always been so considered. He therefore founded his American practice, instead, as a urologist, or specialist in the diseases of the uro-genital organs, which was his main area of competence. Dr. Benjamin was not, however, a clap-doctor in any vulgar sense, but was basically concerned with sexual problems, and at the beginning gave much more helpful advice to his patients than many accredited psychotherapists ever do. I don't know how good the advice was, but it was very permissive, and he had a very nice practice. Later, however, Benjamin became oddly interested in transsexualism operations, which are merely legal castration, a very dubious subject.

Naturally, he had a large collection of German sexological works, of the great period from the 1880s till the mid-1930s, when Hitler destroyed Magnus Hirschfeld's Institute of Sex Science in Berlin and Leo Schidrowitz's matching Institute of Sex Research in Vienna, these two specializing respectively in homosexuality and sado-masochism. The large, illustrated volumes published by these Institutes, and by other independent German and Austrian sex researchers and publishers, especially since about 1900, and even more especially since 1920, form an enormous and electrifying literature, of very uneven merit. Most of these books are heavily and very frankly illustrated, and for that reason libraries that have them usually avoid placing them on the open shelves. Not to protect the public morals, but to protect the books from being mutilated or stolen.

Dr. Benjamin's library was no exception. His sexological books were kept in special floor-level cabinets with locked wood-panelled doors, just below the open shelves lining his office, which were covered with standard heavy medical works on urology and so forth. Benjamin very much wanted me to catalogue the sex books — for sale, as it turned out — since Dr. Dickinson had flatteringly told him I was the person who knew most about this literature in America. But I could only work with Benjamin's books during his lunch-hours, as he had patients coming in for office consultations all the rest of the day.

Accordingly, he gave me the keys to the locked cabinets, pointed to his secretary's typewriter near his desk, handed me a packet of over-sized 6" by 10" cardboard index cards to work on, and went out to lunch. I worked for the two hours until he got back, and found it very unpleasant indeed crawling around on the floor pulling out and putting back the books. When Benjamin got back from lunch I asked him to tell me in round hundreds how many sex books he felt he had. I then averaged that out with the number I'd estimated from a quick look inside the cabinets, and told him how many lunch-hours I figured the job would take, which came to months. We both agreed that this would be far too long — especially me, as I had no desire to ruin the possibility of doing anything else all the days that would be broken that way at lunch, right in the middle.

We decided instead that I would come in and do the job Saturdays and Sundays, all day, or long half-days; and that was how it was done. This made it possible for me to pull out a whole cabinetful of Benjamin's books at a time and pile them on a desk to work with, something that couldn't be done during weekday office hours, when patients might be coming in. That at least got me up off the floor. As I say, book cataloguing is too close to rock bottom in the literary and bibliophile profession, as it is, for a poor cataloguer to have to endure the further open symbolism of doing it crawling on the ground.

Working for Dr. Benjamin, I got back into the habit of cataloguing books, and began looking around for other work of the same kind. The little Brooklyn bookbinder and bookseller, Rubin Bresler, who was still operating both his professions year after year, agreed to see me for a few minutes when I called him at his official binding office in the basement of one of the big downtown municipal buildings. At his suggestion we made an appointment to meet at a telephone booth by the cigar stand on the ground floor of the building. Bresler liked to keep his two professions strictly separate, and had no time to waste. I tempted him outside, however, by offering to buy him a Pepsi-Cola in the candy-store across the street, which was really a small delicatessen turning into a pocket-sized supermarket. It also had three tables where you could sit down, which struck me as a better atmosphere for our interview than the telephone booth by the cigar stand across the street. Also more private. Conferring in a telephone booth reminded me too much of standing up doing business at the lock boxes in Grand Central Station with jazz music's main marijuana pusher, 'cello-toting Mr. Bop.

As I recollect, Bresler didn't want a Pepsi-Cola — neither did I; the corn syrup they used in it then was too horribly sweet, though at least not carcinogenic — and he settled for an egg cream. This is a northeastern U. S. slang term for a chocolate soda, so called because it contains neither egg nor cream. Well, the chocolate syrup is announced on the large bottle to contain some minute amount of powdered extract of ancient eggs, and they do put a small squirt of thin milk in the glass, so I guess that's the cream. Thus: egg cream. Life in the big city.

Walking out with Bresler fifteen minutes later, after the Pepsi pause that depresses, who should I almost bump into, coming in through the delicatessen door, but the F.B.I. man who had been so interested in whether I was a masturbator. As he was alone, I figured it was an accident and he wasn't working on my case — they were usually always in twos in those days, like Mike & Ike or Italian policemen. He was probably there for an egg cream too, and recognized me instantly.

"You got your draft-card on you?" he asked with a grim smile. I gave him a broad wave of my hand for all answer.

Bresler was immediately alert and wanted to know who it was. I told him it was my lawyer. Why did I need a lawyer? I told him rapidly that some girl was suing me over the paternity of her child.

"It's nothing," he said. "It's nothing. You just get two guys to swear that they laid her too." I filed that in my memory, under "Gallantry – male." Well, it was certainly ungallant and dishonest, but at least it was less humiliating than the defense used by Theodore Dreiser, author of *Sister Carrie* and *An American Tragedy*, in which the trapped young man simply murders the pregnant girl. The defense or excuse Dreiser personally made use of in his own case, was that he was nearly seventy years old and impotent, which ain't necessarily so. You'd have thought, in that case, that he'd have been flattered by the girl's accusation and agreed eagerly. Well they jest at scars — as Romeo says concerning true love — that never felt a wound.

I had never yet made any girl pregnant, never caught a venereal disease, not even bugs; never had any of the accidents of erotic life that other people were always worrying and complaining about. No urologists for me. I had also never but once worn a condom. They cramped my style. Perhaps I should've knocked on wood, or put a black rabbit's hind foot in my front pocket, when I said that about not making any girl pregnant. Live & learn. Later, I made a lot of girls and women pregnant, sometimes at their request, but mostly by inadvertence.

Bresler wanted me to come out to his house evenings to do some cataloguing on a collection of erotic books he'd just bought, from the usual dead collector's widow. A former customer. That meant I'd have to be commuting, by subway, the long dreary hours to Brooklyn and back. To get to Bresler's small and undistinguished brick house, I had to take the subway to Grand Army Plaza; then take a street car quite some distance at a right-angle to the subway line, and after that walk down two further blocks to the left and then three blocks to the right. All this is absolutely authentic, and I also had to do it all again in reverse order on coming back from there at eleven p.m. As my reward, I would find myself in Bresler's tiny, suburban development red brick house, no different in any detail from hundreds of other houses on all sides of it and in every direction, except that the large cellar playroom was lined with book-cases to the ceiling, full to the gunwales and falling off the shelves onto the floor with semi-erotica and fake deluxe press books and a hefty percentage of authentic erotica in English for the knowledgeable buyers.

THE DETAILS about the house are noted above because I have observed over the years that many people are under the erroneous impression that the places where erotic books and similar impedimenta are bought or are collected are fascinating Exotic Temples of Ravening Lust, deliciously different from their own boringly routine parlor, bedroom and bath, and complete with odorous background effluvia of opium pipes and patchouli, with softly treading nautch-girls of various races, with décolletages down to HERE and up to THERE, both back and front, if not simply stark naked and with frond-like peacock feathers inserted fetchingly wherever your fancy strikes.

Or else that they are Nasty Little Dives, something like the recent vulgar sex-shops — all of these modelled on the original such shops before World War I in Kobé and Yokohama, Japan, and other oriental ports, with their delightful illustrated catalogues, all in pidgin English, of masturbatory devices and delights — entered through cruddy-looking hanging curtains over the door composed of strands of used soda-bottle caps squeezed in half, and presided over by shifty-looking individuals with faces right out of French Connection movies, who have just arrived with the collectors' items in dirty gunny-sacks from Port Saïd and Havana, Cuba. In the bad old days.

This is all an error. Except for their standard overcrowdedness, and the general air of it being impossible to find anything in its proper place, most such ceremonial habitats of erotica that I have ever been in, or worked or lived in, have been of the most ordinary and sometimes distressingly middleclass nature. Even occasionally including small wooden animal dolls or plastic statuary, on the radio or sideboard, which wiggle their heads or boggle their eyes when you brush past them. Rubin Bresler's library-parlor, for example, featured in the exact middle of the main center table a large shiny square brass clock mechanism, on which four globular weights turned slowly in a circle. This was wound only once a year, as his wife proudly told me, and was kept under a glass bell.

The botanical and erotic library of the Hungarian millionaire Arpad Plesch, in Beaulieu, on the Côte d'Azur in France, though it had an azure-blue ceiling with the owner's own horoscopic stars flatteringly set out there in silver — but without electronic planetarium clockwork, a nicety added by Arab arms-and-oil millionaires only recently — was in the same way overcrowded and in deplorable taste. Where there was nothing else to show off, there would be six or seven old gold watches, none of them running, laid out ostentatiously on Plesch's library tables, along with some ugly and presumably expensive little limited-edition cast brass statuettes of female nudes scattered about by way of non-literary decoration.

FOR REASONS I can't explain, but probably connected with the enormous fallen meteorite they keep outside the side door of the Museum of Natural History, which was just around the corner from where

I then lived, I somehow became very interested in the engraved Maya inscriptions on stone monuments in Mexico. These inscriptions had never been deciphered since they were first discovered in the jungles of Yucatan in the early nineteenth century, and described then to the world in John L. Stephens' *Travels in Central America.* I got hold of that beautifully illustrated work, and another by Stephens; also Sylvanus Griswold Morley's rather cold and schematic *Introduction to the Study of Maya Hieroglyphics*; and I vaingloriously made up my mind that I would be the new Champollion who would decipher the Maya inscriptions.

I think the mad ambition was set off in me by Beverley Keith, whom I was now seeing occasionally, and who'd been telling me about Mexico and these very pyramids and statues, some of which she had seen on bus-excursions. She only told me a little at a time, and diffidently as that was her way; but I was fired by the high intellectual challenge of the thing. If Champollion could solve the mystery of the Egyptian hieroglyphs after they waited mutely over three thousand years, surely the Maya code could be broken after only five hundred. Some clues should still exist.

Of course, I didn't understand a word of Spanish, but that didn't matter, since neither did the Mayas, and most of the very sparse literature on the subject was in English. I wasn't able to afford the other large quarto publications by S. G. Morley, giving the main body of the inscriptions, and had to use these in the Natural History Museum library. The curator there was extremely kind to me, and did not at all pooh-pooh my pretentious plan, though he did allude to the fact that it might well take twenty years of my time even to do the preliminary studies such a decipherment might require. Plus a trip or so to southern Mexico, to see the actual surviving inscriptions engraved in stone, something I wasn't even considering. He was right too. What could possibly be done by an untrained, strictly book-oriented person?

And yet, only a few years later, the Maya inscriptions were at last successfully deciphered, by an eighteen-year-old Russian boy — ten years younger than me — through their similarity to ancient Chinese numbering petroglyphs, which is what he was actually studying. This also had the side effect of demonstrating finally the origin of the Mexican culture in the Orient, though when or how, and whether by land-hopping along the Aleutian Islands, or by rafts across the Pacific, is still uncertain. So that's what an eighteen-year-old boy could do, and did do, only through books and without going to Mexico at all, just on the inspiration of the intellectual challenge of the unknown. But it wasn't me.

While entertaining myself studying the Mexican doll-faced wall pictures and inscriptions, I was still working hard on my history of censorship, *Taboo*. The largest effort of English censorship, I found, has always been against Shakespeare. The first expurgated edition of his plays — by Alexander Pope — was nearly a century before Dr. Bowdler's. In fact, as studying the variant folio texts showed me, Shakespeare had expurgated himself. Nothing daunted, I now set out to study the earlier texts of several of Shakespeare's plays, known as the Bad Quartos, and to prove that these were really what Shakespeare wrote, though in garbled form, owing to having been stolen by short-hand reporters in the theatre, helped along by the memorized parts of one or another suborned actor. This is completely in opposition to the now current theory, that Shakespeare originally wrote the very much longer and different forms now usually printed, known as the Good Quartos — to be sure — and that these are what the Bad Quartos garble.

My theory was and is the opposite: that the Bad Quartos were in fact limping copies of Shakespeare's originals. And that when they were pirated and published, without Shakespeare's permission and by other publishers than his own, he simply revised and enlarged the stolen plays, thus getting the copyright back into his own hands when the new form was published. This re-copyrighting trick or subterfuge is still being used today, though more often by the pirates than by the original authors. Check back a few chapters here to Erich Posselt's revised and re-copyrighted collection of soldier songs, under the name of 'Edgar Palmer,' though the songs themselves hadn't changed meanwhile.

I spent a great many months on the comparison of the Quarto facsimile texts, and on studying the whole literature of the controversy about them. *Hamlet* is the crucial play here, because the later "Good" quarto is enlarged to nearly twice as long as the earlier "Bad" quarto — as the "Good" quarto title page brags — and is far too long ever to put on the stage. The play actually played before audiences even today is always cut back to something much closer to Shakespeare's original and more stage-worthy Bad Quarto text. All Shakespearians know this about *Hamlet* but refuse to admit it. Eventually the thing seemed to me such an open-&-shut case of revision to regain copyright, that I wrote up an elaborate monograph proving, as I felt, that the Bad Quartos are better than the Good, in the sense that they are self-evidently closer to what Shakespeare originally wrote.

I never published this monograph in any of the learned journals, though it wouldn't have been difficult to do so. What stopped me was the appearance just about then of a book on the attempted pre-dating of Shakespeare's *Sonnets* and the identification of the rival poet flouted in them, by an English writer, Leslie Hotson. Even though the *Sonnets* were in no way central to what I was doing, I was deeply disgusted by the enormous crust of this author, and what I felt was his evident urge to astonish the scholarly world with a sensational reversal of the accepted theory for a century or two, since the great Shakespearian critics and scholars like Edmund Malone. I was not alone in my disgust. On the publication of Hotson's book, the best Shakespearian scholar of the moment, or at any rate the leader of the prevailing school, gave the author his comeuppance in just the title and four opening words of his critique: "Elementary, My Dear Hotson!"

That presumably settled Hotson's hash, in the British critical and military tactical fashion, at its height during World War II, of attacking wherever the important area of battle is *not*. But it didn't satisfy me at all. I was still angry and upset about Hotson's ridiculous book, on a subject that interested me not a whit, and even though the best man in the field had absolutely demolished his impertinent nonsense, about which no one has heard another syllable since except maybe right here. Because the real worm in the apple, as I saw it, was not anybody's errors of concept or chronological miscalculations, but this bumptious urge to astonish, by means of which almost anyone can, and many do leap into well-paid prominence , simply by loudly and self-importantly announcing the titillating opposite of some long and placidly accepted idea. Such as, for instance that the world is round and not flat, that Mars & Venus have never struck each other on the beezer during their separate passages through the heavens around the sun, or that Johann Gutenberg really did adapt a very valuable invention from the Chinese when he imported the idea of printing to Europe. Nobody can get their pictures on the covers of national newspapers by maintaining the above long-accepted ideas. However, if you turn them on their heads, and shout loud enough; well . . . . Look what happened to Copernicus and company.

I began to wonder, therefore, for the one & only time in my life, about my own sincerity. I wondered whether I too might not merely be touched by this presumptuous urge, in my work on the Bad Quartos — beyond just my evidently overweening and unjustified ambition, as with the Maya inscriptions — to make a violent splash simply by maintaining the *opposite* of what all the Shakespeare fuddyduds-in-the-saddle believed. The bottom dog water-boy vindicated! I therefore never published this monograph though I was completely sincere in what I had studied and written, long and arduously, and had no conscious desire to astonish anybody — least of all the current crappety Shakespearian crew. James Joyce remarks somewhere in *Ulysses* that Shakespeare is the happy hunting-ground of all minds that have slipped their tether. Except his.

Meanwhile, on this preparation, and again by sheer accident, I was soon to interest myself profoundly in the strange and violent erotic career of this mysterious red-headed young noblewoman who stands out in a lightning flash of bitchery, scandal, death and the execution of the innocent — in a whirlwind of court hangers-on, magicians and poisoners — in late-Elizabethan and Jacobean history of England: Frances Howard, Countess of Essex. *Ever . or . never.*

AFTER the breakdown of my work on the "Bad" Quartos because of Leslie Hotson's wrong-headed book, it was with a certain instant recognition that I ran into the next windmill I was to tilt at. This was the question of the first edition of the first book printed in England, *The Dictes and Sayings of the Philosophres*, an English translation of an Arabic conspectus of Greek philosophy printed by William Caxton at Westminster in 1477. Though certainly of no world-shaking importance, this book was of central importance to me as the opening item in taboo, my proposed history of sex censorship in English literature, since the first book printed in England was, as it happens, also the first book expurgated there for its sexual content. Originally written several centuries earlier during the greatest period of Arabic literature, and drawn from ancient Greek writers and traditions by one Mubashshir ibn-Fatik, this "Book of Wisdom" had first been translated from Arabic into Spanish, from Spanish into Latin, from Latin into French, and from French into English by Anthony Woodville, Earl Rivers, who was the patron of William Caxton, the first English printer.

Caxton was originally a silk merchant, in Bruges, Belgium, and had first learned printing on the continent, at the age of fifty, in order to publish there, by Gutenberg's then-new process in Europe, his own translation from the French of the *Recuyell of the Historyes of Troye*, the first book ever printed in English, two years before *The Dictes and Sayings of the Philosophres*. Being therefore conversant with the French language, as he explains in a short and curious Afterword to the *Dictes*, he was very surprised to notice that Earl Rivers had gallantly omitted from his translation a number of passages in the original French text, in which certain crude statements were made attacking women. So that the reader should not be cheated of these titillating doses of misogyny, Caxton translated the missing passages himself, and printed them in a sort of outhouse supplement to his Afterword. There he also explains to the reader with an unmistakable wink of the eye, that if the reader should perchance be shocked by these passages — nothing very scabrous, I should add — as Earl Rivers had been, he could simply take a knife and cut the offending Afterword out of the book.

It was with this extraordinary passage, and some note on its further importance as marking the importation to England of the anti-woman literature of the ancient *Querelle des Femmes*, which of course starts with the Biblical story of Eve, that my history of

English-language censorship, *Taboo*, was to begin. I wanted to quote Caxton's explanation in full, from the first edition of course, and in all the amusing quaint old spelling. As there was also an undated reprint of a year or so later, which Caxton had entirely reset in type, I naturally had to know precisely which the first edition was, in order to quote from that one.

With all its incredible wealth of printed books and long runs of learned journals, The New York Public Library is not rich in rare British incunabula of our historical era, most of which survive, in the one or two copies that still exist, only in the library of the British Museum, and elsewhere in England. The moment World War II had begun, however, the English librarians had taken the precaution of microfilming all their oldest old books, and sets of these microfilm copies were deposited in certain main American libraries, as in New York. I was therefore easily able to make the transcript of the passage I wanted, not merely from William Blades' quatrecentenary edition of the *Dictes,* but also from the microfilm of both the original editions. No problem.

Well, there was a slight problem however. The library catalogue noted the existence of an article on *The Dictes* in the British Museum's journal, *The Library*, by a Dr. Curt Bühler, curator at the Pierpont Morgan Library in New York. On looking this up at once, I found to my irritation that Dr. Bühler seemed to be doing the same thing for Caxton that Leslie Hotson had done for Shakespeare. With all the best intentions in the world, I am positive, Dr. Bühler had examined the two original editions of *The Dictes and Sayings of the Philosophres*, and had come to the conclusion — the opposite of the obvious conclusion long accepted by William Blades and all other Caxton specialists — that the first edition was really the second edition, and the second edition was really the first edition, if I make myself clear. Or so Dr. Bühler seemed to be saying.

So now where the hell was I? Which edition was I supposed to quote from? Would I have to study not just the passage about the expurgations that I was after, but the two entire texts from the first to the last page, collating the two folio editions page by page and line by line, to try to check the typographical and other evidence for their dates and precedence adduced by Blades and Bühler, and to determine, if I could, who was right? And this only for the purpose of knowing which edition I was to quote, for a twenty-line citation, in all the quaint spelling in which each edition differed wholly from the other though the actual *words* were the same. Come ON! How much of the conspewkious consumption of scholarship was I supposed to be laying out on a project like this?

But there I was, willy-nilly, for a week or two, with my head stuck daily for a couple of hours deep inside an odd, unpleasant, guillotine-shaped microfilm reading machine, like an oversized metronome, at the crowded book-delivery enclosure in the Public Library, with pages and librarians bustling busily about me every minute: exactly the wrong place to have to do a pesky collating job like that. And for so picayune a reward. Yes, there I was, with Blades' fine large facsimile of what everyone knew damn well was the original edition open on the table before me. And me cranking through the film-viewing machine at the same time, or trying to, the British Museum microfilm of that goddamned second edition, which nobody in the world but Dr. Bühler had ever even thought of wasting a second breath on. I was furious at my chaining myself, out of some misplaced notion of conscientious research to such chickenshit activity, checking all the flyspecked *i*s and clubfooted *f*s in the two funny old printings, line by line, merely in order to make my first firm half-page quotation on the history of modern sex censorship.

The real paradox was that, being a born censor and Savonarola myself, I thoroughly approved of what Earl Rivers had done, in expurgating his text of the anti-woman passages he'd found in the original. After all, that was exactly what I'd done myself — wasn't it? — in omitting the even more literally sadistic anti-woman passages from Bob Sewall's overwritten pornographicum, *The Devil's Advocate*, when I was typing up the mimeograph stencils for that lazy son-of-a-gun. And would do several times again in later years, as with one nastily cannibalistic chapter in Restif de la Bretonne's otherwise wholly erotic *Anti-Justine*, whose intention his title makes clear; and just recently in a German erotic video film on the orgies Catherine the Great of Russia, called *Catherine the Naked Empress*, horribly punctuated between its super-elegant orgies, as I found to my surprise, with long, really hideous scenes of rapine, manhunt and torture. The leopard and his spots.

I ruthlessly scotch-taped Restif's cannibalistic chapter shut — my girlfriend was reading me the book aloud in bed, and I didn't want her to read me *that* by accident. And for a very similar reason I taped over the accidental erasure tab on the film tape of Catherine the

Great so I could rerecord over the torture scenes, and blanked them out blithely with irrelevant orchestral interludes taken off the air from a television program. Go thou and do thou likewise. You can begin with Toby Hooper's ultra-popular film with the midnight cult-crowd, *The Texas Chain-Saw Massacres*, which I admit I've never seen, but a cultivated young lady who inexplicably stayed watching it to the end, tells me that the final scene is a vengeful long-shot of fellation. If so, just leave that in, and blank out the whole rest of the film for starters: the opposite of the way the director did it. Every man his own Savonarola.

Anthony Woodville, called Earl Rivers, the gallant translator who expurgated *Caxton's Dictes*, was no wrinkled old scrivener any more than I was, but dynamic young and highborn nobleman who had fought a famous tournament with the Bastard of Burgundy when he was twenty-five — it was declared a draw — and only forty-one when he was beheaded at Pontefract Castle by Crouchback Richard III, against whose usurpation of the crown Rivers had plotted after the repellent murder in the Tower of London of the royal children, whose protector Richard was supposed to be. Rivers' execution and his curse and defiance of the evil king — "We give thee up our guiltless blood to drink!" — are one of the noblest moments of Shakespeare's tragedy on this vile history.

And in the midst of all this life of action, Rivers had found the time and interest to translate an Arabic work of philosophy from the French, and to recoil from insulting women therein. It was easy to admire a man like Rivers, and yet there it was: he had expurgated the very first book printed in England, and so we were at least technically on opposing sides, even though it was I who had expurgated the most recent erotic book printed in English. Thinking ruefully about all my contradictory stances, as I whirled the crank of the microfilm machine reels, there were moments when I felt more like the Bastard of Burgundy myself.

As to the knotty problem of the two competing editions, fortune smiled on me. When comparing the two texts, I had the luck to run into numerous passages in the second edition, as we all understood it to be except Dr. Bühler, in which there were long blank white spaces in the last lines on various pages, even though there was plenty of room for the three or four following words to be fitted in. By means of this standard typographical ruse, the text took up again identically on the top of the next page in both editions. This could only mean one thing: that the second edition had been set in type page-for-page to match the first, when it was found that more copies were needed. But that, owing to the narrower face of the recut type now used, the typesetter of the reprint hadn't always been able to arrive at exactly the same spot as his original at the foot of each page. He therefore had to copyfit, and quad and pad out these short pages with extra blank white spaces in their final lines. Dr. Bühler's revisionist theory, at that point, fell heavily to the ground.

Well? I went to see Bühler at the Morgan Library, to talk it over with him, phoning him in advance for an appointment. He turned out to be one of the librarians I knew there by sight, but had never known his name. We met with measured tread, Dr. Bühler carrying a magnificently bound copy of Blades' quatrecentenary facsimile of the *Dictes* — I guess Pierpont Morgan hadn't been able to afford a copy of the original edition — and me carrying a deceptively slender manuscript envelope containing nothing but two white-on-black photostatic copies of the several page-endings in the two editions confronted, with the second edition showing the silently accusing blanks.

Dr. Bühler remained standing during our entire interview, which was brief. I had told him by phone what I was working on, when making the appointment with him, which is why he was carrying the facsimile of the *Dictes*. He glanced only very briefly at my two confronted photocopies, and then became entirely frozen and rigid. He told me with extreme politeness that what I was showing him was extremely interesting and that he assumed that I would be publishing my findings. I understood at that moment exactly how it must have felt, for German university students at Nuremberg and Heidelberg, to face each other in insane *Mensur* duels with their bodies and throats carefully protected from each others' broadswords with heavy padding, but their faces bare to be cut to bits by their opponents' slashes.

The article I wrote for submission to *The Library* in London, under the title "A Word on Caxton's *Dictes*," to confute Bühler's theory and present my typographical evidence, was long and highly detailed. I traced every passage I cited through the English to the French, through the French to the Latin, the Latin to the Spanish; then stopping there, as not only I couldn't construe a single word of the Arabic text, but I didn't think *The Library* would print quotations in Arab anyway, or I would have calligraphed them all blindly out with tracing paper. All this polyglot wealth of ancient texts had been printed in full in the various learned philological series and journals of the nineteenth century. And so I would be there now, day after day and evening after evening in the Public Library, with these very odd volumes spread out before me on my favorite table in the high-ceilinged South Hall reading-room, searching out the matching passages in these various languages, like the library bum I was becoming catching fleas with a finecomb. And sometimes chuckling like a drain as I asked myself chortlingly why on earth Isaac D'Israeli and H. Spencer Ashbee had both fished up that great passage about literary research having in it some of the pleasure of wrestling with a fine woman — and observed how heartily I agreed with them.

The editor of the British Museum's bibliographical journal, *The Library*, who had the curious name of Frank Francis, wrote to tell me that he would of course run my article, and that it was of prime importance to British incunabular bibliography. But he added that he found my querulous and contentious tone — which of course he didn't call by those names — somewhat inappropriate to their pages, and would have to edit my article severely. As good as his word, Francis pruned the thing wholesale of every, er, inappropriate syllable. Of all my contentiousness he left in only the opening words of my article: "Dr. Curt Bühler . . ." in which I called out my opponent in what I assumed was proper Teutonic duelling style.

Francis had obviously been particularly upset by some unseemly levity on my part in which I alluded to, and continued a debating joke originally cracked by no less a pamphleteer than Karl Marx, the sixty small pages of whose *Communist Manifesto* still have the power, after nearly a century and a half, to keep all the billionaires of the world and their paid brain-boys at the universities and "Institutes" shitting pins and needles.

Marx and his co-author Friedrich Engels knew every trick in the parliamentarian orator's pack, to be sure. And when some turgid apologist for mad-dog capitalism had the crust to write a book and entitle it *The Philosophy of Poverty*, proving with Voltaire's Dr. Pangloss that everything is for the best, in this best of all possible worlds, so the poor might just as well shut up and starve. Marx riposted with a reply urbanely spoonerized, entitled *The Poverty of Philosophy*. (And it ain't changed much since.) Elsewhere, Marx refers with similar heavy sarcasm to the theories of another of his opponents, named Bühler as it happened, in the phrase *"Dr. Bühler's Umwälzung der Wissenschaft"* – his upskydownskying of science. I admit it: I just couldn't resist this, since it said exactly what I had been feeling about Leslie Hotson on Shakespeare's *Sonnets*, and other similarly cute *Verblungeter und Umwälzungener* theories of the publicity-oriented research kind. So I built the phrase like an exploding firecracker stuffed up somebody's ass very carefully into my article, in a nice, unexpected climactic spot where it struck like a high Teutonic enema or gong: *"Dr. Bühler's Umwälzung der Wissenschaft"*

With perfect and unconscious British superciliousness and duplicity, the editor Frank Francis never gave me even the slightest opportunity of seeing how he was going to gut my article, beyond the generalized word of warning in his letter of acceptance that his editing would have to be "severe." Obviously, he should have allowed me the option of withdrawing the article, if I didn't like it edited *his* way, and have it published somewhere else edited *my* way. Learned journals don't pay you anything for your contribution to their pages, after all. You're supposed to get your pay in roundabout fashion, through the better university job they dole you out after you've published a few such scholarly articles — if you're careful not to rock the boat. I had no university job to polish, and so writing for these jacks-in-office at all was just charity on my part, to give them The Word, and of course to make myself look good and feel big meanwhile. But you would expect a little scholarly courtesy from the editor. Apparently not in England.

My article, "A Word on Caxton's *Dictes*," as it appeared in print in *The Library* a year or so later was entirely cut to bits. Passages of it were even rewritten in an entirely different style, never in order to strengthen or improve them but in every case to modify and qualify and meech them down almost to imbecility, making half the article, and all the work with the polyglot texts seem like meaningless boondoggling. In which case, why had it been published?

The *Umwälzung* climax had of course been aborted and completely cut out, and a whole preceding half-page was peppered full of holes and sheared away, where my clever and overbearing editor saw I was marshalling an overlapping *accelerando* approach to it, exactly the way Beethoven's *Third Leonore Overture* finishes, and all the overtures Rossini spent a lifetime imitating from him. Watching the editor pitting his mind and his blue pencil against me in this way, via my helpless manuscript, was very educational. If I hadn't been positive before that I didn't ever want anybody editing my stuff, I was now. They can make their own discoveries and write their own books. Let mine alone.

All I can say for Francis' editing is that at least he printed my confronted facsimiles from the two editions, and that was the main thing and the essential proof of what I was claiming. Dr. Bühler, who had been given space in an earlier issue for the erroneous theory I had now demolished, was naturally also allowed further space for a reply in a later issue. It appears he had been shown my article before it was even published, and for all I know, may even have assisted in cutting it up and rewriting it. Why not? The whole point and handling of the affair was clearly with the idea of protecting Bühler from any embarrassment over his unfortunate blunder. Rehabilitating Caxton and Earl Rivers — let alone Caxton's true bibliographer William Blades — very evidently didn't matter much to anybody but me. What I learned from this was that the rules of literary courtesy are different in England than everywhere else. The main thing isn't what you know or what you do, but *who* you know. You have only to read a few British book-reviews to understand that, something I had never yet done. It's important to have friends, and friends of friends, everywhere in the literary and university game. In England apparently that's all that's important.

Actually I suppose I shouldn't complain. My article on Caxton, as printed, was still perfectly creditable, very long and detailed — and a perfect example — almost a priggish parody, now that all the *sæva indignatio* had been drained or rather clipped out of it by the shears-bearing editor — of what a learned journal article on an abstruse and quite unimportant bibliographical matter should ideally be, especially on a subject occurring five hundred years before. I hated my article now, all thirty pages of it, except for my opening call-out challenge, mercifully still there perhaps with the thought that it was good advertising for Dr. Bühler; and my final line or *quietus*, for which I mock-innocently reprised the closing colophon line of Caxton's book itself: *"Et sic est finis."*

In his reply, also in *The Library*, Dr. Bühler curiously denied that the page-end blanks I had reproduced in facsimile, and confronted in facing columns, in any way proved the priority of the first edition of Caxton's *Dictes*. This was something of a stunner, even in the way of pure bulling-things-through. But he also stated that he did now agree with the standard position I was defending — though only on the basis of "new evidence" *he* had found since his original and erroneous article putting it into question. I couldn't quite understand an *amende honorable* this roundabout and equivocal, but you can't have everything.

To chasten me for my formal duello call-out opening, good advertising as it might be, Dr. Bühler arranged to give me no scholarly advertising at all and did not mention me by name in his reply even once, not even in a footnote. He referred instead at all times, with perfect obliquity, to "the article" — meaning mine. "The article" had said this; "the article" had claimed that. No names. The British folklorist, A. L. Lloyd told me years later that Bühler's reply reminded him of a fight to the death with knives he had once witnessed between two Gypsies. When the survivor was asked what it had all been about, he answered, pointing to his now stabbed-to-death opponent: " 'e said me *article* was dorty!"

CHAPTER 44

BEVERLEY

SHY little Beverley Keith and I had been keeping company in a muted way since the night of the unfortunate marijuana party that marked the exit — an exit marked MUD — of her mannered friend Athena Besterman. Beverley and I were shy with each other because Beverley was shy. I learned a little about her, not much. She was a Canadian, now becoming a naturalized American citizen so she could work in the United States. Her family came from Toronto. Her parents were divorced: her father, an army officer and inventor, now lived in Florida; her mother lived in New York but was away right now. She also had an older married brother in town, a museum curator. She had very little to do with her family, she said, except her mother, because the only members of the family who had tried to understand her were an uncle, named Ernest Macmillan, who was the conductor of the orchestra back in Toronto, and his wife. All sides of her Protestant family originally came from Scotland. She knew no one in New York except her mother and her brother, and Athena. When I asked about her mathematical boyfriend I had so liked at our first meeting, she said he wasn't her boyfriend but someone Athena knew and had invited for her to meet some while back. Beverley had never had a boyfriend.

BEVERLEY KEITH 1940S

After digesting that last statement, which I believed to be literally true, I told her she'd probably need a job more now than a boyfriend, because she said she hated to be dependent on her mother who'd soon be back from her summer holiday which had lasted several extra months as her mother had been living with some man she met then. Beverley was always very frank and direct like that, in a simple way, and I don't recollect ever hearing her tell a lie or catching her out in one. She had nothing to gain by lying, and nothing to lose. In addition, she was peculiarly innocent about all practical things, a complaint she also later made about me. This was not a pose on either of our parts. In that, at least, we matched perfectly.

BEVERLEY KEITH 1943

I tried to find out why she had gone to live in Mexico, but she couldn't really explain it. She said she didn't like any of the jobs she was able to find after she graduated from Barnard. In any case, she hadn't studied anything but Greek primitive philosophy, and the only real career open to her was becoming a teaching associate. One of her professors had very much wanted her to stay and to do just that, but when she learned it would mean more years of classes and writing an M.A. and then a Ph.D. thesis, she preferred to drop out at that point. People used to say to me in later years that Beverley was "the original hippie," but actually she was more like Goncharov's ultimately unworldly and indolent Oblomov, or rather like Melville's *Bartleby the Scrivener* — a story Beverley introduced me to — who has withdrawn internally from life and whose mild-mannered answer to every offer and suggestion is: "I'd rather not."

And what had she lived on in Mexico, I asked her? She had lived on nothing. She taught English to the daughters of the Indian family she lived with in Oaxaca for her board, and gave lessons to a few other people for pocket money. Her needs were extremely sparse. She made her own clothes, which just consisted of cotton underwear and two blue denim jumpers which she had sewed herself and washed alternately every couple of days. She cut her own hair in bangs by simply lopping it off at each side with a big pair of scissors, borrowed from her hostess. She had no other friends and seldom spoke to anyone. She read a great deal, mostly non-fiction. Towards the end, when she had become proficient in Spanish, she was reading

Manuel Gamio's various large works on the ethnology and history of the Mexican people.

When she came back from Mexico, all of Beverley's belongings other than the clothes on her body were packed loosely into a small mahogany wood cigar-box exactly ten inches long in each direction, and three inches deep — I measured it one day out of curiosity — plus a volume of Gamio's and a new novel about Mexico: it may have been Malcolm Lowry's *Under the Volcano*, which she carried in her other hand. These she read alternately on the various busses back to New York, which she preferred to trains as weaving more intimately through the towns they passed. She observed everything; she said nothing. And she smoked cigarettes incessantly.

Beverley had lived in Oaxaca for two years, while the government was building a road there from Mexico City, where she had already lived part of the first year. As the contractors were paid for building the road by the mile instead of by the job, they arranged for the road — which is still there — to wander about in broad loops in a strange gerrymandering fashion even where the land was perfectly flat. It therefore took a very long time for the building of the road to be finished and arrive at Oaxaca. The day the road was opened, a busload of officials and tourists arrived for the ceremony of inauguration. Beverley put all her little sacred things, and an extra pair of cotton under-drawers and woollen stockings such as the Indian girls wore, into the cigar-box; said goodbye to her hosts, and used her saved-up pin money to buy a ticket back to Mexico City on the same bus. Oaxaca had been her sanctuary and refuge, and was now to be debauched. She did not want to stay to see it.

Back in Mexico City she telegraphed her mother for enough money to come back to New York on the bus and did so. She would stop occasionally in whatever town the bus-drivers would let her off, and check into the smallest hotel she could find in order to wash and dry her clothes in the hotel-room sink. For shoes Beverley had been wearing on her feet, over the woollen socks, and was still wearing when I met her, though now over cotton bobby-sox, two heavy, rounded pieces of worn-out automobile tire, sliced off the original tire with a machete, and with small wire loops twisted into the edges and cleverly laced with Mexican leather thongs. She had no other shoes. These were the kind her Indian hosts and their daughters had worn in Oaxaca, and did not think of them as primitive or quaint, but as cheap and practical on the Mexican dirt roads. They didn't live in any wigwams or hogans either, but in a one-story-high wooden apartment house. Plenty of people still live in apartments like that in Los Angeles today, the outside walls roughly stuccoed over like the latter-day pueblos they are. As a matter of fact, the prevailing architectural style in southern California, that even the richest people now live in, of flat-top cheese-boxes in rambling "ranch" style, really comes to the same thing.

Beverley's unwillingness to live according to the white WASP world's rules was very consternating, even to an outcast like me who also didn't live according to those rules. I wondered how long she could survive in New York if she was really going to cut loose from her mother now, as she said she planned to, again not giving any reason. It was obvious that Beverley did not love her mother, and didn't even approve of her; and when I finally met her mother I found that those were her mother's exact sentiments about Beverley too. Her mother being a decayed, would-be society woman flapping around on the edges of the fashionable world and wishing and pretending that she was rich. Her husband had divorced her years before, made a small settlement on her, had now remarried and wanted to hear no more about her. Thinking it all over, I felt I ought truly to take a total innocent like Beverley under my protective wing, such as it was. After her mother got back and Beverley did move out of her apartment, I saw her much more frequently than was logical, since we were not lovers and I found her childlike and unattractive sexually. So, in a way, Athena had been right to introduce us.

One day — I was now seeing her at suppertime at their apartment every other or every third evening — I thought I should speak to Beverley about her heavy smoking, which not only looked ungraceful in a girl so young, but was unquestionably bad for her health since she smoked continuously, though for some reason her fingers were not stained as yellow as some I've seen on modern girls. She told me she had already been smoking for twelve years, and was unable to stop.

"You must be joking!" I said. "How old were you when you started – eight?"

"No. Eighteen."

Beverley was thirty years old when I met her, four years older than me. No one could have suspected it. She looked, at most, as though she were still in her late 'teens and seriously underfed, being very slender and flat-chested. I had assumed she was the youngest member of the class with Athena at Barnard, probably some genius child who had been pushed on fast very early on, because she had a fine mind, though she did not care to show it off. *Bartleby the Scrivener* indeed. The only things she would ever say more than a few words about were Greek primitive philosophy, and music, both of which she understood well and loved very much.

Music especially she didn't turn into many words, but I was close enough to both her and music to see that Beverley experienced it deeply and viscerally, in the same way I did. I listened to music with her, in her mother's furnished apartment on a little radio she had accepted hesitantly from her mother. Of course I mentioned my records and high-fidelity phonograph to Beverley, and she said her father had also had a large collection of the old shellac classical records when she was young, and allowed her to play them; nor had she ever broken a single one. I immediately invited her to come and hear my best records too. We sat on the bed together in my room, and I played my nicest records for her, including the exquisite "Jesus, Joy of Man's Desiring" by Bach. It made her smile with pleasure, the first time I had ever seen Beverley smile, and she told me her Uncle Ernest used to play it on the organ for her after his orchestra rehearsals at the concert hall in Toronto.

That Uncle Ernest was quite a one. He also played the organ occasionally on Sundays in church, and would mischievously play things like "The British Grenadiers" and "Pop Goes the Weasel," but so slowly and solemnly that nobody ever caught on. When he practised in the organ loft he would also prop an adventure book open in front of him on the music stand and read it while his fingers played automatically. Beverley became quite animated telling me about her uncle's musical mischief, and I put one arm around her as I listened and began to stroke her hair.

"Are you going to make love to me?" Beverley asked, turning to look into my eyes unblinkingly. I told her I was. "I'm a virgin," she said. "I suppose it will hurt."

I assured her that if it hurt I would stop. We played more records, and I let night fall before I did anything that might seem inartistic to her or shock her. That way we were in the half-darkness, which I thought might be wise the first time. However, it was not possible to enter her body, as her hymen was too resistant. I told her not to think anything of it. Some of the world's greatest women had been that way, for instance Queen Elizabeth. Beverley said nothing now. We listened to more music, and I gave her some of my special Greek wine, as I always lyingly called it, because it was really only plain cheap wine with a few drops of oil of cinnamon in it, which gave it a lovely, musky taste. We drank up most of a bottle of that while the music played, and then I tried again to make love to her, but it was still impossible.

The next time I saw her she had moved. Her mother had come back now, and Beverley immediately moved in with her soft spoken, slightly older brother Graeme, who was a curator at the Cooper Union Museum over at lower Fourth Avenue near all the bookstores. Her mother had given her the little radio to take along with her. Graeme's wife Isabel was shocked by my visiting with Beverley in her room, and assumed we were lovers, which apparently she believed to be wrong since we weren't married to each other yet. We also weren't really lovers, but it wasn't our fault we weren't.

Isabel would purposely make as much noise as possible doing the dinner dishes, every evening when I was there and alone with Beverley in her room. She'd be crashing and banging like the mad duchess in *Alice in Wonderland* and *Through the Looking Glass* in the kitchenette on the other side of the wall. I got the definite impression she was angrily, if unconsciously trying to stop or spoil what she thought was our fun. I asked Beverley what she thought about Isabel's boiler-factory tactics, which were effectively ruining all the music we listened to, on WQXR.

"She's jealous," Beverley said. "Because you're so wild-looking, like Heathcliff. And Graeme is such a milquetoast."

I wanted to bust into the kitchen and have it out with Isabel, but what was the use? It almost isn't possible to walk up to an intense, visibly repressed woman you hardly know and say to her: "I know you think I'm making love to your sister-in-law on the other side of the wall, but I'm not. So will you please stop banging the goddam dishes that way. It spoils the music we're trying to listen to on that little radio." So I said nothing. Beverley decided to move out. Maybe that was what Isabel wanted. It didn't matter, Beverley said. When your baggage is a cigar-box, it's easy.

Her brother Graeme, for all his soft-shod politeness, had both feet solidly on the ground at all times, and had made his dreamy sister see, better than I ever could, that she was going to have to get a job and earn some money. I believe he did it by the simple expedient of informing her that he wasn't going to be supplying the plain cash money she might be needing otherwise, because Isabel wouldn't like that. Graeme was obviously aware — there was never anyone who didn't notice it instantly — that Beverley was someone quite as unworldly, if not as agitated, as Rima the Bird-Girl in W. H. Hudson's *Green Mansions*; but it didn't impress him a bit. So Beverley got out.

As she was unable to do anything employable except typewrite, and female typists weren't much in demand just near the end of the war, Beverley bought a newspaper and looked through the classified ads. She observed that there were large advertisements for men and women at the shipyards just across the river in New Jersey, and also in Brooklyn. Without discussing it with anyone, she simply went and got a job in the first Jersey shipyard she applied to as a marker-helper, whatever that may be. She told me the large flat panels of metal for building cargo ships in a hurry were marked out with wooden templates and chalk; then cut loose by someone else with an oxy-acetylene torch and assembled by welding. They welded together a couple of ships that way, at high speed. The work was hard, dirty, and often dangerous underfoot and overhead — a little like playing hopscotch in a madhouse, Beverley said — but almost half the employees seemed to be women, and happy to get the nicely-paying jobs.

The marker and welder Beverley was supposed to be helping, a tough young woman from Moscow, Idaho, named Faith Craig, became good friends with her — no one but her brother could resist her helpless innocence — and helped her over the difficult training period. Beverley told me about all this with the utmost simplicity. She complained about nothing. When she got her first fat little pay envelope she left her brother's house on Hudson street, near the old square church of St. Luke-in-the-Fields, and moved into a hideously bare and cold furnished room around the corner on one of the side streets, one flight up and right close to a street light which shone mercilessly in through the window at night. There were thin scrim curtains but no shutters that could hold or even filter the light out.

I came to see her there, and was shocked by the room. She said it didn't matter. She was going to put as much money in the bank as she could from what she earned at the shipyard. As soon as the war was over she hoped to go back to Mexico. She also told me she had gone to a doctor that day, and had asked him to stretch open her vagina with some instrument so that I could make love to her. She had no idea what he did. It hadn't hurt. He said he might have to make a slight cut. She asked me to try to make love to her again. She made no attempt to excite me, or to romance me or herself. She didn't try to get me to kiss her, and didn't think of trying to kiss me. Just asked me flat out like that, please to try again.

"Because it's time," said Beverley. "I'm thirty years old."

I looked at her very hard when she said that. I knew it was true, but it was impossible to believe. She looked about sixteen, with her dark hair in those amateurishly cut bangs, and wearing a man's overcoat in the cold little room. She had bought it for two dollars in a pawn-shop down by the ferry slip where she took the ferry to the ship yard. It was cold in the early mornings and evenings crossing the Hudson River, she said. I'll bet it was. The coat collar was too large for her, and she had simply sliced it off the coat with a razor blade. It now made her look almost exactly like tiny orphan Jackie Coogan in Charlie Chaplin's *The Kid*, except without the big floppy railroad-cap. I said to myself that making love to a girl like that would probably feel like debauching a particularly helpless minor, but I thought I ought to do her the favor she was so soberly asking for.

She was perfectly docile when we opened the bed and lay down naked together in the half-dark with the street light blazing in over the other half of the room. It felt as though we were about to make an erotic stag movie under ultra bright Klieg lights, except that it was also pretty darn cold. I had difficulty raising a hardon, and did not feel the slightest passion. I tried to force myself into the mood by kneading and caressing the flesh of her buttocks roughly and sucking her flat little breasts.

When the moment of truth came, Beverley did not bleed – the doctor had taken care of that. It was also obvious that she felt nothing at all. I didn't feel very much of anything either, except pity and a sort of far-away embarrassment for us both at such a sad little comedy. Beverley did not seem tense or nervous, but lay beside and under me completely passive and willing, as though I were some further doctor operating on her. But she was also completely frigid. I couldn't expect much else the first time, I told myself. I didn't express any disappointment, and neither did she. I told her she'd like it more as she got more accustomed later to making love. I told her that appetite would come with eating, as the proverb said, and I believed it too.

Beverley took very much to heart the fact that I didn't like her room, and found it frightful, especially the street light blazing in at the window and making that enormous bright white square on the wall opposite the bed, even when we pulled down the ratty little starched cloth shade and drew the dusty scrim curtains, as of course we had to. She asked if I thought there were any better rooms up on the West Side near where I lived. When I answered distractedly that I thought there might be, she surprised me very much the next time I saw her by ringing my doorbell and telling me she had just moved in across the street. I can tell you, it was a real surprise.

MEANWHILE Alma had reappeared again after over a year. I could no longer remember how long it was, exactly. She hadn't come back after my purported trip to Washington, and had obviously got the idea correctly that I was phasing her out. Alma had been going to night school at City College, in the hope of getting out of working in the necktie sweat-shop forever. And also clearly in the hope of finding another, better boyfriend, which she had done. The boyfriend had now been called up in the draft, for the army, so Alma had come back to me. She was about twenty-four now — I was twenty-seven — and she had very definite sexual needs, which wanted satisfying. She was deeply troubled because she wasn't married yet, and I got the impression that the relatives she still lived with in Brooklyn, just beyond the Delaney Street Bridge, were now making fun of her a little for not having yet caught a man.

I began making love to Alma again Sunday afternoons, for a brief while, as making love to Beverley distressed me somewhat owing to her almost total lack of response. I was also taking notes heavily then on my sex life, because it worried me. I was not used to cold women, and they hurt my sexual pride greatly, even though I was very tender and understanding about it. Beverley was also willing to do anything whatever that I might want in bed, but Alma still drew the line at sucking me, though she was still wild about being sucked herself. I told her frankly I had another girl who was not so narrow-minded, and so unfair.

"Oh," she said lightly, "I was sure you had another girl while I was gone. I had another fellow too." So there!

But when I told her that Beverley was now actually living right across the street, I could see from Alma's sudden tense expression that she knew even better than I did what that meant.

"Are you going to marry her?" she asked, biting her lip.

I explained to her again — it wasn't for the first time — that I wasn't marrying anybody. I wanted to study and to write. I had only published one book so far, of which the edition had been almost entirely destroyed, and some minor journal articles and stories, and things of which I wasn't particularly proud. I wanted to live for my writing, and have a career. I was born to write and speak. I was not a family man. Alma almost looked as thought she understood, and pulled me over on to her brightly to make love. This time she actually did try to suck me, but drew back after having started, and knelt there naked on the bed, her fists clenched close by her breasts, her throat wracked by spasms of dry retching. Yet she had swallowed nothing, and had hardly more than touched me with her lips.

"I can't!" she wept. "I can't! Please, please! Don't ask me to!" I waited till the retching stopped before speaking.

"*Why* can't you do it, Alma?" I asked gently. "Millions of women do it, and they like it very much. Even animals do it, so it must be natural."

"I can't!" she cried. "I can't! You touch goyishe women with your penis, and it's *treyfeh*!"

This was really too much for me, and I thought I'd break down in a spasm of laughter myself. So that was it. I was ritually unclean, even if I washed between women. What about my tongue? Why wasn't that taboo, because I kissed Christian women too?

"But Alma," I told her, as seriously as I could, "I'm not food. You're not going to swallow me." She wrung her hands and shook her head, swaying her whole upper body in lamentation from side to side.

"Oh yes I am!" she wept. "That's just what you want! And besides it's *despoiling nature*. The juice is meant for making babies — not to eat!"

She bit her knuckles to try to stop herself from crying, or perhaps really to protect her mouth from me. The whole thing seemed crazy. If ritual uncleanliness could be removed at the vaginal end by bathing in the congregation's *mikveh*, couldn't she just gargle with the sacred water too? I decided it would be kinder not to discuss sexual and food taboos with Alma.

"I can't argue with all that much theology," I told her. "Where did you get that stuff from? Is it in the *Shulkan Arukh*?" That was the standard code of Jewish life and laws.

"Yes," she said. "My aunt's husband looked it up for her." I didn't believe it; I had already looked up cunnilinctus too.

"Well, what does it matter?" I argued. "Jews don't believe in Heaven and Hell."

"Maybe you don't," Alma said, "but *I* do!" A pause.

"Writers never go to hell;" I said; "they suffer enough in this world." Silence.

"Alma, we could never be married, could we?" I pointed out to her. "We'd fight like wild things. It's tragic enough this way." I meant comic, of course, but it's hard to tell a naked, kneeling woman, retching and filled with misery because she's trying to bend herself subserviently to what she considers your perverse erotic needs, that she's being comical. In fact, maybe she wasn't.

Somehow, I had the feeling that I wasn't outfitted with the kind of girlfriend I really wanted. This one was a hysterical prude, and at the same time as hot as a little red wagon. The other one across the street was sad and solemn and totally willing, and just as totally frigid. Something had gone wrong somewhere. And I couldn't blame it on the war, either. Well, at least Athena was out of my hair. She was really dangerous, behind her cool posturings of sincerity. And Mel's leftover Elena — ouch! Nevertheless, these two were just not the kind of girl I needed.

The next Sunday when I saw Alma she had come to a decision, but didn't tell me so. She had the grace to want to end nicely, and without any scenes, or not any worse than the one we had just had. Either she had decided I wasn't ever going to marry at all, or anyhow not her; or else I was too set in my sinful sexual ways for her ever to be able to live with, and still get to Heaven later. Either way, I was a bad investment, and she was about to write me off after eight years of waiting around and trying. She wore her nicest dress, of gold lamé cloth, which she told me she had found at the tie factory when the bolt came in, and got enough yards of it for a dress before the cutters started on it with their enormous shears. She had to work three weeks, without pay, to match the wholesale cost of enough cloth for a dress. Each square yard cost more than she was paid for a week's work.

Her aunt, who was a dressmaker, had cut and fitted the dress, and Alma had stitched it herself by hand, with incredibly tiny invisible stitches. She showed me all of this with care, flipping up the skirt to show me the painstaking work she had done, even on the hidden hem underneath. I understood what she was trying silently to say to me, about her abilities as a wife. I had sung it often enough with my family Friday nights at home, formally addressed to the woman of the house. Solomon said it, to end his Proverbs. He had seven hundred wives, so he must have been speaking from the heart: *"Who can find a virtuous wife? For her price is far above rubies. The heart of her husband shall safely trust in her . . . She seeketh wool and flax, and worketh them willingly with her hands . . . She maketh herself coverings of tapestry; her clothing is silk and purple."*

Alma wanted me to take her out in the park and photograph her in her beautiful gold lamé dress. She said she needed pictures for her family in Scranton. I took my little square mock-Rollei, and when we went downstairs I bought two reels of film at the candy store, fitting one into the camera before we went out into the bright autumn sun. When we came back to my room the sun was still high and I had a few frames left I hadn't shot in the park. I photographed Alma sitting kneeling on the bed, with the skirt of the golden dress spread carefully in a circle around her knees. This was the one picture that came out best later.

Then she stripped off her dress with a sweeping motion of both hands, from the knees right up over her head, and unsnapped her brassiere and shook it off her arms. She threw herself backwards on the bed, lifting her hips for me to pull her panties off her, and to begin our lovemaking by licking her pussy, as I always did. She had perfumed her pubic hair, something she had never done before. And I was sorry she had, because I much preferred her own natural vulvar odor to any perfume, but I appreciated the intended nicety. Though Alma was too proud to say so, and kept a calm and smiling air, I understood very well that this was goodbye. I was careful to give her several orgasms in a row before I allowed myself to come. I would leave a mark for the next man to shoot at.

When I took her to the subway later, by the park, Alma asked me if I would take her to a Broadway show next week. I was surprised by this evident postscript, but of course promised I would. We had seldom gone anywhere but to movies, or walking. If she felt she deserved a Broadway show for farewell, I couldn't argue with that. We had been to only two or three in all those years. I realized I was pretty cheap with my girlfriends, because I always thought of myself as poor. So rather than go Dutch, which I didn't like, we went nowhere but to bed. Whenever I did have any money, I spent it on books, and not on entertainments. This time I got tickets for what was supposed to be the funniest show in town, a variety show called *Hellzapoppin'*. It was pretty funny, but it tried much too hard, and the two showmen who ran it like circus ringmasters were very offensive, with their fake yoicks and pretended belly-laughs in overloud appreciation of their own humor.

As we came in the entrance, two ushers started herding us officiously down the orchestra aisle at one side, without even looking at our tickets, crying "This way, please! This way, please!"

"Hey, wait a minute!" I said. "Our seats are in the balcony." I pulled Alma back, who was already starting to follow the ushers' directions.

"Oh, please don't make a fuss!" she said, very tense, though she had been all smiles a moment before. "I just want to have a good time tonight. Please?!"

I told her firmly that I *knew* I had bought balcony seats, and that if we wandered down into the orchestra stalls the way we were being herded, we'd only be put out finally when they looked at our tickets, and sent back up to the balcony. I really hadn't had money enough for orchestra seats, and was getting tense myself and feeling shamed.

When we got to our balcony seats finally, Alma tossed up her gold lamé skirt in back and sat down on her panties instead, so as not to spoil the cloth. And what did we then see on the stage but a highly-amusing curtain-raiser entertainment in which embarrassed-looking men and women holding tickets in their hands were being herded out on the stage from the wings by the ushers; casting confused glances behind them saying more clearly than words, "How the hell did we get *here*?" Just innocent chumps, there for a good time, like us. And the jolly ringmaster, with his hat on, looking at their tickets with mock sobriety, at which point — WHOOSH!! — a burst of air, as at Luna Park in Coney Island, up from under the stage. And the man's hat blew away, if he had one, and of course the woman's skirt — high over her head! And the woman screamed, every time.

One woman realized what was happening — so similar to the innocent "showers" at Auschwitz, for our pleasure — from seeing the woman ahead of her with her skirt over her head and hearing her scream. She balked and absolutely refused to advance with her escort and their tickets to the ringmaster's outstretched hand. Instead, she got out of the line sideways and climbed down off the stage clumsily over the footlights, with her mortified escort helping and following her the best he could.

The ringmaster, whose name was either Olsen or Johnson, was piqued that she had got away, and advanced to the footlights to shake an admonitory forefinger at her. "All right, honey," he brayed. "Next time *you'll wear them!* Ho, ho, ho!!" I thought of this scene often, the next year, when all of us in the country were stunned — except the State Department diplomats who had known all about it for a year or more, but had carefully kept the secret — by the discovery of the German death camps by the advancing Russian army, and the details of how the Jews had been herded quietly, without any fuss, into the large gassing chambers stark naked, with the explanation that they were going to "the showers" for delousing. Yes, it was a very funny show. The funniest in town.

At the intermission I had to pee, like everybody else, and went out and lined up after a couple of dozen other men outside the restrooms. Inside the urinals, the little chunks of camphor that were dropped loose into the drain to absorb the odor were in the shape of large gambling dice, with spots of color. Against the back of each urinal, where the piss hit, was a life-sized caricature in colors, obviously painted or put on by decalcomania, of Hitler, Mussolini, or the Japanese premier Tojo. After I pissed pleasurably in Hitler's eye, I waited around until a toilet booth was free. I wanted to know, for when I would write up my notes when I got home, how the toilets were no doubt matchingly decorated. Yes indeed. Inside the toilet bowl was painted another portrait of Hitler, looking up, this time with his mouth wide open around the drain hole, so that when the toilet was flushed the shit would shoot down Hitler's throat. The funniest show in town. King Louis the Sixteenth had a chamber pot like that made with Benjamin Franklin open-mouthed inside. Ho, ho, ho.

When I got back to my seat, Alma lifted her spread-out skirt slightly for me to sit down again beside her. A lovely, graceful gesture. I didn't bother to tell her about the toilet room decorations. Suddenly, to my intense astonishment, my father walked up the aisle with a big smile, and sidled along in our row to say hello to us and to be introduced to Alma. He had been sitting on the other side of the balcony, and noticed us during the first act. Alma said very little except for how-do-you-do, and put her foot lightly on my instep to stop me when I started telling him that she came from Scranton too, and had lived in The Flats. But why was my father there? The outfit he worked for in Scranton, which was then the state liquor store, was given two sets of free tickets each week for a Broadway show by one of the big liquor companies, to sort of remind the clerks to push their brands. My father and another employee had come to New York in their car with another couple. My mother was not with him. Her legs had been hurting her, and she didn't want to travel away from home.

My father added that my mother had been working very hard in the garden to help the war effort. Under the shadow of the two big oak trees where the squirrels flirted their umbrella tails in our back yard, the ground was just right for clematis and lilies-of-the-valley, and my mother had always grown them there. Most people couldn't succeed with them. At the annual Spring charity dinner for the Jewish Home of the Friendless my mother was always prouder of her bowls of lilies-of-the-valley, in the centerpieces on the tables, than of the embroidered tablecloths she had slaved over for them and the clothes she had been knitting for the orphans all year. Now the government medical services had announced with signs in all the post offices that they wanted lilies-of-the-valley — not the flowers, but the long pointed leaves which contained a special drug that was needed for the wounded soldiers, to replace some other drug now impossible to get because of the war.

My mother planted all our back yard with hundreds of bulbs of lilies-of-the-valley — the government medical service would give you the bulbs free if you'd try to grow them — and she was on her knees there now, most of every afternoon, coaxing and cultivating the plants with a tiny steel hand-claw and hoe. She kneeled on a rubber floor-scrubbing pad, of course, my father said, but it was very bad for her arthritis. My father had tried to get her to stop, but she insisted. The next month when I was home for Thanksgiving, I congratulated my mother on her lilies-of-the-valley. She said it wasn't anything much, and that while she worked she used to recite in chronological order the names of all the presidents of the United States, which she was memorizing. Whenever she read the terrible news about the war, she thanked God she was in America now for thirty-five years. She was worried about her family in Rumania. She said Daddy had told her about meeting me by accident at the show in New York. He hadn't liked Alma, my mother said. He thought she looked too *Jewish*. Now I understood. Leaders in Israel should not have wives who looked too Jewish.

GIRLS dropped from Heaven sometimes. Beverley and I weren't married yet, and it never even occurred to me that we would marry. She was just one more girlfriend at first, and certainly the most gauche and least interesting one in bed, but I felt she was an unhappy waif and somebody ought to be nice to her. Pity is a damn poor emotion to base a marriage on. I didn't realize that then. Anyhow, I kept going meanwhile with all the steady girls I had — which was about two or three then — and didn't hesitate to take up with new ones. I tried to avoid one-night stands, but it sometimes happened that way. You can't please everyone. The girls are shopping around, just like the men are, though mostly for marriage and not just for affairs. Marriage wasn't at all what I had in mind then. The only girl I had ever even thought of marrying, red-headed goddess Magdalen Currie, I had let move away to Chicago and then to California. Without often saying it aloud, even to myself, I was waiting for true love. Meanwhile, I was willing to settle for sex and tenderness when I could get them.

One afternoon I came back to my room from lunch at the Japanese curry joint on Columbus Avenue to find a message scrawled on the telephone pad at the top of the stair landing: "Mr. Legmun. Girl colled. Geniver." That was old Mr. Nossiter's best telegraphic style, and you couldn't ask for more. As usual it drove me wild, especially since I couldn't imagine why Jennifer had called me. She was the tall, cute younger sister of one of my girlfriends named Helen Carlen, and both sisters were honey-blondes of the clean shicksa type that wasn't really my favorite but that made all the other guys stare jealously when you paraded one of them on your arm. But Jennifer never called back. I didn't really think she would. She was always a bit feather-headed and the family pet because she was the youngest and so sweet and cute. I decided it had probably only been a message from her older sister. However, when I finished my afternoon's work and went downstairs, figuring to go and have supper with Beverley on Grove Street, I found Jennifer Carlen standing on the stoop outside my door in conversation with Wally, a Cuban-Spaniard who had a room downstairs. Wally was a somewhat older man with terrible teeth and always very flashily dressed who was one of my best sources for offcolor wallet cards and novelties.

"Oh, there he is now!" Jennifer trilled brightly. "I won't need these after all, but thank you." And to my astonishment she handed Wally back a long zoot-suit chain at the end of which was a ring full of keys.

I took Jennifer by the arm in a more or less proprietary gesture and with a very lukewarm smile to Wally, started down the steps with her, walking her quickly toward Columbus Avenue. I knew I wasn't going to take her up to my room immediately after a tableau like that, which I wasn't even sure I understood. She explained that Wally had helpfully assured her that I wasn't home, and when she then confided to him that she was stranded in New York that day with nowhere to stay, he had gallantly unhitched his key chain from his belt and given it to her – in case she didn't find me. He was a smooth worker, I must say. I would settle him later, the son of a bitch!

Jennifer and I had coffee sodas at the drugstore that served Ricciardi ice cream, which I assured her was the best, and then walked the long way around the park and back to my room. She was indeed stranded in town, where she had come to stay the weekend with her new boyfriend, who she explained was a jazz musician. She didn't say anything about his color, but I understood from her references to it taking place in Harlem that he was colored. They had made love perfectly nicely all night, she said, but then in the morning he suddenly turned ugly and wanted to beat her. She had grabbed her clothes and shoes and run away, thinking she would go to her sister Helen's place, but found when she got there that Helen was out of town, and the superintendent wouldn't let her into the apartment. So she had called me, because she said she knew I wouldn't let her down.

Of course I wouldn't, I assured her, not saying anything about her having calmly hedged her bet for a bed for the night with Cuban Wally. As I often stayed at the Public Library till closing time at ten p.m., I knew Beverley wouldn't be worried about my not coming for supper, and would also go to bed if I weren't there by eleven, as she had her job to get up for in the morning. Jennifer and I talked for a while, and of course I played her all the few blues records I had, and *Strange Fruit*, which she adored, especially the throaty contralto. Now that I had discovered Conchita Supervia, I understood the tremendous attraction and excitement of that kind of voice, which had never touched me particularly on the blues records. The controlled, ripping intensity, like Spanish Flamenco singing, was really what hit me hardest in Supervia's voice — that and her sudden descents into deep, powerfully passionate utterances, almost in another voice.

After a while, Jennifer said calmly that she was terribly hungry, and had used up most of her money the day before, on subways, and on telephone calls today. We went out again to eat, all the way over to a Chinese restaurant on Broadway, to make things a bit gala for her weekend in town. I didn't suggest going out to a show, or even a movie, because the meal for two would eat up all the money I had. I honestly couldn't afford to constitute myself an entertainment service for loose blondes in New York. Over the rice-bowls and fun with the chopsticks I asked her cautiously if she was in love with her musician boyfriend.

"Oh no," she said brightly, "I'm just having adventures! I'm young!"

"I dunno," I surmised, "getting beaten up in Harlem by a black jazzman doesn't seem like much of an adventure to me."

Well, he had been lovely until then, Jennifer assured me, and so had all his friends, the other musicians. I tried to explain to her that she should be very careful, and could end up getting gang-shagged or prostituted by her boyfriend before she really knew what was happening. Little did I know then that she had taken them all on. It wouldn't be exactly white-slaving, I went on stupidly, but surprisingly close. I touched on this as lightly as I could, but tried to make it definite. Jennifer was pleasant to be with, but distinctly dumb, or let's say shallow under her bright and pretty air. I wasn't sure I was entirely pleased in the knowledge that we were of course going to sleep together. Mostly it wasn't very flattering to get her just because she had nowhere else to go. Mr. Wally would clearly have been satisfied with that, but I wasn't. I also caught myself wondering if I really wanted her — if she had perhaps picked up some disease or other in her adventure in Harlem. I was ashamed of thinking this, since I understood perfectly that I was feeling racial prejudice. On the other hand, there is certainly a lot of venereal disease — and every other kind — in Harlem, and that's a fact of life too.

Sloppy seconds or no, Jennifer in bed was an absolute dream. She was not passionate in the way her older sister was, but she was tremendously willing, and anxious to please in every way. It wasn't exactly authentic — something I always cared about very much — to be sexually serviced in this way by a woman, instead of two people flowing and exchanging together their mutual passion, but it was enormously pleasant and flattering. I wondered if the women I made love to experienced in the same way my intense need to satisfy them sexually, if necessary *forcing* them to orgasm. Jennifer's specialty was anything oral, and she began by pouring up her saliva into my mouth when I kissed her, something I have always thought of as the man's prerogative in its evident symbolism, but after all why not? Then she curled up on the bed between my legs and began sucking my penis and lapping my balls in the most artistic and refined fashion possible. I saw this was never going to excite me in the deep way I wanted, so I began studying her art instead, in the way of taking mental notes to write down later.

Jennifer drew her head away with a long pouting kissing sound as her lips drew off the head of my prick, and she looked up at me fetchingly. I had left the light on, on purpose, with a dark red woollen cloth thrown over the top of the lamp, on the pretext that I needed the light to change the phonograph records, but actually to enjoy the sight of her blonde prettiness and pink tits. Then she spoiled everything with her next question.

"Do you think I do it well?" Jennifer asked, dangling her tongue out at me in invitation. "My friends say I'm wonderful at it."

This would have infuriated me if I could have taken her seriously, so I pretended to be infuriated and threw myself on her, going through a pretence of rape alternately orally and vaginally. The moment I became rough with her, Jennifer's artistic flutiness disappeared and she was real. Her body bucked up against mine violently at every stroke inside her vagina, and when I changed to her mouth and throat she took me deep and hard, her fingernails sinking into my buttocks to pull me even deeper into her throat and of course to get back a little violence and mild cruelty of her own. The artistic foreplay had left me cold, really; but fucking her violently this way, as though it were a revenge, was very powerful and exciting. I wanted to pull out at a certain point, and go back into her cunt, to make sure she would come too, but she wouldn't let me out of her mouth and kept raking my loins with her nails until I came. Whoever taught her had taught her well.

Jennifer lifted her mouth out of my crotch very lingeringly as I rolled off her, her lips still pouting and savoring and unwilling to end. I lay back on the pillows thrown against the wall, waiting for her to come up to me, but she didn't move. "I love it so!" she breathed in a dark voice. "Oh, I love it!" When you can't say "I love you," I guess you can always say that. It's some kind of love, anyway. She licked her lower lip as though to find a drop still there, but of course there was nothing there, as she had swallowed it all, and would have swallowed quarts more if I'd had it. How many gallons of jism does a woman swallow or accept into her belly in a lifetime, I wondered vaguely?

Anyhow, it was Jennifer's turn now, according to all the rules, and I pulled open her legs like a wishbone and began to suck her pussy to make her come, using all my fingers and thumbs somewhere at the same time, in or out or who knows what. Making another person come when you yourself have come already is a sort of social heroism, but one always has to hang on and try anyway. *Noblesse oblige.* Jennifer's feeling was still all in her mouth, though, and not really in her clitoris or anywhere below the bellybutton.

Above the mountain-line of her breasts — my horizon as I lay there with my face between her thighs — her nipples stiff as pink stalagmites, I could see Jennifer's mouth still kissing and yearning and accepting, with her open lips mouthing the air, eager to be orally involved in everything I was doing to her with my mouth. Now she was sucking or biting her bent knuckles too. I bit her thighs lightly a few times, and tugged on her pussy lips harmlessly with my teeth. I was pretty sure her touch of masochism would go at least that far, and maybe a lot further, and felt no sin. She came slowly but abundantly, whimpering in low happy bursts and grunts. I was glad to see her artificiality stripped away. When we rolled apart after a while, to sleep, Jennifer grabbed my face and licked her juices greedily from my chops. Then she curled down again and fell asleep with her head on my thighs, my penis soft against the side of her mouth and cheek, like a stubby mushroom now, waiting for next time.

It was late. Down alone at Grove Street, Beverley would be asleep by now. Jennifer was asleep too, her breath soft but raucous. I pushed her hip to one side a bit, to press down my pillow, so I could sleep too. My women were all tucked in. Not true, of course, but that was how I felt. A harem was a responsibility, not just a delight, and don't let anyone tell you differently. Along the hairline between Jennifer's buttocks a tiny grummet of shit caught my eye, high up toward the dimples of her back. Not clean, that. It saddened rather than disgusted me. I slipped off the bed and turned out the floor lamp, then came back and wiped Jennifer clean with the corner of the cloth I had taken off the lamp. If that accidental grummet was all the disease she had caught in Harlem, I was well out of it. We slept.

Dressing together in the morning, I asked Jennifer if she'd go back to her hometown if I gave her money for a train ticket, or if she'd hightail it immediately up to Harlem. She told me frankly she wasn't sure, so we settled for me going downstairs in my bathrobe and phoning her older sister Helen, who for a miracle had now come back. We arranged that Jennifer would come to see her for lunch. After that it'd be her baby. I refused to give any details. Jennifer and I made love again, very simply, and then finished dressing. She was twice as pretty by daylight as I had remembered, and I had the vanity to sling the little camera over my shoulder and trot her off to Central Park, where I took Jennifer's picture by some high rocks with her skirt naughtily perked up with both her hands, and one knee bent in pure pinup style. This was for my sex scrapbook, I admitted. "A tribute to your beauty," I added weakly. Jennifer smiled. "You won't need my picture for your own scrapbook," I told her. "I bit my initials inside your thigh. With a heart."

"Yes you did, you devil!" she laughed. "I *never* bite."

I wondered what Helen would say to her at lunch about Jennifer jealously stealing her boyfriend, and whether I was the first man the two sisters had ever shared. That stuff in *Ezekiel*, in the *Bible* about incest with sisters and their mothers is just bunkum, of course. Everybody knows that real incest is only with your own sister. Plenty of boys and men have done that in every country of the world, and with their daughters too, when the time comes. As Freud remarked, no one would bother to forbid something that nobody wants to do. Jennifer had confided to me at supper the night before that she was also secretly sleeping with her brother Lance, an adolescent drunk. He was mostly homosexual, but was now madly in love with Jennifer, and violently jealous of all her boyfriends. That was one main reason she had lit out for New York, to relieve the pressure on them both. Their father, a confirmed romantic, had named all the children out of history: the first daughter Helen, for

Helen of Troy, and the later boy and girl Lancelot and Guinevere – that was Jennifer. They had all simply succumbed to the erotic pressure of their names.

❦

MY FAVORITE girlfriend Magdalen Currie was in New York for a week at Christmas with her new lover, Stavros Nicolaïdes, whom she'd met in San Francisco. Stavros was great. He was a short, stocky Greek-American, with powerful hands and shoulders like the half-man half-bull of Minos. He had lots of dark hair, and wore his shirt collar out over his jacket, without a tie, altogether very much like myself. He looked like a good-natured truck driver, but was actually a poet, and worked for the Greek Consulate in San Francisco. Magdalen had met him in connection with a stevedore strike in the port there, when her advertising agency was called in to do public relations for the strikers' union, most of whose members were for some reason Greek-Americans.

Stavros had explained to Magdalen the strikers' position, and then all about Greek bouzouki music, and had taken her to special waterfront bars where she could hear Greek music and singing. By midnight he had of course become her lover, and was now explaining to her all about Greece. He also pointed out to her that her name was Greek, which she had never realized before, and Magdalen was now well on her way to becoming the first blonde Greek patriot.

When I met him, Stavros was interested only in talking intensely about the war, which was just then approaching its victorious crisis. But the background machinations were about what you might expect. Especially in Greece. The Anglo-American forces had been stopped all autumn by the Germans under Von Rundstedt, after their first invasion successes, and the Germans were now counterattacking at the "Bulge" of Belgium and Luxembourg. But the Russian forces — two hundred divisions — over five times as large as that of the combined Allies, were inexorably rolling west, mopping up the Germans as they went, and Nazi Germany was *kaputt*. Roosevelt, Churchill and Stalin were to meet a month later at Yalta in the Russian Crimea, to divide up the spoils of war, while the mere soldiers did a couple of more months of the necessary killing and dying.

Winston Churchill, whose Empire was now lost, was rushing about everywhere performing his final gesture of putting in his puppets, such as De Gaulle in France, most of whom he had kept eating high in London the whole time for just this purpose. Namely, to make sure that the withdrawal of the defeated Germans would not mean the triumph of the Communist parties allied to the victorious Russians. In Greece, for example, the British Army was now fighting side by side with the Fascist forces, against the leftist factions, exactly as they had done at the end of World War I; and Churchill and his foreign secretary Anthony Eden had just arrived in Athens with the necessary gold and political clout to try to stymie the leftist victory. Stavros Nicolaïdes, whose diplomatic job gave him more information than the newspapers gave us, was in a violent turmoil about all this. I was trying to learn what I could from him, but also to calm the poor guy down.

He apparently did not know that I had been Magdalen's lover before him, or if he knew, he didn't give a damn. He did not act like someone who, at that historical juncture, was thinking primarily about pussy at all. Presumably I was just a writer, a professional acquaintance of Magdalen's through her agency work. She now had a very good managerial job, which was bringing out the tendency to be bossy in her private life that was the only thing I had ever disliked about her. I prefer to be boss myself. Stavros paid no attention to Magda's various impractical demands. And sometimes rather imperious nonsense, but treated her like a lover as he understood the art. If she got in our way, while we were passionately discussing the fate of Greece and the war, he would give her a hearty slap on the ass which I would have thought would fell an ox. She loved it, and stood there canting her ass a bit higher as though daring or begging him to do it again.

"No!", he said. "One's enough." Then turning back to me: "I have to get to Greece. People in Paris during the Popular Front would say to me, 'Oh, you should have here before the War of 1914. It was magnificent then.' Well, Athens is like Paris was before 1914."

"You must be older than me if you were in the Popular Front," I said. "I wanted to go to Spain with the International Brigade, but they turned me down for being too young." In fact, he was five years older than me, and had been twenty-three at the time of the Popular Front.

"Isn't it strange?" Stavros said — he was calming down a bit — "all of us were so much against the war until Hitler and Franco came along."

"Yes," I said, "and carrying posters and writing articles against the 'Merchants of Death,' and Krupp and Schneider."

"And then the war against Franco came, and it was the right war. And we were the first ones to sign up." Later Stavros had worked on the Greek ships smuggling Jews into Palestine, he told us.

Magdalen came over and stood with her arm around his shoulder and her other hip casually touching me. She rumpled Stavros' hair and recited in an Irish lamenting sing-song: *"For men must fight, and women must weep, And the sooner it's over the sooner to sleep."*

Stavros had to leave then, for some professional reason, and left us to talk about our presumed mutual work. We had all had lunch together in her sister's apartment on Horatio Street. The minute he was gone she said, "Isn't Stavros wonderful?" I was examining the massive silver chess set her sister's husband was now manufacturing.

"He certainly is," I agreed. "Now that's the kind of man I really like! If we ever hear that Churchill's been assassinated we'll know who did it. But if you were still mine, I'd never leave you alone in an empty apartment with another man. Does he realize — ?"

"Sure he does," Magdalen told me with a rippling little laugh. "I told him I wanted him to meet you because you were the greatest lover I ever had before him."

"Well," I said, "I admit I'm flattered. It may not be very original to say, but I don't know what I admire most, your memory or your nerve. Does that mean he's better than I ever was?"

"No, no!" she assured me. "You're both the same. You even look alike. But he's more broadminded than you are. For one thing he isn't jealous. When he's away he doesn't care if I have other lovers, as long as I'm there waiting for him when he gets back."

"I'm the same way," I expostulated. "How many men do you know that would have gone away and left you in bed with little Susan?"

Magdalen brought out a bottle of Greek brandy that Stavros was teaching her to drink. The first swig nearly killed me — it tasted like liquorice: my favorite hate — but she seemed to love it. I sat nursing my glass so she wouldn't refill it. Magdalen wandered off now into a long tale about her older sister Josette, who had loaned her the apartment, and told her that the *acme of human sensation* was for a woman to have two men making love to her at once, simultaneously. Not top & bottom that is, but front & back. The effects of the bouzouki brandy cleared off me instantly, and I gave Magda a reproachful look.

"Why not three men?" I asked. "You have three holes. And then there's your armpits."

"Because it's too darn hard finding three men that want to be friends. You know, darling," she said, pouring more brandy, "I'm not really joking. I may get married one day. I want to have tried *everything* first, before I have to learn to be sedate. Why not? We did everything with Susan, didn't we?"

"That's different," I said.

"Sure! Because it's two women, and one man mastering them both. Double standard!"

"That's right," I admitted brashly. "The double standard. You don't mind my plain English, do you? You're the finest woman I ever fucked, but that doesn't mean that I want to play out this little bedroom comedy you have in mind, with you mastering me, and another man too, like a queen bee and a couple of her drones. Just because your sister says it's the *acme of human sensation*. I didn't know you were so jealous of her." I wasn't really sore yet, but I was getting there.

"I don't think it would be me mastering anybody," Magdalen said, not argumentatively, but dreamily. "I think it would be more like both of you mastering *me*. And I'm willing!"

I did drink the Greek brandy then, and it was still awful. "Is that why you phoned me to come for lunch? Just to make up a threesome?"

She nodded. "I want to try it," she said simply. "You once said that everything is permitted between Christmas and New Year's. I want it to be with you and Stavros because I trust you both. I don't mean trust you not to tell — you can tell if you want. I mean the idea is kind of scary, too. Both of you charging at me madly, maybe hurting me."

"I saw how he hits you. Where's your feminism gone? I'm going to hit you myself in a minute if you don't stop!"

"So hit me," she shrugged. "Anything is better than being neutral."

"I'm not neutral. I'm against it!" I felt at a loss. Had it been knowing me that had changed Magdalen? We should never have gone to that Lesbian party. But that was years before. I didn't want to fight. I took her and kissed her. "Be nice, sweetheart, I said cajolingly. "Be nice."

"I'm not nice anymore," Magdalen said ruefully. "I have a job where I boss a dozen people around all day. Pretty soon I'll just be a slave-driver grinding de woikus for de benefit o' de bosses. I'm losing my femininity. I want to throw myself into sex again, like a total woman — the way we used to do when you weren't such a goddamned prude!"

"It sounds to me," I said grimly, "like you want to offer yourself up as a sin-offering front and back, so you'll be punished by his prick and mine for one week of slave-driving, and be shriven so you can start on another — another week of slave-driving. Will you go to confession first? Do you want us to whip you too?" But I was already whipping her with my tongue, and figured I'd better stop. We were both silent for a while.

"I'll tell you the truth," I said, beginning again in a much quieter tone and concentrating hard on trying to say it right. "It's too homosexual for me. I'm not prudish — you know me — but I just can't do things to you with another man plugged into your opposite end. I'm not even sure I could get it up in a situation like that. I'm not afraid he'd bugger me. I just don't want to see him bugger *you!* I'd be strangling inside. So we toss a coin for which ends we take, right? For starters, I take your mouth and he takes your pussy, because maybe you'll marry him later. Now it's great for *you* — I don't deny it — but whether you're on your back or your belly, there I am staring into his eyes the whole while, and him staring into mine. What the hell do we talk about – the Popular Front? He kisses one titty; I kiss the other. You love it; you're just rolling up your eyes. But the truth is, he and I are really fucking each other, using your body."

"Keep talking, darling," said Magdalen, with her long rippling laugh of long ago; "I could listen to you all night."

I was in my anger now, glaring at her with my eyes fixed, not able to stop. "Yeah! We're all charging away at you. And at each other! Because we'd be ashamed to leave you out, and bugger each other straight. Anyhow, not the first night. The second night we wouldn't be ashamed, and we *would* leave you out. Just like you and Susan when I wasn't there. I'm sorry, I can't go it. With another woman, yes; but I can't do it with another man. *I don't want to see another man fucking you!* Bad enough to know about it! Sure — then we trade ends. Set 'em up in the next alley! Well, I just don't want to put my prick in your pussy when it's full of another man's come! And I won't suck it out again, either. Not my style."

"Why is come so terrible?" Magdalen asked, looking me right in the eye. "I love it."

"It's different for a woman. Double standard! You're a woman. I'm not. You were born to receive a man's semen into your body; yes, and have a baby because of it. Everything else you do — everything else you ever did with me — it's just marking time. What is this crap about *the acme of human sensation!?* You really think it feels so different from having two fingers or a dildo up your ass at the same time, with a prick in front? I mean, pardon my crudity."

"Well, aren't there other ways?" Magdalen said quietly. "Surely there must be some position in the Golden Book —"

"No, that's the Silver Book!" I interrupted her, angry and impolite.

"— the Silver Book, where *I* can experience what you used to have with Susan and me? You certainly seemed to like it. So would I."

"I don't deny it," I said. "And didn't you have it at both ends with Susan and me, too? But with another man you'll never have it with me! What is all this anyhow — just jealousy? Male protest? Penis envy? The works?"

"Oh darling!" she cried, "you know that's not me."

"That's just what I told you," I snapped. "It's not *me!* So we're not at both ends — him and me — top and bottom. It's front and back now. Me in front; him in back — he's a Greek, isn't he? He's been buggering your ass off for months, hasn't he? And what happens? The two of us just *squash you flat*, swapping spit with each other! Get another Greek!" Wild denunciations like that of the people I love are my worst fault. This was really just a mild one. But neither of us was really angry, and we kissed when I left her uptown later.

It was the first time I had ever been alone with Magdalen without making love to her, and I assumed I never would again. Too bad. She was the best. But the ruckus over Stavros, and my total unwillingness to share her in a trio with another man — I had found it hard enough at first, I remembered, to master my feelings of jealousy, even with intense little Susan as third party in bed — didn't really cause any coldness between Magdalen and me. She understood perfectly why I was refusing, anyhow she accepted it as jealousy and not as fear. Maybe she was too gullible. I hope she found her "acme of human sensation" later with Stavros and some other pansexual Greek. I'm not built for that work, and I know it. Too proud.

Instead we made love together sweetly and beautifully, just the two of us, a few days later — it was for the last time ever — when Magdalen phoned me suddenly to say that she was still in New York, and that it was her birthday and she didn't want to spend it alone. I did not ask about Stavros, but she told me anyhow. He was in Washington in connection with something about the Greek civil war, in which Churchill and the British evacuating forces were making Greece accept a monarchy, which meant fascist government by the generals. The usual thing: it would "prevent communism." Stavros was doubtless planning to get to Athens to assassinate Churchill for real this time.

As I was going out the door at 76th Street, I met Beverley trudging up the porch stairs. Now that she was living across the street, she came over whenever she liked, without any prearrangement, and the truth is it disturbed me quite a bit and prevented me from working. Perhaps that was why I had the unkindness to tell her with brutal candor, "I have to go. It's Magdalen's birthday, and she wants me to make love to her. I can't refuse an appeal like that."

Beverley did not turn a hair. She walked back down the stairs with me, reached forward her face for me to kiss her when we parted at the sidewalk, and trudged back across the street, saying quietly, "Come back to me."

Magdalen was very passionate. She said she was just over her period a few days before Christmas. I didn't inquire how many days: she had always kept perfect track of that. Her nipples and areolæ, which were always big, seemed simply enormous. I wondered if she was really kidding me and was really pregnant. I had brought along a bottle of white Niagara wine — I couldn't find any French wine — and a pretty little birthday cake, really a decorated cheesecake from a small French bakery I knew in the East 70s, where they also made little round balls of bitter-sweet chocolate rolled in powdered cocoa, called truffles in French. I brought some of those too, as I liked them even better than the exquisite cheesecake, though of course they're bad for the arteries. As my ultimate ambition sexually, like every other man, is to die of a heart attack at orgasm in the arms of a passionate woman — not much fun for her, pushing me off, I admit — it's hard to worry about arteriosclerosis while buying erotic dainties.

We naturally found a moment in our lovemaking for me to push one or two of the little truffle chocolates into her pussy and eat them out again. This was originally Magdalen's own idea, though other people may have thought of it too, and it was supposed to appear in *Oragenitalism*. But Magdalen had insisted it was too good for the *hoi polloi*, and that we should keep something secret for ourselves. So instead I mentioned only using strawberries, sweet cherries (pitted), and sections of orange, and slices of apple dipped in honey. I also accidentally forgot bananas! — pure jealousy, of course. The honey and apple proved to be a real disaster when we tried it for the second time, because the honey got into my eyebrows. I put out a much enlarged edition of *Oragenitalism* — in 1969, of course. My publisher was even threatening for a while to put out an illustrated edition in which none of the men are to wear beards: too confusing. But if there is ever another revised edition I plan to put in the chocolates and leave out the honey. *Let 'em eat cake!*

Owing to the loose cocoa that the French chocolates were rolled in, we pushed a pillow under Magdalen's bottom, as we would have anyhow as I sucked her, to keep from staining the sheet with chocolate. She was wearing Blue Chemise II, daughter of the original blue nightgown of years before, and just for fun I sucked her first through the silk jersey of the chemise, pulling the clinging thin wet silk into my mouth together with her long pulpy pussy-lips, and tongued her clitoris as best I could through it. It didn't really feel as sensuous to the tongue as it does to the hand, but the idea was very exciting to both of us. Then I dragged the chemise away with my mouth and began dipping the chocolates into her one by one, and with only my tongue and lips, sucking and eating them out again. Of course, it was pretty hard to get them out, but that's part of the fun. Eventually I had to use my fingers and all, but Magdalen loved that just as much or more.

We had drunk up all the wine with the cheesecake, and I was a bit heady. Half a bottle of wine is my limit — after that I get tipsy. As I was lying there with my head on Magdalen's thigh, listening to the music on the radio, and lazily dipping the chocolates into her and eating them out, all beautifully improved by her own flavors and juices. I must have forgotten at a certain point to give her any.

"Beast!" she said finally, "where's my share?"

I rose up between her thighs and lay down on her breasts to bite into the chocolate with her, half and half. "Isn't it a pity Susan isn't here now?" I mused — it was the wine — "She always thought pussy-chocolates were the manna of heaven. And they are."

"What nerve you have!" Magdalen admired. "You and your double standard! You're afraid of another man in bed, but you'd like to have Susan bothering us now. Are you still seeing her?"

"No," I admitted. "I got jealous of her Lesbian friends. The same as if it were a man. I'm even jealous of your vibrators."

We made love. A little of the chocolate had melted inside her and we found it later on me, so Magdalen had a taste of that too. We rested a long while, and listened to music on the radio. Not many announcements: WQXR was always wonderfully discreet. Then we made love again. Magdalen came very powerfully, two or three times to each orgasm of mine. I thought of her womb all open and desirous, just like the rest of her was, and drinking up my semen.

Afterward Magdalen was sitting naked at the mirror, making up her mouth for us to dress and go out. Her lips were so full that when I kissed her they would turn outward and leave a faint line of lipstick all around her mouth. Her pussy-lips were the same; often I had to spread them with my fingers before entering her, to keep from tucking them inside as I drove in. I looked thoughtfully at those lovely large nipples and those dark pink areolæ as big as heraldic shields.

"If you have a baby with those French chocolates," I said stupidly, "it's sure to be a Negro."

"I'll name him after you," Magdalen promised, smiling. "That way, if you ever hear about a famous Negro scholar called Gershon Anybody — you'll know."

We kissed again to seal the bargain, and fell back together on the bed. She took my prick through the cloth of my trousers and moulded it, closing her eyes and yearning toward me with her open mouth and hands as eagerly as if she hadn't made love for months. We made love again, this time with our clothes on and all disarrayed. When I tried to get up, Magdalen pulled me back with her.

"Shall we go out to dinner?" I asked.

"Yes," she said, "yes. But stay with me a while longer. The dusk is so sharp. It's hard to endure."

Magdalen and I never saw each another again, though we did correspond for many years, even after she was married. She was very unhappy, because she and her husband had to live in Washington for some job with the World Health Organization. She didn't marry Stavros; she surely should have. And she now found Washington a cold, cruel place, at once frantic and very dull. She wrote to me once that she saw a small ad in the papers, about a "Non-Conformists Club" being started. It was the first ray of hope she'd had in years, Magdalen said. She rushed off to join, and was stupefied when the entire first meeting was spent electing officers, all of whom made little campaign speeches about their idea of how nonconformity should be done. Magdalen was livid with fury, she wrote, and challenged one of them after his little speech.

"It seems to me," she said, "that you stand for exactly what *he* stands for" — pointing at the speaker before.

"Of course I do," he told her patiently, with a smile all around at the other members. "The question is just: do you want *him*, or do you want *me?*"

They then all sat, raising their hands, up & down, in perfect order, doing the electing; and ended by voting on all the rules and regulations of the club, according to which the Non-Conformists would non-conform. When the meeting was over, Magdalen went home and got drunk.

BEVERLEY was a mysterious being whom no one but me had ever been able to understand, or even approach. Why I was able to approach her was also a mystery, to which I never really knew the answer. I guess she was ready — rotten-ripe under her child-like exterior. Two more dissimilar people never tried to love each other and be happy together. It was not easy. Under her ostentatiously visible surface air of shyness and withdrawal — flown silently but incessantly, like a desperate S.O.S. signal from a ship in distress — Beverley was as fiercely private to herself as any small animal at bay. Her struggle against the world, by the time I met her, was intended only to hold it out and away from her. She wanted nothing else. The world had almost nothing Beverley wanted anymore or would accept from it. If it had broken roughly through her fragile outer integument of silence, she would have had no defense but suicide, which would not have been so very different from the monastic life she lived. But in another sense, Beverley wanted and was waiting for *everything* from the world, like a suckling child. But she was too proud, and too badly hurt from long long before, to ask for anything. It all had to be forced on her.

When I considered all the people on whom psychoanalysis is uselessly thrown away, simply because their families can afford to waste it on them, though the patients themselves flout and reject the whole thing and refuse to be cured, it drove me wild to realize that Beverley was ideally someone whom psychoanalysis could have helped. She was certainly blocked, and intensely repressed, but she and I consciously knew where her trauma had been, and that it was her parents who were the heart of her problem. I guess that's almost every young person's story. Perhaps for that reason both of Beverley's parents, whom I implored separately when we were at our most impoverished to advance us the money specifically for her analysis, even if only a month at a time, frigidly refused any such thing, or for that matter ever gave us a penny for anything else. No money, no little family presents, never any help of any kind, except an occasional small kitchen gift or dinner when they happened to be in town. Her father, a former army-officer, as I learned for the first time four years after we were married, had quite a large fortune which he intended to keep strictly for himself and his young second wife, and did so. He was an engineer and inventor, of gas refrigeration, among other things. He visited us once, and kissed Beverley lightly and distantly on the cheek when he arrived and when he left.

Her mother Kathleen vampirized Beverley whenever and however she could. I later found that she tried to vampirize everyone. In effect, her mother Kathleen was the anti-model that Beverley dedicated herself not to be like. I always got on very well with her, until almost the very end, when she became too big a problem for other people and in a very unappetizing way. And arrived in France, after her son and daughter-in-law were being driven nearly crazy by her, where she proceeded to try to drive her daughter and this son-in-law crazy. But I wasn't having any.

Far from wanting to help her daughter or anyone else, Kathleen Keith was strictly and only interested in what she could get out of whom, and how fast, and as much as possible, not excluding cash. She had once been an attractive woman, maybe twenty years before, and liked the adulation of men's company. So, after her husband divorced her for adultery in Canada decades before, she simply became a high-class gold-digger and hetaera, and supported herself — between vague department store jobs, when available men were scarce — as companion and mistress to the richest men she could snag. She then continued as an occasional prostitute of lower and lower class; finally, and before the distressed and astonished eyes of Beverley and myself, to young American sailors on leave in the harbor of Cannes, France, when she was nearly seventy years old, possibly a world's record.

At the beginning, we had no ostensible mother-in-law problem whatever. If Kathleen was no particular help, she was also no trouble. She lived her separate life of a middle-aged divorcée with many men friends. She did not act offensively flirtatious when I was around, and we seldom saw her. When she was in town she would sometimes invite Beverley and me to dinner. Kathleen was a very fine cook, and had learned her cooking professionally at a *Cordon Bleu* school in Paris, just after World War I, when she accompanied her husband who was then a Canadian army major, with their two small children, Beverley who was six, and her brother. Her Paris dressmaker, Mademoiselle Jeanne, whom I later met and knew, a little old hard-working *couturière* in a bleak apartment five storeys up, told me with shock — forty years after the event — how Kathleen would cleverly ditch the two kids at the dressmaker's apartment. And then go out on the spree to make whoopee, or *faire la bombe*, as Mademoiselle Jeanne precisely expressed it, helling it up around Paris with various British officers and other men friends behind her husband's back, under the pretext of her *Cordon Bleu* cooking-school lessons every afternoon.

However she herself learned, in spite of these distractions, Kathleen never taught Beverley how to cook, nor did she know how. Kathleen had naturally planned for her to marry a rich man, and to have servants, and did not think it necessary for Beverley to know anything. Beverley was in any case a great disappointment to her, especially in her absolute refusal to wear fashionable clothes or cosmetics like her mother — ever or at all. Kathleen had explained to Beverley that she couldn't expect to catch her a rich husband unless she at least dressed prettily, to which Beverley answered that she never planned to marry at all. That was how it happened that I met her, still unmarried when she was already thirty years old and looked like sixteen. Her mother didn't think much of me as a catch — no money — but at least I wore pants and laughed at her jokes, and now Beverley would not be an old maid for life. What I thought about Beverley's peculiar clothes, no one asked me.

We got married because Beverley was pregnant. It was my own fault. I was naturally trying to do the impossible, in holding on with my teeth while making love to her, to try to bring her to an orgasm. But I never succeeded. Meanwhile, this one time, I guess it must have been a combination of the music and my desperation, and I just did not pull out in time. When I felt myself coming inside her, I did not try to withdraw, because I knew it was too late, but hugged her even tighter and whispered to her, "We're making a baby now!" That's the Sunday punch that sometimes makes a frigid woman come, even when they only *imagine* it. This time it was true, although I didn't know it then, but even that didn't work.

When Magdalen left, just after Christmas; Beverley told me she was now two months pregnant. I thought over how much Magdalen had changed in four years, and how little I had ever wanted to marry Alma. Or anyone else. I had taken up with Beverley to protect her, and that was true. I couldn't let a waif like that have a baby without a husband. So we were married. I was never sorry, and felt I had done the right thing for her, and continued to protect her the best I could for the rest of her life. But I destroyed much of my own normal sex life in doing so, as I was continually tormented and depressed by Beverley's total frigidity. She was as willing as any woman could be in bed, but it meant nothing to her except as a sort of tenderness, and she was only trying to serve me sexually. I could not accept that.

I was prey just then, and therefore, to a lot of complicated emotions about her, and did not want Beverley living across the street from me. We would have a place down in the village, I insisted, where we would live and sleep together, and I would keep my furnished room uptown as an office or studio and go there every day. For a brief while our place was her mother's apartment, since Kathleen was again out of town. Then we found a small square back room on the ground floor at No. 68 Bedford Street, just where it touches Seventh Avenue, looking out over a tiny unkempt garden hidden behind the large billboard of a gas station on the Avenue.

There was a small Italian grocery store on that corner, and I would arrive every evening, when Beverley was back from working at the shipyard, and we'd have supper together. We mostly ate things like canned chili con carne, with a long, crackly bread and a salad I'd pick up in the Italian stores on Bleeker Street across the avenue. We drank milk; we couldn't afford wine. None of this involved any cooking ability. You just had to plug in the electric plate; not even strike a match. In the morning I would make scrambled eggs for both of us, with grated cheese or sometimes ham if there had been enough money for that. Then Beverley and I would walk up towards the ferry-slip, where we would meet her friend and co-worker Faith Craig, who was a folk singer, and they would take the ferry together to the shipyard. And I would continue on up to West 76th Street, to my room, now studio where all my books and papers were. And music. At night Beverley and I met again at our little room on Bedford Street; first every night, then later every other night.

Beverley's mother gave us two small heavy aluminum cooking pots for a housekeeping present. The tops fitted almost hermetically tight, so we called them Hermy I and Hermy II. That was Beverley's total dowry. One night we left the chili beans in one of them, and the cooked escarola salad in the other on the little electrical hotplate, because we were too tired to wash up. In the middle of the night we were awakened by a terrible noise, like a powerful gong. The cold chili beans had fermented, and had blown the tight top right off Hermy II and part way across the room, landing on the hearth with the great clangor that woke us up. It woke up the elderly maiden lady in the apartment above us too, and from then on we had trouble with her about every little thing, especially when our fireplace smoked. Her fireplace was connected. I guess she thought we were keeping out sexual score with a gong, and it excited and made her jealous.

When Beverley was nearly three months pregnant she told her mother for the first time. Her mother was very perturbed because she knew neither of us had anything in the bank, and that I had no steady job. She saw clearly that the moment Beverley's pregnancy would be so far advanced that she couldn't go to the shipyard anymore, some real help and maybe money would start being demanded of her, or at least needed. Beverley never demanded anything of anybody. She just stood there in her impoverishment until you couldn't bear to watch anymore, and forced everything on her that you knew she needed. Anyhow, that was how it had been with me. And her mother didn't know any better than I did how to resist this kind of terrible, almost suicidal, silent pressure. She assured Beverley it was madness to have a baby in our circumstances, and just at the beginning in this way. She told Beverley she could help her get an abortion.

Beverley did not want an abortion, but she said that if I agreed with her mother then she would agree too, and would have the abortion. I know I did wrong, but I agreed too. I had felt terribly nervous and trapped the whole while, by the idea of the baby. Especially since neither of us had planned it or wanted it. Could there really be a lullaby that goes, "Go to sleep, my little miscalculation"? Maybe more than one thinks. Anyhow, I agreed to the abortion; I didn't urge it — and the rest of the problem was to find an abortionist.

Before trying that, Beverley got some absurd powders from a druggist, without telling me, and took them. They had no effect but to make her quite sick for a day or two, but she was still pregnant. Her mother told her she might kill herself that way, and promised to hurry up and find an abortionist. However, even all her fancy contacts failed to turn one up. Dickinson was not around to ask, but I asked all the other doctors I knew, or had ghost-written for. Nobody seemed to know anything, or want to, and everybody reminded me gravely that it was all highly illegal.

A girl in the shipyard gave Beverley an address, and again without telling me she went there with this girl on the way home from work. That evening she arrived home at Bedford Street late, when I was already there several hours and quite worried about her, and she told me what had happened. The abortionist's address was in Harlem, and while the other girl had waited in the miserable little outer office, Beverley had gone into the examining room with the purported doctor, who was a middle-aged Negro with a continuous smile. He asked for his money in advance, which was fifty dollars. Beverley had prepared this, and was about to give it to him, when he patted the operating table, which was only a couch with a sheet on it, and told her with his endless smile that part of his price was that he wanted to have sexual intercourse with her before he performed the abortion.

"I can't do that," she said. "I'm in love with my husband."

"Don't be a little fool!" he told her. "Your husband isn't ever going to know. Come on, hop on here!" And he patted the operating couch again, encouragingly. "You want the operation, don't you?"

"No," Beverley said. "I've changed my mind."

She started to leave, but he ran out in front of her and barred the door. She began pulling at it and calling out her girlfriend's name. The friend pushed wildly on the door from the other side, and between them they got it open. The Negro abortionist stood glaring at them, with his back up against the wall opposite. His endless smile had ended.

"Now listen, you two bitches," he snarled at them, as they rushed to the outer door, "it's my word against yours! I never saw you, anyhow!" They got out the door, and he slammed it after them.

Beverley was too shaken up emotionally to go to work the next day. I took her over to her mother's in the morning, to keep her company. She told her mother the story of the Negro abortionist, of course. That night when I got home, she told me that her mother had been on the phone to one of her former boyfriends, a doctor in Massachusetts who was referred to only by his first name as Gilbert, and who said that Beverley should take the next train and he would help her, which he did. I took her to the train, and she was gone three days. She phoned me when she was about to come back, and of course I met her at the train too. Dr. Gilbert had performed the operation himself. He didn't know much about it, he admitted to her, but he understood the theory of the thing and did his best, and she was now no longer pregnant.

That evening she told me who the Dr. Gilbert was. He was much younger than her mother, and only a little older than Beverley. Two years before, when her mother had met him on a trip to Boston and taken up with him, she had suggested that he would be a good man for Beverley to marry, and that he liked her very much, having met her at dinner at her mother's apartment. Beverley had said she certainly couldn't marry a man she didn't love, and hardly even knew. But her mother waved all that away.

"You won't have to sleep with him," she told Beverley airily. "I'll take care of all that for you."

After that, I would look at Kathleen, and listen to her when she spoke, as though she were some kind of entomological specimen or stinkbug.   She also became much more chummy, now that she had proof that someone had finally deflowered her daughter, and would tell me all the latest dirty jokes that she heard from her rich boyfriends.   She never told them in front of Beverley, however. One went like this, and I wrote it down at the time, as I wrote down everything then, the staccato style being due to the fact that Kathleen always seemed to be just ever-so-slightly drunk:

"You know this one? *Society lady in Paris goes to the drugstore and says, 'I got bugs in the bush.' The druggist gives her a green pomade. Says, 'That'll kill the bugs in the bush.' Next week she comes back again and he asks her, 'Did it kill the bugs?' 'Yep! Killed the bugs, killed the poodle dog, killed two Argentine millionaires, and took all the hair off the bush!'* "
I tell a lot of jokes myself, so maybe I can't complain, but I remember thinking there must be better ways than that of entertaining your son-in-law at tea. Who knows, I figured? Maybe it was pure autobiography.

THE WAR was coming to an end. The American Army crossed the Rhine by March, and Russian mechanized units were within thirty miles of Berlin. By April the Russians had fought their way into Berlin, where they found Hitler's final bunker guarded by *French* — I repeat *French volunteer troops* of the so-called

Charlemagne Brigade. Hitler committed suicide there by Mayday, with his mistress Eva Braun, and so did his crippled Minister of Propaganda, Joseph Goebbels, along with his wife, having beforehand poisoned all their own young children with their own hands. This is not something I am making up to be shocking, but attested historical fact. The war in Europe was over. The total of dead would be added up later.

There was a wild mob surging around in the streets of Times Square, just like New Year's Eve, blowing tin horns, and continuously in motion, no one knows exactly why. There was also an official celebration a few days later, referred to in the newspapers as Victory-in-Europe day, to remind people that the Japanese hadn't yet been completely crushed. This would obviously come soon, as their main industrial centers were being bombed now from Okinawa, only three hundred miles away. I never quote newspapers if I can avoid it. One serious and very succinct history text states concerning that month: "United States battleships moved in to shell the densely populated cities with impunity, and the Twentieth Air Force dropped 40,000 tons of bombs on Japanese industrial centers in one month." In other words, Japan was already being mopped up. Why they shelled densely populated cities was never stated.

Roosevelt died in April at Warm Springs, Georgia, but lived long enough to know that he had been one of the main architects of the destruction of Nazi Germany. Just as Hitler's suicide was accompanied by rumors that he had not died at all, but had been spirited away and was now living disguised as a lady's maid in Argentina, etc., Roosevelt's death also gathered its moss of folklore, though not quite as flattering as that concerning Hitler. One day just then, I met in the hall of the Public Library an occult book-collector and private dealer named Frederick Glück who had always made himself pretty offensive with anti-Roosevelt jokes. His red, pompous face simply bulged out over his tight collar — he still lived and dressed in the 1920s mentally —and he stopped me to talk about books for a moment, and to obtrude his latest anti-Roosevelt item. This was his moment of triumph. His enemy, Roosevelt, was dead. Alive or dead, Hitler never perturbed him.

"Say, Legman," he asked, his eyes greedy with scandal, "did you notice the *mysterious* circumstances about Roosevelt's death?"

Me: "What mysterious circumstances? He was pretty sick at Yalta."

"*Oh* yes! But did you know that he was *alone* with a woman at the moment he died? A portrait-painter, they called her."

"You think she killed him? How? Nobody shot him, did they? What did she do, poison him with her paint brush?"

"Not at *all!*" Glück assured me, twinkling mysteriously. "There are *lots* of ways a woman can kill a man. He liked that sort of stuff, you know. Have you ever noticed the way his wife's teeth stick out? She could really eat corn on the cob through a picket fence. *Hah!*"

"Well, Mr. Glück," I said, "I'd believe your story except for two things. I already heard the same story, but without Eleanor Roosevelt's teeth, about the President of France in 1899."

"That doesn't mean it couldn't happen twice," he said quickly.

"No, but why is it you never tell any stories about Hitler? He died under pretty mysterious circumstances too." Expert on oragenitalism as I was supposed to be, I was really nauseated with this Nazi bastard. Why are all occultists anti-Semites too? Nothing was going to satisfy him but to get to Roosevelt's grave in the night, and dig up the body and piss on it. He was doing his best right now with his mouth. He wasn't the only one, either.

There is something about coming to the end of a long period of tension that makes a lot of people go nutty, who have been holding on fairly well during the crisis itself. In the rooming house I now worked in there was a pretty sad case like that. Most of the large rooms, except mine, were taken by married couples now. One flight down was a young couple with peculiar ass-to-face sexual habits. The husband worked at a mathematical war project at Columbia. Two flights down, in front, which was the best room in the house, though I didn't like it, because it never got any sun, the fairly young editor of one of the liberal magazines lived with his wife. I'll call her Deborah, although that wasn't her name. I had a very brief affair with her some months before, when she was living there alone. She told me that she was separated from her husband because he was impotent, and would probably divorce him.

One day the husband turned up, named Shelby, trying to patch things up with her. Deborah introduced us, and we all went out to have Chinese food together. In the course of the conversation,

Chinese bird's nest soup came up. I said I didn't much like eating birdshit, and that the Chinese only ate it because they believed it was an aphrodisiac, something that I claimed didn't exist. "Women are the only aphrodisiac for men," I said. "Especially a *new* woman."

Whatever his deficiencies as a lover, Shelby was a fairly nice person and an extremely interesting talker. The word aphrodisiac galvanized him, and he held forth on the subject for quite a long moment, finally admitting he had tried them all and that they weren't worth a damn. A day or two later, meeting him on the stairs, I told him frankly that his monologue on the subject suggested that he was talking about himself, and I told him I knew a fairly good Park Avenue Specialist — I purposely avoided using the psychiatrist — who had quite a lot of success with cases of anaphrodisia. Again, I avoided saying "impotence," of course. He admitted that the subject interested him, took down the address, and said he might drop in on my specialist friend to discuss it with him one day.

He went there that same afternoon, and the next morning came up to my room to report jubilantly what a success it had been. A great success! Here's what happened. He went to see the psychiatrist, who was a cripple and must have been in an impatient mood. He listened to Shelby's story and told him that a highly intelligent man like himself ought to be able to face the truth. Namely, that he probably wasn't impotent at all, but just hated his wife. Shelby was furious and punched the crippled psychiatrist in the face, he told me, and rushed out of his office. He found himself on Lexington Avenue, walking north looking for a crosstown bus home. Hardly a block up he passed a vacant storefront in which a Gypsy fortuneteller had set up temporarily, with a curtain of bright cloth over the doorway, and some paperback dreambooks scattered in the otherwise empty window display.

The fortune teller was standing in the doorway, with her hand on one hip, smoking a cigarette. She hailed him with a strange look, he said, and asked him why he was eating his heart out. She told him to come in and she would read his fortune. It wouldn't cost him any money. She liked his face. On impulse, he went in. She dropped the bright cloth over the doorway, and sat down opposite him, and took his hands in hers to read his fortune. After the usual remarks about being crossed in love, which he admitted to eagerly, she said that the fortune was free, as she had promised, but that if she wanted she could sell him a small bottle of Gypsy Secret Remedy for only five dollars, which would make any girl in the world fall on her knees before him. "Even me." She added.

When Shelby expressed his doubts about this, and told her he had already tried every aphrodisiac known, she made him a sporting proposition: Double or nothing. He would drink the little vial of Gypsy Remedy, and if it didn't make him potent *immediately* — with her — it wouldn't cost him a penny. If it worked, though, the price would now be ten dollars, not five. Struck by her fair offer, and also somewhat admiring her swarthy beauty, he drained the little bottle in one gulp.

The Gypsy woman looked in his eyes, "with a strange smile," he told me, and reached out with both hands and unbuttoned his fly, taking out his penis, and leading him by it to a pillowed section of the store in the back, which was her bed. She pulled up her dark, voluminous skirt now with one hand, and started sinking backwards on the pillows, drawing him with her.

"Come on, Big Boy," she said in a husky voice. "Stick it in!"

He was completely potent with her, the first time this had happened to him in over a year. He started stammering his thanks, but she would not let him get up and said, "Come on, do it again for the ten bucks!" He did it again. He then gave her all the money he had on him, which was closer to fifty dollars, in return for the secret of *what was in the Gypsy Remedy?* She said she did not want to tell him because the other Gypsies would probably kill her for doing it, but finally admitted that it contained nothing but bull's blood. That was all. She also gave him another bottle of the Remedy for his money, making a special mystic gesture with it over his head as she handed it to him, explaining that it was really the Gypsy gesture that made the blood work. "But of course, that's all the bunk," he assured me.

He came home, drank the other bottle, and leapt on Deborah, and was completely potent with her too. They both wept in each other's arms half the night, and fell asleep entwined like honeymooners. That was his story. It was all owing to my having given him the psychiatrist's address, and he didn't know how he could ever thank me. I didn't say anything, but I was hoping he hadn't told the psychiatrist who recommended him. He was probably the only person who wouldn't wholly appreciate the miracle of the Gypsy Remedy.

From then on Shelby was completely potent with Deborah all the time. This required, however, that he should eat an enormous steak dinner every evening, practically raw and dripping blood. As the Nossiters didn't let them cook in their room, it had to be in restaurants, and he took me with him whenever he found me in. I was now only going down to sleep at Beverley's room on Bedford Street every other night, and so the alternate nights there I would be with Shelby in one of the restaurants on upper Broadway, devouring an enormous steak of my own with him. He paid for everything. The only thing was, I felt like throwing up half the time watching him chew on the raw meat, with the blood often trickling out of the corners of his mouth as he talked. He didn't mind. He was a different man, and a marvelous conversationalist over the dinner table. I could see how he had gotten his job as a liberal editor. He threw away some marvelous editorials talking to me at dinner. Deborah for some reason seldom came with us.

He kept getting his steaks less and less well done, until finally he could hardly get them chewed. He tried steak Tartare, but was very dubious about it, as you couldn't see the blood drip. The steak Tartare he announced the next time, had not worked! As Shelby was Jewish, I wondered whether the intense Jewish ritual prohibition was perhaps catching up with him, but said nothing about it. He went back to the half-raw steaks, which again worked like a charm. His potency never failed after that. But there was one problem. He began to complain about headaches, to which I suggested that he should lay off poor Deborah, who had begun by adoring his new cure, but was now terrified of the monster with an endless hardon she was married to. I told him he was perhaps overdoing things, and that I had had the same experience with headaches when I made love too often. It could cause high blood pressure, you know. But he said he couldn't stop. He had to do whatever the steak revved him up to. How about smaller steaks, I suggested? No, that wouldn't work. *It was the call of the blood!*

Within a few weeks he had pinpointed the cause of his now unremitting headaches, which started every morning at exactly nine o'clock. They were caused by a machine in the Bureau of Printing and Engraving in Washington, D.C., which was exactly on his, Shelby's wavelength. When that machine was turned on every morning — he buzzed. I asked him tentatively how he knew all this, but he just looked mysterious. Deborah told me privately that she was now really afraid of him. I told her what I thought was happening, and that he was becoming paranoid. Neither of us knew exactly what to do. About a month later he attempted to wrestle the owner of his magazine out of the office window, twelve storeys up. He was locked up at once as insane. Deborah moved away, to go back to her parents. She looked as though she was pretty nearly crazy herself by now. I guess I helped that family real good.

❦

NOBODY was prepared for Hiroshima except the people who did it. Like the German death-camps, about which we were hearing more and more now, for better or for worse, the secret had been kept. From the general public, anyhow. Thousands of people, in fact, hundreds of thousands had been involved in the preparation and the delivery of the Atom Bomb that wiped out over half of the Japanese city of Hiroshima, on August 6th, and the next one Nagasaki three days later. But theoretically, at least, *no one knew what they were doing,* except a few score of the head British and American scientists, and of course all the dozens of necessary politicians and generals whose choice it was. Even the crew of the Enola Gay, named for the captain's mother, that dropped the first atomic bomb, "Little Boy," presumably did not know that the result would be any different than any other bomb. Anybody who believes all that is welcome to believe it.

And even if it were true — which it wasn't — that you could get six hundred thousand scientists and "supportive personnel" under one thin physicist, J. Robert Oppenheimer, and one fat general, Leslie R. Groves, at the direct orders of President Franklin D. Roosevelt and Winston Churchill, to prepare in that way the end of the world, without any of them but a few score demanding to know, or knowing, what in Hell they were doing, and where in Hell they were going — that was really the worst part of the whole thing. That was the real human atrocity. Worse, in a way, than the hundred thousand Japanese killed in one lightning flash of Atomic radiation and explosion at Hiroshima, and seventy-five thousand more killed by the second plutonium bomb, "Fat Man," at Nagasaki, the name taken from a murder-mystery by Dashiell Hammett. Meaning that it took three scientists or supportive personnel, blindly obeying orders, to kill each person done to death with those two first amusingly named atom bombs. How was that different from Auschwitz?

Besides, it was totally pointless, since the Japanese were already licked, with American battleships moving in on their coast for over a month before "to shell densely populated shoreline cities with impunity." Plus the thousands of tons of aerial incendiary bombs being dropped by American aircraft based on Okinawa which had already destroyed the Japanese war industries and potential. It was simply and visibly and before the eyes of the whole world the standard cliché of the Western badman who has shot his enemy to death, and who then strides over to the fallen man twitching in his final agony, and kicks him violently in the face with his cowboy boot, knocking out a clutch of teeth and an already dead eye.

My mother could kneel on the ground if she liked, repeating by rote the names of all the presidents of the United States, and thanking God she was an American for thirty-five years. That day I changed my mind. It seemed to me then, and it still seems to me today, that Hitler really won the war in the creation of the Atom Bomb. He had promised to *sow mud*, and he did. I saw it as though in a bad dream: like a *dybbuk* or soul-eater that leapt from his corpse to live on in the souls of the living. In the effort to destroy Hitler, America had turned itself into a nation of rotten, insane killers and puppets, from the top down, no different in any way, except perhaps the overt anti-Semitism, from the Nazis. The war against Vietnam, later, proved this. And we are all waiting helplessly for our punishment now.

I went down to Times Square, to bathe in the enormous mob, surging in their cry of victory. I felt like a visitor from Mars. They were all so sure we had won, and were screaming that we had won. And I knew so totally that we had lost. And I was frightened. I was frightened and I was forlorn, and I was helpless, and I was terribly alone. While the mob screamed and surged, and blew its dinky tin horns, I kept repeating to myself the childhood prayer I had somewhere learned, though not as a child.

> I am a stranger, and afraid
> In a world I never made.

After that I could never sleep a whole night without waking up suddenly with overpowering sensations of strangling, or my throat burning, and with horrible evil dreams still swirling in my head. I was becoming an honorary victim of Hiroshima, and knew that too. But I didn't know how to stop it. I tried large doses of aspirin, but didn't want to start with sleeping pills since it was notorious that they were all habit-forming. I tried to work out ways of going back to sleep again. I would heat myself a glass of milk to drink. Or sometimes, if I was sleeping with Beverley, I would wake her up by tickling her from behind, and simply strop myself crudely in her vagina until I came. Often she hardly even woke up. And I would eventually fall back to sleep.

Later I found that a better way was to get up and work, whatever the hour might be, and then take a long nap the next afternoon when I found myself worn out, and work again in the evening. You got two hours of waking time for each hour of sleep, however you divided it up. I went on like that for years. Then, slowly, when I got away from America to France, eventually, I was able to sleep the whole night long again. But when I came back to America briefly, to earn money when Beverley was sick, something else happened to me — I fell in love with a witch — and again that gave me terrible dreams and prevented me from sleeping a whole night through. And that is the way I still am, and know I will be that way until I die. She ate part of my soul, and I cannot get it back. At least I get a lot of work done, waking up at three and four and five in the morning, with nothing around to disturb me. But what is the work worth? Well, the muezzins know: "Prayer is better than sleep."

My undesirable friend, Bob Mexico, turned up at my rooming house one day, during that August of the Atom Bomb. He was the same as ever: lanky, with his mock-Mexican moustache drooped over a hanging cigarette; his long, strangely dirty fingers with their incredibly long and dirty fingernails, making continuous gestures not very well synchronized with the points they were intended desperately to underline. This time he was totally euphoric and excited, and was clutching a still-damp set of page-proofs which he had brought triumphantly to show me. He was now a published author! The thrill of it was suffocating him, and had to be shared, especially with me, who had never had but one book published and that under a pseudonym and underground. This was his moment of triumph, and by comparison I was obviously to admit that I was shit.

It was a book about the Atom Bomb, the very first book that would ever hit print on the subject. He had been writing day and night ever since the first newsflash came over the radio. The publisher was wild to get the book out as soon as humanly possible, to 'cream the field,' as Mexico told me. He had flung the manuscript at the printer when Mex was only half finished writing it, and the other half had to be written even faster, to keep up with the typesetter. There had been no galley proofs. The book was set directly in pages by the printer, to get it out at superhuman speed. They were already printing it. I noticed three typographical errors just on the first page I opened to, but of course it didn't matter. No one had thought, in their hurry, to bother about reading proofs.

His book was a cheap journalistic rehash of everything about the Bomb that had been printed in the newspapers since the first newsflash had arrived, including all the oversimplified, ununderstandable, and contradictory journalistic explanations of how the god-damned thing worked. This was for paperback publication, with a sheared back and gum binding instead of string sewing, and for newsstand distribution. Mex had received a cozy two hundred dollars for his superhuman, totally ignorant rush job, and had been promised another hundred dollars if it sold more than one hundred thousand copies on the stands, at twenty-five cents apiece.

I pointed out to him cautiously that even if he got the three hundred dollars this was a royalty of hardly more than one percent of the gross, but he didn't mind. Do literary agents get more? He was a published author at last. The Atom Bomb had made him! Actually, when the end of the sales period came and the pamphlet disappeared from the newsstands, it had been reprinted at least twice, since Mex picked up on various newsstands copies with two different cover titles, and three different variants of the title-pages, and he was fit to be tied.

He was really screaming and gesticulating, totally furious, since of course he never got paid anything more than the two hundred dollars, meaning even less than one per cent royalty. On the other hand, they all printed his name on the title page. When he angrily stamped into the publisher's office with his variant editions and title-page variants — positive proof of the publisher's perfidy — right in his hand, the publisher told him to get lost and threw him out. Publishers yearning to make dough out of the instantaneous deaths of hundreds of thousands of pulverized Japanese women and children, could hardly be expected to have their piles bleed over the literary rights of one cheap little plagiarist calling himself a Mexican. When you work for the Devil, you get paid off with a sharp stick up your ass. Every time.

Mexico wasn't the only one who wanted to cash in on the Atom Bomb. By the end of the year I saw at least two other tawdry publications of the same type, one of which Mexico claimed was pirated word-for-word from his own masterpiece! I also noticed at least two Atomic Cleaning & Pressing establishments, both in Harlem. But my favorite was The Atomic Shoeshine, spelled out on the rickety wooden chair-platform in white buttons, which the proprietor assured me shone in the dark. There were dozens of others, just in the nomenclature department, but I didn't bother to note them all down. The feeling was very powerful in me — then and now — that the Bomb had been absorbed into the soul of the nation, not just into its shoeshine signs, and would fester there forever and destroy us. We'll see if I'm wrong. If I'm right, we won't see.

On the basis of his Atomic Bomb pamphlet, Mexico got a few assignments to write other things, in particular, a pulp magazine story or two. But he found himself in trouble immediately, when he did not have all the materials lying before him in printed form to copy from, as he had done with the pamphlet. His story idea was quite good, of a demon violin that makes great but mad violinists out of all its owners; and that the great Paganini had merely been the first of these.

This idea came out of our discussions of the Bomb, and my describing it to him as a *dybbuk* and explaining what that was. The story was of a *dybbuk* violin, and he called it "The Devil's Fiddle." But he couldn't get it written, and finally offered me half the money if I would flesh out the idea and make a story of it, which I did. It appeared in some semi-science fiction or horror-fantasy magazine, and the editor and readers adored it and wanted more. Even the editor's wife wrote us a fan-letter, which Mexico assumed was an erotic invitation. Who knows? They also wanted a follow-up published, explaining how the story had come to be written. I had to write that too; the usual fake publicity buncombe about the story being written in Peru, by the shores of Lake Titicaca, etc., and how the author had been found dead under suspicious circumstances. I was really thinking of the tragic suicide then of Stefan Zweig.

But our author wasn't so easy to kill off. Mexico was now supposed to do a whole follow-up story, and he had neither idea, plot, nor the ability to write it up. I refused to collaborate any further, as I was disgusted by his merely clawing some crude cash out of the dybbuk idea, instead of trying to understand it. His soul, too, had been eaten. In fact, he was proud to claim that his had been the very first, as his Atom Bomb pamphlet proved. I explained to him that writers are born, not made, and that what he had dome on that pamphlet was merely editing, not to say plagiarism, from a dozen newspaper stories strung together and rewritten as fast as he could typewrite. Very close to my ghost-written biography in Washington, D.C. of the World War I notable, truth to tell.

I suggested to Mexico that he would be better off continuing with his Latin-American biography work, translating and typing, because that was certain money; whereas if he launched himself into writing without any ability he could easily starve to death! Or even *with* ability! But I could see that he felt sure he would be able to swing it, by concerning himself solely with getting the assignments and contracts, and letting ghosts like me sweat out the plots and the dialogue. There are plenty of faked and exploitative writing careers that are based on nothing more than this type of operation, especially in the movies, of course. My final offer was that I would give him story ideas for half the money, and he would have to do the rest. I could read in his eyes that he was planning to lie to me about how much he would be getting on each story, and told him he would have to show me the check he received, and give me half that amount.

The first story idea I gave him was the follow-up of "The Devil's Fiddle," with a miraculously-discovered copy of one of the Sibylline Oracular Books, which would be any book in the world that one wanted. The possessor could therefore recover in this way all the lost books of antiquity, all Bach's lost music, the Great Library of Alexandria burned by the Caliph Omar, etc., and could photocopy them all, page by page for sale to all the research libraries of the world. I figured that would be commercial enough to suit him, like hitching Pegasus to a milk-wagon. But he still couldn't figure out what to do for a plot, and finally had to plagiarize H. G. Wells' "The Time Machine," and have the hero try to play the stock-market with the Sibylline Book, by ordering it to become tomorrow's newspaper and photocopying the stock-market page! This certainly suggested what authorship and literature really meant in his mind. He isn't the only one.

In addition, Mexico asked the magazine editor, when he brought in the finished story, to give him two checks, on some poppycock explanation of having two bank-accounts to aliment. The editor of course immediately understood that this meant that there was a hidden ghost-writer, namely me, being screwed. He gave Mexico the two checks, each for half the total amount as Mexico wanted, and then asked him casually if he knew any other writers who might work for them, as he had a great deal of work to hand out. Mexico sent me in to see him, and the editor opened cold with these words:

"That Spick friend of yours is screwing you, you know?"

"I know," I said, "but what does it matter? I have more ideas dripping off my balls every day than he'll ever have in a lifetime. You can give me those second checks direct, if you want. Anyhow, he isn't a Spick. He was born in New Jersey."

What the editor really wanted, was to fire Mexico, and to assign the stories to me directly, but I assured him I didn't like writing pulp. Actually, I didn't see that he was being any more honest than Mexico was, and I figured he'd work out some method of screwing me too. I left them to their honeymoon with each other, and Mexico was very grateful, and no longer asked for double checks. Even the checks were a bother to him, because his real name was Robert Bragg. Why he changed this to Mexico, and sometimes put on an accent to match, I don't know. The accent he learned from seeing Cantínflas comedies in little Hispanic movie-houses. I also told him that "Robert Mexico" lacked the necessary drama to sign his stories with. He assured me that his *real* name was Nuñez Roberto — and a long string of phoney names here — de México y Braga. I told him that Nuñez wasn't very sexy, and changed it to Nuncio Roberto de México for him. All the stories were therefore signed N. R. de México. He was glad of any help, and had no pride of any kind, even about his resounding pseudonym. Watching him operate was like watching bugs under a magnifying glass. Like Oscar Wilde, he didn't have any real enemies, but all his friends detested him.

One day I made fun of him, as an imitation Mexican, when he admitted to me that he had never smoked marijuana, despite his admiration for the scenes on this subject in Bob Sewall's book. I told him I'd help him out and get him a couple of sticks. He was terrified and assured me that he wouldn't touch the stuff. And that on his many mythical trips to Mexico he had seen countless poor devils leap out the window under the influence, or rush to the bullring to impale themselves on the bulls' horns. I told him that was a lot of bull, and that if he wanted to help out his limping powers of invention maybe marijuana would be his only way of ever getting free of me. I shouldn't have said that. It worked too well.

Like all weak characters, Mexico was very suggestible, and also like many, he yearned to be strong and evil. Or rather, he thought of evil as identical with strong. Millions of people labor under this same confusion, especially when they see monsters like Hitler in their moment of triumph. That, and simple fear, are the secret spring of the favorite American motto about *joining 'em instead of licking 'em*, and all the rest of that craven identification with the aggressor. Like anti-Semitic Jews.

When Mexico read in Sewall's *The Devil's Advocate* the branding and flagellation scenes that were apparently the first such he had ever seen, he set out to imitate them on his wife, to the degree that he dared. Gerri was a plain, unpretentious girl, with no nonsense about her, very conscious of her Polish origin and quick to resent anything that she thought of as a slight. He couldn't have picked a wronger person to whip, even on the cockamammy explanation he gave her that it would make them both ever so much more passionate in their immediately-following sexual delights. When he started that crap, she got a lawyer and divorced him for mental cruelty. His experience with drugs was even less fortunate.

After my diabolical suggestion, about finding inspiration in The Weed, had worked on him for a few days, he came back and begged me to help him get started smoking the stuff. His presumed Mexican contacts evaporated when he tried to buy even one stick, and he was nervous about going up to Harlem and standing on a street corner. I dug out the three remaining sticks in Beverley's little Mexican envelope in the cigar-box suitcase, and figured this would be a good way to get rid of them. But I didn't want Mexico to know I was supplying them to him, as I didn't trust him any further, anymore, than I could throw him by his gangly prick. I told him I had a friend who might let him have a few sticks as a favor, and took him up to visit another friend of mine trying to become a writer, whose name was John Del Torto, and who had a furnished room on the less fashionable bottom part of Riverside Drive. The marijuana would come, presumably, from a friend of John's.

Del Torto was mixed up with a tall girl who lived in the same rooming house, and who stated that she had a pair of Mussolini's authentic underpants, which Il Duce had worn, and which of course she would never launder, etc. You know the type. Although she was very tall, if you argued with her about anything, she would teeter up even higher on her toes, to try to dominate you. Perhaps you know that type too: I've also seen it done on horseback. I told Del Torto, that as an Italian-American himself, he shouldn't hang around with such an obvious proto-Fascist, but he couldn't resist her easy availability in the room across the hall. It would be in Del Torto's room that Mexico would have to make his *début* with the Weed of Inspiration. It certainly wasn't going to be in mine. I told Del Torto he could have a stick too. He smoked two of them, and got no effect from it. The sticks were pretty old by now, and very crackly inside the paper, and probably falling to dust.

Mexico, who was a habitual cigarette smoker, with long yellowed fingers, took the final stick and turned it over several times in his hands nervously, before he could make up his mind to try it.

"Look," he said, his face pallid, "if I do anything foolish after I smoke this, you stop me, see!" We assured him that we would both leap on him and overmaster any foolish impulses he might have, such as jumping out of the window. Thus reassured he laid down on the floor — I guess he was confusing it with opium, and lit up.

After only about two puffs, which he dragged down maniacally deep, he gave every symptom of floating away, and began shaking with the ague. John, who was not a smoker, was getting no effect, and couldn't understand how a hardened tobacco-man like Mexico could be under the influence so soon and so deep. I didn't bother to tell him. Instead, I laid down on the floor next to Mexico, and put my arm around his shoulder, trying to reassure him. I felt ashamed of having touted so impressionable a jackass into this.

Later, I was even sorrier. Mex became a habitual marijuana smoker almost immediately, with all the usual soundtrack about the finer types of weed, the difference between hashish, hemp, and that bad ordinary stuff we're getting lately, etc. etc. In an unguarded moment one day — I believe I had a headache and was trying to turn off his clack — I told him that if you wanted good stuff you had to grow it from seeds yourself, as I did, in a window box. Where was the window box? He wanted to know immediately, looking at my empty windowsill. Well, it had fallen in the wind. Besides, people notice it growing, as it gets pretty tall. And I foolishly added that I had replanted all my seedlings with tender loving care out in the gravelly soil by the Lackawanna railroad tracks in Hoboken. I could have bitten off my tongue the minute I let it slip. Not only I could see he believed every word I said, but I could almost hear the mental click as he registered the location.

"When are you going to harvest it?" Mexico asked excitedly.

"I'm not going to harvest it," I told him. "I think the field is under surveillance. There's a lunch counter on the edge of it, and I have a feeling the lunch counter man is really a nark."

"I'd take a chance for some really good stuff," Mexico insisted. For a drug everybody tells you isn't really habit-forming, he was terribly avid, as all the non-habit-formed smokers of it usually are.

"I wouldn't do that," I warned him solemnly. "It's a bad rap if they catch you." I knew instantly he was going to get caught, probably the first hour, and would drag me down with him the minute the squeeze would come. I could have shot myself for having told him the location.

Naturally, he immediately rushed off to Hoboken with a suitcase and a knapsack, and — to make things perfect — a brand new shiny hand scythe that he bought in a hardware store and carried in the knapsack. He went into the lunch-counter first, as he told me later, and told the counter man a long cock-&-bull story about how he was a roving plant expert and studying weed specimens. Other than hanging a large arrow on his back, I don't see how he could have made himself more conspicuous. But Mexico even found a way to do so.

Having filled his suitcase and knapsack to the brim, he tucked the now black and grimy hand scythe in with his harvest of hemp, and marched down the street to the Lackawanna Ferry back to New York. However, as the price of the ferry-ride was ten cents, he thought of a clever method of avoiding paying that. Instead of buying a ferry-ticket, he walked around through the railroad station and down the passageway leading to the ferries, which arriving train passengers were allowed to take free as a final service on their railroad ticket. As he started under the great overhead boom onto the ferry platform, a large hand clamped down on Mexico's shoulder and a voice said, raspingly:

"Awright, wise-guy, where's your train ticket?"

The ticket collector at the ferry-slip had seen him getting off the ferry from New York an hour before. How could he have missed him? With that stringy moustache à la Cantínflas, and the odd loping walk Mexico still affected at the age of twenty-eight coming down on the toes of his feet instead of the heels, which he believed the Indians also did.

Mexico naturally offered now to pay the dime fare he had so brilliantly skunked the ferry-line out of, but they didn't want it. Instead they turned him over to the police, who immediately looked through his suitcase and knapsack, shook the location of the marijuana field out of him without delay and turned him over to the feds the same day. He had spent the night in jail, was now arraigned and out on bail, and came to see me at once, blaming me for everything and demanding a letter of recommendation of his character to a certain justice Joseph McLaughlin, who was going to show clemency if Mex could get three such letters, including one from a minister or priest.

He also wanted me to forge a further letter, as from a minister, but I assured him he was in enough trouble already and told him to try the closest Catholic church to his furnished room in the West Village on Bethune Street. He could say he was a Catholic, and in danger of loosing his faith if they sent him to jail. I told him to act very emotional when talking to the priest, but to avoid any of his usual witty Spanish imprecations, such as, "By the twenty-four testicles of the twelve apostles of Christ!" or "By the blessèd cunt of the Virgin Mary, that I would have fucked — if I had had the time!"

Incredibly enough, they let him go. I was glad they did, because I had no way of knowing whether he implicated me or not, and, if he had, I was at least as far in the clear as he now was. Anyhow, I hoped so. The next Thanksgiving, when I went home to Scranton, I examined the field very carefully as the train began gliding out through the Hoboken yards. As I knew it would be, it had been entirely burnt over by the police and the lunch-wagon stood out stark and strange, like an etching, along the edge. But it didn't matter, of course. The seeds of the year before would be in the ground, and it would all grow back eventually. Except that now the police would have their eye on the field. Anybody that harvested it now would net a free ticket to jail, even if he had the intelligence not to try to cheat the ferry-line out of ten cents, with a suitcase of marijuana in his hand.

Mexico laid off hemp after that, which he told me he now considered childish, and the mere and mildest of narcotic drugs which were going to be a whole new world of inspiration for him. He got hold of a book which I have to admit he had first seen on my shelves, though I now refused to lend it to him. It was called *Phantastica*, a translation of a serious work by a German toxicologist, Lewis Lewin, on narcotic and hallucinatory drugs. Mex tried out everything in the book that he could get hold of, using bribed doctors' prescriptions, which he filled easily in the drug-addict area of the West Side below 72nd Street.

Fortunately he tried everything only once, looking for Milady Inspiration, just as Baudelaire had done, and did not get hooked on anything. However, he ran into me one day on Bleecker Street, where I was buying vegetables for supper for Beverley and me, and told me with great animation that he had somewhere got the idea that snake-root, an East Indian plant which reduces the blood pressure, would give him a new and unknown thrill, which is certainly untrue. As the source of his misinformation had not told him how big a dose to take, and what to beware of, he took who-knows how big an over-dose, which evidently dropped his blood pressure like a falling kite, and he died then and there, alone in his small furnished room on Bethune Street. It was in the papers two days later, a very small item. The new and unknown thrill was death.

Mexico's last hack-job had been an admiring biography of the shitass Broadway columnist, Walter Winchell, who by then didn't have another friend on earth, and was later to be cut to bits on paper in a serious biography written by Lyle Stuart and published by Samuel Roth. Winchell decided immediately, on learning of his admiring biographer's sudden and inexplicable death, that he had been rubbed out by Criminal Elements who were doubtless after Winchell too. He used his influence with the police to have Mexico's body autopsied *post mortem*, and of course nothing was found. Anyhow, nothing that could save Winchell. I guess I didn't help my friend Bob Mexico much, either. And this time it was really my fault. That's one thing I can't blame on the Atom Bomb.

CHAPTER 45

CATERPILLAR'S END

IT WAS ironic that I had no proper job in Manhattan all the while I was supporting Beverley's *pied à terre* on Bedford Street and my own workroom on West 76th, but that the moment we found a cottage with a yard and a tree nearly an hour's subway-jump from Manhattan I immediately got a steady job downtown and had to commute back & forth daily. Meanwhile, since my ghost-writing work tapered off to almost nothing during the war, I had been making the best part of my living for several years travelling all the way up to the Bronx Park, to precisely that same cottage, to catalogue for Tim Trace; and out to the other end of Brooklyn in the evenings, to Rubin Bresler's rumpus-room cellar fitted up to be an erotic bookseller's showroom. Book-cataloguing was in fact my real profession, laced with an occasional job of ghost-writing now & then, just as it had been over the two happy years when I spent most of my time in the Public Library preparing the international homosexual bibliography for Will Finch half the day, and my own erotic bibliographies and lexicons the other half, till the library closed at ten o'clock at night. But now most of my cataloguing for hire was being done out at the end of Brooklyn for Bresler, and up at the arse end of the Bronx for Tim Trace, and the hour-long and two-hour-long subway rides each way ate up all the free hours I would otherwise have been able to spend in the library on my own biblio-lexicographical work. This threw me back on myself and my own mental resources in the few hours left to me in the subway and elsewhere. I began writing again in my mind during those hours. It was this that saved me from becoming what I was otherwise turning into: a library-worm or bum, like Trace's preceding cataloguer and God knows how many others.

Instead, I began writing again — no longer absorbing endlessly and uselessly, but expressing something. Not in, but out. I kept the phonograph combo going in my room most of the time when I was home, with powerful symphonies and concertos for backdrop. Generally, I would knock out a personal letter or two in the early mornings till I felt my motor begin to turn and my stubs of wings beating at the same pitch as the music. Then I'd begin working on my manuscript. Bad mornings, when I couldn't get going because of something wrong the day before about sex or money, I'd keep writing letters until noon — throwing my strength away on them, I realized, but what's to do?

If a particularly good line or worthwhile phrase or insight dropped into any of the letters, I'd copy it off before sealing the letter, sometimes onto index cards for the sex-slang dictionary that-was-never-to-be, or as the start of a later-to-be-continued manuscript sheet. That would often get my motor turning over. So even the enormous correspondence I kept going then and for years after wasn't entirely a waste. I still have most of the carbon-copies. Emotional, real letters to women, including my mother, I would write late at night in pen & ink. In those years I wasn't able to typewrite a love-letter. Not a real one. So I have no copies of these. The main thing was to keep working, even when I wasn't working well. The bad first-hour stuff would get edited out during the endless revises later.

I started hammering away seriously on my manuscript, writing up what I now knew and felt about the comic-book plague on which I had been researching and collecting so long, and how clearly I saw it had to end in mass-illiteracy and the sick thirst for violence in the whole eventual adult population. And it has, hasn't it? Have you seen any recent movies? Like Oliver Stone's *Platoon*, the horror movie of the Vietnam war.

This began to fit itself into the history of censorship, *Taboo*, that I had refused to finish for E. Haldeman-Julius' "Big Blue Book" series when he made it clear that he planned to expurgate my manuscript at the dozens of pages he marked with a heavy marginal thumbnail gouge while reading them. His way of living up to his self-applied reputation as the main and noisiest apostle and mock-practitioner of free speech. What a faker! A censored history of censorship, or expurgated study of expurgation, did have a certain *Through the Looking Glass* logic, I had to admit, but I was too proud to accept any such nonsensical tampering with my work, and I haven't ever changed. Too castratory for me.

There were meetings now, here and there, concerned with the comic books, and especially with their obvious violence. One or two newspaper columnists sounded an alarm, especially a woman named Judith Crist on the *Herald-Tribune*. I went to see everyone like that who got into print in New York, and wrote mammoth letters to those out-of-town. A professor named Harvey Zorbaugh at New York University held a panel there on the comics, consisting entirely of comics-industry publishers and artists, like Al Capp who drew "Li'l Abner," and their on-salary "psychologists." I sat there indignantly listening to their bullshit and defensive bromides, when a young man sitting next to me touched my elbow and introduced himself as one of Ring Lardner's sons I had known briefly at college in my days as a chess-terrorist. He said he was working on a magazine.

"What are we going to do about this?" he asked in an undertone, in an easy, smiling voice.

"We're going to fight it! It's ghastly!"

"Who'll win?" he grinned.

"They will, but I'm going to fight 'em anyhow. What about you?"

I don't remember what Lardner answered, or if he answered at all. I never saw him again, nor anything published by him on the subject. But he had precipitated in me something that was important to me, asking who would win. It was going to be like *Cyrano de Bergerac*, I realized now: all the more beautiful for being useless.

After the comic-book article, or chapter of *Taboo*, as I still thought of it, was drafted and rewritten two or three times, I began to be carried away in lovely exhilaration over this tremendous contradiction in the culture, as in its censorship, that I was now hewing away at like a sculptor, blocking it out in all its absurd domination of the scene. Like the monumental stone head of another King Ozymandias, broken off senseless and dead, but nevertheless dominating the literary and human desert all around it as far as eyes could see. The contradiction, that we were being told — had been told now for centuries — that sex was wrong, and that violence and murder were right. On paper anyhow. That a writer of books about sex was a pornographer and a presumed degenerate, while a writer about murder, violence and death was a Literary Man and had a fair chance of ending up rich. Meanwhile, in the realm of action, not words, sex was still moderately legal and murder presumably totally forbidden.

I was certainly not the first person ever to notice this contradiction. Montaigne, three centuries earlier, had flung out the cry, in his essay *On Some Verses of Virgil:* "We bravely say 'Kill, rob, betray,' but *that other* we only dare pronounce between clenched teeth?" One or two other writers more recently had also touched on this flabbergasting hypocrisy, always in only a sardonic sentence or two, so far as I knew: George Bernard Shaw in *Killing for Sport;* Claude Houghton, himself the author of a famously gimmicked mystery novel, *I Am Jonathan Scrivener,* and my favorite dramatic critic and stylist George Jean Nathan, who added the shrewd insight that in murder-mysteries it is really the murderer who is tracked down as the victim — the readers' victim, that is.

Even in so gross a writer's handbook as Jack Woodford's *Writing and Selling,* there was a clear realization of the profitable psychological transfer Woodford recommended, though he didn't practise it himself: Why write about sex unprofitably and run into

censorship trouble all the time? Write sexless murder-
mysteries instead, and clean up the cash! Listening to
the radio one evening at Bedford Street the winter
before, on one of those Author Meets the Critics
programs, I even heard the particularly foppish bearded
murder-mystery writer, Rex Stout, toss off as a
presumably witty reply to some question about the sex-
motivation of the characters in a story: "If by *romance*
you mean love . . . I'm out of it. I'm a writer of
murder-mysteries, and I'm not supposed to know
anything about it."

All I was really adding to these clear-enough
statements was the total picture of how this cancerous
transvaluation of libidinal interest had spread through
literature, in the two centuries since Pope and Addison
and Dr. Johnson had successfully tidied up and totally
bowdlerized down English letters to sexless milk-&-
water beginning with their editions of Shakespeare.
And I was insisting too on the point that this really was
a *transfer:* that it was specifically the banned erotic
emotion driven offstage that was being imported back
secretly, in classic Freudian style, and bloated up into
enormous best-sellerdom, but now in the form of the
infinitely more dangerous sadism.

My real luck in all of this was that I hadn't done
my research well enough. Unknown to me then,
Maurice LeBlond, the son-in-law of Zola, had
published in the 1890s a superb article in French in
defence of Zola, taking the war into the censors' camp
under the proud title, "The Pornography of Murder."
LeBlond had pre-empted almost every point I wanted
to make, and wrongly thought I was making for the
first time. He was also writing — just as I was trying to

do — with all the power and fury of moral outrage, of a man who knew well that what was normal and right was being mocked and prohibited, while what was dangerously perverted, evil and wrong was being substituted and glorified.

Only a dozen years later did I run across LeBlond's powerful article for the first time, tucked away where one would hardly have expected it, in the long introduction by the translator of Carrington's unfinished edition in English of the Arabian love-book *The Perfumed Garden* by al-Nafzawi, issued early in this century *[transcriber's note: the twentieth]*. I still have never been able to find LeBlond's original French text. Probably it appeared in a newspaper during one of Zola's many run-ins with the censorship. But it was clear that if I had ever found LeBlond's article or even known of its existence then, I would never have sat down to write another article, in fact a whole book, on the very same theme. That was my luck. Like the Good Soldier Schweik getting mobilized into one army while trying to desert from another, *Love & Death* was written "by misteak."

Long before the comic-book article was finished to my satisfaction, I'd realized I'd also have to handle murder-mysteries, which were an even more obvious example of the same kind of perverted substitution, but for grownups instead of kids. And I began pencil-drafting and writing at high speed on a matching chapter on murder-mysteries to open with; then jumping in conscious contradiction, to a violently denunciatory final few pages — condemning violence — in which I suddenly found myself writing my title: Institutionalized Lynch. This had just the kind of tight-

clenched verbal sadistic whip crack I liked —
hypocritical me — the polysyllabic mock-elevated
Latinity of the adjective to build up tension; then the
one-syllable smash of the noun!

High in my third-floor furnished room on the
sunny back-side of 50 West 76th Street I was tearing
along like the wind, pounding it out on the same and
identical black upright iron-framed office typewriter on
which I am writing today with a plain black cotton
ribbon, a mere three and a half decades later: Royal
Standard KMM-2516590: old, heavy, indestructible,
non-electrical and with piano-key action like a trip-
hammer. Cost, $140-. Consider this an unpaid
testimonial in love and gratitude for a splendid
instrument. If the typeface ever wears out I'll get an
Olympia, which is even better.

Yes, high in my top-floor bed-sitting room,
baking shirtless under the New York summer sun by
the open window, with Artur Schnabel in his big, bow-
windowed ground floor apartment down across the
areaway from me, practicing the same passage over and
over hundreds of times from the finale of Beethoven's
Sonata Appassionata until I thought I'd go mad, I would
laugh and chortle and stamp on the floor in time to the
music, in shameless self-appreciation of some of my
more orotund phrases and wild denunciations of half
of the other writers in the world. All the time thinking
to myself without a blush that, for an apostle of literary
love and not violence, I was certainly hammering out
some intensely loveless, violent, sadistic prose.

No help for it. If any of the sadism-loving
readers had the crust to complain, I'd tell them that I
was a helpless victim of all the sadistic comic-books I'd

been reading by way of research. A martyr to my work. And I would laugh and chortle and stamp even louder on the floor. What did it matter? The mathematics and physics expert, Carl, who lived downstairs under me, wasn't home daytimes. He still had his job at Columbia University where he had worked on the secret Atom Bomb project. What Manhattan Project were the bastards working on now, I wondered. We'd find out, wouldn't we, the day it exploded and took another hundred thousand people with it — and maybe us too — to perdition. Rotten sadistic me.

Just as I had with the comics research, I tried now to meet all the murder-mystery writers I could. They had a club, and I got myself invited to some of their meetings. These "mystery" writers were really disgusting, without knowing it, under their cheery pose of being mere businessmen types, in the blood business strictly for the money. When I tried to bring up the moral point, and the contrast with the total obloquy of pornography, they laughed and hooted, assuring me brashly that they knew very well that their job was peddling bloodlust to sexually depressed readers, and that I had nothing whatsoever new to tell them.

One writer, whose name I didn't catch and wish I had — actually seemed humanly piqued by my moral attack and snarled at me in a furiously restrained voice, "Exactly who made *you* the keeper of our collective conscience?" None of the others showed any doubts whatever, or were bothered about their consciences. And practically all of them pointed out that, after all, they were making MONEY out of murder-mysteries, so how in hell could I possibly complain?

"In other words," I finished for them, "the touch of dirty money purifies everything."

"And how!" shouted one. "You said it!" laughed another.

"So the only authentic degenerate in the field was Edgar Allan Poe, is that it? The rest of you are just plain businessmen."

"Right!" they shouted, whiskey glasses clinking.

"That's progress!" somebody added. Everybody laughed again.

In other words, I thought, self-confessed murder-pimps. But that would have been too unfriendly to say in such jolly company. Somebody handed me a tall drink. I drank. One of the writers even invited me later to come around and see him at his studio. He wanted to discuss the matter further. I took him seriously and went, one afternoon coming down from the library.

His place was out at the extreme end of West 14th Street, almost at the Hudson River, in an area full of vague grey factory buildings in among ice-houses and trucking plants. As I approached I suddenly had an intense feeling of *déja vu* outside the building at the number he'd told me. Men in long white coats, soiled and streaked, but with crisp, flat straw hats on their heads were standing and milling about in front. Straw hats! *Straw hats!!* Suddenly I was back at the Franklin Beef Company in Scranton, shovelling up the dried cow-shit on Sunday mornings in the killing-pens at Minooka. Straw hats for bald-headed middle-aged butchers to go into the enormous, house-sized ice-boxes, of course. No mistake there. The address the writer had given me was a slaughter-house.

This guy must be Mickey Spillane under a pseudonym, I said to myself rather illogically. Spillane was the most outrageous of the murder-mystery writers then, his proto-fascist stuff purposely ultra-violent and bloodthirsty, and naturally selling in the millions. There was another one like him in England, "James Hadley Chase" — really one René Raymond — of *Kiss the Blood Off My Hands!* And a French imitator, Boris Vian, pretending to be a Negro Faulkner-cum-Hemingway presumably named "Vernon Sullivan." Spillane had opened up a new vein for many. Maybe an artery. Well! A slaughterhouse! Defiant gestures like that were nothing new. I often did the same sort of thing myself. *Say it isn't so!*

I trudged up the wooden steps and knocked at the door with the writer's real name thumb tacked to it on a neat white card. He pulled the door open, all smiles, whipping off heavy eye-glasses to invite me in. An old-fashioned wooden business desk, a typewriter, a stack of yellow second-sheet paper, a few reference books piled at the corner of the desk. He certainly had stripped things down to the essentials. I had almost a twinge of jealousy for anyone who could travel that light, thinking of the massive, oppressive files spreading out tidally over my bedroom floor

I didn't bother to waste time, just in case he really was Mickey Spillane. "Is writing your books in a slaughterhouse intended as a defiance," I asked him for starters, "or a confession?"

"What are you talking about?" he asked, visibly puzzled. "This is the only place I could get in the neighborhood. I live across town, over near Gramercy Park. It's nice and quiet here. I can work."

"Yes," I agreed. "It's quiet. They hit the animals on the temple first with a sledge-hammer. Otherwise they scream terribly when you cut their throats — worse than 'The Murders in the Rue Morgue'."

I forget what else we said. He told me he was definitely not Spillane, and I believe I told him he could surely get a nice little studio office ten blocks closer to his own neighborhood, and very cheap too, in the Flatiron Building. But then he'd have all the traffic noise under his window, he objected. There was nothing more to say. The straw hats and the slaughterhouse had said it all. *Say it isn't so!*

❦

MAYBE I shouldn't admit this, but the next step of my research into murder-mysteries was rather peculiar. I decided I would write a mystery myself, or at least the beginning of one, and see how it *felt*, really, to the writer. Whether it was actually done ice-cold, the way these phoney bastards were claiming, or whether at a certain point one would feel coming to the surface the repressed bloodlust out of which the writing of a crude murder-mystery — and the reading of it too, of course — obviously had to be done. The best of the writers were the frankest about it.

Dorothy Sayers in England, a truly splendid stylist in the lapidary tradition, and more than worthy to rank there with John Collier and Walter de la Mare, even has her impossible androgynous snob detective, Lord Peter Wimsey, announce often that he is an amateur murder-fancier in just the same way that Hemingway openly gloated on the death of bulls in the ring. In one of the Sayers stories, about a bearded man whose throat is cut with a straight razor on an offshore rock, there's even a fantastic passage in which Wimsey and Miss Sayers — of course, he's really just her in pants — excitedly discuss the state of juiciness and coagulation of the blood in the dead man's beard. I thought I would try to write one like that too, but with somewhat less juiciness about the blood, maybe, to try to find out what the writers really felt.

This is all just a rationalization, I suppose. Maybe what I was actually doing unconsciously was trying to get in on the profitable racket the murder-mystery writers had been cushily bragging about to me. The raw cash bucks. They must have mixed something into my drink. That had to be it, because I went almost to publication before something happened that brought me to my senses.

Both the subject and the title fell readily to my hand in a medical article on psychosomatics I had recently seen by Dr. Walter B. Cannon, on 'Voodoo Death,' explaining how intense fear or excitement raises the blood pressure in the victim especially if his arteries are clogged with fat, as most are, and he died of self-induced heart-failure, whether as lung edema or apoplexy. This would avoid any blood-guilt for me, at the top level anyhow, I felt, since there'd be no visible blood and the victim would actually be killing himself. Anyhow, you could say he was, and that it was that way. They'd straighten out my real guilt or innocence in heaven later. What else is heaven for?

After all, thousands of lucky men have died just that way in a woman's arms, from the over-excitement of orgasm. No one would ever seriously suggest that the woman killed them, would they? Like Meg Steinheil and the French president Faure. Or a more recent Rockefeller. It was a kind of glorious accidental suicide — the French even had a name for it: *la mort douce*, sweet death. Isn't that what Wagner's *Tristan & Isolde* is all about? With the music underlining every pant and groan, both of the lovers' orgasm and of their "Love Death."

Since I didn't consciously think of *Voodoo Death* as a book for publication, but only a sort of literary and psychological exercise, I simply started knocking the thing out one hour a day on the typewriter, when my day of real writing was over and I felt a bit fatigued and off my stride. The plot was absurd, involving a voodoo cult having their secret death-orgies at night at the foot of the Palisades cliffs in New Jersey along the Hudson River. The villain was my favorite heavy-set shish-kebab restaurant owner in the Syrian section downtown near Radio Row. The standard seedy private detective, or outlaw killer-of-killers was the only character with any special quality to him, or any dialogue I bothered to take any trouble with. For him I used the bit of tough street knowledge I had picked up in the years I lived in Harlem, with drugs and Negro strong-arm men all over the place. But to be true to the theory of libidinal transfer, I left out completely all the equally realistic Harlem pimps and whores, since this murder-mystery was to be almost entirely without sex, according to formula. Except of course for the mild flirtation between the detective hero and the shish-kebab villain's perfectly innocent daughter. You could hardly call that sex.

This was even more of a pain in the ass writing than my usual ghost jobs, since I didn't even have any rational hope of payment at the end of the necessary weeks of drudgery. To entertain myself meanwhile, I laid out the plot and the chapters to match exactly the moves of a famous chess game played by the Danish champion nearly a century ago, in which the end-game is a smothered check-mate, as it's called, where the white knight — my detective, of course — who has already lost practically all the other powerful pieces on his side of the board, suddenly lunges across the black king's defending lines and puts the king not only in check, but in constructive check as well, by the same knight, if the immobilized king then tries to move into any of the spaces left open for him. End of game.

Of course, chess always ends with a sort of repressed king-killing like that, since the opposing king is the one piece the scared pantywaist players never have the Œdipal guts to take. But this Danish game was a particularly heroic *coup de maître*, and all the more so in that the white knight who tracks the king down, like the standard detective, to his implied suicide is almost entirely alone & unaided on the board at that point. It was the showpiece in one of my chess books, and I made a hand-drawn chessboard diagram of the game position just before the white knight moves in — this for a preliminary leaf in the book that was never to exist at all — and then another drawing showing the end-game, for tailpiece to the book, with the smothered king and the triumphant white knight. Each chapter had a simple italic headline to start the action, showing the chess move to be made in that chapter, such as "Kt to Q4," and the action of the chapter of course more or less matched the move.

While I was working on this, Bob Mexico dropped in on me one day, and was very excited by the idea of a story based on a chess-game, even though I pointed out to him that it's the oldest gag in the book, being used by Lewis Carroll for the framework of *Alice in Wonderland* and *Through the Looking Glass*. Mexico and I had never done any more writing together, after our imbroglio with the editor's wife over *The Devil's Fiddle* story and its sequel *The Sibylline Books* which was never published. He very much wanted to start collaborating with me again, as he could never work out any satisfactory plot ideas or action, although he could hammer out cheap dialogue by the yard at the overslick wiseguy level the pulp editors loved. He was now doing comic book captions for a living, an art-form which also specialized in witty rejoinders and ho-hum asides while the extralegal avengers' ham-sized Rambo fists knocked out the victims' teeth.

Mexico tried to convince me that I should let him sell *Voodoo Death* to the pulp pocketbook publisher who had just done a similar action-mystery novel for him entitled *Madman on a Drum*, a title taken from a line in Oscar Wilde's "Ballad of Reading Gaol." I confess I was seduced surprisingly easily by the idea of making some money on all the work I had done. Somehow the moral objections I knew I should raise died a-borning. I had enough shame though still uneasily budging somewhere in me, to flip the title-sheet into the typewriter and add an author's pseudonym: "Arthur Madigan," I think it was, though later I changed it to something else.

The pulp publisher accepted the book immediately, and, as might have been expected, Mex told him that he himself was "Arthur Madigan." On the basis of this lie Mex promoted a contract for still another book, as yet unwritten and untitled, and walked out with an advance check on *Voodoo Death*.

Things moved so fast then, that Mexico never came back to tell me what he had done in the way of screwing me, till type was all ready to set and my beginning and ending drawings of the chessboard were actually made into zinc cuts and proofs pulled. The end-game chessboard drawing had made the publisher believe that the book was finished, but everything suddenly jolted into reverse gear when the typesetters informed him unexpectedly that only half of the chapters were present. That was when Mexico arrived at my place for the rest of the manuscript, offering me grandly half of the advance he had swung. The other half he stated was to be his as "agent's fee."

In a simple and friendly fashion I told him to go to Woolworth's five-&-dime store and buy a rubber duck, which he could then stick up the farthest corner of his grimy ass and give it a left-hand turn. This he understood as persiflage or friendly insult and replied in kind. When I persisted, answering nothing at all to his remarks but "Up your ass! Up your *ass!*"— he decided I wanted more money and agreed he would accept a twenty percent agent's fee, to which I of course replied, "Up your ass."

"All right, you bastard! Ten per cent!"

"Up your ass. In fact, up your gigi with a furlined shit-scoop." I was beginning to get bored.

Mex was now sincerely confused, and asked what the hell I *did* want. I quoted to him D. H. Laurence's remark about the piracies of *Lady Chatterley's Lover* in "My Skirmish with Jolly Roger," in which Laurence observes that Judas is always there with his kiss, but that it's hard to have to kiss the traitor back. And I also told him, which was the truth, that I never intended to write the whole book, which was only a research exercise for the book I was really working on. Not only that, I insisted, but I had no intention of ever finishing it and would kill him dead if he tried to finish it for me. To clench the matter, I told Mex finally that I would be phoning his publisher the minute he left, and would tell the publisher exactly what had happened, and that his fine new writer, N. R. de Mexico, born Robert Bragg in Dunellen, New Jersey, was a plagiarist and a crook.

Mexico became violent, insulting, and finally tearful. He begged me not to destroy his budding career in this way, as he was going to go insane if he had to keep writing dialogue for comic-books. I hustled him down the stairs and walked him to the subway and made him take me to his bank down on West 14ᵗʰ Street, which happened to be the same as my own. But to the contrary of me, I knew he always kept a decent-sized account in the bank as he was terrified of being broke, and admitted it. I made him take out the amount he had received from the publisher as an advance and hand over the whole sum to me. I also told him there would be trouble if it turned out to be a penny less than the whole sum, and I would certainly find out.

As soon as we parted company, I went back to my room and got out the further chapters I had written in the intervening weeks, and looked them over with a coldly critical eye. They weren't badly done, but much too violent. I would have to be careful another time about purposely unleashing the demon in me that way. Then I went to see the publisher myself. He was in a printers' building over in the East 40s. I gave him back his money with the appropriate haughty gesture, and asked for my manuscript. As I had said I would do so, and hadn't promised Mexico anything different, I told him exactly what had happened, except that I tried to cover Mexico a little bit by saying he had been acting as my agent but had exceeded his authority. *Voodoo Death* was already contracted for with a big paperback house on Madison Avenue, I told the publisher, pulling the best name I could think of out of a hat.

"Exceeded his authority, huh?" the publisher growled, flipping over with a thumb and forefinger the extra chapters I had brought along to show him as proof that I was the author. He walked over to a set of floppy cardboard file-boxes against one wall and pulled out my manuscript, with an inky string tied around it and the title page already marked up by the printer for typesetting. He threw it down on his desk in front of me.

"Take a look at that!"

On the title page, neatly printed in tall, spidery letters, I read: "VOODOO DEATH, by N. R. de Mexico, Author of *Madman on a Drum*." The money, all in crisp banknotes, was still lying on the desk in a stack.

I pushed it toward the publisher again, feeling like Pontius Pilate shoving at Judas Iscariot his thirty dirty pieces of silver. There was a great scene like that in John Ford's *The Informer*. I picked up my manuscript silently and started to leave. The Publisher followed me to the door.

"I knew it was too good for that Mexican bastard." he grumbled. "Did you write *Madman* for him too?" I shook my head no. "Listen, how much did that pocketbook house give you for an advance? We can match that. Lookit our loss on all that set type! We need good writers. We can give you newsstand distribution all over the country like they never even heard of."

Carried away now by my own fiction, I assured him it was impossible. It wasn't just a question of a mythical thousand dollars one way or the other. My contract with the pocketbook house, I told him, stated that I had to submit my next book to them before anyone else, and the same with every following book they took, so that actually I was enslaved for life. "The only way I'll ever get out of that contract," I told him, "is to take it to the Supreme Court and claim it's against the Constitution — the Fifteenth Amendment, the one against chattel slavery!" As I'd never in my life seen one of the pocketbook company's contracts, I could speak freely, every word being a lie. Also, I don't think it's the Fifteenth Amendment — it's the Thirteenth.

Just to protect myself from any further unfortunate *contretemps*, in case this grubby guy got so worried about his loss on the already-set type that he decided to commission Mexico secretly to finish the story off somehow, I warned him in a polite way, as I left, that my mythical other publisher was so perturbed by the whole mixup that they'd already sent a photostatic copy of the manuscript to Washington with the necessary six bucks to copyright it in that form.

"That way they're protected against Bob Mexico and his tricks," I said significantly. "And so am I."

PREDICTABLY, after that, the manuscript of *Voodoo Death* was burning a hole in the lemon-crate filing box where I threw it all when I got home. On an evil impulse, I then spent a couple of mornings knocking out the few chapters necessary to finish it; as much, I told myself dishonestly, out of a compulsion to finish the built-in chess game as for any other reason. In a pig's ass! Then I began asking myself, unconsciously I suppose, what to do with it. In fact, I knew exactly what I wanted to do with it, which was to sell it and get the money, now that I knew there was over a thousand dollars in it.

What I was really asking myself was how I could possibly justify trying to peddle a murder-mystery — even though there was no actual murder in it, just mystery and a death by apoplexy — while I was simultaneously writing a hammer-&-tongs attack on the whole genre, presumably the first ever written. There was no way of resolving a contradiction like that in myself, so I just shoved it down under the level of thought. Meanwhile, though *Voodoo Death* was finished now, I didn't do anything with the manuscript. Just left it in the crate. I guess that was my way of fighting my dishonorable urge to join 'em and cash in, since I knew I couldn't lick 'em.

But was it really certain that I couldn't lick them? I hadn't even tried yet. My article, which I knew now would make a small book that I planned to call *Institutionalized Lynch*, hadn't even been published and wasn't really finished. Shouldn't I finish that first, and somehow get it published? Hit the rotten bastards writing and publishing murder-mysteries right where they lived! Including me. The paradoxical result was that I now stopped writing on my real book, not able to deal with myself any longer as so total and contemptible a hypocrite. If I was a murder-mystery writer, or evidently wanted to be one, under the cheap disguise of a pseudonym, then I couldn't at the same time be writing attacks on murder-mysteries, or any other kind of literary sadism for that matter. Very well then, I was a murder-mystery writer. That's what I was and that's what I would write. Needs must when the devil drives. I had the cheapest excuse of them all — the one I had always laughed at the most scornfully in other people, as paid and prostituted minds. I needed the money.

It was funny. In the years when I wrote pornography for a living I hated the work, and knew it was having a bad effect on my own sexuality. But I had never felt particularly soiled by it. Probably because I'd never written any more sadistic a passage than one once when my hardon-bearing hero, carried away by his passion, bites his girlfriend savagely on the inside of her highly erogenous perfumed thigh — representing the tender, thuriferous tissues of her juicy vulva, of course. You can hardly call that sadism, can you? *Please* say you can't call it sadism! Just a normal, up-standing, thoughtless virility. Some girls would call that a rough caress. The *Kama Sutra* has a whole straight-faced chapter on that very art of scratching & biting as a special erotic technique. It's an art.

And now, for having written one rather short murder-mystery, begun strictly as a literary exercise to try to *understand* the thing from the inside — or so I told myself — I felt like a total whore. Well, it wasn't the writing that was the whoredom, was it? That was an intellectual game. Maybe. The whoredom was in trying now to sell it. And I had refused to sell it, hadn't I? Had nobly thrust back his stinking two hundred and fifty bucks — you call that an advance? — at the funny little publisher in the decaying printers' building on the East Side who pretended to have the best distribution in the country. Yes, that was true. But I had finished the manuscript since, and was now carefully thinking over who to try to sell it to. No question about it. I was a whore; a murder-pimp just like all the others. Maybe I ought to rent a studio over a slaughter-house, on West 14th, just like What's-his-name — if there were enough to go around. A real stylist: the dying grunts of the cows calmed and inspired his soul. But would they calm mine? Don't let Tinkerbell die!

One thing I was sure of was that I certainly wouldn't go to the little guys, like Mexico's publisher, with their ridiculously low advances and their highwayman contracts demanding that you sell them your manuscript outright. Half the advance when you brought the manuscript in, and half on publication. If you got it. Many a slip with the little publishers, some of whom opened up under a new business name every couple of months. Jake Brussel wasn't the worst crook in the publishing business at all; just the one I knew best in the sex-book field, and he was crooked enough. I thought I'd try taking the manuscript of *Voodoo Death* around to a few of the big pocketbook houses myself, but they put me right out the door with it, explaining with what I guess was supposed to be kindness that they never dealt directly with authors, only with agents. I had no agent, of course.

In the end I did give it to a fairly small house, but one that had been in business quite a while, feeling like Professor Garbage in *The Blue Angel* when I saw the place. They were on East 23rd Street, right over Uncle Phil Lewis's big, drafty slum-shop bookstore, which also sold magazines, magic tricks and legart calendars and novelties — not to mention under-the-counter pornography, of course — the biggest emporium of that kind in town.

I felt vaguely certain, going up the stairs, that maybe Uncle Phil was actually the money *down*stairs behind the publishing firm *up*stairs, which also published all of Jack Woodford's mild sex-novels, their main standby. But who knows? The editor turned out to be someone I knew, named Alan Wilson, whom I remembered as the manager of my favorite midnight remainder bookstore in the Paramount Building on Broadway years before.

The minute I turned over the manuscript to him, I went into total writer's block for the first and only time in my life. It was absolutely dreadful, like slow death, worse than anything I had ever imagined from the occasional references to it in the writers' magazines. I felt like someone whose legs and prick had been chopped off by falling into a threshing machine. And I was pushing myself around for weeks after like an emotional cripple on an imaginary little pushwagon for the legless. Not only I couldn't write anything — not even a letter: some writers don't have it that bad, and instead waste *all* their time on letters — but there was nothing I could throw myself into to forget how awful, and how abysmally useless and castrated I felt. I didn't drink, I couldn't stand the cheap Hollywood movies beckoning sleazily on every street corner, and I was being relatively faithful to Beverley as I always was when I was working hard. That meant that sex wasn't much of a wild thrill for me just then, and I made no attempt to find another girl. There was nothing to do but suffer.

The idea of turning back now to library work, and the endless drudging out and piling up of more thousands of 3 X 5" index-cards, wholly disgusted me. What I wanted to do was write, and I couldn't. The only thing left for me was music, and every record I put on was a reproach to me. Look how Mozart had to suffer with his mad wife — and Beethoven, though of course that was all his own fault, as with most of us. And Schubert worst of all, and him the sweetest singer. At least Mozart died surrounded by his friends, singing his Requiem with them from the manuscript parts he hurried to sketch out with a quill pen sitting up in bed, while the black wings of death slowly enfolded him and his ink-wet manuscript together. That's the way to die! Who cares about his unmarked grave? That's only the dead meat and bones. Mozart lives! And Schubert who died syphilitic and forgotten in some gypsy wagon? And Smetana and Schumann in the nut-house. Well, who cares how you die? What counts is how you handle living. I wasn't living.

I went out and bought some planks of wood and a small crosscut saw, and started building a three-tier cabinet for my phonograph records, to get them out of the disorderly cartons on the floor. For a hammer I used the head of the handsome little hand-axe with the laminated leather handle that I'd bought down at Browny's that time I planned to go camping with the student-nurse, and ended up abandoned on the mountain-ridge in Vermont by Del Torto and Company, the high-speed hikers. No matter. Mountain tops were just where I liked to be. I was born on a mountain top, wasn't I? Or was Scranton the crater of an enormous extinct volcano? If so, Harrison Avenue up in the hill section was nearly the highest rim. Besides, a volcano is a kind of mountain too, like Fujiyama. So thinking, I gave myself a violent whack in the head with the cutting edge of the hand-axe as I hammered, nearly taking my ear off better than Van Gogh. I patched it up with court plaster tape and decided to be a bit more careful in future.

The court plaster reminded me that the electrical cord of my work lamp with the whirling top was frayed through and needed to be taped. This would be a good time to fix it. I sat on the floor examining the frayed part of the cord, and decided I would have to cut away a whole section first and begin with two fresh ends. Reaching up, I got my library scissors from the edge of the typing table and took a big, decisive cut into the electrical cord. As I had completely forgotten to pull the plug out, I felt instantly a powerful shock as the shears cut into the live wire, and my right arm went completely numb up to the elbow. I dropped the shears, lurched carefully over sideways and got the electric plug out of the wall with my left hand. Then I lay there on the floor a while thinking. The scissors had an ugly blue-black burn, probably a hole, where the two cutting edges met. The phonograph had gone dead instantly when I shorted the wire, and the music had stopped with a slow, repulsively falling tone moaning down the scale.

I struggled up and sat on the bed and battered at my right arm till it began to have some tingling feelings again. Then I went and got old Mr. Nossiter the landlord, and told him I had blown a fuse. The fuse-box for the whole house was in his apartment, so he could turn off the current on anybody whose rent was too far behind. I went out, not caring anymore about my work lamp. I wouldn't need it anyhow, since I wasn't able to do any real work. Between the axe-trick trying to hit myself in the head, and my attempted self-electrocution with the lamp wire, I realized I was now a psychosomatic danger to myself, just the way Dr. Cannon had described. Evidently I was trying to commit suicide, or at least was moving fast into that area. I didn't know what to do. I got on the subway, carefully staying far away from the platform edge in case my accident-prone suicidal mood hadn't passed yet, as I had no reason to believe it had, and went downtown. I'd change my mood listening to some new records at Rabson's near Radio City. That was still my favorite music-shop and the only one that would give me credit. Sophie Rabson who was the boss and her brother Bob, who was the manager and the main record-clerk, both liked me. God knows why.

While I was listening to music upstairs in the big record department which had excellent little listening-booths where you could play records all day without anyone ever asking you to buy anything, one of my favorite people came in, named Irving Kolodin. He was a lot older than me, and had a job as music columnist on one of the literary magazines. I respected his musical judgment very much. Kolodin was preparing a revised edition just then of his phonograph record guide, which was by far the best then, and the only one with lively critical notes. Some of his notes were brief sardonic gems. Rabson's was where he went to listen to all the new records, since his book competed with the Gramophone Shop's guide. Otherwise he might have listened to the records there.

Kolodin was a 101% diehard Arturo Toscanini rooter, and didn't know or didn't remember that Morton Gould once got me a brief job on the N.B.C. publicity staff for the Toscanini concerts at Radio City years before, in the acoustically dead Studio 8-H. But I had left under a cloud when I confided foolishly to one of the other lobbygows — who immediately tattled on me to Toscanini's son Walter, who was the straw-boss — that I hated Toscanini's compulsively fast tempos, that his readings of Mozart and of Haydn's "Clock" Symphony were ridiculous jokes, and that I thought he was becoming just a stiff, vain, mad old man, and that

Bruno Walter could conduct rings around him and up his ass. I still think so. But it was perhaps undiplomatic to mention it when my job was to promote the Toscanini concerts. Maybe I was trying to loose that job, or change over to Bruno Walter.

At that time Bruno Walter — whose name really was Bruno Schlesinger — had just arrived in America when the Nazis overran Europe and he had to get out, being a Jew. He was now conducting a new orchestra created specially for him by the Columbia Broadcasting Company, who also issued all his records. Guy d'Isère, the secret erotica printer, played clarinet in that orchestra. Everybody knew that Bruno Walter was the greatest conductor in the world — he and Wilhelm Furtwängler, who had stayed behind in Germany, not being Jewish, to conduct the Berlin Philharmonic for Hitler. I tried to get a job on the Columbia concerts staff instead, but failed utterly. When I admitted I had worked for N.B.C. they figured I was just an industrial spy, and showed me indignantly to the door.

Anyhow, my clearly expressed opinions had got me fired then — not the only time. But Kolodin seemed unaware of this now, or maybe hadn't identified me with the brash youth of ten years before, which was before I had grown the moustache. We would talk affably now about the new records, with Kolodin pointing out all the specially good sides in all the new albums, and me complaining about why didn't anybody ever put out a Conchita Supervia memorial album and all that. We kept crossing each other's paths politely at the counter, and going in & out of the listening booths with the big, heavy five-record albums and the brown-enveloped singles in our hands, and an occasional blue-shanked chromium record needle that big Bob Rabson would deal out every hour or two, so we wouldn't ruin the music on the records. But this day, suddenly and unreasonably, I started knocking and mocking Kolodin's judgments, arguing bitterly with his wittily expressed choices, challenging the excellence of all the record sides his guidebook found so admirable. He stood it for quite a while, listening courteously.

"You know," he said finally with a pained expression, "you don't really have the right to persecute me like this, just because you bought a copy of my book for two dollars and ninety-eight cents." That would have stopped anybody sensible, but it didn't stop me. Kolodin began avoiding me at Rabson's, but I refused to take the hint and continued to pursue him with my impolite anti-judgments and negations.

The end came a day or two later when I told Kolodin perfectly gratuitously that some tremendous choral and orchestral climax he had been enthusing about in a review of a new recording of one of the Wagner "Ring" operas wasn't much of a much, and sounded to me like the Harlem Hamfats grinding chopped mud. Kolodin went absolutely white, popped back into his listening-booth with a tight-lipped and certainly very cutting reply which he unfortunately delivered in so tensely refined a pianissimo that I couldn't understand a word. That was the last time we ever spoke. His nasty musician friend, Oscar Levant, a third-rate pianist specializing in playing Gershwin in movie musicals could come into Rabson's and insult people that way all day long, and worse, but not a nobody like me. You're only witty if it says in the gossip-columns that you're witty, like Levant.

Otherwise you're just an undesirable boor. Also like Levant, and many another.

After that, I got completely out of hand. The Harlem Hamfats grinding blue mud were only the beginning, some sort of inner breaking point I had come to. I started acting like a mad dog, my nastiness and verbal aggression quite out of my own control, though I tried to disguise it at first as wit, teasing, hilarious humor, and practical jokes. Inside I knew better but I was unable to stop. I had a dream then that told me what had happened, but again there was nothing I could do about it. In the dream I lost my temper at Artur Schnabel endlessly practicing across the areaway from me in his luxurious bay window, at that magnificent grand piano, and I had suddenly flung my typewriter out the window at him to silence his clack.

The typewriter sailed in a slow arc and broke into a thousand pieces three floors down in one of the backyards separated by little wooden picket fences, and I rushed down to try to salvage it. I was stamping up & down under the billowing white sheets of somebody's laundry hung out on the lines, trying to climb over the picket fences and pick up the pieces of my broken typewriter — THIS typewriter, the one I'm writing on this very minute! But at every step I took I was grinding some hooklike key or wheel of it into the mud.

The paper-white sheets were blinding me and the fence-pickets stabbing my legs as I climbed them. I couldn't see anything I was doing, except that I realized I was losing even the inner pieces of my machine into the mud. The frame and roller too were strangely twisted and beyond repair where I was plunging and stamping on them blindly. Then I woke up dripping with sweat, fighting the bed sheets in which I had become tangled in my sleep, and rushed over naked to the typewriter table. There, to my horror, I found that my big square royal had actually disappeared, and had been replaced by a narky little Underwood portable!

Then I woke up completely and realized I wasn't in my room at all, but had been sleeping down at Bedford Street with Beverley, and this was her portable on the wooden kitchen table. I threw on my clothes without even waking her, and rushed to get the subway to my own room. The typewriter was all right. Outside the window that morning, Schnabel was practicing serenely — Chopin preludes this time, for finger exercises. I sat down in wonderful relief at the keyboard to start writing. Nothing came.

❦

AS I SAID, I spent most of my time in record-stores then. I didn't spend much money, in fact none at all, because I didn't have any. The two hundred and fifty dollar advance I had wrung out of Bob Mexico and given back to the pulp publisher was the last cash money I believe I saw for quite some time. I had earlier put in a whole case of cheap canned red chili beans, behind the low screen that marked off the kitchen corner and tiny sink in Beverley's room, and that was about what we ate. Beverley was working part-time at some kind of advertising institute or business adviseering service run by one Leo Cherne at Madison Avenue and 40th Street, and what she earned bought us bread and milk to put in her coffee. Whatever milk she didn't use, I drank. That and beans. And an occasional head of lettuce and loaf of Italian bread from one of the little stores across on Bleeker Street.

Living on my wife — which is how I described this to myself — was also adding to my fury. I lived in a perpetual internal rumble, and would often have sensations of burning, more and more frequently, running up & down from my stomach to the back of my throat. I knew this was purely psychosomatic, because I felt so rotten about being in writer's block, and so did nothing about the burning pains. Drinking hot milk would stop it, I found, or even cold milk in a pinch; but only for a moment or two. *Mama!!*

Down on Chambers Street in the radio and electrical appliance part of town, my friend, Fred Petras, clerked in a record store in a partly dismantled old building soon to be torn down. It was just a dump with a high ceiling and mostly pop records, but Petras would put aside good blues records for me when they came in, and an occasional repressing of good New Orleans jazz or boogie-woogie piano. Petras was trying to prove to me that not all recent jazz was piss-poor garbage, as I maintained, and of interest only to superannuated white snobs. I had picked up this prejudice over the years, mostly from dislike of Bob Sewall's *aficionado* approach to jazz records, and the whole, obvious fake-jazz and "white jazz" money-business of recent white bands like Paul Whiteman and

Benny Goodman, and many another hoke artist. Jazz was a Negro art, I felt and knew, and it was real and powerful when Negroes did it. White jazz was invariably either big business or pure shit, or both.

One day Petras pointed something out to me that was very important, I could see, though I didn't know then where to file it or how to use the knowledge. When I came into the store one afternoon, after most of the day back at my old haunts in the great South Reading Room of the Public Library, he said, "Listen to this," and snapped a little ten-inch jazz record on the counter pickup.

"Strictly nothing," I assessed it grumpily.

"Right! Now listen to this. — Same piece, same band, same players; all except one." He put another little ten-incher on. It was marvellous! The band was playing like demons possessed. The whole store throbbed with it. Obviously the same piece of music, but what a difference! Petras showed me the labels on the two records. They were identical, except on the second one a single final line: "Trumpet solo, L. Armstrong."

Petras grinned at me. "We have with us tonight . . ." he said.

Not much consolation for a lone-wolf like myself. And getting loner all the time, too, as I drove off one after another of my few friends with my new verbal savagery which I had once known enough to keep on paper only. Petras and I stayed friends a while longer than most, but I ruined that too. Our friendship was under a strain anyhow, because I was now planning to collaborate on a phonograph record index-guide with another record clerk I knew, named Ferdinando, who worked in the big Castellànos-Molina Spanish record store on West 72nd Street, right near my room. Petras had already moved up into the same neighborhood on my recommendation, where he had a much larger and more luxurious room than mine.

The index-guide planned was not to be like Kolodin's book, and would contain no critical remarks — there were too many new records coming out for that. Only an alphabetical listing of every recording commercially available of each piece, both classical and popular. I would have made it only classical, if it had been up to me, but that was too much like the older Gramophone Shop catalog with which we were going to compete. Also, Ferdinando had already begun with a very careful listing of all the Hispanic records in print, on all labels domestic & imported. That was going to be our sample, and I took fire on the project and worked up a current matching listing of all recordings by Mozart available in America. Then I typed the whole thing up into a very decent-looking manuscript which I took around to all the technical book-publishers looking for a contract.

It was good for me to work at this, because even if I couldn't write anymore at least I could make lists. I was almost a perfect typist when doing copying work: seldom an error and very very neat. I felt like the fallen angel I was, doing work like that, but I kept plugging at it, and running around with the manuscript to publishers, mostly on foot to save the nickels for streetcar and subway fare. Nobody wanted the Record Index-Guide; everybody said the idea stank, was too specialized, that no one but the record stores would buy it — which was exactly the idea, I tried to make them see. It would also have to come out in an updated revision at least twice a year, which would be admittedly an enormous production expense.

That was the whole idea as far as I was concerned, because that would mean steady jobs, maybe for years ahead, for both Ferdinando and me, as editor-compilers of the popular and classical sections. But no one wanted it — anyhow, not then. A firm in Boston made a fortune with the same idea when long-playing records came in ten years later, and are still publishing it quarterly. Computer typesetting and automatic alphabetizing reduced their production problem to zero, but of course electronic conveniences like that weren't available to us then. That was always my problem: being twenty years ahead of time. Lucky they didn't hang me.

Maybe I misjudged Petras, but I got the impression that he was irritated by my new collaboration with Ferdinando, who was also very distant with both Petras and Bob Mexico. Especially Mexico, whom he recognized instantly from his accent when he tried to talk Spanish, as only an "imitation Spig;" as Ferdinando put it cuttingly. With me maliciously reporting this immediately to poor Mexico, who always fondly imagined he was getting away with his Hispanic masquerade, and had even learned to play the guitar very badly.

One main problem in collecting anything is always your fellow collectors, who are generally out to get there ahead of you and snap up all the good finds and bargains before you can get to them. Vultures! One has to lie to them, or at least misdirect them scientifically, just as they do to you; and friendships in your own field are always a bit poisoned by this mutual competition, concealment, shameless lying, and suspicion. Trading duplicates and wheeling and dealing also cause a lot of bad blood. Even the mere showing off of one's latest finds with insufferable pride — a sin few collectors are innocent of — is also not calculated to make your collector friends like you any better. So it happened that following up a secret spoor, after seeing Westermann's big German bookstore in Radio City practically thrown into the street by the F.B.I. when the war started, as a propaganda importing service, I began searching privately for German record-importing houses that might have remained untouched by the War.

One day I found the Telefunken record importers, moribund now in a sleazy little walk-up under the elevated train structure on Third Avenue in the German section of Yorkville. I went through their boxes and bins for hours until evening, and found endless treasures of symphonic music mostly, all on beautifully machined imported pressings with bright yellow labels and the shellac edges silken smooth – not like the crudely turned out American recordings for the mass market, with rough, scratchy edges that cut like a circular saw. In one of the bins, to my delight, I found a copy of that rare treasure, Sibelius' *Maiden Coming From the Trysting Place*, Telefunken A-1900, of which I had already found one several years before. But now I had that ultimate desirable: a duplicate of a fine piece, for trading purposes; the one sort of key that best unlocked the jealously-held rariora of the other collectors' troves, mere money being a poor second-best even if you had it, which I didn't.

Naturally I took the new record around to Fred Petras' room in triumph the night I found it, and we played it over a couple of times on his rumbly rig while we began diplomatic negotiations for the ensuing trade. To begin with, of course, I told him I didn't plan to trade it with him at all, but had only brought it around for him to hear and appreciate. I planned to keep it safe, as a duplicate of my own, in case I broke my earlier copy. After all, these records were only shellac and eminently breakable, though the curious thing was that I never broke a phonograph record in all the years I collected them, though sometimes you found new ones in the albums cracked and it took months replacing them. Petras was driven almost to desperation by my dangling in this way the Sibelius record he so much wanted, and I started moving in ruthlessly with a brief triple-star want-list of some of the old Flamencos he had, now no longer available in the Columbia record catalogue for decades. To whet his appetite to frenzy, I told him we could play *The Trysting Place* just one more time; then we'd have to get down to business with the trading.

This time the record brought out of the adjacent room Petras' two new neighbors, with whom he shared a luxurious private bathroom. One of them was a very hotsy-totsy female Hungarian refugee of the ZsaZsa Gabor type, in her early forties and fresh from Vienna, and the other her perfectly gorgeous daughter of about eighteen or twenty, with the most delicately articulated face and body. You could see instantly in the mother what the daughter would look like in twenty years, and in the lovely daughter what the mother must have been up to ten years before. Petras gave me the high-sign with his eye-brows up to here when the ladylike neighbors tapped and came in. We gave them the royal treatment, sitting them down in armchairs while we played *The Trysting Place* over yet one more time. What did I care? It was Petras' copy we were wearing out!

He had already mentioned something about his new neighbors to me, and that the daughter was sensationally pretty. She was indeed. Naturally he had been trying discreetly to squire her around. Unlike me, Petras always had his shoes perfectly shined, and clothes natty, owing to his record-store job. The mother had evidently sized him up as a brown-haired, sharp-nosed acceptable head of male, or ticket buyer *Amerikanischer* swain or *schwein*, and I believe he had already been allowed to take daughter Maria-Teresa to a movie or a concert or something, and bring her safely back to mama at a proper eleven p.m.

Shined shoes or no shined shoes, that girl was just too beautiful to be wasted on Petras, I felt. He couldn't appreciate her. He had doubtless noticed her lovely binocular bosom, of the juicy apple type, but I'll bet he hadn't even observed her delicately tiny feet, and the insidious little ladylike sway of her butt as she walked. That eminently edible ass of hers was jewelled like a watch! I did everything I could to charm her, but was too young and inexperienced then to know the rule that in situations of that type you have to vamp the mother first. The portcullis then slides smoothly up — you don't actually have to lay the mother, in most cases; you just flatter he with the idea that you seethingly *want* to — and you get the letched-for daughter on the second time round. All you have to struggle with now is her jealousy of your attentions to her mother, and her leftover Elektra complex. Men have ended up murdered by the daughters that way. Listen, I didn't ever say it would be easy.

Some people say that that kind of mother is much better in the hay than her inexperienced daughter ever can be, but you'd be surprised how fast a talented and affectionate young girl can learn. Also, there's something about a fresh young face and a tight young ass that's hard to resist when you're young yourself. Or when you're old. Anyhow, I didn't know all that then, and made my pitch directly at the daughter, taking off to be sure from the intensely beautiful and erotic yearning of the Sibelius song. The result was that the mother was furious at me, took angry exception to some overfrank Latin term I used, and flounced out, taking the ravishing but wholly dutiful and intimidated Maria-Teresa with her. She had of course psyched me and my nefarious intentions on her daughter from a mile away, long before I undiplomatically spelled it all out in Latin.

"You bastard!" Petras snapped at me. "Now you ruined everything! Why in hell did you say a thing like that?! I'm surprised you didn't ask Maria-Teresa if she's guaranteed cherry." Cherry meant a virgin, because hymeneal blood is red.

I refused to be remorseful, and told him I hated that middle-aged Hungarian bitch-mama anyhow, who had probably collaborated with the Nazis. Petras calmed down a bit and we played some more records. Suddenly, there she was again! The mother stuck her head inside Petras' door, and stated frigidly — though you could tell without a telescope she was a real steam-boiler, and nowhere near frigid — that if he didn't turn down the music she would call the landlord and have him put out the next day. I wish I could remember what it was I said to her daughter: it must have been more obvious or rougher than I imagined. Some words and ideas are hard to disguise, even in Latin and in pairs. Like when you call a book *Peregrine Penis*: both Latin words.

Since I saw that there would now never be any hope for me with the beautiful daughter, I decided to revenge myself on the bitchy mother for protecting her daughter so well. But how? As they still shared the bathroom with Petras, with interconnecting and locking doors at each end, that was obviously the place to attack. I went in and took a healthy leak, carefully not locking either door, and hoping one of the two women would walk in on me. I waggled my prick around in the air awhile, authoritatively, with my best John Balls air, but there was no one stirring. I would have to think of something else.

Hanging from the shower-curtain bar I noticed a pair of blue rubber gloves on glove-stretchers made of wire like a coat hanger shaped like hands, and I had an inspiration. I stripped one of the gloves off, and bent the middle finger of the wire hand up at right angles to the palm. I though I would leave it for a Finger gesture sign, "Up yours!" on the sink. Then I had an even better idea. Carefully turning up the toilet seat, I attached the wire hand and the inflated glove in the Finger gesture underneath the toilet seat by means of the hook, with the finger sticking up. Either the rubber finger or the wire one should do the job, I figured, and went out rapidly. I invited Petras to come over to my house with me to hear some more records, so it wouldn't be him that'd stumble into my trap.

Few of my phallophoric *macho* inventions have ever been more successful. The Viennese mama slithered into the bathroom only a few minutes later in a blue silk floral wrapper tight-held at her waist, in the process of going to bed, something we found out the very next moment when she came charging into Petras' apartment through the connecting bathroom door screaming like a banshee in hysterical German. Poor Petras had no idea what happened, and had to accept the full force of the storm on his head — wild cries, unknown curses, evil gesticulations, and violent threats in badly accented English to call the police — while I sat fiddling quietly with the controls of the phonograph, looking disapprovingly at him for whatever crime it was she was blaming him for. At a certain moment the absolutely frantic woman, who had now been joined by her lovely daughter, also in the most fetching dishabille, rushed back into the bathroom and tore my infernal machine loose from the hinge of the toilet seat where I had wedged it, and started waving the twisted wire hanger under Petras' nose, the inflated rubber glove bobbling about idiotically. It must have gone in to the hilt.

"Und doss you call beink a *chentleman?!*" she screamed. "Bummler! Pig! Schweinhundt!" The daughter clutched her own silk wrapper intensely with both hands, somewhere between anger and silent pathos, and also managed simultaneously to look as though she had just been raped by a troop of Austro-Hungarian hussars in full uniform including the sheepskin jacket over one shoulder. The scene was too painful. I left.

What really bothered me was: what is the relation between gross horseplay like that, and the deeply sincere emotion I felt at the same time for Sibelius' tragic and passionate song, "Maiden Coming From the Trysting Place"? I wondered if I were really two different people, mixed together inside one skin. I guess I am.

Mark Twain has a delightful story that expresses even better than Freud ever did this problem of the war between the cultured and polite Ego and the untamed and ravaging Id. Twain's story, "Those Wonderful Twins," tells of a circus-freak which has two torsos and heads, but only one pair of legs. One of these conjoined twins is a drunken brawler, while the other is polite and refined. They have it worked out that each twin has control of the legs alternate days, and on his day the drunken twin always hits it out for the nearest saloon, and gets them *both* dead drunk, since they share one stomach. He finally gets in a brawl, where he is challenged to a duel for the next day. But the next day the legs belong to the other twin, who naturally runs away. I wish it were so simple. One way, as Twain's story is certainly saying, is to call the cultivated half of yourself Samuel Langhorne Clemens, and to call the unavowably awful half of yourself that vulgar humorist, Mark Twain..

SOME WEEKS later when my money ran completely out and I had to sell Petras my square painting by Mahlon Blaine of four nudes standing with their backsides to the viewer, one vertically at each yard-square edge, representing the Four Seasons or Races of Womankind, or I don't know what.

I can remember paying Mahlon fifty dollars for that painting, one day when I was very flush, and sold it to Petras for thirty. It'll be worth thousands eventually — I believe it's changed hands already for a couple of thou — just as Mahlon prophesied when Magdalen and Susan posed for him that time naked. I had five or six of Mahlon's paintings at one time or another, mostly of American Indian women, all resembling his divorced wife Duskal, and posed in secret magical rites. Although he made many erotic line drawings, I never saw but one erotic painting by him, after the one of Magdalen and Susan. This other is a small gouache showing a male demon standing vertical and impaling a woman on his mammoth prick. I think he may have made more than one macho item in that style, later on, when he was old and broke, for private sale at the Washington Square art show every spring. But, as I say, I never saw any but this one, found recently and which I still have.

Well, it didn't take me a week to spoil things for myself at the other record store I then started hanging around instead of Petras' place. It was just a block north on lower Church Street near Chambers or Vesey, in the next rundown block of old office-buildings near the passenger entrance to the trains to New Jersey running under the Hudson River. All that is the area torn down to make space for the ghastly Square-headed twin towers by a Japanese architect apparently using children's toy blocks for his snob model, which now dominates the lower Manhattan skyline and makes it look like cubist shit. My new record-store was a fairly high-class joint specializing in new records, both popular and classical. It was run by two brothers, fairly young, and I got along quite well with them as they realized that I loved and wanted music very much even though I was chronically dead-broke most of the time and could seldom buy anything at all. They didn't care. Record-store bums like me were like bookstore bums: they gave the place background and charm.

The last album I got there — after that I could never go back again — was a tremendous new recording, anyhow just newly issued in America, of Beethoven's Fifth Symphony played by the great Wilhelm Furtwängler and the Berlin Philharmonic, with the accompanying rumor that Furtwängler's matching recording of Beethoven's Choral Symphony No. 9 would also soon be issued. This, the older brother at the record store told me confidentially, was supposed to have the finest choral singing of any record ever made of it. The chorus is the part that's usually done worst, beginning with Beethoven's basso invocation to peace: *"Oh, thou Burning Ones, cease these warlike sounds!"* The swinging into the chorus of Schiller's spoon-fed pap about *"All Mankind shall be as Brothers; Brothers all Mankind shall be!"* Faithfully promised by the Brothers' doughtily screaming girlfriends, or Daughters of Elysium, like it says here.

"The salesman told me it's really powerful," the older brother confided to me. "They sing like mad."

"Well, they *are* mad, aren't they?" I replied dourly. "He means the Heinies are now going wild about singing the Brotherhood of Man so everybody'll forget about them frying the Jews at Auschwitz. Anyhow, I always hated that yodelling part." And I began to intone the great chorus from Beethoven's Ninth, which I certainly love as much or more than anyone else, but in a heavy German comedy-accent remembered from Der Baron back home, and in parodied words:

"BLACK! ist rising schmoke from Ausch-vitz,
Schmoke from Ausch-vitz *black* does rise!
Brothers vee heff made a blun-der,
Giff us beck our o-vens, pleeze."

The two brothers both looked at me as though I was crazy too. But was I? Unabashed, and louder now, I went on intoning:

"O-vens! O-vens! Schmoke ist rising,
Giff us beck our Ausch-vitz dear.
Bro-thers, Bro-thers vott a blun-der,
Schmoke from Ausch-vitz BLA-A-ACK!!
Doth rise!"

If I had sung it one more time, I'd have been in total paroxysm. The older brother grabbed an unopened album from the counter and shoved it at me.

"No kidding," he said hurriedly. "Say, this one is really for you." And he pushed into my hands the fresh new album of Beethoven's Fifth Symphony, still in its brown kraft paper wrapper. I tore it open eagerly and took it into the listening booth.

After just the first four electrifying notes, twice repeated, which Furtwängler took with unusual speed and intensity, almost like a snarl of defiance instead of the usual slow, pious sancrosanctity befitting "Fate Knocking at the Door," which had been helping us Win the War for years now — with Churchill standing there in all the newsreels, sheepishly holding up two fingers in the international "V" gesture of cuckoldry, now rebaptized "V for Victory" with the Morse-code opening of Beethoven's Fifth surging up each time for background music — I knew this was the recording we had forever been waiting for. We could now burn the wooden old standard recording by Felix Weingartner, guaranteed to contain every single note Beethoven had written but not a goddam thing more. I listened to the whole five minutes of the first side, transfigured; then stumbled out into the store to pay my last five dollars for the album, and rush home, positively pauperized but glorying in this new treasure. The BLACK schmoke of Auschwitz was temporarily forgotten.

But the store was now suddenly crowded, and no one was paying any attention to the record-counters or seemed to want to take my money. All the clerks, and the customers too, were crowded around a tall, handsomely smiling chap who was signing autographs for everyone with a seigniorial air on bits of paper and cardboard they were thrusting at him.

"Who is it?" I mumbled to the nearest clerk at my elbow. He mumbled back a name I hardly recognized — some white jazz musician who I seemed to remember was married to the soldiers' favorite pinup girl of the period, and with the biggest bosom as they believed, Betty Grable.

You would have imagined that listening to that transcendent Beethoven's Fifth would have made a better man of me — never mind what it did or didn't do for Beethoven! — just the way art is supposed to do. But it didn't. Instead, I mingled in with the autograph-seekers, determined to insult the musician, whose name was Harry James, the worst way I could think of. His crime? Presumably being a mere white jazzman, but really for being married to a sexier-looking girl than any I had. What a bosom on that famous pinup picture, the way the photographer had it airbrushed in! And what a butt! You could found a religion on an ass like that. In fact, that's what the lonely soldiers had done.

When I worked my way up in front of him, James smiled at the record album I seemed to be holding out, still clutched in my hands. "You want me to autograph that?" he grinned.

"No!" I snarled. "How about showing us your prick? We all want to see the prick that's been in Betty Grable."

There was a split-second of deathly silence; then the crowd suddenly sheared open in back of me like the Red Sea before Moses and the fleeing Israelites. I dashed out of the store with Beethoven's Fifth still clutched in my hand and Harry James in fierce pursuit, shock and bloodlust written large on his face when I cast one desperate glance back over my shoulder. I could hear a faraway voice behind me shouting, "Aw,

Harry, he's only kidding!" You wouldn't think an old vaudeville joke like that would upset anybody so.

James was much taller than me, and by all rights should have had longer legs and caught me, but the angels of desperation hurried my own legs along. I streaked up Chambers Street like a madman, ducking into the little cemetery that's for some reason plunked down there near the foot of the Woolworth Building. Then I ducked out again by one of the side entrances, and so lost my pursuer. I hid in busy side streets by the Brooklyn Bridge for nearly an hour, thinking about having been chased there by older, bigger men too, at frightened midnights years before.

After a while I crept back into the same cemetery — I don't know why: maybe searching for punishment — and sat down calmly on one of the benches. My shirt was dripping wet, my armpits stinking with the bilious green sweat of fear, just like that time with the stolen typewriter at Michigan. Oh, I was searching for punishment, all right — somebody to knock all the shit out of me. Big bastard, that guy Harry James. But there was no one around in the cemetery but a few women calling vaguely after uncaring children running up & down the paths, and seedy old men feeding the pigeons. Poison, no doubt. It's those sentimental pigeon-lovers that poison them, every time.

I sat a long while thinking, wondering what the hell was the matter with me, which I knew perfectly well, and asking myself urgently if I ever planned to come out of it. I haven't actually told here half the crude, idiotic things I did. The truth & nothing but the truth, please note; but not the *whole* truth, maybe. I can't remember them all, anyway — mercifully blocked out. They were all pretty lousy. Stupid too. But I finally realized, sitting there in that graveyard, that I had no intention of stopping until I had no friends, no money, no prospects, and was probably beaten to a toothless pulp as well. Never mind about love and lovers. I had also obviously disgraced myself forever at the Chambers Street record-store, where the two owners had been considering the possibility of putting out a test issue of my proposed Record Index-Guide to compete with the Gramophone Shop uptown, just for prestige.

Come to think of it, I hadn't tarried to pay them for the Furtwängler album, either, though I didn't think anyone would hold that against me under the circumstances. I went home and played it as loud as possible — it was glorious! — exulting childishly now in my awfulness, and pointing out to myself in my defence that Beethoven had an even more famously nasty and uncontrollable tongue and unpardonable character than I ever could, which obviously made us equals at least in that sense. I tried to scrub out the green sweat from the armpits of my shirt but it wouldn't come, just like that time years before at Michigan.

About a week later I got a letter from Alan Wilson, the head or perhaps only editor at the small publishers where I'd finally submitted *Voodoo Death*. He apologized for not writing to me earlier, owing to an exceptionally large load of manuscripts on hand for reading, he said, and asked me to come in and see him. I was all exultant the day I went, but really fierce, with my face rigidly set in my angry lion stare of suspicious pride, and counting up all the extra hundreds of dollars

I was going to demand for the advance, beyond the basic thousand dollars the other schmuck up on East 42nd had already offered to match. But Wilson was all smiles and almost deferent charm when I sat down in his office. There was an indefinable air about his smile, though, that I didn't like. A sort of half-hidden triumphant twist that I couldn't psych. His smug tone of fresh new affluence and success also didn't set too well with impoverished me, but I tried to repress what I felt as best I could. After all, publishers have got to be richer than authors, just like it says in the Golden Book of Heaven.

Not only publishers have to have the loose capital to print the books, but they therefore can & do take twice as big a percentage of profit on the gross as the author's modest insufficient little ten per cent — if he gets it!. They also make it on all the ten or even a hundred books they may successfully publish every year. Whereas an author is blessing himself for a damn lucky year when he can write and sell just one. That's the comparison, all right, and that's why lots more publishers have country homes in Bucks County and Connecticut, and yachts too, than authors ever will. Well, since that's the way that Heaven evidently wants it, who was I to complain? Karl Marx?

I sat studying discreetly the handsome worsted pattern of my editor's coat lapel, jealous of the modest elegance of his small-figured tie. He'd hit Madison Avenue soon enough, I figured, even if he was maybe still buying his suits cut-rate at Klein's or Barney's. After all, neatly but shabbily dressed as I was — and I couldn't even afford Klein's bargain basement on Union Square — I had no real kick coming. Wilson *was* accepting my book, which they expected to have out within four months to catch the next season's sales well ahead, he said. And he wanted another book from me too, right away.

"We really liked that scene where the detective roughs up the Negro counterman with jiu-jitsu," he said enthusiastically, riffling through my manuscript on his desk looking for the page.

"He doesn't rough him up," I corrected him painfully. "He just throws him clean." I wasn't even sure that was true.

"Good writing," Wilson insisted. "Strong!" He gave me that indefinable smile again. "We figure we've got a new Mickey Spillane."

That moment was the watershed of my career. Something went through me like a clarion trumpet-call. I froze, with the words "Mickey Spillane" coming at my eyes: two burning icicles about to plunge into me. With those two words — perhaps artless, perhaps malicious — my lifelong smiling enemy Alan Wilson saved my life, as both writer and man. I am grateful to him to this very hour. Who cares about his piracies of my uncopyrightable books his companies may publish? Just money. I'm still grateful to him. I only wish I had more uncopyrightable titles, so I could unwillingly pay him more. I could have killed Wilson then. Today I love him. — You know what I mean. But at the crisis of my life he unwittingly saved me.

The air slowly emptied out of my lungs as he sat back behind the cluttered expanse of his desk, slyly smiling at me, and me smiling vapidly back with only the turned-up corners of my lips. *The new Mickey Spillane*, that was to be me, was it? Something clicked inside: I could hear it opening in my soul. I had the feeling of being some kind of wiggly bug or fuzzy worm whose carapace of horn and slime has suddenly split down the center, liberating at last a winged creature about to step out naked and free. I took a deep breath suddenly, my chest filling up to bursting like Prometheus Unbound.

The editor — what was his name, Wilson, was still smiling; talking too, I think, but I wasn't listening any more. His mask had fallen, just like mine, but we were travelling fast in opposite directions now, listening to very different madmen on different drums. I smiled back at him, I know — mine an enormous, truly sincere smile. What a pleasure to think that I would never have to see his sly smirk again. I told him I had just a few final touches and improvements to make on the manuscript, and got it temporarily away from him on that pretext. I could already hear the presses rolling and see the rotten voodoo incantations of my own death whisking out over the ant-magnetic flames, if I left the manuscript in his hands even another hour.

Wilson gave it back to me temporarily. I would have to bring it in, he said, ready for the printer, chess-moves and all, the next week. Temporarily forever! I walked out of his office clutching the manuscript in a death-grip under my arm. Reborn. — *Reborn!!* I floated down the shabby staircase and out into the street, past the rough wooden boxes out in front of Uncle Phil's slum shop — slum for slumgullion — offering paper back cook books for a dime. The legart magazines and postcards were kept under strict surveillance inside, so horny teenagers and derelicts couldn't steal them on the smash-&-grab. I would now never be that *slum*. I had fallen as low as I would ever go. *Voodoo Death!* Mine.

I floated along for a couple of blocks and stopped finally with my back up against the Flatiron Building at Broadway, still sucking in great lungsful of air as though I had just been born on Creation Day in the morning. I believe that day was the closest I ever came in my life to a true religious experience: an authentic Epiphany. The only way I can describe it is that it was like falling in love, or being dragged back from a suicide cliff. Being liberated unexpectedly from some deathlike dungeon cell by a magic word, after having already given oneself up as dead. And hearing the heavy shackles struck from one's wrists and ankles in the clear, bright music of a cold chisel and sledge hammer. *"We figure we've got a new Mickey Spillane."* Mickey Spillane! — The same four opening notes as Beethoven's Fifth.

I put away the typescript of *Voodoo Death* in one of the two open-topped lemon crates by the window of my bed-sitting-room studio that served as my filing system in the folder marked "JOBS — CURRENT" It was dead now, like a cast-off skin, but that's what the folder said. I believe it's still there. I don't say that I became a butterfly that day, but I know I was never a caterpillar again.

CHAPTER 46

KINSEY & CO.

ONLY A FEW MONTHS before the end of the war, Beverley and I decided we really hated New York and wanted to get away. But where would we go? We didn't know. Nor how we would live when we got there. Well, we'd find work to do. It seemed better not to ask ourselves too many questions. The main thing was to get away. I had this continuous idea, which also came as a recurrent bad dream at nights, that I was strapped to a smoking volcano. Not anything beautiful like Fujiyama, but a dirty, slag-covered, smouldering, dangerous mountainous heap.

I suppose this dream was a hybrid, somewhere between the legend of Prometheus chained to the mountaintop with his liver torn out eternally by an eagle for having stolen the lightning from heaven, and the true story I had read recently in Charles Fort, of the catastrophic eruption of Mont Pelée in Martinique in 1902. There the population had been prevented by armed force from abandoning the island before the explosion that killed them all. The savants of the French Academy of Sciences, far away and safe in Paris, had telegraphed reassuringly that Mont Pelée was only smoking, as it sometimes did, and would not erupt. There was no danger. They knew. Thirty thousand strapped-down victims then died in the explosion, including the soldiers and policemen ordered to prevent them from escaping. Science had spoken.

I didn't tell Beverley anything about my recurrent dreams and fantasies, which I found sufficiently alarming by myself, without having her upset and wholly depressed too. Her personal sadness and silence were enough of a bringdown to me, as it was. As the gas station on Seventh Avenue, on the triangular corner behind our little room, was a perennial crucifixion to us, I just kept expressing the idea to Beverley as wanting to get away from New York and the stink of the automobile exhausts. Naturally, I didn't say anything about the perennial stink of the cigarettes she never stopped smoking, brooding silently hour after hour. Presumably we would take that lesser stink with us wherever we went.

But where to go? And what to live on? As to the money part of the question, I didn't know how to solve that without simply robbing a bank. So I attacked on what seemed the more practical and interesting side: where to go, dead broke as we always were? That part of it didn't matter, I assured Beverley cheerfully. We'd always be able to get up the bus fare, no matter how far away. I had lots of books. I'd sell maybe half of them, if we had to, and put the rest in storage; and there we'd have both bus fare and our grubstake for the first few months while we got our new bearings and found work. There wouldn't be any problem. We were young, we were strong, we could work. The only question was where to go?

The right place to start studying a question like that, I felt, was the map room at the Public Library, gorged with thousands of maps of all the world. The

American West was the most interesting and the roomiest, of course. Nobody there but a couple of thousand Indians not yet satisfactorily massacred or shut on reservations in the less desirable parts. That would teach them a lesson about owning a big country that gun-bearing Europeans wanted. And what about Canada? Too cold. Then I got side-tracked for a while by the discovery in the map room of the glorious relief maps of the Grand Canyon, maps of which I was by some miracle able to feel and understand the stark beauty of their plummeting concentric lines in sepia brown.

I ordered a complete set of these beautiful maps from the Government Printing Office for some pittance — a dollar and a quarter apiece, or something like that — and tacked them up on the walls of Beverley's little bed-sitting room, where I could voyage through them while lying looking up at them in bed, floating leisurely high up in the endless sky like Nils Holgersson on the neck of his tame wild goose. What did a contradiction like that matter, as long as I floated? The Grand Canyon maps reminded me somehow of Bach's so strangely passionate concertos — we didn't know yet that they were really by Vivaldi — though of course in another idiom or way of couching ineffable beauty on paper.

Half-blind Sacheverell Sitwell wrote a fabulously illustrated book — there's an even better one by Jurgis Balustraïtis — on strange and baroque artists and their visions, their *trompe l'oeil* and extravagant perspectives; but all the art critics and historians seemed to have overlooked the frozen movement and tactile beauty of topographic mountain maps. Have they maps of the

Alps too? They must, and older. I'll bet those are glorious too. And what about the Himalayas? Who cares about the cheap competitiveness of their mere *heights*, and grabbing off all the tallest ones for the invader's flag by changing the native names into French or English: Chomolungma into "Mount Everest," and only because it's a few yards higher than mere mathematical "K-4." Talk about misplaced patriotism!

Beverley and I finally decided, strictly from studying the maps, that the very best place would be Salida, Colorado, just southwest of Denver and Pueblo. We chose it for its name, partly, which means escape or leaping off — to be sure — and the fact that it was in a river saddle just at the crest of the highest peaks of the Rockies. If it was cold nights, Beverley would learn to knit and make us some sweaters. We weren't the first to discover that area, of course. Taos was only a few hundred or so miles south, in New Mexico, where D. H. Lawrence had lived, or at any rate been dragged off for an unwilling reburial after he was dead, by some obnoxious bitch who wasn't even his wife. She didn't feel it was appropriate for a novelist from the coal-mining area of England to be buried in Vence, in the south of France. The American southwest was more appropriate.

In truth, there were some lovely town names there: Powder Horn, Wagon Wheel, Cimarron, and more. In fact, there were a couple of Cimarrons, which Beverley said was Spanish for wild. We would scout them all after we got there, I assured her. I was worried by the high Rockies the maps showed just west of Salida; whether that might not cut off our sun too early in the day. Nobody wants the sun to set at two in the afternoon, and dark days without the sun depress me very much. Well, if the sunlight wasn't quite right we could always go on to Taos where the artists' colony was, and there might be quite a few nice people to get to know. I could see from the map that Taos had its back to the Sangre de Cristo mountain range, and a perfectly clear view to the west. There would be no problem.

Well, you know the rest. Just a few months later the Atom bomb was exploded over Japan, twice, at Hiroshima and Nagasaki. And the newspapers were filled with the gloating details, how the bomb had first been tried out near Los Alamos, very close to Taos. And how they had moved the Indians out forcibly, as a precaution; and then there was this great black, burning mushroom of unbridled destruction bulging up into the sky — as destructive as twenty thousand tons of Chaim Weizmann's mere little liberating T.N.T. of the war before. That black scenic mushroom, as everyone now knows, became the glorying sign of the new dispensation. To me it looked more like the last despairing globule of water erupting into the sky at the stern, when the immense ocean liner of earth would have dived — shipwrecked and now forever lost — below the uncaring waters of forgetfulness. One thing was sure: that mushroom was the poisonous marker on the world's grave, if the world will have any grave.

After that, Beverley and I never said anything about Salida again. I don't believe I ever even pronounced the word for forty years, until I was reading aloud the preceding few pages today for rhythm. We understood then that Salida was over for us. There would be no escape. Not for us and not for anyone. Beverley replaced the maps of the Grand Canyon with some colored Van Gogh prints of fields and old churches, all of which I liked well enough except for one desperately cockeyed picture of his little unadorned bedroom, with the bed sticking out at you all out of perspective like big feet in the foreground of a photograph wrongly composed. When I said something about it, Beverley informed me that this cheerless bedroom picture was her favorite. I accepted it as the silent message it was, crying out her mute disarray and withdrawal from the world, and the empty-handed melancholy of her soul.

As the weeks went on after the Bomb went off, when we learned about the corrupting and polluting of our Last Chance Inn that was Salida, she became very depressed, even more so than usual. I realized we should do something — budge — anything — if only to give Beverley the feeling that all our plans had not been knocked into the mud, that we could still move and act, that we were not helplessly trapped. And so, late that summer, I put together all the camping stuff I had prepared then and before: two small backpacks, a pup-tent, a frying-pan with a folding handle, a fine Boy Scout hatchet, a felt-wrapped canteen for keeping water cool, and some woollen socks for both of us. I had my strong, low work-moccasins, and Beverley of course wouldn't wear anything on her feet but her perennial sandals. But at least I got her to put away the impractical Mexican ones made out of slices of old automobile tires, and bought her a fine simple pair of leather sandals that she wore forever after.

We agreed we would go scouting for a home closer by, this time, in the Finger Lakes area in upstat New York. I had tramped there one summer a few years earlier, from Binghamton to Buffalo, searching for folksongs and whatever adventure I could find. The year after that I foolishly went south instead, trying to follow in the steps, no doubt, of Cecil Sharp song-catching through the southern Appalachians, and ended up in jail for statutory rape. Never again!

Beverley's mother Kathleen had just received as a present from one of her many admirers — this one a Canadian — a Hudson's Bay blanket. It was marvellously heavy of double length for folding in half, and firehouse red; with two and a half short black marks woven into one edge telling how many beaver pelts the Indian trappers would have to pay for a blanket that weight in the Hudson's Bay company stores. It was far too heavy to carry camping, but we didn't realize and mistakenly imagined that all Indians are migratory and on foot. Besides the bright red was too beautiful to resist. We talked Kathleen out of it, on loan for our trip, and piled it on top of my backpack, with the folded pup-tent on the smaller pack we got for Beverley.

We took the bus up to Albany and Schenectady, and planned to start walking west along the Susquehanna River, figuring to end at Lake Canandaigua. Maybe we'd even push on to Niagara Falls — with a tiny thought there of a classic honeymoon for us too — and cross over to Toronto to meet Beverley's Canadian relatives whom she said were wonderful, especially her uncle Ernest who was the conductor of the symphony orchestra there. Uncle

Ernest and I would get along famously, she said. He and I were the only two people she'd ever known who loved music in such an intense and total way. We picked our jump-off point from the map again: Esperance, for the significance of the name, of course, where the Schoharie River separates from the Susquehanna, which is for some reason known as the Schenevus Creek up there. It was the next bus stop along the road after Clement Wood's ranch for would-be wife swappers, on the Bozenkill at Delanson, where we carefully did not stop.

Except for avoiding Wood and his Bozenkill Babylon, nothing worked out the way we planned. The country was lovely, though pretty tame, but our food was either too heavy or not enough, and it was very difficult getting small cooking fires going in the continuous wind, to set up the folding frying-pan and cook our bacon and eggs. Eggs at least were plentiful, and we hardboiled up a bunch of them every evening at our campfire and ate them out of hand the next day when the wind was too pesky to try for a fire at lunch. We bought our eggs at the farm houses we passed, and the farmers also gave us all the sour milk we could drink or carry, free. I love the stuff, and Beverley would put some of our brown sugar into it and then she could drink it too. We struck out on side roads and the farmhouses got very sparse. One cretinous-looking hired man frightened Beverley by taking one look at her, as we came ankling along the dusty road, and then he went rushing with a wild whoop into the outhouse. Who knows how long it had been since he saw a young woman out there in the boondocks?

Beverley had the art of saying perfectly true but marvellously inappropriate things. "I don't like peop masturbating over me," she observed. "It isn't friendly." We got away from there fast.

There had been quite a lot of wind the first few days, and now the rain came. We managed to get our pup-tent set up, and cowered inside it trying to laugh. No chance of any hot food, but we had our hard-boiled eggs from the night before and were outfitted with small oiled-silk bags of Pennsylvania Dutch *muesli*, which is just raw rolled oats that we'd made up with raisins and hazelnuts mixed into it. You can live a long time on rations like that, if you can get any milk or green leaves to eat with it. People call it granola now: it's always been the subsistence food of shepherds in the high Alps. We also had some chocolate bars, which we broke up into squares and ate with the *muesli* and our canteen-full of sour milk.

"I'm beginning to get my period," Beverley announced. "This is just the right time for it, isn't it?"

We laughed like wild things as the rain pelted down and soaked through the pup-tent, dripping on us wherever our heads & shoulders touched the cloth. I helped Beverley roll over and fasten on a folded-up undershirt, which we pinned inside her panties with our paper of big new diaper-pins. Naturally we had totally forgotten anything like pads for her. We were a long way from any drugstores. How did Adam & Eve solve all these little natural problems, I wondered? Probably used the extra leaves from the Tree of Knowledge.

Rolling around laughing, and pinning the folded undershirt inside Beverley's panties, we also knocked over the main prop-stick of the tent and couldn't get it up again in the rain. We propped it as high as we could on the helve of the hatchet lashed upside-down to one of the rucksacks. And we lay there, locked in each other's arms, with our noses just barely out facing the rain, making love and singing folksongs and laughing as we struggled Beverley's panties on & off her, pretending not to be crying. Mostly we sang *Milady Greensleeves* to new peri-menstrual words I improvised:

> Deep! Deep! Went the arrow in,
> And all for the love of a *laydee!*
> Down! Down! Went my heart's red blood,
> And all for the love of a lady.

IN THE MORNING the rain had stopped, and the sun came up very red and passionate. All the trees were dripping and so were we, everywhere the cloth of the pup-tent had touched as we lunged at each other underneath. We dried ourselves, and hung our wet clothes and towels with diaper-pins on the back of our sacks as we walked along in our underwear. A mile away from where we had bivouacked we found a big, abandoned barn we hadn't seen the night before, and decided to stay there at least one night in case the rain came again. We spent a beautiful day wandering around, with our packs stashed in the barn. It was half full of large, square haypacks, bound around with wire and stacked up two and three high. That night we slept on top of these. They'd been there a long time and had no hay-smell left.

The following morning I woke up early and was admiring the massive adze-hewn beams and joists of the barn roof. Some of them were inscribed with a knife-point with the names of the harvest boomers who had come to work there in the fields some long autumn before. The haypacks must have been piled right up to the roof in those days, where the men had stood on them to engrave their graffiti. There were dates from 1909 to 1912, with the boomers' names and monikers. One message read: "Joey. I am going to Oneonta. Will wait for you. — Curly." Beverley and I agreed that was pretty close to Schweik the Good Soldier's rendezvous with his friend, at five o'clock after the war. And the friend called back after him: "I may be late. Wait until five-thirty." Two world wars had now passed since 1912, yet it was not so long ago.

Beverley climbed down and got a frying-pan full of water from the brook nearby to wash her face in, setting it on one of the haypacks. I jumped down. My left foot caught between two haypacks as I landed, and I fell forward heavily to the floor, scratching my face terribly. But the worst was my foot, which was still caught. The ankle was badly twisted by my weight pulling on it as I fell. When I tried to get up, my foot crumpled under me and would not support my weight. I could feel it beginning to swell.

Beverley said she would go for help, and ran to the barn door. Then she ran back and kissed me, saying she didn't know how long she might be gone. I sat on the floor waiting, dragging myself up against the lowest haypack to support my back. It wasn't an hour before she came back with a young farmer in overalls.

He was exceptionally nice. He said it was his barn, and apologized that I had fallen off the haypacks.

"Damn things shouldn't ha' been there anyhow," he said, "but I lost a bunch o' cows this last year."

He had an old, open touring car outside, with wooden bar wheels. He held me up on one side and I hopped to the car with him. Then he and Beverley stowed in all our traps, and he took us to the nearest bus station. I tried to express our gratitude but he waved it all away.

"You might give me one of your cigarettes, Miss," he said to Beverley, "and we'll call it square. Young gal like you oughtn't to be smoking, anyhow."

He drove off in the touring car, and we waited hours for the bus. Then for another at Albany, to New York. Beverley toted everything at every change. No one tried to help her. I was unable to. In New York we got a taxi down to Bedford Street, and I went to bed for a couple of days. Every change of busses had been a torture to me, and my ankle was now all swollen up as big as a house. Beverley wanted to get a doctor for me, but I refused. I told her I had ghost-written for too many doctors, and had no respect for them. We'd bandage the ankle and bathe it in a bucket of hot water twice a day, and I knew it would get better. I was wrong. It was the same ankle I sprained jumping off the freight-train at Bethlehem, and it still bothers me today.

It was over a month before I could walk on it, and then I had to use a cane. Meanwhile we moved temporarily into Kathleen's apartment so I wouldn't have to clump up and down a whole flight of stairs each time to go to the toilet, as I did at Bedford Street.

502

Kathleen was on an Indian Summer vacation with one of her boyfriends, a Dutchman stationed in New York as purchasing agent for some big Dutch company, and who was learning how to talk English from Kathleen. She said, by way of a joke, that she was his sleeping-dictionary, but what she really liked best was bossing him around and correcting his manners and explaining him How Things Are Done In America. He was a big, friendly, masochistic twerp. The perfect organization man. They too are only obeying orders — like the guards in Auschwitz.

Kathleen's apartment had been changed meanwhile, but in the same building. Instead of the parlor opening out over Bleeker Street at the corner of Grove, now the main windows were in the bedroom, facing bleakly on the backs of other apartment houses to the east. Beverley and I slept in the big bed by the window. As we certainly didn't keep the light on all night, it never occurred to us that people might be spying on us when we made love, which was at least every other night. But they were. Finally some guy actually had the nerve to be peering at us with a telescope in the early evenings, where we could see him far across the back yards. This infuriated me, and I drew a large sign and stapled it to the window shade, where it would appear only when the shade was pulled down. When we saw him arrive with his telescope, just at dusk, I yanked down the shade so he could read the sign, which read very simply, in large capital letters: "GO HOME AND JERK OFF!"

We could hear him screaming and cursing far away. It was like music. This voyeuristic geek really had more nerve than brains, because he then went and complained to the superintendent of Kathleen's building that not only were we being horribly immoral, but we had also put up an obscene sign. The super came up to tell us at least to take down the sign. He hung around quite a while, continuing to explain over and over several times how undesirable it was for there to be any kind of fuss, and I assumed he wanted a tip to forget it. I told him that Kathleen would fix it up with him when she came back — she'd give him a fine present for Christmas. He said that was real nice of us and he appreciated it, but what he *really* wanted to know was what was the specially immoral thing the guy had said we were doing. The peeper hadn't given him sufficient anatomical details, and the super was perishing with erotic curiosity. I told him we made love on a pogo-stick and threw him out.

Beverley wasn't working in the shipyard anymore, as they had started cutting back on ship construction the minute the war with Japan ended. Now she had a part-time job in an advertising research bureau at Madison Avenue and 40th Street, where she typed up results of questionnaires and advertising campaign proposals. It was certainly very dull and stupid, she said, but it wasn't visibly evil. Otherwise she would have refused the job.

We had been shocked to find out how many people we'd been meeting for years, who called themselves mathematicians and physicists and so forth, like the boyfriend Athena had tried to fix her up with, and my ass-to-face friends in the rooming house I lived in, actually worked on the Atom Bomb design teams at Columbia, where it was known non-committally as the Manhattan Project. In fact, my ass-to-face friends were still working there, and it was they who hadn't been able to resist telling me the marvellous news of their connection with this world-shaking new advance in science, after Hiroshima. The main "brain-trust" directing the Manhattan Project wasn't allowed to meet at Columbia or Princeton, anyhow not more than three members at a time, in case of spy attacks. They met secretly for the duration in a second-story office over a bookstore on Fourth Avenue, in a nondescript old building called Bible House. As the project progressed, the bookstore downstairs got to specialize in science fiction. That was what the bomb-scientists upstairs liked to pick up on their way home. Star wars relaxed them.

❦

THE BIBLIOGRAPHICAL work I was now doing for Professor Kinsey at Indiana University, who was building up a splendid library of sexology, didn't pay very well. He didn't mind paying for the books, because that was his own money, but he was very tight about paying *me*, because that was foundation money — from the poor dead-broke Rockefellers, as I remember — and he liked to be able to account to them very exactly for every penny pinched on mere personnel. He also felt it as a profound rejection that I was doing the work from New York, mostly at the Academy of Medicine, which had the best sexology collection in America until then. I steadfastly refused Kinsey's standing offer to let me bury myself in a Midwestern town like Bloomington, Indiana, where the main entertainment seemed to be following the varsity football team around the Midwest as a rooting-section at all the big games. Not my idea of escape.

Kinsey was also giving me a hard time about the Regius/Grien penis measurements, though they had nothing whatever to do with his questionnaire project about American sex habits, and I tabulated for him all the relevant measurements in Grien's manuscript sheets concerning the hundreds of boys & men he (Grien) had fellated. I'd also had the temerity to essay a few amateur statistical remarks about the unusual bimodal curve of distribution of Grien's figures. This was all the more unusual since, if there's one thing statistically positive in human bodily measurements, it's that large people have large organs, on the average, and small people have small ones. How not?

The trouble with Grien's figures was that he was a mad oncer, and had sexual relations wholesale with both grown men and boys — also with women — scientificking things up pathetically by carefully measuring their pricks. Just as Kinsey wanted to do though neither of them ever seemed to want to depth-gauge any vaginas when I suggested it. The non-random heights of Grien's men-&-boy friends therefore inevitably skewed his penis measurements into two rather distant averages. Instead of the standard bell-curve of distribution of any randomly chosen series of bodily measurements, Grien's penis statistics plotted out to a peculiar double-crested curve like a camel's humps.

I tried to make this clear in the tabulations I supplied to Kinsey, but he was furious at me for daring to venture outside my specialty of erotic bibliography into his specialty of sexual statistics, especially on the penis. As I might have prophesied, I got canned off Kinsey's project on the pretext that I wasn't working hard enough at my job, as soon as I had supplied them with the basic information and books they needed to get their library started. And, as I say, at very modest prices for my work, on the same excuse that Dr. Dickinson had used — that I had no medical or other degrees. Neither did Regius, who went on to become the nameless star of the first *Kinsey Report.*

The hack job I'd been working on when Beverley and I went camping out in upstate New York, and which I now took up again while my ankle was healing and Kinsey was kissing me off in angry and very haughty letters, was obviously not very desirable, though perhaps not quite as bad as writing murder-mysteries, unconsciously in the style of Mickey Spillane! The little publisher who gave me this new hack job was someone I was introduced to in Sam Weiser's occult bookshop, which was then on Fourth Avenue. He told me it was to be a dictionary of the occult. I didn't know why this was necessary, as there was a new and very concise dictionary of the occult just published in England, by Julian Franklyn as I remember; not to mention the standard dictionary by Lewis Spence. But obviously this little guy wanted something smaller for the cheapo trade. Not much I could do about that. I figured the job was harmless enough — the occult was certainly a racket and ridiculous, but not on the mammoth scale of organized religion — and I thought it might even be amusing.

The publisher supplied me, as poneys, with two illiterate little pamphlet dictionaries of the kind he wanted, and I made him buy me, right then & there off Weiser's shelves, a copy of Spence's big, square *locus classicus*. The price made him blench, but I refused to relent and told him I couldn't possibly do the job without it. Actually most of what I did for him that could be called original, I was ultimately stealing from a marvellously illustrated old French dictionary of occultism by Collin-de-Plancy that I'd found in Maurice Sloog's shop, and that actually prints, as authentic, grotesque woodcut portraits of all the known demons, by name. Maybe I can be forgiven for this; it took my mind off the annoyance of being laid up with my bad ankle for so long.

One day, when I was about halfway through the alphabet, I decided it was time to get some more money on this deal than the lowly minimum advance I'd accepted when the publisher came through and bought me the copy of Spence. As I still couldn't get around well, Beverley went to see him for me on her lunch hour. His place was somewhere off the top of Union Square, and she came back and told me it wasn't a publishing house at all but a horrid little sales office, in some somber old office building. When you walked in you found half the office was entirely closed off with heavy wire grating across the middle of the room. The publisher was there, sitting at a table behind a small wicket in the grating.

Beverley didn't get a chance to ask him about money. Not knowing who she was, he threw her a crude pamphlet catalogue, which she brought back to show me; and he told her to hurry up and pick what she wanted to buy, as he was going out to lunch. The catalogue was entirely of occult fake medicines and magical de-hexing products clearly intended for rural and urban peasants, with titles like "High John the Conqueror Root", "Rabbit's Foot Anointing Oil", "Mandrake Root Extract Water," and "Guaranteed Love-Attracting Hair Oil," which was in two flavors or odors, Passion-Rose and Magnolia. There were also a few dream-books "with interpretations *in three numbers* of One Thousand Dreams." — meaning they were for trying to win on the daily newspaper numbers gambling game — and *The Sixth and Seventh Mystic Books of Moses*, advertised on the last page at fifty cents each, though stereotype junk like that, dating from the last century, could always be had for only ten cents or a quarter apiece in the usual slum-shop emporiums.

After looking over this catalogue of crap for a shocked minute or two, Beverley finally blurted out to the publisher why she was really there. He told her coldly that I would get the rest of my promised money when I brought in the manuscript, and not before. She left, and while she was waiting for the elevator down; she saw the publisher scuttle out into the hall from another door, not the door of his office, and disappear down the fire stairs. This explained how he got in & out, despite the doorless wire grating.

I couldn't screw myself up to finishing the job, now that I realized that what I was doing was supposed to assist in palming off worthless occult medicines on uneducated victims, black or white, who were surely authentically sick or undernourished, and were giving this crook their money instead of going to a doctor. I wasn't going to a doctor either, for my ankle, but at least I wasn't chewing on, or rubbing my prick with, High & Low John the Conqueror Root, between two evilly smoking green candles, stated in the catalogue to have been manufactured from the grease of *Black Cats* killed at midnight on a Friday night *at the Foot of the Gallows.* Maybe that would help me by working on my childish imagination if all that was wrong with me was being impotent, owing to a jealous neighbor casting a triple-whammy hex on my proud or sinful penis; but what good would it do me if I had t.b. or cancer? Or was eating all the wrong stuff, or had a nice big infected abscess.

The publisher-junkdealer's catalogue didn't state anywhere, when I examined it carefully, what specific illness any of the roots and greases were supposed to cure. That was left to the customer's ailing organism and imagination; and was probably illegal anyway as too specific, and not to be gotten away with. The printed text claimed instead that the items peddled were simply good for all the ills of humanity — for those customers who Had the Faith. What amazed me most were the incredibly high prices for these worthless dollops of suet and mineral oil. Where on earth did these poor boogers ever get the money to pay for them without robbing a bank? Or maybe that's why certain banks — and candy stores — were in fact being robbed.

The markup on the magical trash and medicinal garbage was even higher and more outrageous than on the cheaply got-up dream books and "pre-remaindered" sex books of the type Jake Brussel published, and even lower. Everything was priced three to five times higher than what the same items, without the occult come-on, would cost in a five-&-dime store. The exotica, like mandrake root and whatnot, obviously had no limit on price: the seller charged however much he thought he could get on raw nerve and the customers' ignorant gullibility.

Vaguely I could remember seeing small ads for things like this, in the back-page columns of leg-art and snappy stories and true confessions magazines. Most of the men's pulps also carried the small backpage "occult products" ads. It was like a whiff from an exploding sewer. Who were the customers, I wondered? Undoubtedly that gooney, goatish hired hand in the outhouse in Esperance, and his peers. And this was what I was supposed to be making a living out of . . . . But can you really call that living?

My manuscript was finished up to the letter M — for "Mandrake." This had taken me over a hundred typewritten pages, but I finished up the alphabet from M to Z in two pages more. I concluded the article on "Mandrake" with an extra paragraph noting that the pulverized root, *if*, — but only if — it had been drawn screaming out of the earth under a gallows at midnight, and thus fertilized by the involuntary ejaculate of the hanged man, would cure cancer, epilepsy, stammering, baldness, fallen arches, and all the venereal diseases. I hoped this sabotage would at least get my so-called publisher in desperate trouble with the feds. Stating that you can cure cancer must surely be illegal, I thought, since no one can. The great Wilhelm Reich had just died in a federal prison during the war for going mad and promising to cure cancer with the orgasmic "orgone" energy of the planets.

My final shaft was a hand-lettered titlepage I had prepared, with the presumed author's name taken directly from Carlyle's speaking-trumpet character in *Sartor Resartus*, called Teufelsdroeckh, or Devil's Dung. I credited the work to one "Phil Van Drake," but as I was worried that the allusion might go over someone's head, I respelled this phonetically as "Dr. Phil van Droeckh, Prof. Emeritus, University of Leyden." I then took my first walking trip on my cane, taking the bus up to Fourteenth Street and then over to Union Square.

The little publisher clawed the manuscript in through the slot in the office grating where he handed out the occult medicines and accepted his customers' cash. He sat riffling through it for a few minutes, and obviously didn't see anything odd about it taking a hundred pages to get from A to M, and only two pages from M to Z. But he did finally register the allusion in the author's name.

"What da hell 'uz dat mean?" he snorted, in his tiny little screeching voice, like that of a Mongoloid child, clearly intended to intimidate me. "Dat's dreck, ain't it? — Shit, huh? You a wiseguy? Ya wanna a broken arm? You ain't gettin' anudder dime outa me!"

"Where does it say shit?" I demanded indignantly. "You crazy? Dr. Phil van Droeckh — that's a famous name in occult science. Look, I'll show you."

I grabbed the manuscript from his hand through the slot in the grating, and pretended to be studying the title page.

"All right," I said, knowing perfectly well there was no chance of getting another dime from him, just as he had said. "If you don't like it this way, I'll fix it." And I clumped out of the office with my cane and my manuscript, and pushed the elevator button. Suddenly there he was, boiling out the side door Beverley had told me about, his face all red as a turkey-cock.

"You gimme back my money!" he shouted. "You can stick your lousy book up your ass!"

"Oh yeah?" I snarled, lifting my cane menacingly. "I worked for my stinking money, didn't I? I'm gonna fix this manuscript like you want, and you're gonna gimme the rest of my money!"

I guess that's why there are literary agents. In fact, I think it's terrible that all they get is one percent of the action: only ten percent of the author's piddling ten percent. One day I'm going to start a crusade for my idea that literary agents ought to get two percent of the gross. But out of the publisher's share, not the author's. And save the authors' highly-strung nervous organisms from these distressing scenes.

The elevator arrived, and I clutched my manuscript fiercely under my arm till I was down in the street. Then I crossed over to Union Square, sat down on a bench, and looked at the manuscript again. It really disgusted me. *I* really disgusted me. How could I have written such an atrocity? Was I asleep? Crazy? What could I have been thinking of? I wanted to fling the awful thing into a trashcan, but I was afraid my little man might be following me, and would recuperate it when I was gone and maybe publish it. Doubtless under *my* name! I carried it all the way back to the apartment on Grove Street with me, and there tore it luxuriantly into ribbons, a few pages at a time, looking occasionally at the text as I did so, and clucking my tongue in hideous appreciation. Then I carried the mess out into the hall and dumped it all down the garbage disposal unit. The only regret I had was that I never found out what High John the Conqueror Root is.

Nevertheless, that ridiculous mock-occult dictionary or sales catalogue of mail order fakes and frauds, A to M, by Dr. Phil van Droeckh, Prof. Emeritus, University of Leyden, was very important to me. Following on the way it did after my *Voodoo Death* chess caper, in which I was saved only at the very last moment from becoming "the new Mickey Spillane," it marked the watershed, or maybe I mean the continental divide of my career as a writer. I had always been pretty picky & choosy about ghost-jobs, but obviously not enough. After that, I would never again accept a commercial writing job, whether ghost-written or to be signed — in fact not even manuscript typing for someone else — unless I was positive that the subject was at least harmless. And not too idiotic either. Pushing idiocy hasn't helped the human race much. If it was my own honorable lunacy, well, all right. But not for money. Their enemies always said that Jews were money-crazy. At least they wouldn't be able to say it about me.

We were all, especially the radical thinkers, profoundly moved and pulverized that year by the Atom Bomb. For me, one of the worst of the returning shock-waves was when the laudatory articles and books began appearing, and I learned to my horror that almost all the top scientists who had created or promulgated the Bomb in America — beginning with Szilard, Einstein, Teller, Fermi, Frisch, Wigner, Peierls,

Segrè, Rabi, Oppenheimer and the rest of them — were all Jews. So that's what Jewish brains were good for! The standard explanation given was that Hitler had driven all the Jewish scientists out of Germany and Europe, and this was the job that was offered them when they got to England and the United States. In other words, dead or alive, Hitler had come through on his promise: he had sowed mud! And all of us, and our children, are eating that mud.

That's an explanation for goyim. For a Jew, that's not an explanation. Who said these imbeciles had to prostitute their so-exceptional brains to murder? And why — just because Chaim Weizmann had done the same thing in 1917 for T.N.T.? Couldn't they have sold *falafel* on the streets of Miami beach? Or wasn't the real explanation that they were simply trying to beat Hitler to the Bomb? Then why, after they created the bomb, and watched the test explosion in dark glasses — two months after Hitler's Germany had surrendered, if you please! — did they nevertheless manufacture more, and then turn them over to the military and the politicians, who were imperiously demanding something to show for their two-billion dollar investments to drop on Japan? Satisfying themselves with circulating weak-livered intramural petitions, that the bomb they had ruptured themselves inventing should not now be dropped. Like nervous girls muttering at the last minute, "All right, you can put it in, if you're careful dear, but only *half way!*"

After the second bomb was exploded, over Nagasaki, I took down the topographical maps of the Grand Canyon that Beverley and I had put up on the wall over the bed in Bedford Street. I didn't want to see that anymore. My upside-down flights in imagination through the lovely concentric lines of cliffs and valleys were over. Salida, Colorado, had been an evil joke played on us by fate. Some dark guardian angel, with a misplaced sense of irony, had let us pick our secret jump-off point of escape precisely in the Sangre de Cristo Mountains — well named — where Robert Oppenheimer and his crew had also chosen to assemble and explode the trial bomb. Then quoting in his notebook from the invocation of Vishnu in the *Bagavad Gita*, and certainly not in self-condemnation since he then went on to agree with the unanimously assembled generals and journalists, that the bomb should be used against Japan and as soon as possible: *"I am become Death, the destroyer of worlds."* Some people would brag about a wooden prick. Also, as is well known, all American atom bomb professors spend their spare time studying up on Hindu heroic poetry.

When I took down the Grand Canyon maps, I felt solemnly that I was now no longer an American. I was taking back my membership. Later I realized that out of the same gut-deep revulsion I felt for what we had done, and what I was sure would come of it, I was now no longer a Jew. I was nobody. I belonged to nothing. I was alone. I did not feel any hatred, except against the Germans. That same summer we had the whole horror of the German death-camps to swallow too, when the Russian tanks got to Germany, and the horrible truth came pouring out. But I knew that something had died inside me. Some social impulse, of loving the world and finding it beautiful and wanting to be part of it and even to improve it.

All of us radical kids of the 1930s, and plenty of grownups too, believed sincerely in Progress; in acting and agitating tirelessly, making the world a better place to live in for millions of little people who had no voice. That was an essential tenet of our faith, and it was over now. Progress was dead. There was no hope left, not really. No one would ever believe in anything again. We would all just be marking time, cynically making our living and rolling our foolish little hedonistic hoops, waiting for the return of Vishnu who had *become Death, the destroyer of worlds*. But why blame Vishnu? We had done it ourselves, in collective madness.

As for me, I was just one more Man Without a Country. Philip No-land, as in Edward Everett Hale's so heavily moralizing story. I looked vaguely at the map of the Grand Canyon as I folded it away forever behind my filing boxes: the swirling brown whorls representing the rising and descending cliffs that had once thrilled me so, as I floated up and down through them. The little printed legend in one corner explained the coloring system used. Brown was for topographical levels, green for vegetation, blue for water. And at the end, one last sly, significant line: "LETTERING AND THE WORKS OF MAN ARE IN BLACK."

ALFRED KINSEY

[Kinsey came to New York, and he came to see me in connection with the book scouting and bibliographical work I had been doing for him. When I asked him what entertainment he especially wanted to have in New York, he replied that he wanted to go wherever he could eat the Best Ice Cream. He was accompanied by two surprisingly young male helpers. After the ice cream, we went back to my furnished room. This explanatory text added by transcriber.]

AFTER THE BOYS left I put away my scrapbook and Kinsey got down to business taking my case-history. Kinsey's method was the ultimate in worthless, soulless x-scratching in prepared boxes. He did not want any refinement of ideas, nor any subjective discussion of anything. It was all *did you do it*, or didn't you, and *at what age* did you start? Exactly like Roman Catholic confession, not forgetting a certain amount of *how often* per week or month for each item. He kept this going at machine gun speed, since he had far too many questions to ask, having much enlarged Hirschfeld's basic questionnaire to homosexuals, which was mainly what it was, along with some additions from the earlier American questionnaire studies of sex.

No questions of any kind were asked about any emotional levels or responses to anything. The approach was totally physical — organs and apertures. And "outlets," meaning orgasms expurgated. I bothered to interrupt the flow to mention this anti-emotionalism to him, but Kinsey looked pained, with his put-on gymnasium instructor prunes-&-prisms mock smile, and assured me that it was hard enough to gather the FACTS in his present research, and that "attitudes" would have to come later. Meaning, never, if at all. I understood and kept answering my machine-gun interrogation duly. Kinsey was not interested in anybody's love-life; the raw sex-life was as much as he was geared to handle. That was his attitude, but he didn't know it. His Midwest hick bow-tie fascinated me: it wiggled when he talked. I kept my attention focussed on that.

The only twitch of actual interest in any of the answers that he showed nearly caused us to upset the apple cart. When he asked me if I had any sexual relations with children and I said yes, I could see the sudden guilty flush of interest he could not repress, the cremasteric muscles at both sides of the jaws, which were already heavily overdeveloped with his held-in aggression, suddenly beginning to flex and crunch unconsciously.

"At what age?" he asked almost through gritted teeth, trying to mask his tension. And then the letdown when I had to answer, "Till I was twelve. After that I got more interested in girls my own age and young married women — you know, mother images." His disappointment was so visible it was ludicrous, like the unhealthy, self-elected father confessor he was.

Kinsey made a moue of distaste at the intrusion of outrageous Freudian concepts like "mother-images," and the inquisition was over shortly after. Then he wanted to see my scrapbook some more. He was particularly interested in the series of erotic photos I had made of my friends Bill and Virginia Mulholland, and complimented me on the quality of the photography. I admitted to him that I had had very little to do with that. A professional photographer had set the whole thing up for me, including placing the camera. All I had to do was push the button, and think up the poses.

"Even so," Kinsey began musing, "you could do that work professionally. We very much need a photographer on our staff."

"Not me," I told him. "Changing lenses every once in a while and pushing a cable release isn't enough of a challenge for me. Besides, I hate doing things I can't do well." I wondered what he wanted photographed. Obviously it wasn't just a question of doing recording photographs of documents and erotic artworks. A photostat machine could do that. He was certainly after doing some kind of human plastic poses, but didn't know how to be frank. Everyone else had to take off their autobiographical pants for him, but he wasn't unbuttoning anything. Not even his bow-tie. The way he had leapt at my accidental admission of sex with underage children I suspected it might be that, and I hinted around the evident point that all such photography was of course illegal. Not to mention half the acts photographed! Could his two inappropriately young helpers be mere pratt-boys, I wondered? Well, the difference between my age and Dickinson's was even greater, so that didn't prove a thing. Though Dickinson wasn't trying to make America safe for homosexuality with statistics, as Kinsey was.

I began describing to him some of the dangerous photography Regius-Grien was doing in the Southwest with kids, and pulled out a few of the examples he had sent me, that he had been afraid of letting Dickinson see. Kinsey became livid with sudden interest, but tried to drawl casual remarks of half-ass anatomic and scientific nature as I turned over before him the photos of Grien holding some ten-year-old kid's pants down, and pumping up an erection on the kid's prick for the camera, tripod-held a yard away. Kinsey asked me cautiously if I could give him copies of these photos for the files at Indiana, and I assured him that when they had a staff photographer he was looking for he could make copies of anything I had that he wanted. What the hell! All for science. I also gave him Grien's real name and address to write to him direct. He later became the anonymous sex-hero of Kinsey's eventual book. I warned him about Grien's own activities and pansexual life, and his specializing in hotel voyeurism and so on, and I added that he was sure to get in trouble sooner or later about kids — which he did. This got Kinsey off onto one of his main hobbyhorses, that if everybody who did anything illegal sexually under the present laws had to go to prison, there wouldn't be enough room to hold them.

"Don't you worry," I told him cheerfully, "they'll build new prisons. Every governor of the state has a brother-in-law in the building trades. Have you ever seen any of those forty-eight state capitols?"

I was just talking to hide my feelings. I was already disgusted with Kinsey's primitive amoralism and mock-statistical sound track. He was clearly some kind of sex freak, possibly heavily repressed and just as possibly not, and was as blinded by his own sex problems as Hirschfeld had been. I much preferred Regius-Grien's bold candor. He admitted he was a sexual wildcat, had screwed both his mother and father, not to mention goats, chickens, little boys, *et cetera* — your true and total sexual sociopath, but still trying to salvage something maybe of scientific value out of it. Kinsey's uninflected provincial flatness and scared phoniness couldn't compare. Kinsey's dominant idea was that anything people did must be right *because* people did it. That included him in. It had statistical existence, so it was o.k. This was the "Nothing human is alien to me" crap with a vengeance. If statistical existence makes things right, then what was wrong with leprosy and murder? That exists too. I wondered how Kinsey had ever gotten a job in a college with so total a blank as to human values. Even a junior high school civics course should have forced him a little higher than that.

Well, of course, he had done his main work on the taxonomy of insects, as he was proud to relate. Hardly a humanistic background. Kinsey had spent years on that stuff, which he referred to as biology. He had caught and chloroformed about a million helpless oak-gall wasps, and then done eight or ten standard millimetric measurements on each and every one: nose-to-pippik, pippik-to-pecker, pecker-to-antenna, left-right, right-left, you name it. Doubtless with plenty of young assistants out there in corduroy britches and high boots in the boondocks with him, to relax with around the camp-fire later reading off the measurements: "Pippik-to-pecker, 0.006; very fine example," and so forth.

Except for my disappointing case-history, and due to my uncharacteristic diplomacy, I obviously impressed Kinsey very favorably. My homosexual glossary had also made it clear to him that I knew all the urban underground ins-&-outs he was searching to learn. He asked me if I would consider moving to Indiana and taking a job on his small but select staff. I repressed the mischievous urge to ask whether he didn't think I was too old, being all of two years older than his helpers, and asked instead what the life was like out there in the Midwest, as if I didn't know! I mentioned politely all the vague cultural advantages I had, living in the big city, and with a wave of my hand around us at the cases of records, I added that what I truly cared about most in life, after books and sex, was classical music.

"Well, I'm the same," Kinsey said earnestly, "and I hope you won't think I'm bragging if I say I have more records than you do."

"Really?" I asked, a bit astonished.

"Oh, yes. I see that you have some of the same records that I have," he said, looking at the cases. "Sometimes I have as many as three or four different recordings of the same piece. There it is, you see, the problem of *human difference*. Each person plays it differently. It's the *differences* that are significant, not the similarities."

He was so sincere about his propaganda I didn't feel like arguing that I felt the exact opposite, and cared most about the similarities. And that's what the composers wanted too! Instead I asked what he did with all those records. Kinsey explained that he had private record concerts for his staff and friends one evening a week, where he played only the best classical music. That made it sound almost tempting: there would be sure to be some nice girl-cousin or niece turning up at the Thursday-night cottage concerts once in a while.

"What do you play for them?" I asked.

"We follow the Victor catalog." He said proudly. "Alphabetically. We're up to Lalo!"

That finished the possibility of my ever being on the Kinsey Institute staff in Indiana, but I said nothing. The poor hick meant well. Anyhow, he was willing to buy books and build up his library, and was even hoping to get Rockefeller Foundation money to do it with. No matter what kind of crappy book he might put out himself, the library would be there later. I said I would help in every way I could short of leaving New York, and that I was sure I could be of much more use to them right where I was. We then started downstairs to find his two boy-assistants.

As I was holding the door open for him to leave my little furnished room, Kinsey suddenly remembered something and handed me a numbered return-card on which he explained I was to write the length of my penis in inches, both soft and stiff, the following morning, and send it to him later. I told him I knew it already and wrote him out the figures from memory. He looked doubtful about that, as though the real, human peter-pulling activity over his little slip of cardboard was a very important element for him. It made things more exact, he assured me. I accepted another slip and told him I'd check it out in the flesh later.

With the younger boys he said, some "direct measurements" had already been done, like those that Regius-Grien had sent to Dickinson, including the use of judging-eggs to estimate testicle size. I realized then that you had to walk on eggs talking to a person like Kinsey, and repressed the two questions that immediately came to my mind. First, what in the hell relation did little boys' prick-&-ball measurements have to the ostensible purposes of his research into sex life? Or big boys' either, for that matter. And second, wouldn't that kind of approach eventually attract only homosexuals to his staff?

Instead, as it was obvious that Kinsey didn't have a grain of humor about him, I asked him perfectly straight-faced whether there was any intention of making matching depth-gauge measurements of the vaginas of the "female cases." I didn't dare say "girls and women" — too unscientific, that — and I also didn't add that, in that case, I might reconsider taking a job on their staff. That "statistic" didn't interest them,

Kinsey said, Women didn't require an erection to accept the male.

"But the problem isn't acceptance," I said; "it's orgasm!"

"Only for the human female," he told me grimly. We left.

CHAPTER 47

FIRETAIL

LOGICALLY, I wouldn't ever have made a mistake again like that with *Voodoo Death*, but in fact I did it all over again, and in spades. Almost immediately after. Except that this time I took a few more precautions against myself, and drew back before my feet were actually sliding over the edge. It was my work on the Shakespeare Bad Quartos that entrapped me. This is how it happened. There was a young woman in Beverley's office, named Betty Shapin, who had taken a master's degree at the University of London just a few years before with a thesis on literary censorship in Shakespeare's time. She and Beverley got to know each other eating lunch together at the office; they recognized and appreciated each other's quietly repressed British way of not talking much.

Well, since I was studying Shakespeare every evening then — I kept my set of the Bankside edition of the parallel folio and quarto texts shelved in Beverley's fireplace on Bedford Street — and was also writing the history of literary censorship, which is how I always described then the book I was working on, born like the Phoenix out of the ruins of *Taboo*, Beverley told me all about the other girl's thesis and her about me. She also arranged a meeting between us in the dingy side-office by the reception desk, intended for parking bigshot clients from the Midwest until some official could be spared to butter them up.

Betty Shapin was more than quiet. Slender and dark with an unhappy face and lips held bloodlessly tight, she was depressed by her job which was far below her abilities. And she told me with sudden animation how much she looked back to the fun it had been at the University of London with all the other lively young students and witty professors studying Elizabethan and Jacobean literary history a mile a minute to forget about the War. She was flattered by my interest in her unpublished thesis, and had brought along her only carbon copy of it to our meeting, which she allowed me to take away and have photostatted, white-on-black, the only reproduction process other than photographs available to us in those years. When I brought back her thesis she said she really couldn't get over finding anyone in America who was interested in these historical things. I assured her I was more than interested in literary censorship; I was deeply emotionally involved.

The way she kept turning over the point verbally made me certain that she wanted to make friends with us, and was probably very lonely in New York. But as Beverley hadn't taken the initiative of inviting her over to supper some evening, or lunch on Sunday at Bedford Street, I didn't think I should presume. One of the two women would be sure to misunderstand my gesture as a sexual interest in Miss Shapin, which was not the case. I asked Beverley if she'd like to invite her. And, if she thought Miss Shapin might not appreciate our plain pine plank table without a cloth, and wooden trunk to sit on, and our brown ceramic plates, I suggested we could invite her to Beverley's mother's neat middle-class apartment one evening when Kathleen would be out — which was most evenings. I guess I must have seemed too eager, or too bossy about it. Beverley was not enthusiastic. She saw Betty every day in the office, she said. That left me out. Plain. Anyhow, how did we know Betty would like chile beans? I began to feel this was all turning into a delicately unexpressed reproach against me for not being a better provider, and I became very stiff.

"Well, she's your friend, not mine," I said in a carefully controlled voice. "When I want to entertain my friends, they'll eat chile beans if I have to shove 'em down their throat with a stick!" No answer — Beverley's standard reply, and hard to deal with, like fighting water. "Everybody likes chile con carne," I urged her. "We'll mix in half a pound of fried hamburger and have beer. Or a bottle of that Chilean wine that Harmen brought a case of for your mother." I smiled at her cajolingly. But nothing came of it. Beverley and I did not entertain. Beverley was not domestic. I did not insist.

Betty Shapin's thesis, when I sat down to study it, was tremendously interesting to me and extremely well-researched.. But it had the peculiarity of being only half about censorship in Shakespeare's time. The other half, overwhelming the original and announced subject, was a very full history of the remarkable Overbury murder case in London in 1613, in which the main characters included Sir Robert Carr, later made Earl of Somerset, the handsome young male prostitute

of the homosexual King James, and his friend the sententious but not very diplomatic Sir Thomas Overbury, who ended up dead in the Tower of London. His error was warning Carr against continuing his side-affair with the principal lightheels at court, the passionate young Lady Frances Howard, daughter of the Lord Chamberlain and just then wife of the Earl of Essex, son of Queen Elizabeth's executed former lover, Robert Devereux.

Lady Frances had only one wish: to be rid of her husband and to marry Carr, which she did. This marriage destroyed him, since the riotously homosexual king was naturally jealous of Carr's amours with a woman, and immediately replaced him with the even handsomer page-boy George Villiers, created Duke of Buckingham for his bedroom services to the monarch. Lady Frances had not hesitated to have her marriage to the young Earl of Essex annulled, claiming that she was still a virgin and that the marriage had never been consummated. This was considered the joke of the decade in London, and numerous bawdy poems and songs were written on the subject, though it was too dangerous for any of them to appear in print until two centuries later. The joke turned sour, however, on the discovery that Overbury had meanwhile been murdered in the Tower of London by a poisoned enema, almost certainly on secret orders of the king.

Both the Countess of Essex and her new husband Carr were charged with complicity in the murder, along with her occult confidante, Mrs. Anne Turner, who was hanged for the crime along with a few other small fry. All the titled participants were pardoned, of course, the Countess of Essex at once, but Carr only after serving six years in prison though obviously innocent. The whole purpose of the imbroglio about Overbury's death in the Tower seems to have been to frame his friend Carr and get him out of the way of the king's intended advancement of Villiers. Fellow antiquarians and paleographers, let us all now rise and sing the well-known anthem; *"Tis arsehole rules the navy! Arsehole rules the sea! You may get your bloody bum from the King's Grenadiers — but you'll get no arse from me!"*

I had never heard but vaguely of the Overbury case and the Countess of Essex before, though they had been used as background for a superficial historical novel by one of my favorite authors as a boy, the adventure-hack Rafaël Sabatini, rather frankly titled *The King's Minion*, but otherwise giving an outrageously glozed and expurgated version of the story. For myself, I found it all fascinating and joyously followed up at the library all Betty Shapin's careful references to the original sources, including none other than Sir Walter Scott. The one thing made most clear by these sources was the wholly repellent, cowardly, and treacherous character of King James I. Henry VIII had been bad enough — but James! The rest of the story was extremely complicated, as befits a court intrigue with noble titles, castles and great fortunes at stake. And the cast of characters was fabulous. My favorite was the court astrologer and quack, and probably also poisoner and abortionist, Dr. Simon Forman, whose incestuous daughter was precisely the Mrs. Anne Turner involved, and whose former mistress had been Emilia Bassano Lanier, the religious poetess and mysterious Dark Lady of Shakespeare's Sonnets. (Not my discovery: credit the great and bumptious Professor A. L. Rowse.) But it was the personality of the clearly vicious and unprincipled young Duchess of Essex that motivated and dominated the whole tragic story. Perhaps that was why it so fascinated Betty Shapin, and many another historian as well.

I finally became very enmeshed in the secret story of the Countess of Essex, and spent hours and finally months tracing down all the complex background intrigues and personalia. Until then I used to spend my evenings after supper with Beverley, poring over the Shakespearian texts, comparing the oldest folio and quarto readings in parallel in the Bankside edition and the few modern Quarto Facsimile editions that I then owned. But after my first week in the library chasing after the wilful and noble tail of Lady Frances Howard, the new project came rapidly to take up most of my spare time, and Shakespeare was dropped. After all, I had already written my painfully detailed and scholarly article, "A Vindication of the 'Bad' Quartos," which none of the Shakespearian journals wanted to publish. They were all on the side of the "Good Quartos" theory, which denied that Shakespeare had rather turgidly revised and enlarged these texts to regain his pirated copyrights — a riposte still available to authors today. Anyway, my work with the parallel texts of Shakespeare was really just boondoggling too, I knew. Mostly I had been doing it to keep from going crazy evenings with Beverley, who seldom ever read a book or even sewed; watching her silently drinking syrupy coffee and smoking cigarettes hour after hour until bedtime. Who knows? Perhaps it was just The *Gift of the Magi* problem. Maybe she thought she was just trying not to disturb me while I poured over my Shakespeare texts?

Now I had this passionate new project and would spend my evenings systematically reading The Concise Dictionary of National Biography, hundreds and hundreds of pages printed on bible paper in minuscule type, which I was going through line by line, alphabetically, looking for characters — quickly observable by their life-dates — whom I would use in the historical novel I was now going to write about Lady Frances Howard, Countess of Essex, my new if long-dead flame. At least, I was going to write a few chapters of such a novel, really by way of research for what was planned as the next section of my work in progress, now titled definitively *Love & Death*.

This would be a study of the bitch-heroines in recent American popular fiction, beginning with the tremendous success of Margaret Mitchell's *Gone With the Wind*, and the whole question of sex-hatred between men & women as a main focus of the rising tide of sadism in the popular arts. The title of my pretended — only pretended! — bitch-heroine bestseller would be *Firetail*. The Countess of Essex like most evil women of history, was supposed to have had red hair, and that gave me the hidden pun or two-way allusion of my purposely inflammatory mock-title.

For a while there, the two jobs were being done together. My writer's block was now a thing of the past, owing to the accidental blitz-psychiatry of the editor of *Voodoo Death*. And I was sailing happily along, writing my bitch-heroine article odd mornings, and on the others working out the plot and suitably upstage archaic dialogue to clothe the authentic and historical bitchery of Firetail. I really had it down to an art — a schizophrenic art, that is. But honestly, I must say that writing that bitch-heroine novel certainly did make me understand, to a degree otherwise impossible to me, exactly how the current crop of bitch-heroines in imitation of Margaret Mitchell's Scarlett O'Hara got the hook into their millionfold female audience. The only difficulty, technically, was that I had discovered that bitch-heroines on paper were all intensely frigid and used their sexuality strictly to dominate and destroy men; whereas Lady Frances, my own burning-arsed Firetail, really seemed to have been too erotic — too, er, headstrong — for her own good. The daughter of the richest and most powerful family of England, her downfall was not caused by ambition or greed, though obviously it had been a pretentious tactical blunder to steal the king's boyfriend. What she did, she did out of frankly sexual passion, and was only lucky she was too high-placed to go to the gallows for it. Anne Turner wasn't that lucky.

Eventually I had to give up reading the *D.N.B.* looking for characters for my proposed or pretended bitch-heroine novel, as I already had over two hundred and fifty marginally marked with the secret sigla, ft, and was only up to the end of the letter *G*, at page 550, not counting the many central characters of the actual story, such as Firetail herself whose family name of Howard began with an *H*, and all the rest of the alphabet. I stopped there. The one thing I promised myself to avoid, was putting in that unendurably stiff and phoney standard scene — an embarrassment in all the historical novelists like Scott and Dumas, and even Victor Hugo — of any too-famous literary characters boozing it up at the Mermaid Tavern, and especially not Shakespeare! The real story already had too many of these authentically, since Ben Jonson was the official poet of the Essex faction and had produced the masque and the epithalamium on Firetail's first marriage to the Earl of Essex; while Shakespeare's arch-enemy and rival poet, George Chapman, actually hacked out a long mythological piece in verse, *Andromeda Liberata*, to celebrate the annulment of that same marriage, doubtless paid for by his patron Carr, her new husband.

To give me something to do now in the evenings on the pine plank table after supper, I got a big piece of coarse brown wrapping paper about a yard square and designed on it in colored ink a minutely exact map I called Shakespeare's London, from the best contemporary cartographic sources, with all the main streets and monuments and royal and noble mansions in cute little perspective projections, mostly along the muddy Thames meandering through. This was to give me a correct feeling for the motion and action of my story, without ever having set foot in London; and I found the map a very great help indeed in the writing. It was also rather pretty, and when the topographical wall map of the Grand Canyon came down, I replaced it for years after with Shakespeare's London. It was no masterpiece of the cartographer's art, but I was fond of it.

The iconography of *Firetail* was actually the easiest part, as all the main actors had been magnificently painted and portrayed more than once by the best Dutch artists of the period, and all these portraits were available in color in all their gem-studded lace and finery, in the standard big lives of Queen Elizabeth and King James. The lesser characters were much harder to find: the best was a marvellous if imaginary black-&-white cut of Mrs. Turner, in somber black dress and gorgeously starched yellow ruff on her way to execution, which I found at the head of a broadside ballad about her in the George Daniel collection catalogue. More than any of the richly beruffed and bedizened portraits of Carr and Firetail and Villiers and King James, that stark broadside portrait set over Mrs. Turner's goodnight made me realize what a movie that story would make. And I began picking actors for the parts.

The men were all schlubs, so that would be easy for Hollywood to cast. Firetail, as I would explain to David Selznick or whoever would be our producer, would have to be played by Susan Hayward, who had just the right peppery character and full-lipped mouth, along with a forest of splendid red hair. And I wondered if we couldn't get in a naked bath for her somewhere in the story, maybe in the castle stream along with a bevy of naked maids of honor, in Technicolor, of course. People didn't bathe much in those days; even Queen Elizabeth only had two baths in her life. But surely a big bathing romp on Firetail's wedding morning would fit perfectly into the scenario. I even began to worry: was Susan Hayward a real redhead? Nobody was going to spoil my movie with inauthentic redheaded merkins in the naked bathing scene!

Somewhere about there I began to realize that I was getting run away with. My historical bitch-heroine was about to bitch me too, and possibly burn up my real book *Love & Death* again. For there was nothing unrealistic or megalomaniacal about my Hollywood dream, except that maybe I wouldn't be able to force Selznick to use the actress I chose. Firetail was obviously a natural for the bitch-heroine best seller market, and would certainly make a great movie and a terrific pageant in color — banned in England at first, of course, which would also be fine publicity. But when I saw that I was loosing track of my real intention, which was to expose and excoriate the bitch-heroine best sellers, and not to cash in on a formula that I knew perfectly was the merchandizing not of sex but of sex-hatred, I decided — no! not to stop — I was already too deep in for that, and madly in love with my own bitch. But I would at least build a safety valve or an alarm button into what I was now so joyously writing day after day, which would make it positively unsaleable. Like a sort of moral condom, that would protect me from any dishonorable consequences of my evident infatuation. Bitches are easy to understand, and even excuse. But why are otherwise sane men so crazy about them? I guess it's partly masochism; but mostly it's the unconquerable challenge of the frigid woman. With my Golden Penis, I can tame even that bitch!

Accordingly, I rewrote the first page of each of the chapters already finished, adding a big ornate initial to the first letter of the first word of each chapter, and so throughout. And these first letters now spelled out a secret acrostic, proving that the whole book was only a legpull and a spoof. The opening words of Chapter One, shouted out in standard historical novel style by the green-uniformed seneschal, watching of course with the feisty young Firetail on the castle parapet for the arrival of the outriders of the king's visit and royal procession, were to be: *"You, trumpeters!"* All right, goddamit! — Scene 1, Take 1; *roll!!* And, approaching, beyond the green line of the forest, the tremendous slam and swirl of Scottish pipes and drums, boiling up along the dusty road. Well, that gave me the letter Y to start my acrostic. Which would then read, when traced out chapter-head by chapter-head — the gossip columnists would naturally be alerted to it — *"YOU DIRTY HATEFUL WHORE!"* That doesn't seem very brilliant, I admit, but I figured it would do the job.

There would also be a stanza of the main bawdy song about Firetail at the time of the trial, to the tune of *"Whoope, doe me no harm, good man!"* at the head of every chapter, to distract attention (at first) from the acrostic initial. The song had never been published that I knew of, and was considered by all my sources to be too unseemly to quote in full. So off went my letter to the British Museum for a rotograph copy of the manuscript, hidden away in somebody or other's miscellaneous papers. And two weeks of struggling to learn to decipher the old chancery handwriting, when the copy finally arrived. In those days there was time for everything.

As it happens, it was the acrostic that stopped me. The further I got into the writing of the chapters spelling out the indictment w-h-o-r-e, the more and more clearly I began to realize who the whore really was. Not my heroine, surely; not the hypothetical lending-library lady I was so cleverly trapping; but me, myself, & I. And that was the end of *Firetail.* I went a long way with her, but over the falls I wouldn't go. So, that's just one more unfinished manuscript in my files. Got lots of those. And an enormous mass of research materials, photostats, and character sketches for the book I never finished. God! Those glorious Elizabethan costumes, especially the incredible gem-studded and *petit point* lace ruffs. The world has never seen anything so sumptuous before or since, except maybe in Pazyryk. Nor ever will. Firetail is the one book I'm still sorry I didn't have the crust to finish with all the bells ringing, and Devil take the consequences! Frances Howard is the one woman I have to admit I left hanging, for all my Golden Penis, and I certainly can't say it was her fault for being frigid. I admit it — I'm still sorry. I don't care about the royalties I never earned. I had the right red-headed heroine picked out to play the part, and I would have liked to see the film. It's still waiting for someone to make it. I'm supposed to hate self-willed bitches, but I kind of like them too. Firetail forever! I'm no angel either.

CHAPTER 48

MAYA DEREN

IN GREENWICH Village itself there were then only two intellectual bookshops, odd as this may seem, that dealt in second-hand books. One was Pete Lader's, just in from the corner of Sixth Avenue on West Fourth Street, which was small and pleasant, very much like Briggs'; and the other was Joe Kling's enormous cavernous hall on Eighth Street, that had been there since the Bohemian and Pagan period of the early 1920s, of which Kling himself was a relic. This was the best place for buying unusual books. Kling was a brilliant man, but much soured by becoming old, and he visibly yearned for his youth that came back no more — as we all do. Especially that part of youth that means lots of girls and sex, and the touch of magic this lends. Kling sold his store just about then, to a marvellous earth-mother type of young woman named Toschka, who changed the name of the store to The Four Seasons, and started putting in new books and even a line of greeting cards and novelties, including "hate-cards" — her own invention with her husband. We were never friends again after I told her that publishing the hate-cards made her marriage very suspect.

There were already two other stores selling new intellectual books in Greenwich Village, but that was a rather different thing. You went in there to buy a book you needed; not to hang around as in Briggs' or Pete

Lader's. Joe Kling would never let anybody hang around except female persons. They seemed quite welcome. One of the new bookstores on Eighth Street was run by Eli Wilentz and his brother, whom I got along with very well and liked very much; and the other by a plump, rather pompous fellow named Lawrence Maxwell, who somehow never seemed at ease with me. His little shop was just across Sheridan Square from the subway stop where I got off almost every evening, coming home to Beverley, so I got to hanging out there a bit too.

Maxwell never quite put me out, but often made me feel much less than welcome, explaining to me once that his other customers did not always enjoy my then habitual combination of extreme frankness and not-too-tamed aggressiveness. In addition, I was a real buttinski. I admit it. I did not talk particularly dirty, and still don't, but if the *mot juste* was crude, that's what came out, instead of some wishy-washy circumlocution. It was mostly my aggressiveness that bothered him. Like many people who are deeply convinced of the meaningfulness of Literature and especially Modren Literature, he had no idea of what direct and racy speech of ordinary people sounds like, and felt uncomfortable hearing it spoken, unless one were consciously slumming. Curiously, Maxwell was also the only bookseller in those parts who seemed at all politically aware, but in a vague soft-focus way. Positively nothing radical. You know the style.

The day I asked him why he thought Henry Miller's books were so remarkable — even if only under the counter — when he found my own conversation so shocking and distressing, though I was miles from being anywhere near as aggressive as Miller's standard dialogue in his books, Maxwell explained to me with angelic simplicity that the reason was that Miller was Literature, but I was just *talking*. He admitted, however, looking rather dubious about it, that I would no doubt have the same sacrosanct status if I put all the same remarks on paper instead. I reminded him that Jake Brussel had gone to jail for doing exactly that, and with none other than Henry Miller's book. We agreed, finally, that Paris was perhaps a better place altogether for my kind of candor than New York. Maxwell also looked as though he wished that I would leave for Paris soon. I asked him jokingly if it would be worth twenty dollars to him to see me go: a sort of Society for the Prevention of Legman. This was the first time that the idea had ever crossed my horizon that I too might go to Paris like Henry Miller. But where would I get the money? Paris was for head-down spongers like Miller, or for vaguely rich idlers, with no work to do, ever — the kind of disconnected people Hemingway was always writing about.

❧

MEETING PEOPLE on Broadway by accident was common in those days, even in the daytime, and sometimes on Fifth Avenue too, or in the subway. You never ran into anyone you knew anywhere else, except indoors. Those were the two main drags. The night the crowds celebrated the exploding of the Atom Bomb, I wandered among them at Times Square like an untouching ghost. Three young soldiers on leave, lurching along happily, and obviously pretty drunk, stopped me. One of them grabbed my arm.

"Hey! You're my uncle!" he shouted.

"I'm your uncle?" I repeated dully, coming back from $E = mc^2$, light-years away.

"Sure you're my uncle!" the young soldier shouted again. "I'm Geney Rothman, don't you remember me? From Scranton!"

"That's right," I said. "I'd never have recognized you. I remember; I was at your circumcision."

The other two soldiers exploded into laughter at this, and poor Gene looked as though he wanted to sink through the pavement. I don't know why I said it. Maybe stupidity. Maybe because I was feeling so totally evil that night, and hating everyone on earth. The two other soldiers started a pantomime with each other, bowing and scraping, and saying, "Will you cut first, Rabbi?" and the other replying, "No, you!" I guess my nephew Gene doesn't remember the dropping of the Atom Bomb on Hiroshima with the happiness it ought to bring to a good Jewish boy's heart. If only they could have dropped Oppenheimer and Fermi and General Groves *with* the Bomb, and maybe Secretary of War Stimson and President Truman too, who chose the target cities, that would have improved the situation all around. At least for me. Like Dr. Guillotine being given the first legendary cut on *his* new invention.

Another day I met Ivor Colfax — his stage name — whom I'd known years before as an amateur magician. Colfax was a marvellous hand with cards, and could do the famous cascade or waterfall riffle, spreading out a deck with one sweep of his hand along his other arm, and then suddenly flipping the whole deck over like a train of dominoes, by snapping up on the last card with his fingertips. Try it. He told me he was now in the theatre, and would be going to rehearsal in an hour. He was the actor-director. The show wasn't exactly on Broadway, but it wasn't off Broadway either — it was nearby. We went to the tiny delicatessen on one of the side streets, where you could barely sit down to have a corned beef sandwich with dill pickles, or some hot frankfurters and beans. That's what I always took. I figured you got the most protein that way for your money. Daytime people on Broadway are generally broke.

Colfax told me how hard things had been the preceding few years in the theatre. Musicals were in big demand, and troupes would go out entertaining the soldiers. But it was slim pickings in the legitimate art theatre, now, and that was all he cared about. He was planning to try to get to Hollywood, to direct pictures there. He had big ideas and knew he could do a great job, if he could only break in. If he couldn't direct, he'd have to work as an actor. Or write scenarios — that was apparently the bottom.

I asked him if acting and directing had been a living in the bad years just gone by, and mentioned my own brief period writing for the stage now nearly ten years before. No, he told me, it was no living at all. He had been able to get through, however, by card-sharping. He gave me a big, frank smirk as he said this.

"What? Automatic elbow-handouts up your sleeve, and all that?" I marvelled. I had thought that went out with the dodo.

"Oh, no!" he said, "that's too crude. Besides, if you're caught with a gimmick like that, the other players will kill you. Half of them are gangsters, anyhow, in the games you can get on Broadway. You'd end up in the river in a cement overcoat."

He explained to me that his method was imply to pretend to be a novice player and to fumble the cards a lot, and even drop a few while dealing or shuffling. Then, when he'd be dealer, playing Blackjack, he'd notice the low cards carefully as he raked them up and put them on the bottom of the deck. That way if he needed some special low card to make twenty-one pips, or to hit his secret partner with when he played with a confederate, he would flip the deck over invisibly just long enough to deal off that one prepared card. In my mind's eye, I saw Colfax as I had seen him years before, with me an admiring fellow amateur magician, as he flipped over an entire deck along his arm in the incredible gesture of the waterfall ripple. Now magic was just an adjunct to card-sharping. Maybe it always was, historically. I wondered whether Shakespeare and Ben Jonson could do the waterfall ripple. Or gypped at Blackjack.

"Well," I said, pretty lamely, "they say Christopher Marlowe got killed in a barroom brawl for dealing from the bottom, so be careful."

"Oh, sure," Colfax told me grandly. "I'm playing mostly bridge now, anyhow. The whole trick there is to keep people thinking you're a dub. There's no prestidigitation at all. You've just got them completely overmatched, playing against you, but they don't know it until it's too late. And then they figure it was just my dumb luck."

He held out his hand to shake with me when we split up after the sandwiches and franks, so I had to shake his hand, but I checked carefully on my wristwatch at once. After he was gone I realized that he had never said a single word about anyone but himself. Well, that's show-people, all right. He would go far.

You also often met people you knew on the subway platforms, though for some reason never in the cars. I guess the mathematics there would run it too fine, but the platforms and staircases have a lot of people passing through all the time. Going down the subway stairs at Fourteenth Street and Eighth Avenue, where my bank was then, early one morning I ran into the fat girl who lived with Trevor Paulson, a British homosexual poet that Sewell had introduced me to. Paulsen wasn't basically a bad poet, and had a certain amount of guts too, but he was a ghastly drunk, and during our first meeting he actually fell into the cold fireplace, face down, and we all had to drag him out and brush the ashes off him. He was still holding his glass in a vise-like grip.

While the fat girl, Martine, was washing him off a little in the kitchen, Sewell got down a poetry anthology from the one and only book shelf in their apartment, and showed me one of Paulsen's poems. I guess he wanted to prove his friend was an authentic poet as well as a repulsive drunk. The poem was the usual meaningless unrhymed drivel in broken lines that passes for poetry since Whitman began imitating the

King James Bible prose. The last line was a good joke though. It was about success: *"If at first you don't succeed — keep sucking."* Typical homosexual camp, of course, but courageous too at that date.

When I met Martine on the subway staircase that morning, I was carrying folded over my arm the mate of the magnificent red Hudson's Bay blanket, that Beverley wanted me to put on my bed up at 76th Street, so our rooms would be the same, and connected by the two blankets. They had in fact been woven together originally, and were sold double-length and cut apart. We would be like the Adam & Eve hermaphrodite before the Fall, connected by our red bellybutton blanket all day. Like the song about "that little piece of whang."

Martine went wild about the blanket the minute she saw it. You could see the interior-decorating permutations and possibilities clicking along through her mind. She wanted to know where I got it, and I told her they had to be imported from Canada. She looked at me calculatingly, and pursed her lips slightly.

"Let's have a cup of coffee," she said.

We walked back up the steps and had bad coffee in a drugstore. We spoke of nothing in particular. Of Paulsen and his poetry readings in some New Jersey university town, where he now was for the weekend. As we walked out of the drugstore Martine made her pitch.

"I'll screw you on that blanket if you'll give it to me afterward," she said, with a look intended to be sexy. "I really like a man to screw me *hard!*" she added.

I felt terribly embarrassed, especially because I found her so unappetizing and didn't want to have to say so. "Why are you living with a fairy, then?" was all I could think to counter.

"Oh, Trev has his manly moments too," she assured me. "How about it?"

"Look, Martine," I said, trying to sound reasonable instead of as disgusted as I felt. "My wife just gave me that blanket a half an hour ago, for a love gift. I haven't even put it on my bed yet. I just can't use it to buy a prostitute with at nine a.m."

"Oh, yeah!?" she snarled. Then she spat right in my face, and hurried on ahead of me. Actually, for a fat girl, she was rather graceful in her movements.

Morning in Manhattan. I wiped the spit off with the back of my hand to keep it off the blanket. It was probably rabid, I figured, and would hold its poison for years. And it has. You can't beat the old proverbs: Hell has no fury like a woman spurned. Not to mention if at first you don't succeed . . .

One afternoon just about then I got off the subway one stop up from Forty-Second Street, to walk over to the Gotham Book Mart to see a book I needed. I wouldn't be able to buy it, but the Public Library didn't have it, and if Frances Steloff did, she wouldn't mind my taking notes. It was on Dadaism and Surrealism, my pet hates. Just as I came up out of the subway staircase I practically bumped into my sister Matilda, whom I hadn't seen for years, as she didn't usually come home for Thanksgiving. She couldn't make even a one-day truce with Dad, the way I had learned to try to do because my mother wanted me to

"One day a year without making any snotty cracks won't kill you," my mother would say. And so I would try. Matilda found it harder to try, and had no special reason to try. None of my sisters loved my mother the way I did.

I asked her what she was doing, and told her how beautiful and striking she looked, which she did. She said she was the cigarette girl in a big upstairs nightclub just at that corner. I think it was called the Latin Quarter. The usual thing, a reconverted speakeasy, no doubt, but now strictly legitimate with a floor show, chorus girls and all. Matilda said she went round in tights and very long silk stockings, with a tray of cigarettes on a ribbon around her neck.

"Well, I guess it's a living," I ventured.

"Oh, much better than a living," she told me happily. "All I need is one good drunk a night that gives me a twenty dollar bill for his cigarettes and tells me to keep the change. They never know the difference."

"Why do they do that?" I asked.

"Just to feel big," Matilda said. "I guess they like my legs."

I changed the subject, and asked her if she ever met any interesting men there. I recollected that her movie types had all been gangsters on the Lloyd Nolan and Humphrey Bogart pattern. No-emotion gangsters for no-emotion girls. She said the men were terrible, but mentioned that she had met one girl — a guest at a table one evening, not working with her — who recognized her name and said she knew me, and of course asked if we were related. The girl came in occasionally after that, and they would always talk. Matilda cudgelled her memory for the girl's name, and finally recollected that it had been Chigi Roth. Well, well, I guess I said, and what's Chigi doing now? It appears she was married, to a very nice Frenchman whom she had met when he was living in America the last few years. They now lived in a penthouse opposite the Hayden Planetarium.

"Wow!" I said, "everybody I know is succeeding except me." I made a mental note to phone Chigi and find out how her father, Sam Roth, was doing. Maybe he'd have a ghost job for me that wouldn't be too repulsive. Only after Matilda had scampered upstairs to her nightclub did I realize I hadn't asked her Chigi's married name, so I wouldn't be able to call her after all. It didn't seem worth going up and bothering Matilda for, and also she might put the wrong construction on my interest. I went on to the bookshop, and before leaving I asked Miss Steloff if she knew where I could find Sam Roth, who I knew was now out of prison and operating again, but wasn't listed in the phone book.

"Oh, stay away from him!" she cried immediately. "That man is pure poison!"

"Everybody knows it," I agreed, "but he might have a job for me."

"Well, he's sure to cheat you," she snapped.

Aside from whatever business dealings she may have had with him, and in the old days everything underground that had any literary pretentions at all flowed through the Gotham Book Mart — it was the one main outlet then, as its outside sign wittily implied: *"Wise men fish here"* — Miss Steloff's feeling about Roth was of course based on his shameless piracies of Joyce's *Ulysses*, Lawrence's *Lady Chatterley*, and everything else he could lay his hands on, owing to the copyright law which then refused protection to "obscene" books. If Steloff knew about Roth's *Jews*

Must Live, she never mentioned it. But that was really what I hated Roth for, not his piracies. From his piracies I had learned, at least, to be tremendously careful to prevent Brussel in New York and Abramson in Chicago from pirating Henry Miller's *Tropic of Cancer*, and got them to handle it on a standard, paid royalty instead. Nobody ever thanked me, but it had been done right.

In fact, Roth never did cheat me. He actually seemed to have quite a good deal of affection for me; which was a great embarrassment since I was bound to hate him after *Jews Must Live*. In a prison memoir of his which I have seen, a sort of imaginary dream biography of the life he would have liked to live, I appear under the name of "George Lerner," and am showered with compliments, up to and including accepting me as a sort of honorary son, matching his daughter Chigi, but for some reason ousting his son Richard, who was the person in the family I actually liked the most. I am then cast into outer darkness owing to an attack of erysipelas, with a resultant rash on my forehead, which Roth apparently confuses with syphilis.

However, after a wild and completely mythical scene of fever in the hospital, during which I start a long and marvellous tirade which runs on for pages — I assume Roth got this all down with a tape-recorder, years before they were invented — I am cured, and restored to my former standing in the dream family. The implication is also rather strongly present that I am going to be married off to Chigi, though in fact Roth once chased me out of his office, threatening with his cane, when it came to his attention that I had on one occasion tried to snatch a kiss or something from her. That was as far as it ever went.

I think the truth is that to Roth I represented the sort of young Jewish intellectual that he had once been. But I had not forever destroyed my ties with my emotional and religious past, as he had done with his insane book. As such, he found himself identifying with me, except of course in the matter of money, of which he always had a sufficiency and I never did. So he was always good for a brief writing job of some sort or another, when things were very tough. This was unfortunately combined always with a great deal of pompous and very wearing conversation on his part, seldom about literature and never about religion, but always about things he thought made him look good to discuss, such as philosophy. He was really a total *poseur*, but absolutely certain that no one ever suspected him for an instant. *He* certainly never suspected himself, and that was his strength.

Roth was always a customer, therefore, for ghost-written books, though I never ghostwrote but one book for him, and then was surprised when he wanted his name, or rather his staff pseudonym, stuck on it, as I had expected to sign it myself. He would also stalwartly deny that anything was ever ghostwritten for him, even to the ghostwriter himself, and would describe what was being done as "editing" his materials. This is standard. Anyhow, I needed his money now. And I was willing to keep studying him from close, like the dangerous microbe he was, as I had been studying him since ten years before when we first met, with the idea of writing about his strange and significant case one day. That day now need never come, as all the public parts of Roth's long literary and publishing career have been superlatively recorded in a thirty-page essay entitled "Nobody Knows My Names," by Leo Hamalian, in the *Journal of Modern Literature* for 1974.

Of course, as his title implies, Hamalian was able to learn almost nothing, from his carefully discreet sources, as to Roth's secret erotic publications, and even as to the man himself. So perhaps I still have something to contribute to literary history here. At the time I am writing about, Roth had mostly hedged his bets, or thought he had, and was publishing mere junk, but nothing secretly. It is sardonic that the final trouble he got into had to be on the legal pretext of fraud, not obscenity, when he tried to pretend to his mail-order customers in his circulars that the mildly naughty stuff he was now peddling was really the pornography they were slavering for. As Hamalian puts it, "Roth had pulled the fire out of his chestnuts," by comparison with the hair-raising erotica coming into America after the war, from France and Germany and later the wholly hairy Danish pastry of pictorial erotica, in both stills and movies. If he had not attacked Walter Winchell then, no one would have bothered him. In fact Roth was basically dead and had no function left to perform; yet it was then that his case finally broke the censorship in America. Because he, or his family, now had the money to fight that case up to the Supreme Court.

Since my sister Matilda had told me his daughter Chigi now lived opposite the Hayden Planetarium, I walked over there on Sunday afternoon, when it was too sunny to stay indoors. The apartment house opposite was called the Hayden House, so I just walked in and asked the doorman, expecting some problem as I did not know Chigi Roth's new married name. But there was no problem. Sam Roth's name was on one of the doorbells. They had the front apartment on the first floor up, with big windows in the sun. Chigi apparently lived with her new husband's family in the penthouse. The doorman imparted the information to me — true or false, I had no way of knowing — that they also owned the whole apartment house, as is often the case with people who live in penthouses. Maybe Chigi, now Mrs. Adelaide Kugel was the real Dark Angel of the New Freedom in America.

Roth was delighted to see me. The old scoundrel waved me in, having answered the door himself. Jail hadn't changed him a hair's breadth — he was getting accustomed to it by then, like a long sea voyage, he told me — and he still affected all the same airs of a phoney Britisher, except the accent. His wife Pauline, however, was grievously changed. In the years when I knew they had lots of troubles, she had always been cheerful and coping bravely. Now that fortune had seemingly smiled on them, and they had come to rest in a luxurious apartment with presumably a going business, she was tense and jumpy, and obviously far from happy.

I had always liked Pauline before, but now I could not get close to her at all. She was like someone who has kept up their courage during all the worst hours of a shipwreck, but who, having finally arrived safely in port, can now barely hold back all the anger and tension they had never allowed to come to expression when things were grim. If I had always, in my own mind, been a secret observer in my dealings with the Roths, I knew I would now have to redouble my prudence or Pauline would sniff out the phoneyness of my position at once. Roth's jail sentences had changed innocent her, not guilty him.

And yet I couldn't help feeling that he was also still as suspicious as hell about me, and was trying to make sure I wasn't just one of the new generation of snoopers and spies unquestionably being sic'd on him. He really had me squirming inside, in my consciousness of almost total guilt, with only the one saving grace that I hadn't been working for his censorship enemies, anyhow; I had never turned him in to anybody for anything.

From that day on, I also never thought of myself as spying on the anti-Semitic son-of-a-bitch, no doubt to bring him one day before some non-existent Sanhedrin of Jewish justice, the way Eichmann was kidnapped to Israel and exposed in a glass cage before they shot him. A hell of a lot better than the Nuremberg Trials, anyhow, where the Germans' responsibility for up to ten million civilian execution deaths, of Jews, Gypsies, Russians and Poles, was presumably all straightened out by executing thirty Nazi officials. Maybe a life for a life would be too much to ask, but is one executed Nazi per 333,333 executed victims a fair shake? Well, Justice has been done — *Fiat Justicia!* I suppose Roth's case can be ciphered out the same way. He went to jail, didn't he? Who am I to try to drag him to any further justice, like Javert hounding Jean Valjean in *Les Misérables?*

❧

NATURALLY, Roth had a new book in the works, also some further jail memoirs entitled *Bumarap*. From something he let drop, I gathered that the new book had been ghosted for him by a minor literary light of the *Partisan Review* school, named Harry Roskolenko. Roth was now of course touching up and ruining the ghostwritten manuscript, in his standard way, to support his illusion of being the author. He may, however, actually have written this book, as will be seen. Roth awarded me the job on the spot, of reading and improving this new manuscript as it then existed. As was Roth's habit, it was neatly typed up by someone else, but with his additions and corrections splattered in the margins, between the lines, and on intercalary pages. That was how he always worked. My own manuscripts look even worse, I admit. But I do my own typing — and retyping; yea, unto seventy times seven.

I naturally refused offhand the amount of money Roth offered me for my, er, collaboration, without even paying much attention to how much it was. Operators of his type, I was aware, have no respect for anyone who does not realize that they are invariably chiselling and must be chiselled right back. As I realized he had recently been in jail, though I didn't say so, I simply assured him that things were now entirely different than before the War; that prices were now up to beyond double, and that literary fees would have to follow suit.

"Right!" said Roth, with his most seigneurial air. "We'll double it." But I still hadn't registered what the figure was, so I asked him for half in advance, and took the manuscript home with me. This time he had really outdone himself. It was unquestionably the worst book I had ever read, bar none! The most ignorant, the most pretentious, and the most drivelling. Obviously his own work. Roth also had various titles drafted in on the first page, of which the one he eventually chose to publish it under was the stupidest: *The Peephole of the Present.* It was dedicated without permission to Albert Einstein, whose foolish notions of physical science Roth's book was vaingloriously intended to correct, in an effort to "revolutionize the conception of the size and shape of the world as a whole."

If there was any one subject in the world on which Roth was totally incompetent to write even the ten words of a telegram, astronomical physics was surely it; and here was a whole book of riotous and meaningless garbage by him on the subject. For an instant I was almost certain that he *had* written it himself. But still, I was pretty sure that, as usual, he had turned his drafts over to some poor ghost like myself to put it into at least grammatical English. Roth had also sent the manuscript to unwitting Sir Arthur Eddington, the British authority on relativity and the evolution of stars. Eddington had incredibly written a polite letter in response, acknowledging receipt, and then died immediately thereafter. I don't insist this was a result of reading the manuscript, but he was only sixty-two. As Eddington was now out of the way, Roth had "edited" and hoked up the letter shamelessly, and planned to publish it in the book as though it were a commendatory preface. He told me this grinning, and without the slightest disguise

The whole manuscript was so infuriatingly pompous, and so unutterably ignorant and ridiculous, that I was very glad I had casually demanded half-payment in advance. I knew the moment that I started reading it seriously, that I would never see another penny, as under my new private rules since the occult dictionary of Professor Phil van Droeckh, I could not possibly lend myself to any such crocked enterprise, except to try to stop it. I would accept the money I had already been given as a reading fee. After all, I did read this piece of truly eccentric tripe, or at least attacked reading it here and there. And to prove I had done so, I wrote a few carping comments and contentious remarks in the margins of the manuscript, wherever the most pretentious and ineffable howlers occurred that even a total science ignoramus like myself could see. There were surely ten worse errors for every one I caught.

Roth accepted the return of his manuscript with good grace, a few days later, and understood when I said I really couldn't undertake to rewrite it further, as it was beyond my competence. I meant it was beyond his too, and he understood. Later he printed all my marginal complaints in the book itself, in his favorite form of the imaginary dialogue, without my knowledge, and with my initials attached — but thankfully not with my name — referring to me several times as "my young literary advisor, G. L." I guess "literary advisor" means ghost.

I was awfully glad, when I finally saw the thing in print, that my new ghost-writing rules had kept me almost wholly out of it. The ice-cold and lethal review it elicited in *The Saturday Review of Literature* when it was published is a morsel worthy of any anthology of invective and abuse. And even if the review had said twice as much, it would still fall far short of the truth about this lulu. Roth's *Peephole of the Present* is really a curiosity, a museum piece. For published items written by a presumably sane person — I don't mean out-&-out literary eccentrica by lunatics — this is outstandingly the world's worst book. Crack it open and see. See also *The Book of Job*, xxxi, 35: "Would that mine enemy would write a book!"

Roth had lots of other plans for his re-entry into publishing, and suggested I might read over another manuscript for him which was now almost ready to print and was to be called *Waggish Tales of the Czechs*. As the thing fell open in my hands to a presumably Czechoslovakian erotic folktale written in broad Negro comedy dialect, I didn't bother to look at it further, but asked who had written it. Roth claimed it had been written by Alec Wollcott, as a continuation of his puffed-out bawdy story, based on a joke, "Entrance Fee," in *While Rome Burns*, in the style of Balzac's *Contes Drolatiques*.

"Oh come on, Sam," I said, "did you really write it?"

"Well, I had to rewrite it a lot," he admitted. Meaning, I presume, that some other ghost had already worked it over. "It's mostly jokes taken from my old

Anecdota Americana. You know, I brought out a *New Anecdota* just recently.

Roth would not say so directly, but he got across the point to me that the book was actually an old manuscript he had found lying around from the days when he was publishing the magazines, *Secret Memoirs* and *Casanova Jr.'s Tales*, in the 1920s. He walked over to a bookshelf, and pulled out a slender pamphlet entitled *The Last of the Bleshughs* by "the Marquis of Fartanoys," which he offered to me, and told me this was by the same author. It was a secret reprint by Roth, made about 1928, and embellished with erotic drawings in woodcut style, of a humorous piece that had already appeared in *Secret Memoirs* in that year, and which I knew to be the work of a Philadelphia humorist, Roy McCardell. The *Waggish Tales* manuscript was therefore a hoked-up revision of something McCardell had written, but whether he was responsible for the bad taste of the Czechs talking in Negro dialect, or whether he was even responsible for the whole bum-Czech format, there was now no way of knowing. Wholly irresponsible, Roth adored bullshitting up someone else's manuscript or even printed books in this way, when he could get away with it. As in the ineffable "continuations" he published of Lady Chatterley's Lover; and especially in a largely-faked item about incest, called *My Sister and I*, which Roth claimed deliciously was "mostly" by Nietzsche.

McCardell had only been peripherally in this menagerie, as he had his own newspaper job. He obviously liked erotica and wanted to mix sex with his humor, like a new Eugene Field, but he had the same problem that Field was faced with — how to get his erotic humor secretly published. Roth was the answer for McCardell, just as some unknown printer in Chicago or Boston around 1890 had printed up almost all of Field's erotic poems and pieces in a rare little booklet, *The Stag Party*. For this Eugene Field was to be taken before the grand jury and nearly sent to jail, but he was saved by the intervention of an influential friend.

McCardell also did add another odd piece, "The Quimbo Lexicon," playing endlessly and peculiarly on combinations of the word *quim*; and Roth had published this under the imprint "Philadelphia," in 1929, in his *Observations of an Old Man in Love*, which purported to be an interlude from Frank Harris' then notorious *My Life and Loves*. Harris' terribly mendacious autobiography was later lied even further to a fare-thee-well in an equally purported final volume issued by Maurice Girodias in Paris, but actually written by the main Scottish member of the Paris expatriate gang writing pornography for Girodias in the 1950s, Alexander Trocchi.

Anyhow, I already had a copy of the fake-Harris *Observations* volume, and accepted from Roth only the little supplementary pamphlet, *The Last of the Bleshughs*, which was next to it on the shelf. Why he gave it to me I don't know. He probably had a stack of them somewhere. Roth's secret warehouse stocks were always one of his trump cards. When the police would discover them, as they did more than once, and sent him to the pokey, he would hire another loft — or usually two — on getting out, and start building up his stock again. This time, he told me, he was going to keep things strictly on the up-&-up, and publish nothing obscene. I asked him if in that case he'd sell me the copy of Aleister Crowley's White Stains I saw on the shelf, which was obviously far too raw to be republished openly then in America, and dangerous even if issued secretly. But Roth said he wanted to keep it, as a memento of Crowley, whom he had met and admired in an appalled way.

Roth's meeting with Crowley had been odd and disconcerting, as was everything connected with that typical social psychopath, whose occult soundtrack was the least important part of his fatal charm for weak, conscience-bound people. Or even for would-be crooks and strivers like Roth, who just didn't have that much brutal *panache*, nor Crowley's absolutely maniacal, uncaring egocentricity. Obviously, the sex-part of Crowley's mock-occult message, which was the main part, meant a lot to everybody, whether for good or for bad: whether accepted with a plus sign or refused with all the terror of a minus sign.

As Samuel Roth told the story he had met Crowley about 1919 or 1920 in New York, when Crowley was still hanging out in America as many Britishers did to avoid the First World War. Another famous escapee then — there were many more in the Second World War — was the folk musicologist, Cecil Sharp, who spent the difficult war years in the southern Appalachian mountains with his New Chastity secretary Miss Maud Karpeles, hunting patriotically for surviving old British folksongs. Roth was at that time only a young poet of the Pagan group, and had not yet fallen into publishing semi-erotica and beyond. He had one of intellectual bookstores in Greenwich village at the corner of West Eighth and McDougall Street. It was still there sixty years later, though it had changed hands half a dozen times.

Roth had trouble about Crowley's poems, in *White Stains*, which Crowley called his "poetic reply to Krafft-Ebing," meaning that he was glorying there in everything Doctor Krafft-Ebing described as simply awful in his *Psychopathia Sexualis*, that standby of old drugstore remainder counters' Lowprice Library of cutrate Erotica. Charles Carrington must have had the distribution of Crowley's book originally, as he cites and quotes from it in his 1900s sales catalogue disguised as an imitation of Ashbee's great erotic bibliographies under the title of Forbidden Books. Roth had secretly reprinted this Carrington catalogue about 1929, and the quotations from Crowley's *White Stains* in it, he told me, were what got him into most hot water when it came to court. Especially the poems "With Dog and Dame," — subject obvious — and "Sleeping in Carthage," which is about cunnilinctus during menstruation, beginning "My month of thirst is ended . . ." This must be the ultimate taboo in the Judeo-Christian west. The riotous motorcycle-riding, secretly drug-peddling gangsters, the "Hell's Angels" in the U.S. in the 1960s reserved it for their ultimate public initiation ceremony, and wore a special red patch like a medal on their decorated cycling jackets if they succeeded in this terrifying test. I like cunnilinctus during menstruation, especially the first and last day, when the flow of blood isn't too overwhelming. Why not? Roth's judge and jury did not take this pansexual point of view. Most men are afraid of menstrual blood, probably because bleeding means dying to the warrior male, and he is scared, and jealous of women who can bleed all day a dozen times a year and not die of it. In fact, putting your mouth to that fountain is a profound and exhilarating experience like drinking brandy, and Crowley is right.

IT WAS fairly late in the afternoon when I walked home from Roth's, down the few blocks along Central Park West to my furnished room. I had my eyes on the façade of the Museum of Natural History, owing to my bad habit of spending most of my attention on what I hate, and not on what I love. My favorite architectural hate in New York City is the high-relief frieze there, and the jingoist Rough-Rider statue of that old fraud, Theodore Roosevelt, which forms the center piece, with an Indian running along at one of his stirrups, and an Afro-American at the other. It ought to be dynamited. I thought several times of doing it myself.

MAYA DEREN

On the steps of the Museum of Natural History, where it faces the park, I saw a young woman sitting staring moodily across at the trees. Her face was rather pretty in a pouting way, and suddenly I realized that I knew her. It was Maya Deren. I stopped and said hello, and asked her what she was doing there. She told me that some friends of hers in the museum were letting her use their movie projection theatre to screen her new avant-garde art movie, which was just about finished and being released. Only these friends and her husband Alex Hammid, who was the actual photographer, would be at the screening. She invited me to come too, and we went in together. She sat in the last row and curled herself into a ball, protectively like a hedgehog I thought, when the lights went out and the film started. We were the last ones in, and I sat by her, watching both the movie and her.

It was in many ways an interesting film, called *At Land*, but shamelessly a showpiece for herself. Hammid's camera never left her for a minute, and exploited at all times Maya Deren's cute little face, and her plumply sexy body. There was no meaningful plot, just a string of embarrassing echoes of Cocteau's movie, *Blood of a Poet*, but without all the offensive surrealism. The film began with her being cast ashore by the waves, and rolling slowly in the shallow water. She is a fish, and we are to see her adventures At Land, where she is continuously approached by various men, for evident purposes, but manages to evade them all.

I have forgotten most of the action, but one openly absurd sequence showed her entering a room in which a man was laid out as dead on a slab, or in a coffin. It was Margaret Mead's second husband, named Bateson, I believe; very British, with air force moustache and all. Although, being presumably dead, he was in no position to make the standard pass at her, he too had to be rejected sexually. This was achieved by the ostensible fish-girl suddenly snatching out of the air a small pussycat which she throws on the supine and immobile masochistic male corpse. Real subtle.

After the showing there wasn't much of the usual standing around and discussing. Hammid was there, murmured hello, and then disappeared. A marvellous cinema technician who had made great films in Germany, he knew only one trick on the human level with his florid wife: Self-effacement and letting her take all the bows. I imagined he was using her sexiness to get him started in America. As there was no one else left around to work off her tension with, and everyone was disappearing, Maya began discussing the film with me: what it meant, why she had created it, why she wasn't satisfied with it, and so forth. She seemed completely unconscious of the fact that it was Hammid's movie as much as hers. I asked her where it had been photographed, and she mentioned some rich art-lover's estate up beyond Yonkers or somewhere. Like Henry Miller, Maya Deren was shrewdly conscious of where the money was, and went there to get it. The patron and foundation grant-chasing art so highly developed nowadays. I didn't hold this against her of course, — it's the reality principle — but it's always ungracious to watch in an artist.

We walked out and she wanted to know finally what I had thought of her film. Having just got free of Sam Roth, I didn't much feel like yessing and ass-kissing Maya Deren — unless she was planning to offer me the real thing, which seemed like a good possibility, as she was obviously quite high from seeing herself on the screen in such massive enlargement. Also, like many artists and humorists with a highly neurotic message, she was all tensed up with anxiety to know if she was getting away with it. My function was to represent the sucker public, and to reassure her. Oh well, she was as cute as a bug's ear, and after all, I lived just around the corner. If she wanted to work off her artistic and erotic tension on me, surely I owed that much to the only new art of our century: the film.

I began with a few minor compliments, which are after all the breath of life to theatre people who are, by definition, both narcissistic and exhibitionistic. I mentioned the evident inspiration of the movie in Hans Christian Andersen's poignant fable of the mermaid who loved the human, and had her tail changed to feet by magic so she could come ashore and live with him. I said nothing about Andersen's stinger in the tail: that every step the mermaid took would be like walking on knives. I also said something nice about the only scene that had spoken to me personally: on the opening beach, where the fish-girl collects more and more shiny stones, until at last the ones she has already collected start tumbling out of her arms, as she piles on more. As a maniacal book-collector myself, I told her, I enjoyed neat symbolic criticism like that. I also added that I found that I lost half the women I really cared about, by trying to collect new ones.

She loved everything I said, and she turned on the sex appeal to hear more. It was pitiful to see how much she needed approbation for what she thought of as uniquely her art, though it was equally obvious that everything that was striking on the film, except her own physical appearance, was Hammid's contribution as photographer. Though she enjoyed flaunting her sexual attractiveness, I knew she wouldn't be able to bear my saying that. So instead I began complaining lightly about the crudely anti-sexual overtones of the film, and especially the throwing of the pussycat on the laid-out male corpse. I pressed purposely hard on the *pussy*.

"That's sort of shooting pussyfish in a barrel, isn't it?" I asked her. "Conscious symbolism that heavy usually defeats itself. Most people just laugh."

She denied that was the intention of the scene at all. But refused to state what symbol she had intended by the dead man, the pussy, and so forth. It became an argument for a while, in which I cited Mario Praz's book on the turning sour of the Romantic movement, which had just recently been translated under the beautiful title, not that of the original, *The Romantic Agony*.

What I told Maya Deren about the book intrigued her very much, particularly that there was a chapter called "La Belle Dame Sans Merci," anatomizing the standard bitch-character that I thought her movie was really intended to glorify in a not very hidden way. She denied everything, but asked if I would lend her the book. When I told her I lived just around the corner, she invited herself over at once. It was evening by now, and as we climbed the two flights of stairs to my room, I watched very thoughtfully the tick-tocking of her extremely handsome bottom going up the stairs before me, in the dim light of the staircase. If I couldn't rightly read the workings of her mind, I could certainly read the tick-tocking of her ass. She was evidently going to triumph sexually, or maybe asexually over me, and bitch the man who had dared to call her an aggressive bitch.

I wondered how many girls I had followed up these stairs in the few years I had lived in that room. Quite a lot, and always to make love to them. This time would be the same. Our cinematic and literary conversation was not fooling either Maya or me, of course. We both knew why we were going up the stairs, essentially, which was not for me to loan her a book. But there was a strange nuance for me. I was a married man now, and really did not like being unfaithful to my wife. Of course, before Beverley and I were living together, I had no hesitation about having several other girlfriends simultaneously with her, and had even told her so. But now I wondered whether it ought not to be different. I was waiting for my conscience to hurt me, but it didn't. I knew I was sexually miserable because of Beverley's inability to respond, but that wasn't why I was following Maya Deren up the stairs to my room. She was an intensely attractive woman — and a new woman — and I wanted her. She was also evidently the fighting type, and would obviously not be easy, but that was a challenge too. Maybe it was the challenge I was mainly after.

Maya was even less easy a conquest than I had expected. All she wanted to do was fight. First verbally, and then physically and in every other way. I took Praz's *Romantic Agony* off the shelf to show her, and her eyes opened so intensely wide over it that I simply told her to keep it as a gift. It was a review copy, I said, which was a lie. Then I asked her if she loved music as I did, and stalked over to put on a record. She began telling me about her father then, and how much he loved music, and her childhood. I could see that there was going to be a long and complex Elektra-complex autobiography to go through before the erotic action would start — if ever — so I put on the radio instead, and sat down beside her on the bed-sofa as she talked.

I admit I didn't listen very carefully after a while, except to the music. I am no Henry Miller character who thinks of women strictly as cunts — and in the insulting sense at that — and discounts everything they say as nonessential trash. But I felt that Maya's movie had given her real message a lot more frankly and a lot

571

more clearly than she would be able to do in all these carefully edited, often reiterated words, that I knew I was not the first man to hear. Of course, what I wanted to hear her body say to me would also not be for the first time, and perhaps be just as rehearsed and artificial, but that was different somehow. I started stroking the line of her bare neck and shoulders as she talked, and murmuring yes and of course from time to time. Finally I touched her fine, full breasts. I was positive that would be better early-evening psychotherapy than listening forever to her gussied-up anamnesis that she'd told a hundred times before.

"I'm not here to satisfy your sexual needs!" Maya snapped at me, but with a profound look into my eyes, trying hard to be severe, that said the exact opposite. She did not move, nor try to push my hands away.

"Why not?" I riposted cheerfully. "I'm certainly here to satisfy yours. Come on! When do you throw that pussy on me, or are you afraid of a living man?"

I leaned my body softly against her, to push her over. But Maya pushed back, and hard. Then we began struggling on the bed, rather violently, but not for real. I could see there would be no problem about the physical outcome. She was all steamed up about her movie and by my calling the cards on her bitch-impulses, and she really wanted very much to make love. Her fighting was simply what her massive male-protest required her to do. She was a lot more cat than fish, I thought, except that female cats don't try to lay on top. Anyhow, once a man and a woman start touching each other's bodies, even under the pretext of fighting, the rest is all just standard mammalian courtship. The bites and kicks hardly count. The

French say: *« Les sabots de la jument ne font jamais mal à l'étalon.»* Their hooves do hurt, actually, but not enough to make any stone-horse change his mind. Verbal insults are a different story. Most men's virility is too delicately poised, too bound up with their self-esteem, to stand up against a cursing, screaming fury who really thinks of herself as being raped, or at least insulted. I'm not talking here about textbook male masochists.

Just this once, I'm going to leave out a certain amount here. The real trouble with Maya was that even when achieved, the physical sexual part didn't prove anything and didn't solve anything. It was winner take nothing. That was the way she wanted it to be. She wanted all a man's maleness, and wanted it deep, but she also could not forgive him for it.. Or rather couldn't forgive him for taking it out, all in one piece, not bleeding, and still belonging to him and not to her. A brilliant woman once said that to me frankly, and I was very grateful to her for the warning, but Maya was not that articulate. The pussy image in her movie should really have been a snapping turtle. I know that's ungallant to say, but I won't draw a picture.

In the end we were both conscious of not having really torn through the curtain, and came out of our sexual struggle as we went into it, still fencing for position — victory, domination — verbally if no longer physically. It felt more like murder done to music than sex. Something like Wagner's *Liebestod*, but without any of the languorous, morbid musical symbols to make the essential lust-murder easier to overlook.

My eyes roamed over Maya's body. She was sitting up now, pushing both her breasts forward with her hands repetitively in a strange, self-adulating gesture, and turning her pouting face from side to side. Grooming herself like a cat, I thought. There was no real way of possessing her except staring at her: that she liked. Eyes were one kind of male antenna she wanted focussed on her, and did not fight off. Though now I could touch her too, Maya was a lot greedier for the caress of my eyes. I guess that's where her father had prudently stopped. No wonder she yearned for the optical caress of Hammid's moving camera, focussing close on her every bodyline and twitch.

She was for all the world like the proud nihilist heroines of some late nineteenth-century Russian novel by Kuprin. Or something out of the batik bedspread and painted cigarette-box period in Greenwich Village thirty years before, when I wasn't there — nor her either. Maya Deren had found her century, but it certainly wasn't mine. I was at least two hundred years further back, the period of Pierre Bayle's one-man encyclopaedia, with long erotic discursions, and fighting the censorship like a tiger to get them in. How could I hope to meet in a mere orgasm with a displaced Russian nihilist female, whose real thrill in sex was the preliminary struggle?

"Let's just make a truce and listen to the music a while," I said, my voice carefully controlled, and refraining with an effort from adding something about its soothing the savage breast. I put on one of Dr. Hornbostel's magnificent Balinese gamelan gong records, which were a rarity in those days. But it was clear that Maya was hardly listening, and yearned only to get back to the struggle. Not the sexual struggle; the verbal one. But I no longer wanted to talk. My delayed conscience had finally got into operation, and I felt depressed and diminished by having had her there, on the heavy red Hudson's Bay blanket that was Beverley's love gift to me.

Stiff prick or no, I asked myself, why had I done it, and what good was it? I might just as well have taken up the offer of that other fat girl that lived with the fairy poet, Paulsen. What was her name? — Martine. What a slob! And the soul of a whore too. Well, I couldn't call any names. I was just a ghostwriter with moral reservations.

Why was I so depressed, I wondered? No matter what the old saw says, I never got post-coitally depressed at times like that. To the contrary, I always feel great. Now I felt rotten. A strange set of ideas, adultery. Sex always justifies itself, but only if it comes out right. If it comes out mean and unsuccessful that way, you just want to murder the other person. For having exposed you to such a defeat, and in what should have been a mutual victory. *Look! We have come through!* If Maya and I had fallen madly in love with each other that night — or even just me with her — I could have run away with her in the morning and abandoned Beverley with a clear conscience. But this way? I was just an adulterer and a bum. And now that the cork was out, would it ever end, and what would my life be now?

I was getting like something out of a Russian novel myself, and when the record ended in a blaze of brass drumming, and hooting mahogany logs from the gamelan gong of Lagu-Keblar, I immediately invited Maya to come downstairs with me on the pretext of going to supper. More plainly than I put it to her, I wanted her out of there now, and me too. And especially *off that blanket!* I handed her Praz's *Romantic Agony* as we left, which was being forgotten on the floor, and Maya tucked it under her arm. I guess going downstairs before a woman is never as exhilarating as going up after her. And there are no promising haunches to watch. I felt rotten. Maya didn't feel the way I felt. I could see she had gone through this same unhappy comedy a dozen times — maybe a hundred — with other men, and even thought of it as somehow a victory for her. Never give yourself completely! Poor fool.

We walked a long way down Columbus Avenue together, first not speaking at all, then hardly answering if the other spoke. Maya began talking again about her father. He was obviously a cultivated man, and had influenced her very much, but she was still totally bound up in the unachieved incest with him that made her want to fight instead of fucking, or both together, and to deny the simple sexual reality of what she felt. I wondered if I had really been insulted by her coming home with me. Women like that will usually only sleep with pretty obvious fall-guys, like her fantasied dead male masochist in the movie. It puts their jealous mothers off the track. I wondered if that was really the impression I gave: of the intellectual white nigger? Which was I, as she saw me: the long-pricked Negro, presumably with no brains, and thus no competition; or the short-peckered white intellectual? With nothing. Either way, it wasn't very flattering, to be reduced sexually to someone else's domineering neurotic fantasy. Yes, and what had I been reducing her to?

Somewhere along the street we passed a Chinese restaurant, and both turned into it without even speaking. When the waiter came, he didn't talk much either. We ordered pork and vegetables or subgum chow-mein or something like that, and then I had to listen to the standard didactic soundtrack Maya immediately dealt me out, about how the stuff you get isn't a real Chinese dish at all. It's true, I thought to myself, and the Mexicans never eat *chili con carne* either. They can't afford it. And the Indonesians never eat rice-tafel, and the Italians never eat spaghetti — which is originally Chinese. Marco Polo brought it back with him to Venice. All the eating, everywhere, is done by rich American tourists like us. And always totally inauthentically. Like the sex.

Maya was telling me about her friends at the museum now. That was quite interesting. They were all young anthropologists, who had been part of the psychological warfare team in the war against Japan. Most of them seemed to have been married at one time or another to Margaret Mead. She told me about Alan Priest at the Metropolitan Museum, whom I had met, and how he had been instrumental in saving the Japanese art-city of Kyoto from the final Atom Bomb when Truman wanted to drop it there.

"They should have given him a medal," I said. "That's the only good thing I heard about the war since Hitler's suicide."

The waiter brought us the food, with tea and chopsticks, and I began eating as I listened to Maya talk. Suddenly she stopped, and eyed me furiously.

"Where did you learn to use chopsticks like that?" she demanded.

"Where did I learn?" I was bewildered. "Eating in Chinese restaurants, I guess."

She seized a pair of chopsticks herself, and began prodding and poking them around wildly in the air with one hand, about halfway between an orchestra conductor and a mad toreador, eating a mythical barmecide's meal in the air. So it was a duel, eh? I reached across into her dish with a gourmet air, and plucked out delicately with my chopsticks one fried noodle, which I popped into my mouth. I smiled. My special, unendurable, rotten male-chauvinist phallocratic smile kept for just such occasions. Actually, it was no harder than plucking out pussy-hairs with tweezers, I thought, but said nothing. Why spoil my Sinological victory? This pale Galilean had conquered with the chopsticks, where my trusty nine-inch six-gun — or maybe six-inch nine-gun is closer to it — had failed to make any real impression. Maybe I had approached her at the wrong end altogether, if she was so food-oriented. My depressed mood suddenly fell away from me, and I began eating with enormous fake gusto.

I thought the poor thing was going to kill me. It was pathetic. Here was this talented, pretty, totally extroverted woman, violently anxious to put a garbled art movie of her face and body before the public, but with so little real self-esteem that she was driven positively frantic by discovering that she was not the only person in a third-rate Chinese restaurant able to eat with chopsticks. I began to feel sorry for her, and stopped scooping up my rice into my mouth like a Yangtze River dredge, north Cantonese style.

"Please don't take it so hard," I said. "There's four hundred million people in China, and they can all eat better with chopsticks than either of us. Even the little kids."

I could see I wasn't consoling her. The Chinese didn't count; they were just Chinks. What counted was lording it over me — ladying it isn't quite what I mean — and I had unknowingly spiked that. My earlier thought had been the right one. It was like white women sleeping with Negroes: that was me. No matter who has the longer prick, the woman always wins because she's white. I picked up a single grain of rice with my chopsticks and ate it.

We got through the rest of the meal in silence, drank our bitter tea, and left. She insisted on paying the check, in a sudden burst of clitorine energy, and I didn't argue. Maybe that would be a new career for me — Hollywood stud. If I couldn't conquer them in bed, I'd wow them in Grauman's Chinese restaurant. Instead of walking, we took the bus together downtown. I told her that I really live in the Village quite near her, and that where we had been was only my studio. We had nothing more to say to each other. It was very sad. The bus stopped a block away from Morton Street where she lived, and I got off there too.

"You don't have to take me home," Maya snapped. A standard line.

"This is my stop too," I told her. "I live right here on Bedford. We went the long way around, meeting each other uptown. But I don't think we'll be meeting each other again. What I want to do is fuck, and what you want to do is fight." That may have been an oversimplification of our positions, but it was close.

"Well, thank you for the book," she said, sharp and rather grudgingly, I thought, not wanting to leave me with the last word. Anyhow, not that word.

"And thank you for your wonderful moving-picture," I answered very gravely. "Isn't it funny, though? In the worst cheap whore house on the Bowery, the man gets to kiss the women when he leaves. And you and I are both so brilliant, and we can't even squeeze out a goodbye kiss."

We stared at each other under the streetlight like two assassins, or maybe more like two clockwork automata, in our helpless attitudes of hatred and competition and inability to love. Maya turned suddenly and strode down the side-street with *The Romantic Agony* under her arm. And between her legs. We never made love to each another again, but once, if you can call what we did "making love." I thought of Edna St. Vincent Millay sleeping with everybody and loving no one in the roaring days of Greenwich Village in the 1910s and '20s that everyone moons over so. I thought I knew now how it had really been. A mug's game: winner take nothing.

When I let myself into our room, I found Beverley asleep already under the other red blanket. I got into bed with her, after brushing my teeth and washing my prick carefully in the sink behind the screen, where the electric plate was. There was a little note on the hermy-pot there saying it was my supper. I wasn't hungry. Too full of Chinese food, and chopsticks. And Maya and her movie. I snuggled up behind Beverley, lying like spoons on our sides, and slid my hand down the neck of her nightgown to hold one of her sad little breasts. What a difference from Maya's planturous great boobs, like a sculptured love-goddess on an Indian temple! And yet underneath it, it was Beverley who was all love and heartbreak. And Maya with no heart at all, except for herself. Just some shrivelled-up crippled thing, I decided, like some residual sexual organ. Or bloated up all on one side with vanity — the vermiform appendix of her equally crippled ego. Nasty thoughts. Where would I fit on a scale like that, I wondered?

I lay awake a long time and couldn't sleep. I turned on my back and pulled Beverley's head over onto my shoulder. She made some soft, wordless complaint in her sleep and cuddled against me. I drew all the differences, in my mind, between the two women. I tried to understand, for the first time in my life, what adultery was really about. And what good it was. Or bad. Also, why I had given up Magdalen, who was clever and beautiful, and had fine big breasts and tons of erotic temperament too. And here I was, in a dinky little rented bedroom in the dark, shoring up the soul of sad little Beverley, who was totally willing and totally frigid. Well, was Maya any better, for all her violence?

There were two opposite electrical poles, I decided, wise with the deep wisdom of being half asleep. Maya and I were the same: both violent positives. Beverley and Maya's husband Hammid were also both the same: quiet and self-effacing. But were they really passive, negatives? Maybe we had just paired off the wrong way. Why couldn't we trade back? Not just for one evening, but for good? Make it legal. — Because it wouldn't work. Beverley and Hammid probably wouldn't help each other at all — they'd just weep into each other's beer. And Maya and I would tear each other apart, the hour after the knot would be tied and we'd move in together.

So that's the way it had to be, like in that poem: one gardener with the watering can, and one flower. One negative and one positive, and then the electricity would flow. But which way did it go? I couldn't remember. Was it always from the positive to the negative? I wasn't sure. Was that fair? Maybe it went round and round. Anyhow, why do us positives have to keep loading up those negatives. Is *that* fair? Or are they loading us in the night, when we don't know? I was getting confused. And why was everything all my fault and my responsibility? Wiving goes by destiny, Shakespeare says. Hanging too. But can't a man struggle manfully against his fate? And woman struggle womanfully? Maya and I were wrestling again. I could taste her neck and breasts on my tongue . . . the red blanket.

I was almost asleep. A car went tearing by, down the avenue beyond, and woke me again. Then sleep was creeping over me, like a cool cloud coming in the window, under a dark cloak. I would start a new religion based on *total sexual equality*. In China. Not patriarchal — matriarchal. I would worship in a temple on a mountaintop, with the pillars branches of great trees uplifted. My worship would be performing cunnilinctus on my ten thousand concubines — really my harem of ten thousand sacred prostitutes, with perfumed cunts as deep as wells. Fountains would tinkle in the background, and birds would sing. Everything would be in bright sunlight — nothing in the dark. That would be the worship of the Magna Mater, and the Great Sacred Cunt.

There would be no phallic monuments, no cannon, no war! Just deep green swimming pools of oval shape — no admission fee but a kiss — and filled, brimming, with perfumed milk and water. With pink fountains at each end, like in Bosch, that geysered upward when you pressed a fleshy button. "Press my button!" the girl had sung in Harlem. *"Press my button! Give my bell a ring!"* I was doing my level best wasn't I? Why had it been a fairy poet who described the goddess most ecstatically? — Blind Tiresias. No, Thomas the Rhymer! *"Age cannot wither, nor custom stale, her infinite variety: Other women cloy the appetites they feed, but she makes hungry."* How did it go? *"For vilest things become themselves in her . . ."*

That woke me up, bolt upright. Or had another car gone past? Couldn't get any sleep in Beverley's place, ever. God-damned madhouse, that Seventh Avenue! Saturday nights were the worst. Wait, how did that go about Cleopatra? *"But she makes hungry where most she satisfies."* Was she really my harem; or was I her love-slave, like Cæsar and Antony? Never!! Still how was it fair for me to have a harem of a thousand concubines, like Solomon, and women couldn't. Not if I was to be one of the love-slaves! Well, they couldn't. I saw them first! Besides, women wouldn't like that at all. Women want love, not sex. Men want everything. There was that little poem that explained it perfectly: *Higamus, hogamus, men are monogamous. Hogamus, higamus, women polygamous.* No, wait; that wasn't right! *Hogamus, higamus, men are monigamous.*

Higamus, hogamus, women pologamous. I guess that was it. I fell asleep.

❦

MAYA AND I did meet again: it was hard to avoid each other since we were both always tearing around the corner of Morton and Bedford, going toward the Village square, or across to shop in Little Italy, on Bleeker Street. One day when we passed each other as I was coming home to Beverley in the early evening, Maya said to me shortly, "I want to give you back your book."

"But it was a present," I reminded her.

"Well, come on up and let's talk about it. That's an important book."

We both understood that what was important wasn't Praz's *Romantic Agony* but going on with our own. I went. It was exactly the same as before, and just as bad – or good. Better, really, because now there were absolutely no pretenses. There were no long sub-acid discussions of anything, of any books or movies — no intellectual pretexts or verbal arguments at all. We just walked up the front steps, opened the door, threw ourselves on her divan-sized bed, which was right in the front room as you walked in, and ripped into each other sexually.

I really preferred it that way — as I had warned her the last time — to the kind of scene where the girl (or the man) suddenly picks a fight with you at bedtime, and whumps it up so phoney and big, with you trying to stay sensible and dignified till you finally lose your temper too . . . .and then the curtain comes down, WHAM! What you thought was maybe, at worst, a perverted appetizer, turns out to have been the whole banquet — for her. Frig that! Really this was better. It was dirty and hateful — almost a hate fuck, though we didn't hate each other — but it was violent and therefore *exciting*. And it was *all sex!* Sex right from the beginning and with hardly a word, neither mock-friendly nor mock foe. I always knew I was a repressed verbal sadist, since I'd first heard of Sade, but I never knew I had such a penchant for the crude physical forms too. Just lucky I don't have bedmates like that too often. Well, I could always say I was doing research for my book *Love & Death*, which I was rewriting for the fifth or sixth time then, honing it down to a lethal cutting edge in its sadistic defense of beautiful sex against ignoble sadism. I allow myself artistic contradictions like that — don't you?

The only thing I really didn't go for, this time, was that Maya started working out with her finger- and toenails on my back at her orgasm, right out of the weirder pages of the Kama Sutra. Except that the tattoo designs she was making on me bled all over the place and I also don't believe were correctly executed on the Hindu patterns of "The Mark of the Seven Half Moons," "The Cockatoo's Beak," etc. My back was in ribbons, and although I hardly felt it when she was doing it, it hurt like a bugger every day after that for a week when I had to douse my back with rubbing alcohol. Maybe that was considered an extra thrill, for real sado-masochists with nobody to torture but themselves. I guess I'm not really very authentic in that line.

When she wanted seconds, and so did I, Maya dove at my softened prick with her eager fangs bared, somewhere between Dracula and a hungry panther-cub. Under a pretext of a caress directed at her magnificent shock of dark hair, I got a workmanlike stranglehold on her from behind, with both hands on her weazand, out of some forgotten memory of Robin Hood's historic struggle with Sir Guy of Gisborne or maybe it was Will Scarlett. And I knew, and Maya knew too, that I wasn't kidding. But just to make sure, I put it into words. I'm not proud of talking like this, and certainly not when I'm simultaneously trying to angle into a classic sixty-nine with a fine overheated woman crawling on top of me, but I can do it if I have to.

"You sweet bitch," I said — I wrote down the words not two hours later on a 3"x5" card, and filed it under SEX-TECHNIQUE: VERBAL VIOLENCE, to remember it to my shame — "you bite that cock *just once*, and the interns are going to be admiring your corpse at St. Vincent's Hospital for supper!"

When I got back to Beverley on Bedford Street, and whatever we were eating that night, it turned out that she had seen me walking down the street with Maya Deren, and she asked me please not to tell her I'd been at the library while she was waiting patiently for me to arrive. She didn't make any scene — that wasn't her way — but she started lapsing into one of her sullen silences that I knew could last for godawful days, and that kept me from getting any writing done. It was too castratory for a writer to be faced continually with the evidence that words don't work, and that nothing could ever get through her wall of silence and frigidity — like a hardrock Sleeping Beauty who doesn't INTEND to be wakened by the likes of you.

As it happens I was in the short strokes, just then, of finishing *Love & Death*, and I knew I couldn't afford to be brought down in mid-flight by Beverley's neurotic clam squirting sticky silence all over me from under some unanalyzed, barnacle-covered rock in her private Throg's Neck Bay. I much preferred Maya's violence, verbal or physical, since I could at least fight back at that in the same way. Whereas Beverley's self-pitying mutism, hour after dreary hour, punctuated only by lighting cigarettes for herself and laying out canned gup for the cats — we already had two — did not leave me any opening at all where I could start shoving in my optimistically prying phallic lever. I decided it would be better to lie to her than to let her stew in the truth, and I assured her that Maya and I had merely been talking lengthily about a movie script I might be writing next for her and her husband Alex Hammid, who I lyingly said was of course present, because he was the actual director and cameraman. Beverley didn't even bother to act as though she were listening.

"You smell of her all over," she said.

"I s'pose! She kissed me goodbye on both cheeks. So did he. All the movie people do that — they think it's French."

No answer. I went on to say that I didn't like people making jealous scenes to me, whether justified or not. I spoke slowly, deliberately, not mad. No male mammal, I told her, can stay potent if you lock him in with one & the same female, even for as little as a year.

It was ridiculous to imagine it could be made into a life sentence for human beings just on sentimental grounds. It wouldn't work. I was a mammal too. It wasn't me that made up the laws of nature. If the time came that I felt any slackening in my virility — with Beverley, that is — I would certainly not hesitate to use the one & only operating aphrodisiac anyone ever discovered: another woman's pussy-juice plastered all over me! A new woman's. Like it or leave it, that was Nature's Law.

"You've got it," Beverley said. She lit another cigarette while I fumed and grimaced, and clenched and unclenched my hands. The next thing I knew, I found I was behind the little screen at the tiny sink, unconsciously washing my hands. I stopped instantly, knowing she'd think I was trying to wash the smell off, though I knew that what I was really doing — because I'm always doing it when I'm mad — was washing away and getting rid of the person that's angered me, and the shackles on my liberty they represent. Or maybe I was washing my hands to shrive me of the murder in my heart? My voice, when I came back, was like breaking glass.

"I — like — sucking — lots — of — women's — cunts," I said. "They all taste different, and I love it! The day I think I need that, to keep my prick stiff, loving you will not stop me."

For all my brave talk, I felt absolutely terrible that Beverley had come so close to catching me, simply because there wasn't any way to bathe between the two women when they lived only half a block apart, and around the corner. Of course, I had bulled it through, but the question wasn't whether I was going to get away with anything — my whole sound track was true: I wasn't anybody's love-slave, after all. The problem was to keep Beverley's heart from being broken. Plain & simple as she was, always badly dressed and without a cosmetic to her name, she had no way of competing with any other woman and she knew it. To ask her to dress up in decent clothes — her mother had closets-full Beverley was always silently rejecting — and to look attractive, let alone sexy, was something she would never temperamentally be able to do. If I was going to protect this poor, frigid or maybe just frozen waif, I was going to have to keep protecting her from the competition. She was too vulnerable for any comparison.

At least I would have to keep lying to her if I went on with Maya or anyone else, rather than keep grinding her into the deficiencies she was helpless to fix. I suppose I was lying to myself atrociously, and trying to make myself seem noble and fine, while retaining the right to be a bareassed adulterer; but there may have been something gallant there too, I think.

The next time I moseyed over looking for Maya and another possible wild ride, when my back was a little bit healed, wasn't a week later. But Hammid was there, and we did talk about a possible scenario I might write. I really liked Hammid — his true name was Hackenschmidt. He was highly intelligent, but seemed quite inarticulate because he would only open his trap when Maya went into the next room or to the toilet. I pegged him as pussy-whipped to a pulp, which was a pity because he had true genius behind a movie camera. The same was true of Von Sternberg, everybody said. What was this masochism of German-speaking intellectuals? Was it the domineering Teutonic fathers or the mothers who were castrating them? One thing I could see was, I wasn't going to get laid there — not that day.

Maya got into an intense phone conversation just then, and suddenly went out without a word, wrapped in her big security-blanket overcoat. Hammid knew she was going to a lover, but either didn't give a damn — as a great German camera artist in exile, stuck with a leading lady of bad character — or was putting up with it on a neurotic basis. You obviously had to be a practising masochist to live with a woman that domineering. As I had found, she didn't want any other kind of man in bed with her, except for an occasional wild sex holiday with evident social inferiors castrated by their skin color or poverty. That was me? A lot of castratory bitches are like that.

And that's how Maya Deren also happened, probably to be the first person to die of AIDS in America at an early age, after having, as she told me once when I me her in the street later, gone to Haiti on a Guggenheim grant, I think, and "fucked a lot of niggers" – of both sexes. Haiti's been a bad place for fucking niggers for a long time. Columbus found that out when he brought back syphilis from there. What else is AIDS but another subform still endemic in Haiti? They say it originally comes from eating green monkeys in Africa, but the Haiti vector is a lot closer.

Hammid and I sat talking a long while over glasses of wine. He was terribly nice, and opened up the moment Maya wasn't there to shit all over him with her fake-female cloying act and sexy bossiness. He asked me politely what I did usually, and whether I made a living at it. I told him about some of the things I was trying to do — and fight — censorship, the comics, murder-mysteries, and all the rest of it — and I added enviously how much easier it was to be a movie-maker in a period when the non-verbal arts were at such a premium, and people were so guilty unconsciously and therefore so terrified of any kind of analysis.

Hammid agreed. "But it was so much better in Europe," he said. "Such an audience! So aware — so intense. And brilliant critics."

"I suppose Hitler destroyed all that."

"Of course." We drank our wine.

"You know," I said, "I saw those Nazi propaganda movies: *Victory in the East*, and the others. That was before the American mop-up services cut them to bits, and tried to make them into comedies. They were really very powerful. Ghastly on any human level, but marvelous cinema! When I walked out of the theatre I was ready to paste on a new foreskin and get a Nazi Party card."

"Here in New York?"

"Yes. They showed them for months in Yorkville, just before America entered the war. I went to see them more than once. I'd sit there in the dark cursing Hitler and being overwhelmed by his movies at the same time. They were breathtaking. And the music — everything! You couldn't help being thrilled. It was like the automatic 'feelies' in Huxley's *Brave New World*. You know: watching pornographic movies where you can *feel* every hair on the bearskin rug. I want to say that about the Nazi movies, because it's *true*. They were as good as *Metropolis* and *Caligari*. Better."

"Of course," said Hammid with a little deprecatory wave of his hand. "That's where they learned everything. And Eisenstein and the Russians too. But you see, Goebbels wouldn't let anybody except Riefenstahl work, like her Olympics film, because she was willing to lick their feet with that kind of propaganda. Everybody else had to run. To Hollywood. And not a single one has ever done anything decent there. Except Welles."

"Who comes from Wisconsin," I added. "All home products. It was Hearst who crucified him, not Hitler."

We drank more wine while I wondered idly about Orson Welles' first name. Could it really have been Gershon? Try his birth certificate.

"So you see," Hammid ended, obviously apologizing for himself and not really advising me, "you *must* go to the foundations. Once they give you the money, you do the kind of work you believe in."

"Except the next year, when they *cut off funds*." I told him about Gorer's three sardonic rules for foundation grants, but Hammid merely shrugged. I could see he figured you could get something done anyhow, meanwhile. But he knew how to talk to the rich. He murmured — I didn't. Those beautiful lawns in his movies for Maya Deren were all rich people's estates up in Tarrytown and Duchess County.

"Time is not money," he was saying, "but money is time. You *must* go to the foundations. You have worlds of work there — years of work to do. A foundation grant will buy you time."

"I'll never get it," I said. "I can't sell myself to the kind of fags that are holding the purse-strings. Like

Willie Rüh. The only pleasure they have is keeping anybody competent *out*. It's the mirror-image of their own failed sexuality."

That made him wince. I guess his next grant was coming from the foundation Rüh was running.

"Well, there are some tough dykes too," Hammid said, the slang sounding somehow oddly in his accent — very forced. "What about the people at the Museum of Modern Art, and Thyra Terry at the Guggenheim? Can you stand her?"

I had never met her, but I used to have bunches of big dyke friends of hers that I ghosted for. "I haven't got the right kind of anatomy for them to swing me a real grant,' I said. "I'd be competing with their girl friends."

We heard Maya on the stairs now, coming back from her quickie, if that's what it was. Maybe she'd only gone to the drugstore to buy a whip.

"It was always that way," he told me. "You think Cellini had it any different? Read his *Memoirs*."

"Casanova too," I agreed. "He began in Venice as a male hustler. But that was then, and in Italy. Isn't there any progress?"

"You are joking," Hammid said.

Maya came in, her eyes enormous, liquid, boiling. Not a word. Hammid and I looked at her, like two haughty anatomists; then melting away from friends into uneasy brother-husbands as we stared. I popped back round the corner to Beverley's room on Bedford and wrote up a lot of notes on our conversation. Hammid was a great movie-maker, all right. I wondered if he'd ever be able to get out from under

Maya's fat shadow without simply killing her. More likely she'd kill him.

&

THE BOOK that I would call *Love* & *Death* was finished. Almost nothing remained of my original plan for a heavily documented history of censorship, that I had started for Haldemann-Julius under the title of *Taboo*. Only a single paragraph tracing the pre-history of comic books, as roughly seen in the bison drawings of the prehistoric cave-dwellers and the hieroglyphic writing of Egypt, that I had given Pilkington and his wife to publish in *American Notes & Queries*. The book I had finished now was entirely different, entirely polemic, wrestling over and over in more and more bitter terms with a single tremendous contradiction: *Why was murder publishable if sex was not?* I had made up a simple title-page, with a brief motto on it taken from *The Song of Songs*. It really said the opposite of my theme; expressed only a desperate hope, watching for the morning star. LOVE IS STRONG AS DEATH.

I took the carbon copy on the subway with me down to Bedford Street that evening. I would read it again when Beverley was asleep — silently, as written words this time, and not aloud, as I had declaimed each page of it, time after time, alone in my workroom, listening and examining. I wanted it to be fulminating and denunciatory — to hell with politely cadenced prose, slipping into the reader's consciousness like a vaselined enema! Well, it was the way I wanted it now, and I was happy. Hardly a hundred pages, and it had taken two years.

As I walked down Seventh and turned in at the hook of Morton Street, I saw Maya Deren coming along in that abnormally big overcoat she always hid out in. We waved to each other absently, but carefully passed on opposite sides of the street. We could never be friends after our fiasco as lovers, but we were trying at least not to be enemies. It didn't matter. Not all women and men are made for each other. Only the anatomy matches, and not always that. You do your best.

Women did not seem very important in my life just then. What really mattered was the realization that was sweeping over me that evening, as I walked the long blocks down the avenue. It came over me like a great cool breeze sweeping in from the sea, that my long, long apprenticeship was finished. My *Lehrjahr* was over. I could write the way I wanted now, and could control my brush. My book was deep and powerful, I knew, and just as I had planned it — burning with sincerity and passion. Everyone would realize that, but whether they would publish it was another question. Also whether the book would do the slightest good. I was not just trying to express myself: I wanted a result! That part wasn't so easy to control. I had done my part.

My subject had run away with me too, because here I was attacking violence in the most violent possible terms. Well, why not? What should I have used, wet bedroom slippers? "Not for Children," the chapter on the comic-books, was far and away the best. It was evident that I wrote best when I was angriest. It was certainly illogical, but that's how it was. I was a lot more passionate about what I hated than what I loved.

Well, let it go with all its faults! I felt like the girl in the fairytale who must sit silently spinning thistles into sweaters to save her six ensorcelled brothers, and is being burnt as a witch for her silence. But the last sleeve of the last sweater is not finished! She knits madly at it, trying to finish, but knows there is not time — the flames are now licking around her and her pile of thistle sweaters with her. She holds her breath; tears at the thistle yarn with her teeth. *"Eh! Va pour la dernière manche!"* and flings the sweaters into the air. Overhead, suddenly there is a great beating of wings, as six wild geese swoop down over her and beat out the flames. And reappear out of the smoke as six strong young men carrying her away. Except that one young man has the wing of a bird.

No. I knew I would never bring down a hundred-million dollar industry dedicated to murder and horror and the perverting of children, just with a hundred-page pamphlet I didn't even have enough money to print a thousand copies of myself. Also, what could you do with a thousand copies, when they were deforesting Canada for the paper to print murder and horror on by the thousands of tons. And films, and the silver on it, to make horror movies — how many thousands of tons of that? The enemy was certainly not going to make space for me in their lovely warm bed of rotted roses. I smiled to myself sarcastically. My job was doing the work, and I had done it. Getting it out into the world wasn't necessarily my job at all.

I let myself into the little house at number 68. Beverley was home already, wearing her little faded blue jumper of cotton chambray. Supper was salmon patties, free twisted-off beet greens from the supermarket on one hermy-pot, and Beverley's inevitable steamed potatoes staying hot in the other. My next book would be called *One-Burner Cooking for Economy-Minded Lovers.* No, leave out the "Economy-Minded." There seemed to be plenty of money around for everyone but me since the War started, and certainly since it ended. You can't have everything. I had made my choice. I would just have to make my peace with not knowing how to snag onto the gravy-train. I ate my salmon patty.

Rabbit-eating paupers, were we? I'd show them! For dessert I dashed back to the little store at the corner and bought us a can of enormous halved peaches, to celebrate finishing *Love & Death.* The peaches were wonderful. We would have put brandy on them, to flambé them and make it festive, but we didn't have any. They were floating in a gooey, oversweet liquid that I wanted to pour down the sink, but Beverley said she would save it for baked beans the next day. We ate the peaches out of the can with the big silver spoon from Beverley's childhood in Canada that we had found in her mother's apartment. We exchanged bites, dribbled the soft yellow pulp into each other's mouths, fell on the bed, made love. The moon came out.

In the middle of the night I woke up and found myself naked. I sat on the blanket-covered wooden

box by the long plank table at the window, and lit the lamp. Great brown moths with fantastic markings on their wings flew against the window, beating their wings, attracted by my light. I opened the window to let them in, and they came and sat on my manuscript as I read. Where could enormous moths like that be living in the gasoline stink of Seventh Avenue? Probably hiding out in the shabby, unhappy trees in the tiny garden with its sour green earth behind the gas-station, just like we were. I read the carbon manuscript all the way through, slowly, savoring my bitter jokes and amused and delighted by my occasional heaven-storming prose. Just the first-page appeal to the honor of writers, as men of truth and custodians of the Promethean fire, would appall every pro who even got that far. Tomorrow I would start typing it clean, to send round to the publishers.

Printed in Great Britain
by Amazon

36189478R00328